Zamani

A Survey of
East African History

Edited by
B A Ogot and J A Kieran

Humanities Press

Published for the Historical Association of Kenya

First published
in the United States of America 1968
by Humanities Press Inc.
303 Park Avenue South
New York, N.Y. 10010

© East African Publishing House and Longmans Green & Co Ltd 1968
Library of Congress Catalog Card No. 68-26079

Contents

Introduction

The work we here introduce has been titled *Zamani* (Kiswahili for ancient times, antiquity or the past) to indicate that it deals with the early as well as the more modern history of East Africa, and it is subtitled *A Survey of East African History* to show that the subject is too vast to enable more than a summary account to be provided by the contributors in the space at their disposal. It is also a survey in so far as it is based on information available at the present time (1967). Continuing research into East African history will fill in gaps in the account and change many of the ideas and interpretations that are here put forward.

Zamani is being published for the Historical Association of Kenya, which hopes to further the study and teaching of History, and to increase public interest in all aspects of the subject. The Association plans to devote itself to the encouragement of research and to the stimulation of historical writing. This is one of the works it is sponsoring.

It is a work of collaboration and the editors are aware that it suffers from defects that all such works are prone to. Some readers may feel that it is too much like a collection of essays and that the chapters are not sufficiently connected, that contributors do not always follow up the themes discussed by their colleagues. This is partly due to the fact that, being a work of synthesis, it also embodies conclusions from the original research of many of its writers. Scholars from many disciplines, archaeology, geography and linguistics, have contributed the results of their studies and investigations into problems that the conventional historian could not have tackled, and their methods of approaching the subject have necessarily varied, both from those of their fellow scientists and from those of the historian. It will be noticed, too, that the final chapters, which bring the history of East Africa up to the present day, have been entrusted to economists and political scientists. Some past historians have been reluctant to accept such a concept of contemporary history and have frowned on its practitioners, but this attitude is now dying out. Furthermore, in a period of such crucial importance as the present, in which the foundations of post-colonial East Africa are being laid, it would have been impossible to omit consideration of how problems inherited from the past are being tackled and what informed opinion sees as the outlook for the future.

The book begins with a short discussion of the methods currently used by historians, an account of the geographical background and a discussion of early man in East Africa, after which the historians, archaeologists and linguists take over, handing over towards the end to economists and political scientists. The contributors have had complete freedom to express their own views. The responsibility for the overall arrangement is the editors'. In the belief that they aid clarity of exposition and frequently make a point better than several paragraphs, a large number of maps have been included. It will be seen that there is a dividing line in treatment, although not a break in continuity, with the nineteenth century. For earlier times contributors write of the several peoples of East Africa; later East African history more meaningfully divides into the story of what once were colonies and protectorates and now are in the process of becoming nations.

The chapters on the peoples of East Africa will show, however, that no tribe or clan can be considered in isolation from others. Neither should East African history be thought of as separate from that of the rest of Africa. Most problems discussed in the pages that follow have to be considered in an all-African context, and the solutions to them will be found in and will affect the history of the continent as a whole.

The difficulty of terminology and of classification of peoples is not exclusive to Kenya, Uganda and Tanzania. It has been necessary, as the later pages explain, to abandon certain formerly accepted terms and to introduce others. It is recognised that these are not entirely satisfactory but they are, it is hoped, freer from bias than those used hitherto. As there is no definite agreement among linguists on language classification, it has been decided to use that of J. H. Greenberg, which has the merits of attempting to be comprehensive.

Zamani is not, of course, meant to be definitive. Research is continuing all the time. Those who have contributed to the symposium will feel encouraged if its deficiencies are recognised and noted by its readers. If some of these should feel sufficiently interested to become historians themselves and to remedy these deficiencies it will be even more encouraging. The book is not exclusively for those studying history. Everyone, not just the historian, needs to know the history of his or her country and to take a pride in what was achieved by the ancestors.

University College,   Bethwell A. Ogot,
Nairobi.   John A. Kieran.
18 September 1967.

1

The Historian in East Africa

J. A. Kieran

History

History, we all know, is the study of the past. It has sometimes
been broken up into social, economic, political, constitutional
and other divisions, but such categorisation is for convenience
only and is ignored when it seems to get in the way of explanation
and interpretation. Similarly, historians have divided past ages
into centuries although fully realising that this is arbitrary.
The subject matter of history is so vast that it has proved
necessary to break it up into more manageable units, to arrange
a system of classification, for example, by continents, countries,
centuries and subject material.

For their further convenience, historians have generally
confined themselves to seeking evidence of past developments in
writings. The historian has become accustomed to handling
these as his source material, whether in printed or in manuscript
form. He is happy when searching in libraries and archives. He
knows what he is looking for there: the works of earlier historians
who, like himself, have attempted to interpret, to make sense of
the past, and the writings which were not intended for this
purpose but which today testify to the daily life and events of
their time. The process of first tracing and then sifting through
these materials, deciding what is a true and what is a false
record, evaluating the particular interest and degree of bias of
the writer, and then of making a further selection, of what is

relevant and significant to his purpose, is something to which the historian is well accustomed. There are rules which help him to detect forgeries and to establish whether his written sources are genuine; his training has equipped him to criticise the historical writings of others, to select and to organise from the material he accepts as genuine his own interpretation of the facts, one which is coherent and consistent and which scrupulously gives references to the materials he has used. Finally, he must leave these materials intact and accessible so that other historians can criticise his theories and hypotheses as he will have criticised those of his fellow-historians, both past and present.

This is never easy, certainly not where East African history is concerned. Material for the early period is lacking and what exists raises many textual problems. Badly edited texts have to be carefully studied. In this volume, Chittick discusses the value of the Arab geographers and the local chroniclers he has used for his chapter on the pre-Portuguese period. Interpretation raises many problems. Sutton shows how the 'Hamitic Hypothesis' has bedevilled much historical writing in the past. Some readers may find that the later chapters by Ogot, Kiwanuka and Iliffe on Kenya, Uganda and Tanzania lay stress on factors and developments that they might have ignored, while devoting less attention to topics previously considered of major importance.

A moment's reflection will show that written documents are not the only materials that give information about the past, nor is writing the only medium in which historical judgments can be made. Man's historical experience has left discernible traces of its passage in material objects to be found in the earth, in the way in which society is organised, in stories and sayings, in the grammar and vocabularies of languages, in bodily characteristics, in the crops that man grows and the animals he herds, and in the various arts and crafts he practises. Historical interpretations can be found in songs and dances, in works of art, in poems, legends and fables, just as in the more formalised written histories. The efficiency of writing as a means of conveying information about the past may sometimes obscure the fact that it is not the only means for such transmission. Where writing has not been of major importance in the life of a society, the historian must search for historical evidence and historical interpretation elsewhere, in the earth, in the structure of society, wherever there seems a chance of finding fresh information.

Much of this information will come from the researches of others, who are not historians and who are not primarily interested in history. Their methods of investigation and of recording will frequently seem strange. The student of history will obviously not be able to master the various sciences which can provide information about the past so as to be competent to carry out original work in all of them, but he should know how they can help him and understand their methods of conducting research. Furthermore, to obtain a balanced picture of the past, it will be necessary for him to draw upon the conclusions of scholars in various disciplines and to utilise evidence provided by them. While a historian can appreciate the significance, for his own purposes, of information provided by a man working in another discipline, he is less capable of evaluating the validity of this information because of his incomplete grasp of the methods, techniques and principles of the disciplines concerned. In this evaluation the colleagues of his informant may be able to advise him.

It will be remembered that historians have already learnt much from other subjects, from geography, for instance. The movements and settlements of agricultural and pastoral tribes can hardly be understood without reference to soil and climatic conditions. Rainfall, tsetse fly belts, forests, river valleys, grasslands: all these are factors to be taken into account. The knowledge of prevailing winds, ocean currents, difficulties of landfall, explains much relating to settlement and trade. Ojany attempts to provide the geographical background necessary for the appreciation of much historical development.

There are other quarters from which help can come. The African historian will find himself more and more drawing upon the researches of archaeologists, anthropologists, linguists and students of the natural sciences. The social sciences have been breaking down old barriers associated with the former rigid classification of subjects into the sciences and the humanities, among which latter history was categorised. A wider choice of source materials than is offered by the study of documentation brings with it an obligation to develop some knowledge of the disciplines which have been accustomed to utilising these source materials in the past, and, in particular, a need to grasp how these disciplines and their discoveries can be of help to the historian.

Archaeology

The historian does not feel too lost when he is confronted with archaeology. Here, he realises, is a definite historical science, with the same object of studying man's past, even if the methods of doing so are different. The archaeologist finds his evidence of the past in the traces that man has left in the earth. In advance of historians, archaeologists came to appreciate the importance of collaborating with the natural sciences. Geology was called upon for information on soil structure, zoology reported on animal life, and botany explained the ecology of the region. Chemistry and physics helped with problems of dating, and medical science gave an opinion on skeletons that were discovered. The archaeologist took not only information but also techniques of investigation and analysis from the various sciences that could help him.

This co-operative effort is clearly seen to be necessary when one considers that the archaeologist studies what evidence remains of the material culture of past peoples and what can be deduced from this concerning them and their ways of life. The evidence for this: e.g. coins, bones, traces of metallic objects, remains of buildings, is frequently the direct study material of another discipline, and the need to extract as much useful information as possible from such evidence requires consultation between students of the two disciplines. Like the historian, the archaeologist is attempting to portray man in his environment but unlike the historian, the nature of his source material has accustomed him to consider the principles and methods of sciences concerned with the same source material as his own.

The study of rock engravings and paintings and the investigation of caves above ground is an important part of the work of the archaeologist, but most of his source material comes from digging into the earth, from careful investigation, excavation and classification. From his study of the artefacts (man-made tools) that he finds and classifies, he formulates his concept of a culture. This is largely determined by stratigraphy, the arrangement of levels of human occupation on a settlement site, each level containing survivals of the material possessions and constructions of a particular people at a particular time. The general principle is that cultures, identified by an assemblage of material possessions, will be found in layers of succession, the oldest at the bottom and the latest at the top. What the archaeologist finds are such things as buildings or traces of them, burials and grave goods (objects buried with the dead), human or animal bones, coins, tools, pottery and beads. The recovery of such objects and the determination of their relationship to one another requires very careful digging, assembly and subsequent treatment of fragile or damaged pieces. Accurate determination of the successive strata or layers of human occupation, with a precise recording of the finding of various objects, is absolutely essential, so that the relationship between various objects on a site can be determined and the concept of a culture, an entity related to and associated with certain such objects, can be built up. From the allocation of objects to their various cultures, a picture can be drawn of the pattern of living at the site successively through the ages. The strata themselves will show the progression, usually from the oldest levels at the bottom; bones, where found, can show what men lived at different times and what animals they kept; their pots, tools and other goods will give an idea of their daily economic life.

Classification follows the careful recovery of material and the determination of culture sequences on a single site. The archaeologist then moves into a wider field and attempts to compare his site, its strata and the objects he has found and grouped, with similar sites, strata and objects elsewhere. By the comparison of settlement patterns, fashions in ornamentation, types of pottery, burial customs etc., he hopes to learn how the cultural sequences he has established for the site he has worked on personally compare with those determined elsewhere by other archaeologists. The comparison of material and classifications of objects can then help in the identification of a culture or cultures common to those who lived at several sites. Past relationships between various cultures, suggestive of trade, conquest, migration, of an influence or contact of some kind, can also be discovered. In this volume, drawing on information provided by his own excavations, Chittick discusses the age and importance at various times of such places as Kilwa. Sutton reports on the burial mounds of the advanced hunters, identified as the Capsian Culture, and what they tell us of their way of life. He also remarks on the evidence for contact between Engaruka and the coast, and writes on possible connections between 'dimple based' pottery, 'channelled' ware, and a cultivating, iron-using people, who may be the Bantu.

Techniques of excavation and co-operation with natural

scientists in treatment of findings may be strange to the historian but the purpose behind these endeavours is the same as his own. The information that the archaeologist can pass on to the historian is limited because his acquaintance with peoples is through their material possessions and their economy, and it is from these that he differentiates them as cultures. He can discuss their patterns of settlement, their technological skills, their level of artistry, their trade relations, whether they were agricultural or pastoral, their social and economic behaviour, aspects of life that can be reflected in artefacts. Some evidence of religious beliefs can be found in rock paintings, and remains of structures can occasionally give information about where rulers lived and how powerful they were. But much information not of such a nature as to leave traces in the earth is irrecoverable through archaeology. Evidence of political systems, languages and religious beliefs cannot easily be found by archaeological methods. The intrusion of one cultural group upon another may be clearly discernible but not the reasons for it, nor the way it came about. It is also obvious that people who lived settled lives and accumulated durable possessions can be better studied by the archaeologist than can those who wandered and whose goods perished. It should be especially noted that archaeologists hesitate to draw conclusions from an apparent lack of findings, which may merely result from an unfortunate choice of a site for excavation. Nevertheless, for the remotest past, the archaeologist is often the only one capable of recapturing history, and for more modern periods his help to the historian may be invaluable where documentation is poor or non-existent.

Anthropology

Unlike the archaeologist, the anthropologist is not primarily interested in the past, although he also studies and tries to understand cultures. He concerns himself, rather, with present-day social organisation and relations, with customs and cultural values. He investigates and explains structures of societies, forms of social organisation, institutions, ideas and forms of government, systems of marriage, inheritance and descent, religious customs and cultural values, as well as such material aspects of life as farming, cattle raising, fishing and technology.

The method of anthropologists today is to live among the people they are studying, to experience their way of life at first hand, and to learn through this experience to appreciate and understand the culture as an entity with all the motivations and tensions expressed in the associated social structure. Even where the historian has a considerable acquaintance with a society as it exists today, he has much to learn from the scientific, disciplined approach of the anthropologist. As anthropologists set themselves the task of understanding, rather than merely describing, the values, institutions and ideas of societies, they are frequently led to portray antecedent situations and to conjecture regarding the process of evolution towards the modern situation.

This social science interests the historian because the anthropologist's description and explanation of the belief and custom of today can help him visualise what the culture being described must have been like in the past. The historian needs to understand how a society functions today and what its key concepts are now, if he is to understand how it functioned at an earlier date. The present is here called upon to help explain the past. Social anthropologists studying the ideas, concepts and institutions of present-day societies, sometimes not very different from historically antecedent societies, can give the historians many insights into the reasons behind behaviour and events in the past.

The historian, then, looks to the anthropologist for information about techniques of research and for evidence which can help him find traces of the past in social structures as they exist today, just as he looks to the archaeologist for information regarding traces of the past in the earth. The anthropologist can tell him of the evolution of particular institutions and ideas. Because of his interest in the way in which various social institutions are interconnected, the anthropologist can sometimes draw the historian's attention to the fact that, while in a certain society most features form a logical and coherent whole (given the presuppositions of that society), there are, none the less, certain features which do not seem to fit in. The tentative conclusion may be that these are relics of an earlier cultural complex which has almost entirely disappeared, or, possibly, borrowings from another, taken over because of their value for a particular function but never wholly assimilated. Such evidence of the past with its indications of societies organised on different principles or having different economic bases, is

obviously valuable. It has been suggested that the anthropologist's appreciation that many distinct and apparently
unrelated features of a society are necessarily interrelated and
express the ethos of that society may enable him to declare,
from the evidence that a certain feature existed in the past, that
other features, evidence of which has not survived, will once
have been in existence also. Behind the isolated features which
we know, some have claimed, the anthropologist can occasionally
discern the pattern of a vanished society.

A comparison of the institutions of various societies over a
wide area, like the archaeologist's comparison of material
culture in the past, may indicate the stimulus of one culture
upon another and the lines of development and diffusion. The
centre where a certain feature originated can sometimes be
traced, the lines along which it spread be suggested, and the
modifications it underwent in varying circumstances be indicated.
Such migrations and diffusions of influence and such evidence
of causal connections are bound to interest the historian. The
reconstruction of a parent culture which has influenced related
cultures may perhaps be possible, and the historian may thus
be enabled to visualise the way of life of ancestral societies. This
reconstruction is arrived at by studying certain modern societies,
concentrating on the relics of the past which their social structures contain, understanding how they are interrelated and how
they have borrowed and adapted from each other and from
others.

Cohen here discusses the importance of the cultural system of
the River-lake Nilotes in their pre-migration homeland and the
larger and stronger political and social units of the Lwoo. He
goes on to mention the influence on the Padhola of their neighbours, and instances the Abasuba clan, a mixed group of people,
mostly non-Luo, who took up the culture of the Luo of Nyanza.
Sutton treats of absorption and assimilation among the early
peoples of East Africa: he finds that the Southern Cushites
have left a deep mark on the society, economy and political
structure of the Highland Bantu and Nilotes. Ehret says that
the Sanye, unlike the Mbuguan and Rift Cushites, who continued
to practise agriculture and herd cattle, were hunter-gatherers
until quite recently, explaining that they must therefore have
become assimilated culturally to a larger group of pre-Cushitic
hunter-gatherers.

A note of caution, however, is necessary. Similarities between cultures may be coincidental or the result of similar response to a similar environment. It is always tempting to isolate certain factors which seem to support an argument, while ignoring others which do not. Most anthropologists, too, have been little concerned with asking questions which interest the historian, who, consequently, had to be content with gleanings from anthropological treatises.

Apart from information about particular societies, the general conclusions of anthropology have much to offer to the historian. Investigations into human behaviour as conditioned by the prevalence of certain customs and cultural values lead anthropologists to predict that certain circumstances may be related to particular human reactions. Their detailed studies of societies can give the historian a much better appreciation of motivations, explain a good deal of what is puzzling in human behaviour, and indicate what are likely to be the consequences of new ideas and new institutions. This attempt at generalisation, of formulating rules, which anthropology, like other social sciences, is moving towards, is of considerable importance to the historian, who constantly faces the problem of finding explanations for human behaviour.

In a more specialised way again, anthropology can be of help— from its study of the motivations and assumptions of societies. The historian, studying the historical traditions of a people, for example, should endeavour to find out from the anthropologist what is their concept of time; this may not necessarily be the straight-line progression we are familiar with but may perhaps be a circular concept of the constant return and reliving of historical situations. What people consider to be the relationship between past and present will naturally affect their interpretation of what has occurred in earlier centuries. Before the historian begins to study the traditions of a society, the anthropologist can help him by explaining in what ways the political, religious or social attitudes of that society and its concept of time are likely to have distorted, consciously or unconsciously, memories of past events.

Oral tradition

The work of anthropologists has indicated the importance of oral tradition as a means of discovering the past. We are not dealing here with a separate discipline, such as archaeology or anthropology, but with something which is much closer to the traditional study of history. Oral tradition is history handed down by word of mouth, the source material being the spoken rather than the written word. There are many parallels here. Just as there are various forms of documentary sources for history, so there are various forms of oral sources. The same broad distinction, between the deliberate work of historical re-creation and the source material which unconsciously testifies to a historical situation, holds good in oral as in written testimony. The same criteria of judgment which the historian is accustomed to use when scrutinising documents apply when he has to consider the validity and importance of oral tradition.

Oral sources, spoken words, which do not deliberately attempt to re-create history can include a wide range of popular material and material associated with the arts and religion: riddles, jokes, anecdotes, proverbs, poems, songs, stories set in the past often contain much of importance for the historian. Allusions, comments, casual references in a mass of other material frequently hold the key to the understanding of events. Attempts at the preservation or interpretation of history can include lists of kings or other notables and similar tables of ancestry for clan groups at one level of information, and more extended histories, stories, sagas, legends and myths at another.

Just as there are certain stylised forms for writings and certain rules of expression that types of documents should follow, so oral traditions, according to their categories, will probably be cast in certain ways. One type of oral tradition, an epic poem, say, may possibly require that heroes act in a stereotyped manner, that laws concerning a certain aspect of life be associated with a certain ruler, that events follow a balanced, determined pattern, and that individual character-istics be subdued to the demands of artistry. Alterations, omissions, repetitions, apparent falsifications in the historical record of events may be related to such demands. Consequently, the historian, studying oral traditions, has to find out, often with the assistance of the anthropologist, into what category or categories his source material falls, and what distortions he can expect to find and must allow for. A process akin to the editing of a text is necessary. All those who know the tradition should be asked for their versions, which can then be compared. The search for and indication of variants, and the identification of corruptions, show the way in which the tradition has been handed down, the distortions and falsifications themselves being important as evidence of judgment of history. However, oral traditions pass through a more human, potentially more emotional channel of communication than do written documents: the historian recording them is taking them from someone speaking to him, one who is not passive as a book or document is: two individuals are communicating in a particular situation, the factors of which may affect the transmission and thereby the text of the tradition. The informant, whose task and honour it is to hand on traditions, may attempt his own elucidation and explanation, and his interpretation has to be distinguished from the text itself. Any commentary he may be making must be understood to be such and not treated as part of the text he is transmitting.

The historian has in many ways to treat his oral sources as he would a document, and for his convenience reduce it to writing. When his investigations have provided a text which he has written down, with variations, corruptions and commentaries noted, he can criticise this as he would any documents he handles. The distinction here between the recovery of oral tradition and its subsequent interpretation should be noted. As far as possible, the material, once recovered, should be made available to other historians for their interpretation and commentary.

One of the most important criteria for evaluating the reliability of the text concerns the status of the oral informant and of his predecessors. There is an obvious difference between traditions carefully preserved and transmitted by specialised informants and those remembered by the common people. All 'Official Histories' must be recognised as such and the element of propaganda and the bias in them established. G. S. Were comments that more is known about royal dynasties than about peoples. The position and function of the informant has to be clarified so that allowance may be made for his interest as an individual and as a member of a profession. The function and purpose, the reason for the preservation of the tradition must also be investigated. The old criterion, 'Cui bono?' (to whose advantage?) will have to be applied. Does the tradition actively uphold, rationalise, support or glorify some institution or existing balance of advantage? Fabricated genealogies or stories of origins are not uncommon. To what extent will this bias the narration? The political is not the only interpretation that may have affected the testimony. Popular accounts and references may have distorted events out of nationalistic, tribal or clan pride, for religious reasons, or from a desire to produce an edifying, excitingly dramatic or artistically balanced story.

The anthropological approach is never far away. Both when establishing a definite text and when criticising it, a thorough knowledge of the society to which the tradition relates will be necessary. Form, content and manner of transmission, and significance attached to the tradition will depend on the political and social features of the society. Myths will be understood only when their function and role in society is grasped. As in the case of all other historical evidence, wide comparisons with other material of a similar nature from surrounding areas will illuminate the study of the tradition, highlighting connections and parallels.

But the amount of material of this nature which may be recovered is likely to vary. Organised societies have taken great care of their traditions or, at least, certain individuals and classes considered it worth their while and had the power to take great care of what they wished to be considered as their traditions. Narratives that can be recognised as being obviously historical accounts will be less easily discoverable among nomadic societies or groups less tightly organised. The complexity of less obviously historical material is daunting. Traditions, too, it should be remembered, belong to a clan or a tribe rather than to a stretch of country. Most tribes know their own history, not the history of those who preceded them. As Were says, very little is known or remembered of the period immediately preceding the coming of the Bachwezi. Conversely, a group, dominant militarily or culturally, may impose its own traditions on another so that what at first appears to be the history of the tribe or clan may, on closer examination, prove to be merely the story of this aristocracy. In any case, most oral traditions in East Africa will be found to go back no further than the sixteenth century.

But whatever the difficulties of tracing, defining and evaluating oral traditions, the historian has the advantage of working in a field where he is not attempting to grasp the principles and methods of investigation of a separate discipline or science: he applies to oral testimony the traditional methods, the criteria of judgment, and the techniques he uses with written evidence.

Linguistics

Language itself is a part of a culture complex, and it can be studied in an attempt to discover what its form and content, its grammar and vocabulary, can tell us about the historical experience of the people who speak it. The study of oral tradition treats language as the medium through which information is conveyed: the study of linguistics, for historical purposes, considers the language itself as the historical survival, to be looked at as the historian, using information provided by the anthropologist, looks at other social institutions. If a language is to fulfil its purpose as a means of communication, it must contain words and grammatical concepts sufficient to deal adequately with the situations likely to arise in the cultural complex that possesses the language concerned. Expressing nominal, verbal and other grammatical functions, these concepts come into existence because the realities they represent are experienced in societies which have to find conventional symbols for expressing them. Multiplicity of synonyms for certain objects and processes indicates their importance in political, religious, economic and social life. Cultural change, bringing new ideas, concepts and institutions, is reflected in the linguistic changes necessary in a language so that the new conditions of life may be expressed.

The historian, therefore, finds his source material in the traces which historical experience has left in language. The frequency or absence of certain words and the subtlety of differentiation between varied facets of a single concept, testify to the importance possessed by the object or institution for which words are either lacking or proliferate. The vocabulary of a language is a record of its past, and frequently, of how society has reflected on its past, attempting to see sense and order in it.

Distribution of languages is of great significance to the historian, as are the relationships between languages. Peoples who speak languages of the same family may be assumed to be themselves connected or to have been in close contact at some time in the past. The assumption is that variations between languages of the same family can show how long ago the break in contact occurred—the greater the difference, the longer the time since the ancestors of those speaking these languages today separated. Careful comparisons can indicate migratory patterns and the spread of influence of a language as a whole or of certain concepts held by the society which spoke it. The plotting of the geographical distribution of language families can sometimes show an original centre of language diffusion, a homeland, and indicate the migration of those who spoke it or its derivatives. The spread of certain language families may represent derivation from a common ancestral language with changes induced by varying historical experience, or it can imply a pervasive cultural diffusion. This applies to particular words as well. The study of the borrowing of words from other languages can show how a neighbouring influence has pervaded one aspect of culture, how a certain feature has itself been borrowed or imposed on others. Ehret, for example, uses linguistic evidence to show that Cushitic influences were weaker on the Highlands and Plains Nilotes peoples than on the Kalenjin-Tatog group. Extensive variations between the modern Southern Cushitic languages lead him to conclude that the ancestors of those who speak these languages today were in East Africa for a long time, possibly 4,000 years. Their influence on the Bantu can be seen in the Bantu languages. Cohen mentions the Lango as a people, not originally Nilotic, who adopted a Nilotic language, and refers to Lwoo arrivals in Kitara who adopted a Bantu language and gave up their own.

Comparison of the grammatical forms and vocabulary of related languages may sometimes make possible reconstruction of the ancestor languages from which they derived. This parent language can then tell the historian much of the way of life of the people who spoke it—of their activities, priorities and preconceptions. Ehret, for instance, finds that the Proto-Southern Cushitic community had some knowledge of agriculture and probably lived in southern Kenya.

One major problem associated with linguistics in Africa is that advanced research depends on accurate classification of African language families. Much basic research for this still remains to be done, and where it has been completed, linguists are in disagreement over what it shows. The determination of vocabularies, the reconstruction of grammar, the degree of importance to attach to borrowed words or other linguistic features—all present difficulties. Language studies, however, hold out some of the best chances of recovering the past.

Genetic studies

The passage of time and the experiences they have undergone

have left their impression on the constitution of human beings, animals and plants. Such traces can be recognised and differentiated by scientists, and when they have been brought to the notice of the historian they can tell him something of the experiences and incidents to which they are surviving witnesses. The way in which man has adapted to the circumstances of his environment and the way in which he has adapted animals and plants to meet his needs can be seen in inherited characteristics.

As far as man himself is concerned, results of the work of physical anthropologists, biochemists, biologists, physiologists and doctors have been disappointing. Attempts to classify the peoples of Africa according to skin colour, bone structure, etc., have not been successful. Human remains provided by archaeology have not been sufficiently numerous to enable any worthwhile conclusions to be reached. Sutton, when discussing the Capsian Culture, remarks that the Caucasoid physical type he tentatively identifies with the Southern Cushites appears to be of Ethiopian origin. There is not the data at present for more detailed speculation.

It was hoped at one time that the investigation of man's genetic inheritance would provide more information than has been the case. Genes determine characteristics that are handed on from generation to generation. The frequencies of genes in a population as a whole can be determined and expressed, so that, in theory, comparisons on the basis of different genetic inheritance should show significant correlations, where peoples have common ancestors or between whom there has been considerable intermarriage. Again, theoretically, it might prove possible to identify degrees of intermarriage and to plot migrations and movements on a map. This may eventually happen when the technique is more refined.

The study of man's susceptibility to disease and consequent adaptive resistance to it has been put forward as a source of historical information. Associating the sickle-shaped red blood cell, as distinct from the normal round shape, with a degree of immunity to malaria, it was argued that this was to be found in Negroes and was also present in other African groups in proportion to the degree of their intermixture with Negroes. Further medical research now throws considerable doubt on all these assumptions. Nevertheless, it seems reasonable to expect human biology and associated sciences to produce in the course of time some more sophisticated tools for detecting the effect of history.

Genetic studies are more useful, from a historical point of view, when they relate to plants. The historian is interested in plants from the time of their domestication, after which, he assumes, their movements and the appearance of new cultivated varieties may be identified with the people of whose economy they form a part. Botanists can suggest where the first centre of domestication was—broadly speaking this having been the region where the largest numbers of varieties of the plant can be found today. The spread of staple crops, with consequent effects on population and cultural developments, can be indicated by the plant geneticist. More detailed studies by the botanists are eagerly awaited. Sutton here discusses food production and its importance, especially that of the banana and its route into the interior. Chittick alludes to the possible connection between Indonesian influence and the banana.

Less attention has been paid to the origins of cattle, sheep, horses and goats than to those of plants. It may prove possible to reconstruct the process by which wild animals were domesticated and subsequently bred for man's purposes. The tracing and dating of centres and times of domestication, of routes of migration and of the evolution of specialised varieties is obviously of great importance. Unfortunately, this is likely to prove difficult owing to man's continued interference in the breeding of domesticated animals. The study of blood grouping in cattle has, so far, not proved useful in such research.

Dating

In such ways as these, then, the historian can learn about the past. Various techniques and methods of research can indicate a succession of developments which interests him. The problem of fitting successive events into a firm chronological structure still remains. Reports from archaeologists concerning cultural levels can enable a relative chronology to be determined, indicating that cultures followed each other in a certain sequence. Linguists can identify the relative ages of languages, and anthropologists and botanists can portray evolution and development. The succession of generations and rulers is to be found in oral tradition. But this relative dating is not sufficient for the historian, who demands the precision of absolute dating, and a scale against which the information from varying sources can be set, so that it may be possible for him to place evidence acquired by different scientific techniques as precisely and accurately as possible in its historical framework.

Archaeology has come forward with radiocarbon dating. Carbon 14 is found in carbon dioxide in the atmosphere. It is a radioactive isotope, produced by cosmic rays, and is absorbed by plants, and consequently by all living organic matter, including animals, during their lifetime. Absorption stops when the organism dies, and the carbon 14, already absorbed, begins to disintegrate at a fixed rate from the time of death. From laboratory examination of samples of various forms of organic matter, a calculation as to the time elapsed since the death of the organism can be made. For example, a bone sample can tell when a man or animal died, while a wood sample shows when a tree was cut down. Dates cannot be announced with absolute precision but, calculated with a statistical provision for error, have a probability range between 50 and 300 years. Contamination of the atmosphere by increased radioactivity may, however, have falsified some calculations, and some other chemical and physical assumptions may have to be revised. Other methods of dating, using physics and chemistry, are used, but the radiocarbon method appears, at present, to be the one most helpful to the historian.

Lexicostatistics is the statistical study of the vocabulary of languages with the intention of determining their antiquity. This study is based on the assumption that all languages have a basic vocabulary which changes slowly at a rate which is the same for all languages at all times, and which can be expressed as a formula. The percentages of the reconstructed basic vocabulary of the parent language possessed by derivative languages are indications of their relationship to one another and to the parent language, and are also signs of their respective ages. Glottochronology, a subdivision of lexicostatistics, is attempting to express rates of language development by formulae precise enough to enable dates for change to be calculated. Such statistical treatments of language have not been pushed very far on the African continent as yet and the method has not met with universal acceptance.

Natural phenomena can, sometimes, be dated. Astronomers can determine the paths taken by eclipses that have occurred at various times throughout history. The time when an eclipse affected a particular part of the earth's surface can be fixed.

If oral tradition remembers this occurrence, the events associated in tradition with the eclipse can also be dated.

Statistical calculations can also help the historian get the most out of the information he can acquire. By a system of averaging, the length of a generation (usually taken as the time between the birth of a man and the birth of his first child) can be worked out for a particular society, and dates estimated for events associated with certain generations. This assumes, of course, that problems of nomenclature of generations are overcome so that the progression in time is clear. Where the number and names of successive age sets are remembered, the same system of averaging can be applied.

Some have attempted to apply this concept of averaging to reigns, to work out the average length of reign, and when the number of reigns is known, to suggest dates. This is a much more doubtful method. Periods of commotion, with rulers dying violent deaths, or long periods of peace without usurpers or rivals are likely to upset the calculation. The question of the rules of succession has to be gone into very carefully.

Method

The growing tendency in historical studies today is for the historian not only to accept information from the scientists but also to adopt some of their methods of research. An example of the adoption of such methods is the recognition of the value of the statistical approach. Attempts to determine dates, particularly where these are probabilities, not certainties, show the importance of statistics to the historian, who must know the margin of error within which he is working. The concept of probabilities and the calculation of degrees of certainty fall within the province of the statistician, and where the historian finds himself dealing with pieces of information of varying degrees of reliability he will have to know to what extent it is safe to draw conclusions from them. Techniques of sampling and measuring will be helpful. Complex data, drawn from the natural and social sciences, not necessarily in the literary form to which the historian is accustomed, will have to be dealt with. He will be handling tables, graphs, charts and formulae. Many factors will have to be studied quantitatively, and this will take the historian into the realm of mathematics. In his attempts to be as accurate and unbiased as possible in his assessments and to avoid the reproach that he is giving unscientific, subjective conclusions, he will follow methods already worked out by the natural scientists in their striving for objectivity.

Terminology that the historian has been accustomed to use in the past somewhat loosely, without much examination of what is meant by time-worn concepts, will have to be re-examined; new definitions will be necessary. The historian must not only learn to deal with the formulae, graphs and tables of the scientists, but must also grasp the precise meaning of the terms they use and employ them himself, with the same exactitude and care for the limitations of a concept. What, for instance, is meant by 'tribe', 'culture' or 'society'? Much of the historian's disappointment with the results of physical anthropology and genetic studies in mankind seems to have arisen from his failure to understand the terms being used, the tentative nature of the suggestions put forward, and his consequent attempt to make assumptions that the researchers in these disciplines would not venture to make. Any attempt to reach conclusions from the work of archaeologists, anthropologists, linguists, botanists and others, that these researchers would reject on the evidence before them, is a temptation that must be resisted. The reconciliation of conclusions reached by scholars in various disciplines, researching along different lines, in subjects with different methods and different concepts of what can safely be inferred from research, will be one of the hardest tasks of all. More and more scientists in related disciplines, however, are becoming interested in the problems of the historian, and are starting to ask questions that interest him. He has no longer to resign himself to picking up the occasional infuriating, passing reference to historical antecedents in the works of researchers not primarily concerned with history. Co-operation between those researching in related studies in the attempt to find the answer to specific historical questions has been tried elsewhere in Africa, with varying degrees of success, it is true, but this still looks like one of the most hopeful ways of finding out about East Africa's past.

The greater precision and objectivity which the adoption of a more scientific method make possible accompanies the opening up of a wider field of study, stretching out far beyond the libraries and the archives. In the future, other possibilities for the recovery of historical information may become apparent. Medical science, chemistry and physics will most probably have more to offer. Metallurgy, as another instance, should produce some significant discoveries. More sophisticated methods of handling information are likely to appear; the advent of the computer, for example, has already had an important impact on the study of Geography but has not yet affected the study of East African history to any noticeable extent. None of these developments essentially changes the historian's task or takes away from him his employment. Neither does it relegate to obscurity the study of written and printed documents which remain one of the finest sources of information. The historian's obligation is still that of discovering and utilising all available source material to give the most accurate interpretation possible of the past. Scholars in other disciplines may help him with information: the responsibility for its analysis and utilisation rests with him.

Further reading

BLOCH, M. *The Historian's Craft,* Manchester University Press, Manchester, 1954.

GLUCKMAN, M. *Politics, Law and Ritual in Tribal Society,* Basil Blackwell, Oxford, 1965.

GREENBERG, J. H. *Studies in African Linguistic Classification,* Compass Publishing Co., New Haven, Conn., 1955.

MOHRMANN, C., SOMMERFELT, A. and WHATMOUGH, J. (Eds.) *Trends in European and American Linguistics, 1930-1960,* Spectrum, Utrecht/Antwerp. H. Hoijer, Anthropological Linguistics.

VANSINA, J. *Oral Tradition : A Study in Historical Methodology,* Routledge and Kegan Paul, London, 1965.

MURDOCK, G. P. *Africa : Its Peoples and their Culture History,* McGraw-Hill, New York, 1959.

MCCALL, D. F. *Africa in Time-Perspective : A Discussion of Historical Reconstruction from Unwritten Sources,* Ghana University Press/Boston University Press, Legon, Boston, 1964.

LYSTAD, R. A. (Ed.) *The African World : A Study of Social Research,* Pall Mall Press, London, 1965.

VANSINA, J., MAUNY, R. and THOMAS, L. V. (Eds.) *The Historian in Tropical Africa : Studies presented and discussed at the Fourth International African Seminar at the University of Dakar, Senegal, 1961,* International African Institute/Oxford University Press, London, 1964.

POSNANSKY, M. (Ed.) *Prelude to East African History,* Oxford University Press, London, Nairobi, 1966.

Journal of African History, Volume III No. 2, 1962, (Special Number: Third Conference on African History and Archaeology, School of Oriental and African Studies, London, July 1961) Cambridge University Press, London.

Azania, Journal of the British Institute of History and Archaeology in East Africa, Volume I, 1966, Oxford University Press, London, Nairobi.

2

The Geography of East Africa

Francis F. Ojany

Although the history of any country and of its people can be influenced considerably by the natural environment, rarely is this fact fully appreciated until times of difficulty as for example when a war has to be fought in the territory. No proper appreciation of the history of East Africa with its twenty-four million inhabitants is therefore possible without an intelligent understanding of the major elements of the East African natural

Table 1 : The size of the East African Countries :

Country	Area in square miles		
	Land/ Surface	Water/ Swamp	Total
TANZANIA:			
Mainland (Tanganyika)	341,150	20,650	361,800
Zanzibar Island	640		640
Pemba Island	380		380
UGANDA	74,748	16,386	91,134
KENYA	219,789	5,171	224,960
EAST AFRICA (TOTAL):	636,707	42,207	678,914

scene which form the stage for man's activities. The purpose of this chapter is to offer this vital background knowledge.

Together, the three East African countries of Tanzania, Uganda and Kenya form a compact block of terrain that extends over some 636,707 square miles of land and some 42,207 square miles of water and swamp. Table 1 summarises this information. The figures should form the basis for useful and independent analysis.

Our region is situated in the eastern part of Equatorial Africa, extending from latitude 4° 30′ N to latitude 11° 45′ S and from longitudes 29° 28′ E to 41° 55′ E. Thus, East Africa extends from the western shores of the Indian Ocean to the western arm of the Great African Rift Valley, which forms a natural boundary along the entire western edge.

Geology of East Africa

Figure 1 shows the main types of rocks and faults that occur in East Africa. The chief rock formations are the ancient rocks, which include a complicated group known generally as the Basement System rocks, the Karagwe-Ankolean, the Nyanzian-Kavirondian-Toro rocks, the Dodoman and other older rocks which in the map are shown as 'Acid gneisses, migmatites and associated granites and granodiorites.' These ancient rocks form the foundation of the African continent and are known to be extremely old in age. In western Kenya, the Nyanzian-Kavirondian rocks have been shown to be at least 3,000 million years old, so that the Dodoman and earlier rocks are therefore much older still. These archaean rocks were originally sedimentary formations that were laid down in great geosynclinal formations which covered much of our region and indeed much of Africa at the time. Later, but still during archaean times, these rocks were involved in intense earth movements during which they were folded, altered and considerably graniticised. As a result of these processes, the rocks became harder and much more resistant in their physical characteristics.

Granites and other granite-like rocks (sometimes known as mobilized granites), are the other archaean rocks in the region. They are best seen in the areas marginal to Lake Victoria. These are commonly assumed to be of igneous origin although they may have been altered considerably by metasomatism.

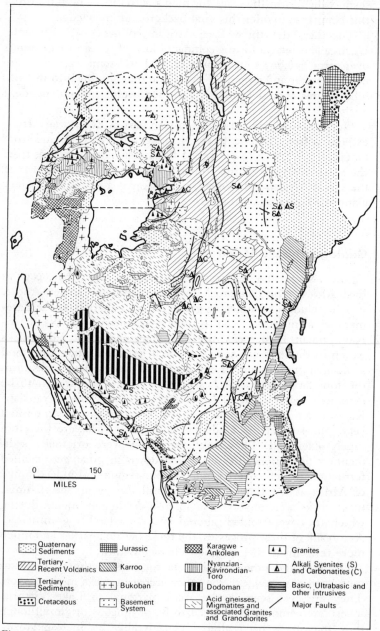

Figure 1 East Africa: Geology

They are much more resistant to erosion and today they form a picturesque tor landscape especially between Mwanza and Musoma and around Bukoba, and to the north and north-west of Kisumu.

Since the Karroo (Carboniferous) era, the coastline of Eastern Africa has been subjected to a series of marine transgressions as can be seen from the record of the Jurassic, Cretaceous, Tertiary and Pleistocene sedimentary formations in the area. From the Tertiary to the Pleistocene, East Africa was included in major tectonic activities involving continental uplift, warping, tilting and faulting. As would be expected with resistant rocks, many responded to these stresses by breaking and not folding. Warping (here down-warping) affected the Lake Victoria basin in particular and this is interpreted as marking the ultimate phases in the process of 'basin and swell structure' so typical of the African structural environment. Tilting is illustrated best by the Uganda drainage as evidenced by the very gentle gradient typical of most Uganda rivers. Back-tilting, involving stream reversal, on the other hand, is best seen in the neighbour-hood of Lake Kyoga which was brought into being following the reversal of the Kafu river during the formation of the Western Rift Valley. Before these events, Kafu, like other main Uganda rivers, probably drained into the Atlantic Ocean. Faulting, of course produced the present day Rift Valleys of East Africa and although it is known that the original tectonic valleys are ancient features, going back into pre-Cambrian times, the present picturesque features with their steep and fresh scarps are clearly post mid-Pleistocene, i.e. less than 500,000 years in age.

The tertiary and later earth movements were accompanied by much volcanic eruption which drastically modified the geography of East Africa. Most of the lava was emitted along old lines of weakness as fissure eruptions although central-type eruptions were also represented as evidenced by imposing composite cones of mounts Kenya and Elgon. Some of the best agricultural lands as well as the better climatic regions are in these volcanic areas; the consequences in the distribution of man in the region will be examined later.

Rocks are important not only in soil formation, but also as sources of valuable minerals. In this connection, the East African rocks so far have proved disappointing in that they do not seem to be well-endowed with minerals of economic value. The pre-Cambrian rocks in Tanganyika have yielded a valuable output of diamonds—mainly from the Shinyanga and Mwandui areas. Also in western Kenya, meagre outputs of gold and copper have been worked but the reserves would seem to be very limited. Uganda has recently found more valuable deposits of copper in Kilembe and this mineral now plays an important role in the national economy. The Karroo Beds of Tanganyika are known to contain considerable reserves of coal but the technical problems involved in exploiting the mineral have so far been prohibitive. The carbonatites of Uganda supply a cement factory in Tororo while along the East African coast, another important rock for cement manufacture is the pleistocene coral limestone. This rock is crushed for cement production near Dar es Salaam and Mombasa and the potentialities are known to be considerable.

The volcanic rocks are also significant in the economic field. The trona (soda deposits—mainly soda ash and common salt) from Lake Magadi in Kenya is the most important in this connection. Between 1919 and 1953, almost two million tons of soda ash were produced and in the twenty years since 1933, nearly a quarter million tons of common salt has been produced. In Uganda, the Katwe Salt Works, near Lake Edward, have also been worked for a considerable period. Of the Pleistocene rocks, we should note the diatomaceous earth which is worked for diatomite at Kariandus in the Kenya section of the Rift Valley. Also a number of the volcanic rocks such as trachytes and phonolites are widely used locally for building stones and for ballast while occasional occurrences of obsidian and flint in the younger rocks were used by early man to make his implements. A number of volcanic rocks were also used for the same purpose.

Relief Features

The physiography of East Africa can be understood only through a thorough knowledge of its geological history. Fundamentally, the area forms part of that section of the African Massif which A. K. Lobeck named 'High Africa', as opposed to 'Low Africa'. 'Low Africa' was generally restricted to land below 3,000 feet above sea level, 'High Africa' being land above that height.

In detail, East Africa has a complicated and highly diversified

topography which, however, can be broken down into a series
of plateau-like surfaces ranging in height from about 1,200 feet
above sea level, to higher plateaus at over 10,000 feet. Figure 2
shows the details of this physiography. The pattern is largely the
result of earth movements involving continental uplifts, faulting,
volcanicity and a series of prolonged periods of subaerial
erosion which have dominated the area right from pre-Cambrian
times. The long periods of erosion, interrupted by a number of
changes in the base level, produced a series of planation surfaces
at different heights above the present sea level. The best known
levels are at 6,000 to 8,000, 5,000 to 5,500, 4,000 to 4,500,
3,000 to 3,600 and at 1,000 feet above sea level. The highest of
these surfaces, now preserved on such areas as the Kisii plateau,
the Kitale-Cherangani Hills, the Machakos Hills, the crests of
the Kipengere and the Livingstone Mountains and probably
the crest of the Ankole Hills, is the oldest of the plateaus (commonly called the Gondwana surface), and is of late Jurassic
age. The well-known, uplifted plateau of Buganda (4,000 to
4,300 feet above sea level), results from a prolonged standstill
and is probably early Tertiary in age.

From Figure 2 it is evident that a proper coastal plain is
generally absent from the East African coast, although a narrow
coastal fringe occurs below 600 feet. This narrow belt widens
considerably in the area to the north of Mombasa along the
Tana River delta as it does also to the south of Dar es Salaam
about the Rufiji River delta. The East African islands of Pemba,
Zanzibar and Mafia belong to this coastal fringe but one should
also note that Pemba island is slightly beyond the continental
shelf due probably to a north-south trending fault which
separates this island from the mainland. Immediately to the
west of the coastal fringe is an extensive and monotonous plateau
which rises inland very gradually to about 3,000 feet above sea
level. This region, commonly known as the Low Foreland
Plateau, includes much of northern Kenya as well as the Duruma-
Wajir Low Belt of Kenya. It is relatively much narrower immediately to the west of Tanga but again widens considerably
below Morogoro from where it extends to include the Kilombero
Valley and the valleys of the Great Ruaha Rivers. Much of
south-eastern Tanganyika belongs to this physiographic region.

Much of Uganda and the interior of Tanganyika, especially
around Tabora and including the Lake Victoria area is part of
a vast interior plateau. In Tanganyika, the height of this plateau

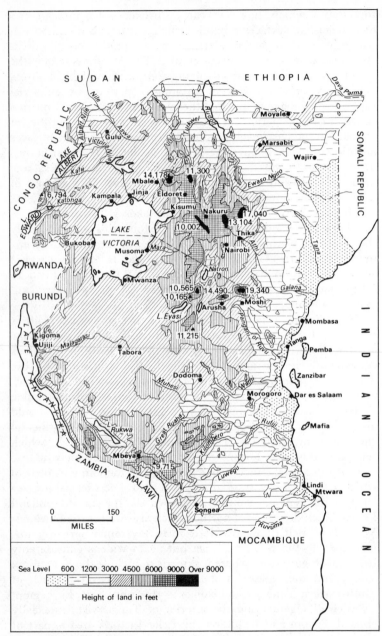

Figure 2 East Africa: Relief

varies between 3,000 to 4,500 feet, although occasionally remnants of a higher plateau rising to 6,000 feet may also be seen. The Serengeti plains and the Masai steppe or plains are examples of this interior plateau. In Uganda, the height of the plateau decreases very gradually towards the north with the valley cut by the Aswa River being just about 2,000 feet above sea level. The land surface also gets progressively younger as one moves towards the north-east from an early Tertiary surface in Buganda to a Miocene level in Kyoga and finally a Pliocene level in Acholi. Some authors delimit the land immediately marginal to Lake Victoria as a separate region but this distinction may be unnecessary from the point of view of physiography. The slight downwarp towards the lake basin—the latest of the 'swell and basin' structure of Africa—has been noted. The present basin is almost certainly a post mid-tertiary feature.

Besides the Interior Plateau, much of Central Kenya, parts of the Northern and the Southern Highlands of Tanganyika, a great part of south-western Uganda and the imposing horst block of Mount Ruwenzori form highland areas which are clearly in a separate class. These highlands rise from about 4,500 to 19,340 feet, the highest point on the Kibo peak of Kilimanjaro. Although these highlands are largely due to the great thickness of volcanic materials extruded since mid-Tertiary times, ancient upland massifs are also still preserved, and these erosional upland plateaus form the Gondwana planation surfaces that we have already noted. The Central Highlands of Kenya are bisected almost equally by the meridional trench of the eastern branch of the East African Rift Valley. The highlands on either side of the Rift Valley are dominated by individual ranges which deserve noting. The Aberdare Range, rising to over 13,000 feet, and the Ngong Hills dominate the eastern portion. The western sections of these volcanic cones were downthrown together with the Rift Valley. To the north-east of the Aberdare Range is the majestic volcanic pile formed by the composite volcano of Mount Kenya, with the Nyeri corridor forming a useful gap between the two. Continuing in the same direction is the Nyambeni Range, a relatively smaller cone that may have been formed by a feeder connected to the main Mount Kenya reservoir.

The western portion of the Central Kenya Highlands is dominated by the Mau Range with its prominent escarpment, the Kericho Highlands, and the Tinderet Hills which continue

through the Uasin Gishu Plateau to link with the other central
volcano of Mount Elgon. These volcanic highlands join imperceptibly with the resistant residual hills of the Cherangani in
the Elgeyo-Marakwet areas to form one extensive highland
environment. Portions of these upstanding areas have also
been downthrown into the floor of the Rift Valley in similar
manner to the Eastern Highlands.

The highlands of Northern Tanganyika are mainly of volcanic
origin and are dominated by a number of peaks amongst which
Ngorongorò Crater at 10,165 feet, Jaeger Summit at 10,565 feet
and Loolmalasin at 11,965 feet are the most important. The
area illustrates especially well the altitudinal influence of
climate, in that, although the surrounding area is almost arid,
the highland region has developed a temperate climate in the
heart of the tropics. Mount Kilimanjaro is really made up of
three different volcanic cones each of which erupted at a different
time but along one line of structural weakness. Shira Cone
(at 13,140 feet), probably erupted during the Miocene era.
It was followed by the Mawenzi Cone (now 16,900 feet) probably during Pliocene times, Kibo Cone (now 19,340 feet) is
clearly the youngest, and is generally believed to be a Quaternary
feature. The different ages of these three peaks are clearly
confirmed by their varying degrees of erosion. Shira, the
oldest, is much dissected and reduced by erosive agencies
while Kibo is still relatively intact.

As in central Kenya, the Southern Highlands of Tanganyika
have a complex topography in which Gondwana planation
surfaces and Cainozoic lava highlands occur together. The
Kipengere Range, the Livingstone Mountains in the Njombe
area, the Udzungwa Range in Iringa and the Fipa Plateau
between Lake Rukwa and the southern portion of Lake Tanganyika are ancient massifs in which some of the oldest erosion
surfaces to be found in Africa are still preserved. Volcanic
materials on the other hand are confined to the Rungwe Mountains between Mbeya township and the northern tip of Lake
Nyasa. The eruption extruded from the point of intersection of a
number of faults as can be seen from Fig. 1. Such an eruption
is quite common in volcanic areas where lines of weakness also
occur. The Highlands of Kigezi in Uganda are, of course, part
of the volcanic province of Rwanda while the highlands to the
west of Bukoba are due to the hard and resistant Karagwe-
Ankolean rocks which outcrop in these parts. The Ruwenzori

Massif is an unusual horst block that was uplifted during the time of tectonic disturbances and is now preserved in the floor of the western Rift Valley.

The East African Rift Valley deserves further attention. Over much of central Kenya its average width is between 20 and 40 miles and its floor varies from 1,230 feet above sea level in Lake Rudolf to about 6,000 feet around Nakuru. From here, the level of the floor drops southwards to 1,900 feet in Lake Magadi. Past the Kenya border, the rift bifurcates, with the southern continuation delimiting the Northern Highlands of Tanganyika to make them into another horst-like massif. We should note also that the Pangani River valley is essentially a continuation of the same system of the East African Rift Valley with the resistant Usambara and Pare mountains forming another block of mountains although details of the fault trends involved have not yet been fully investigated.

The western arm of the Rift Valley is complicated. From the point of tectonic intersection centred around the Rungwe Mountains, the north-eastern trough forms the Great Ruaha Valley while the north-western arm contains Lake Rukwa and the Karu Plains. Another parallel counterpart of this arm defines the Lake Tanganyika trough. It is this Lake Tanganyika trough which continues northwards to include Lake Albert at 2,030 feet above sea level. The magnitude of the downthrow in the valley now infilled by Lake Tanganyika may be judged from the fact that Lake Tanganyika is the second deepest lake in the world.

The general form of the Rift Valley floor also merits examination. Its entire length is studded by a number of saline lakes which are known to be remnants of much larger water bodies that collected in this depression during the wetter phases (pluvials) associated with the last glaciation. In Kenya the lakes are Rudolf, Baringo, Nakuru, Elmenteita, Naivasha and Magadi. Just beyond the Kenya border is situated Lake Natron and further down along the south-western arm of the rift is situated Lake Eyasi, with Lake Manyara occupying the south-eastern arm. The western branch of the Rift Valley has fewer but much larger lakes as is evident in Fig. 2. The reasons for this may be greater initial downthrows as well as a higher rainfall in the area. The Rift Valley floor is also characterised by a number of subsequent volcanic cones of which the Menengai Crater and Mounts Longonot and Suswa are particularly important.

The East African Climate

Highly varied climatic difference is one of the outstanding facts about East Africa, the result of large altitudinal range, the distribution of land and water, land barriers, air movements and ocean currents. The environment is dominated at different times of the year by a number of air-masses and the climate is largely influenced by the character of the source regions from which these originate and by the tracts of country across which they blow. The dominance of a particular air-mass over the region is controlled largely by the apparent movement of the overhead sun between the two tropics, and this provides a convenient basis for an analysis of the East African climate.

From November to March, the main air-stream affecting East Africa is from the north and north-east which, because of its source, is a dry air-mass. It has a drying influence which is particularly marked in the western extremities of East Africa where, as the 'Harmattan' or 'Egyptian air', it blows from a high pressure belt across the Sahara. Over the eastern parts of the area the air-mass, known as the Arabian or Indian North-East Trade Winds or as the North-East Monsoon, is a less drying maritime variety which may bring some precipitation, as we shall note later.

By April, the wind pattern has considerably changed and the region comes under the influence of the Indian Ocean South-East Trade Winds. This air-mass coming from a vast ocean area is moisture-laden and the source of the main rains over East Africa. The air-mass blows steadily, reaching its maximum force in July when there is a low pressure-belt in the northern hemisphere. When these winds cross the Equator; they approach the Arabian peninsula and India as the South-West monsoon.

At this time these winds have completely replaced the North-East Monsoon that blows in November over the Indian Ocean, and this alternation of wind systems provided a natural facility for the early contacts which were established between the south-west Asian sub-continent and the East African coast. The Arabs and the Indians were able to take advantage of the steady North-East monsoon winds to sail their dhows to East Africa, to do their trading in the area while waiting for the onset of the South-west Monsoon winds for the return voyage with their acquired merchandise. Some degree of this traffic is still undertaken, without any appreciable improvements to the manner of construction of the dhows. The historical significance of this early contact will be apparent in later chapters but we may note here the geographical origin of much permanent human record in the coastal belt, of Arabic and Asiatic cultures that is very different from those of the interior of East Africa.

(i) Rainfall

It has been shown that the South-East Trades are responsible for the main rains over much of East Africa, but coastal zones of the region that lie to the south of the Equator also get some rains from the North-East Trades especially where this air-mass has crossed a wide portion of the Indian Ocean. Also, parts of western Uganda get some rains from Atlantic Ocean or Congo airstreams during the northern summer, and Lake Victoria is extensive enough to generate its own maritime climate.

Although the northerly air-masses are drying and not rain-bearing, they are important in that the rains are associated with the zone of convergence between the northerly and south-easterly and indeed the south-westerly (Congo) airstreams. This zone of convergence is conventionally known as the Inter-tropical Convergence Zone (ITCZ), and since its actual position over East Africa is dependent on the position of the overhead sun, the seasonal distribution of rainfall over East Africa also follows this apparent movement of the sun. As a result of the above situation, three distinct rainfall seasons occur over East Africa. A régime of equatorial character occurs broadly over much of the northern parts of East Africa to about 3°S. Latitude over the higher parts of the region and to about 7°S. along the coastal belt. In the coastal belt, a single peak, usually about May, is evident, but inland, a double peak, between March and May and from mid-October to December is the pattern. These are respectively the Long and the Short Rains of East Africa. On either side of this Equatorial régime, there is a tendency towards a single rainy season and a single dry season. Most of Tanganyika and the coastal areas that lie to the south of Dar es Salaam, for instance, have only one rainy season extending from about December to April, the rest of the year being one long dry season. In the northern parts of East Africa, the rainy seasons also tend to coalesce to give a five months' rainy season with July as the wettest month in Uganda. In Northern Kenya

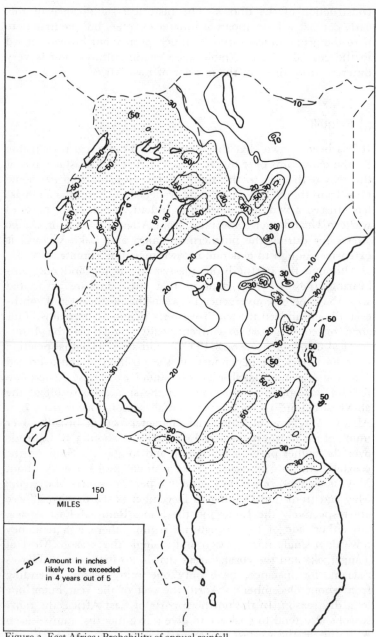

Figure 3 East Africa: Probability of annual rainfall

physiography, especially in the high volcanic conical hills such as Mount Kulal and the Marsabit cones, causes localised rainfall differences and such areas tend towards the equatorial-type régime with a discernible double peak, in April and November.

Relief and inland water bodies, we have noted, greatly influence the amount of rainfall received in various places. A glance at the mean annual rainfall map will confirm this fact especially if it is read in conjunction with the relief map. Highland areas stand out as better-watered islands in an essentially underwatered region. For example, in Northern Kenya, the isolated volcanic cones such as Marsabit and Mount Kulal receive much higher rainfall totals compared with the surrounding steppe or semi-arid and arid vast plains. As one ascends higher, frost may be encountered from about 7,000 feet above sea level while glaciers are permanent on the three major East African mountains above about 15,000 feet. Also the large water surface of Lake Victoria (26,826 square miles), modifies the local climate of the areas immediately peripheral to the lake shores to make them some of the best watered parts of East Africa. The western, northern and the eastern shores are relatively wetter, with an annual mean from 40 to 80 inches (1,016 to 2,032 millimetres).

That East Africa suffers from an insufficient rainfall, is an important fact that must now be emphasised. J. F. Griffiths gives a vivid picture of the seriousness of this problem when he shows that nearly two-thirds of East Africa suffers from a drought of six months or more and that only two per cent of the entire area is assured of a mere two inches of rainfall in every month. Given this unsatisfactory situation and given the fact that much of East Africa is essentially agricultural, mean rainfall totals are of relatively minor significance. Clearly greater consideration from the point of view of planned farming must be the twin factors of rainfall reliability and probability. Figure 3 gives the rainfall probability based on a five year cycle and here again the inadequacy of the rainfall is alarming. Griffiths again shows that 72 per cent of Kenya, 13 per cent of Uganda and 16 per cent of Tanganyika can expect less than 20 inches of rainfall in four out of every five years. He also states conclusively that only 3 per cent of Kenya, 6 per cent of Uganda and 4 per cent of Tanganyika can expect more than 50 inches of rainfall in four years out of every five years. Taking the overall picture in East Africa, 35 per cent of the area can expect less than 20 inches in four out of five years; 20 per cent can expect between 20 and 30 inches; 41 per cent of the area is likely to get between 30 and 50 inches; and only 4 per cent of the entire area can expect more than 50 inches in four years out of five. Although the above picture shows the region as unfavourably placed, it presents but an aspect of the problem. Besides this apparent water shortage, there is the related factor of unreliability, a major characteristic of the rainfall over the entire area. This unreliability concerns both the total amount and the time of arrival and is a phenomenon that applies to much of Africa. The Table below will help to convey the situation better:

*Table 2 : Summary of Rainfall in Millimetres over selected East African Stations.**

Station	Maximum	Mean	Minimum
Wajir	513	249	74
Nairobi	1,570	879	437
Mombasa	1,887	1,204	709
Kigoma	1,214	935	658
Tabora	1,303	866	391
Mwanza	1,486	1,046	721
Gulu	2,035	1,544	1,004
Fort Portal	2,118	1,478	1,067
Entebbe	2,261	1,506	998

Besides the above disadvantages, and the usually torrential nature of the rains, loss through run-off is correspondingly high and combined with a generally high evaporation rate, further reduces the value of the rainfall for agricultural purposes.

(ii) Temperature

Besides the winds and the rainfall, other important elements of the weather which must be taken into consideration in the study of climate are temperature, humidity, sunshine and cloudiness. The first two are particularly important for human comfort. Altitude will help by tempering both, so that higher altitudes have lower and indeed more suitable temperatures and humidities for man, while the mean temperatures for coastal areas are much

*Source for Tables 2 to 5 is the *E.A. Economic and Statistical Review,* 1967.

as Mombasa and Dar es Salaam with 26·3°C and 25·7°C respectively and relative humidity in the zone is always between 79 and 82 per cent. The mean diurnal and annual ranges of temperature are relatively small along this coastal belt, chiefly due to the constantly high relative humidity. As one moves inland into the higher plateaus, the relative humidity drops as does the temperature, and the temperature ranges, both diurnal and annual, are much larger but not as great as in the semi-desert areas. The Table below gives a summary for a number of selected stations, and we should note here that the relatively lower temperatures in the interior highlands served as an attraction for European settlement in the highlands.

Table 3 : Summary of Temperature (°C) over selected East African Stations.

Station	Absolute Maximum	Mean Maximum	Mean	Mean Minimum	Absolute Minimum
Wajir	39·5	33·6	27·9	22·1	15·0
Nairobi	32·2	25·6	19·1	12·7	5·4
Mombasa	37·3	30·3	26·3	22·4	14·1
Kigoma	36·8	27·8	23·5	19·2	13·2
Tabora	35·7	29·5	23·1	16·7	7·0
Mwanza	35·0	27·7	22·7	17·7	10·8
Gulu	37·2	29·3	23·1	16·9	9·3
Fort Portal	31·8	25·3	19·1	12·8	5·6
Entebbe	31·7	25·9	21·5	17·1	10·4

To summarize, a major feature of the prevailing climate over East Africa is water shortage, the result of an inadequate and an unreliable rainfall. Altitude modifies the climate considerably giving an altitudinal zonation of climate with a Tropical Highland climate over the East African Highlands culminating in permanent snow above 15,000 feet. Thus the East African climate exhibits a great diversity, which although providing an opportunity to man for diversification of his activities must be regarded as being essentially a harsh climate because so much of the environment is hot and arid or semi-arid.

Vegetation and Soils

Figure 4 gives a simplified pattern of the vegetation over East Africa. It is clear that, due largely to a lower rainfall and partly to the long established impact of man, the coastal areas of East Africa are covered not by a true Equatorial Forest vegetation but by a poorer Coastal Forest Savanna Mosaic in which the forests and the savanna grasses are not so tall except along river valleys where mangrove forests and swamps also occur. Woodland Savanna Mosaic consists of scattered tree grasslands of low tree and high grass. This vegetation type is a wooded savanna complex in which either moist acacia savanna or combretum savanna may be dominant; in Kenya acacia-themeda is an important member. The Tropical Forest Savanna on the other hand is dominated in most places by elephant grass with only isolated remnants of forest. In Montane and Highland communities of grasslands and forests, the parts actually forested are few in contrast with wide expanses of undulating grasslands in which themeda triandra and Kikuyu grass dominate. Cedar and olive trees are much in evidence, especially in the lower sections of the forests but as one ascends, bamboo forests become more important between 9,000 and 10,000 feet. Beyond 10,000 feet, a mountain moorland is reached and this in turn is replaced by glaciers from about 15,000 feet on Mount Kenya and 16,000 feet on Kilimanjaro.

From the vegetation map, it is evident that over much of the drier parts of Kenya and Tanganyika, a dry bush with thorn trees, a wooded steppe with abundant acacia and commiphora, dominates. This bush-thorn vegetation, gets progressively poorer as one penetrates deeper into the drier parts of northern Kenya until a true desert vegetation is reached in the Chalbi Desert. The dry bush-thorn vegetation is better known over much of East Africa as the *Nyika*—a Swahili word for 'wilderness'. It forms a rough environment which was a major obstacle to early explorers endeavouring to penetrate into East Africa from the Coastal Belt. In addition to the thorn bush and thicket, lack of water and scorching heat within this 'wilderness', together with the malarial coastal belt, made the explorers' task extremely hard and dangerous.

Mention has been made of the role of man in modifying the original vegetation climax. This point needs a short elaboration. Man as a cultivator and as a pastoralist has over a long period

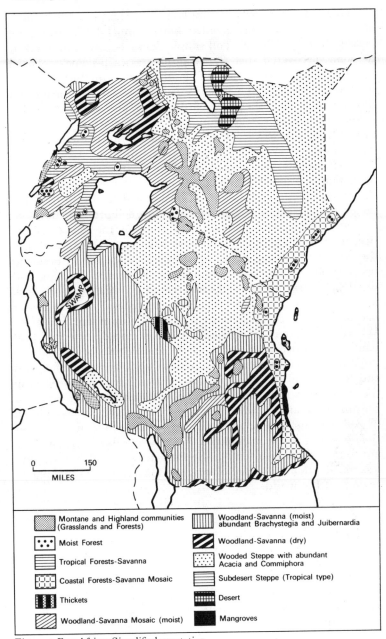

Figure 4 East Africa: Simplified vegetation

altered his environment as simply and as cheaply as his ability and understanding has enabled him. Annual bush fires were clearly the most effective and simple device and, as a pastoralist, he soon discovered that the tropical grasses become too hard and tough (e.g. 'wire grass' of South Africa), for cattle to feed on and need to be removed. The damage which fire introduced did not seem to bother him particularly. The result of all this is that the present vegetation, especially below 6,500 feet, is probably all derived vegetation in which a fire-resistant variety dominates.

A note must also be made here on East African soils. Soil formation is intimately related to climate, the geological formations, the topography, living organisms and finally to the time factor. Time must be available for a mature soil profile to develop. Climate is certainly the most important of the above factors because it influences the rate of weathering, leaching and also the rate at which the living organisms can operate in breaking up the soil. As over most tropical environments, leaching and weathering are intense and, as a result of this, the soils lack nutrient salts and silica so that they are generally red in colour because of the dominance of oxides of aluminium and iron. Where the latter is particularly pronounced, laterites and lateritic soils occur which support little vegetation and are of no value for cultivation. East African soils are generally poor and fragile, and the powerful soil erosion which takes place in the area, due to tropical rains and also to man's overgrazing and burning for many decades, has made them worse. In the opinion of soil scientists these soils need much care and manuring if their yield is to be maintained. Even where black cotton soils are found, these also tend to be hard to work, ill-drained and less fertile than say the *chernozem* soils found in temperate regions of the world.

East Africa as a Habitat

In the foregoing paragraphs, the major elements and facts of the East African environment have been described and explained. That physical environment forms the stage upon which early man, and likewise present man, has lived and derived his livelihood. But man has not been the only inhabitant of the area. Other animals, domesticated and undomesticated, have also obtained their livelihood here and made their homes. The undomesticated at some stage posed a challenge to man but at present an exciting need of coexistence between man and the wild game is recognised by the East African Governments in planning nature conservation programmes so that both flora and fauna of East Africa can be preserved in certain selected areas. Man will get his return through the tourist industry which is rapidly expanding, especially with visitors from developed countries where such natural splendour is no longer to be seen.

But the East African environment also provides a habitat for the tsetse fly, which is a danger not only to man but also to his domesticated animals. As a result of this, large tracts of the country where these flies occur are uninhabited. In Tanganyika alone, different species of the fly cover two-thirds of the country, with the woodland tsetse *(glossina morsitans)* especially in large areas of the Central and the Southern Highland Provinces. Other species, and in particular carriers of the bovine vector, make large parts of the Lake and the Northern Provinces unsafe for stock while *glossina pallidipes* make much of the Lake and coastal areas unsafe for both man and his stock. In Kenya the shores of Lake Victoria, the coastal belt and also parts of the Meru and Tsavo river valleys, harbour species of the fly which are known to be harmful. In Uganda parts of Ankole are also affected by dangerous species.

Population of East Africa

The devoted researches of L. S. B. Leakey in particular show conclusively that East Africa is one of the areas where man first found a home while more recent fruits of these patient investigations suggest that man most probably originated there. This exciting theory of evolution falls outside this chapter but the growth of the present population of East Africa must be included. Space cannot allow the full story to be related and so the reader must be directed to an invaluable chapter on this topic by J. G. C. Blacker (see bibliography, *The Natural Resources of East Africa*).

The first census of the East African population was taken in 1948 and for those interested in the development of East Africa as one political or economic unit, it was the most important

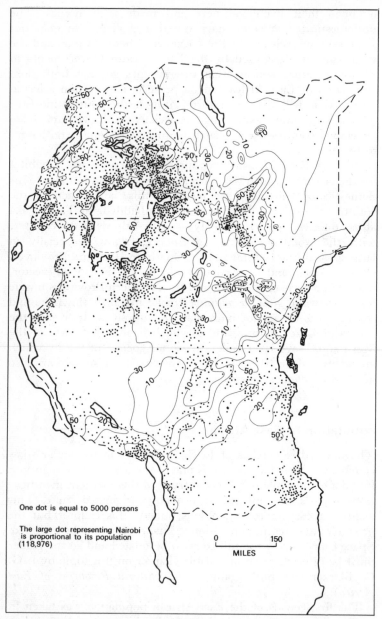

One dot is equal to 5000 persons

The large dot representing Nairobi
is proportional to its population
(118,976)

0   150
MILES

Figure 5 East Africa: Population distribution as per 1948 census, and the mean
annual rainfall

census year for the area, being the only occasion to date when counting of the manpower of East Africa was undertaken as a united effort and at the same time. Consequently, the 1948 population figures can be used effectively in comparison. Since then, Tanganyika has had another census in 1957, Zanzibar in 1958, Uganda in 1959 and Kenya in 1962. The table below summarises the population growth on a territorial basis. To enable a ready comparison of the population totals to be made, it is necessary to estimate the population by taking the same year for all the states.

Table 4 : Summary of population totals over the E. African countries

Mid-year	Kenya	Uganda	Tanganyika	Zanzibar	E. Africa
1948	5,407,599	4,958,520	7,480,429	265,000	18,111,548
1958	7,652,000	6,356,000	8,916,000	300,000	23,224,000
1960	8,115,000	6,677,000	9,237,000	308,000	24,337,000
1965	9,365,000	7,551,000	10,179,000		

The figures in the above table indicate a rapidly growing population especially in Kenya and Uganda. Zanzibar is seen to be the most densely peopled, other countries being essentially under-populated. The mean population per square mile by the 1965 estimates were as follows: Zanzibar 319·4 (1963), Uganda 101·0, Kenya 42·6 and Tanganyika 29·8. But before tracing the distribution of this population over the entire region, a note must be inserted on the composition of the population. The table below gives the non-African population between 1948 and 1965.

Table 5 : Estimated Non-African Population over East Africa

KENYA

	Europeans	Indo-Pakistani	Arabs	Others
1948	30,800	100,000	24,400	3,400
1958	59,000	161,000	32,000	4,000
1960	61,000	169,000	34,000	4,000
1965	41,000	186,000	37,000	4,000

UGANDA

1948	3,700	36,300	1,500	900
1958	10,400	69,600	1,900	2,200
1960	11,400	75,100	2,100	2,400
1965	9,000	85,900	2,100	2,200

TANGANYIKA:

1948	11,300	47,500	11,100	2,200
1958	21,200	80,900	21,400	4,100
1960	22,300	87,300	24,000	4,500
1965	17,300	85,900	25,600	4,200

ZANZIBAR:

1948	300	16,000	248,700*	290
1958	520	18,400	280,900*	340
1960	570	18,900	287,800*	350
1965	650	19,700	298,700*	360

The numerical significance of the various non-African races in the respective countries of East Africa is, of course, related to the political/historical development of each of these countries. It is an interesting case of history influencing human geography.

The distribution of the East African population over the entire area must now be traced. Figure 5 shows the distribution of the population using the 1948 census. The close influence of climate, and especially of rainfall, is clearly obvious from this map on which the mean annual rainfall has been superimposed. Three major regions of high population density are discernible. The concentration around the shores of Lake Victoria is particularly outstanding. Secondly, there is the coastal belt from below Mombasa to the Rufiji River including the outlying islands. Thirdly, there are the isolated islands of high densities in a number of well-watered interior highland areas. This last region includes, the Kikuyu-Kamba and Embu cluster immediately to the north of Nairobi, the Arusha-Kilimanjaro-Usambara group; the cluster in the Mbeya area and the belt of high density running along the border with Ruanda and Burundi, including the Kigezi cluster and continuing as a well-defined

*Includes the indigenous population, i.e. Arabs, Mainland Africans and Comorians.

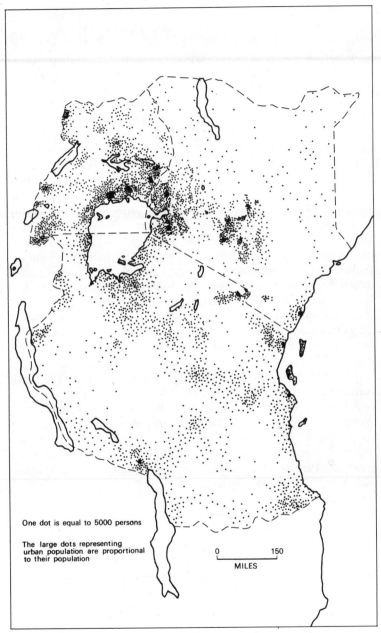

Figure 6 East Africa: Population distribution as per 1962 census estimates

belt with only minor interruptions up to West Nile and Madi. These clusters are even more emphatic from the 1962 population estimates plotted in Fig. 6.

Urbanisation is another aspect of population distribution of much interest to the geographer. With the exception perhaps of the Buganda capital, with a population cluster resembling an urban development, we can say that town development is an alien creation in East Africa. The indigenous African population is largely rural. In 1948, 94·8% of Kenya's population was rural and in 1957, 95·9% of Tanganyika's population was also rural. In 1959, 96·8% of Uganda's population was rural while Zanzibar in 1958 had a 73·5% rural population. None the less, urban areas have grown rapidly—a feature to be explained in terms of a general rapid population growth and increasing realization of the need for employment. This attraction into the urban areas has posed urgent problems which will continue to engage the attention of urban as well as national planners. Nairobi with a population of 266,795 (1962) is the largest urban centre in East Africa. Mombasa follows with 179,575 people (1962) and then Dar es Salaam with 128,742 (1957) and Zanzibar with 57,923 people (1958). Kampala numbered 46,735 persons in 1959. There are seventeen other towns with over 10,000 people each, ten in Tanganyika, five in Kenya and three in Uganda.

The pattern of urban development tends to fit into four main functional categories. There are the coastal towns, some of which are fairly old and originated through early contacts with Arabia and India. Then there are the main ports around the main inland lakes. Thirdly, there are the inland towns which are mainly administrative and collecting centres for agricultural produce. Finally, there are the mining towns such as Magadi, Kilembe, Singida and Shinyanga.

Conclusion

East Africa is primarily an agricultural country where farming and indeed land ownership have brought major problems in development. European farming was naturally directed at the higher, cooler and broadly speaking, wetter areas. In these areas a number of crops such as coffee, tea, wheat, and, later, pyrethrum were grown while in the more marginal parts ranching was encouraged. The African economy in the early phases was wholly at a subsistence level but when Africans began to demand participation in commercial cropping a number of land problems began to emerge.

This survey has shown that the East African environment is that of a diversified area and, although presenting man with opportunity in a number of possibilities, is essentially a harsh one. This harshness is particularly associated with the overall water shortage and with extensive areas in which the tsetse fly keep away man and his stock. The general poorness of the soils is also noteworthy. It is in this environment that man has lived and evolved social and political institutions that have been considerably influenced by the geographical circumstances in which the East African countries are situated.

Further reading

RUSSELL, E. W. (Ed.) *The Natural Resources of East Africa,* East African Literature Bureau, 1962.

H.M.S.O. *East African Royal Commission, 1953-1955, Report, Cmd. 9475,* London, 1955.

OLIVER, R. and MATHEW, G. (Eds.) *History of East Africa,* Volume I, Oxford University Press, 1963, Baker, S. K. J., *The East African Environment.*

O'CONNOR, A. M. *An Economic Geography of East Africa,* G. Bell and Sons, 1966.

LOBECK, A. K. *Physiographic Diagram of Africa,* Columbia University Press, 1946.

KING, L. C. *South African Scenery,* Oliver and Boyd, 3rd Ed., 1963.

LEAKEY, L. S. B. *Adam's Ancestors,* Methuen and Co., 4th Ed., 1953.

OMINDE, S. H. *Population Movements to the Main Urban Areas of Kenya, Cahiers d'Etudes Africaines,* Volume 20, Paris, 1966.

KEAY, R. W. J. *Vegetation Map of Africa South of the Tropic of Cancer,* Oxford University Press, 1959.

MONKHOUSE, F. J. *A Dictionary of Geography,* Edward Arnold, London, 1965.

Survey of Kenya, *Atlas of Kenya,* 1962.

Survey of Tanganyika, *Atlas of Tanganyika,* 3rd Edition, 1956.

Survey of Uganda, *Atlas of Uganda,* 1963.

East African Community, *Economic and Statistical Review,* (Quarterly). (The statistics for the tables are from this source.)

3

The Prehistory of East Africa

Merrick Posnansky

Humanity during its existence has passed through several
drastic and fundamental revolutions of economy and way of
life but those which most readily come to mind are the more
recent, the industrial and the scientific or atomic, by which
mankind has harnessed the power of heat and the atom for
technological progress. More fundamental however, are those
which closely affected man's very existence, the Neolithic or
agricultural revolution by which man controlled his food supply,
the urban revolution which led to the complexities of life in
towns, and the human revolution. It is the last which is fundamental to our whole story, the revolution by which man emerged
as a thinking being, capable of conceptual thought and of
acquiring, assimilating, adapting and transmitting ideas from
and to creatures of his own group. The human revolution was
preceded by the evolution of the primates in which a hominid or
group of hominids emerged capable, first of tool-using, and later
of tool-making. The full description of this evolution is outside
our scope though an outline must be attempted.

The Human Revolution

In recent years, particularly since the accidental discovery by
workmen, thinking it was a baboon, of the first of the *Australopithecines* or 'southern apes', at Taungs in the north-

eastern part of Cape Province of South Africa in 1924, it
has been realised that Africa can claim to hold most of the key
information on human evolution. It has often been suggested
that a missing link exists that would solve our problems and as
each major discovery of fossil human material has been found
newspapers have hailed the discovery as that of the 'missing
link'. It would be far more truthful to say that it is the chain that
is missing whilst the links exist. They have been joined in different ways at one time or another by the world's leading
palaeontologists and it is the ease with which new chains or trees
of evolution are built up which most clearly indicates how heavily
we have to lean on the imperfections of the fossil record. Nevertheless, the relatively abundant discoveries of new fossil material
in east, south and north Africa since 1930, and more precise
dating methods, are enabling agreement to be reached as to the
stages of human evolution and the timetable involved.

Man belongs to the Primates. His particular family is that of
the *Hominidae*. Fossil remains have been found in East Africa
that are particularly relevant to dating the sequence by which
the *Hominidae* separated from the *Pongidae* (great apes, like
the chimpanzee and the gorilla) and Man developed from the
Hominidae stock. It would appear from fossil evidence that the
higher primates had their ultimate origin in an arc running
from western Europe through Africa to south-east Asia, an area
which still contains the largest number of species of present-day
primates. As early as thirty million years ago two distinct
groups had emerged belonging to the genus *Dryopithecus*, the
ancestor of the apes and to *Ramapithecus* (and *Kenyapithecus*)
an early hominid. From then on the evolution of each group
went its own way. The *Proconsul* fossils, from around the
Kavirondo gulf area, particularly Rusinga Island and Homa
mountain, and from Napak and Moroto mountains in Karamoja
in Uganda, belong to the *Dryopithecine* group and the *Kenyapithecus* fossils are probably related to the *Ramapithecus* group.
It would appear that the differences between the two families
were at that time not as marked anatomically as they are at
present. There is still much disagreement between scientists
as to the exact names to give to these various early fossil
ancestors of man, and all we can definitely say is that fossil bones
of ancestors of both the apes and hominids have been found.
Unfortunately the number of fossil finds, except for the
Proconsul material, are few and scattered over a vast period of

time, with most being represented by small jaw or skull fragments and virtually no evidence of such bones as the pelvis, feet and spine which can indicate methods of locomotion and the degree of erect posture, so valuable for reconstructing their appearance and mode of life.

It would appear that from between twenty and thirty million years ago to two or three million years ago the main development was of bipedalism. Different hypotheses have been advanced to explain why an erect posture and two-legged walk (bipedalism) developed. It is possible that the reduction of forest cover in Miocene and Pliocene times, some thirty to twenty million years ago, meant that previously tree-living primates had to adapt themselves to a savannah environment. Part of this adaptation involved defence against carnivores. The small primates, poorly equipped to face the larger predators, had to look up over the tall grass on their hind legs to see if their way was clear. The departure from a forest environment possibly also led to the beginning of hunting, as the savannah provides less obvious protein than the forest with its berries, leaves and fungi.

What, however, are more important than the reasons for bipedalism are its effects. Bipedal locomotion freed the hands. The hands were able to evolve as specialised units, the thumb became separated and the fingers more adaptive. The first bipedal creatures that we know of were the *australopithecines* of which now over three hundred specimens, comprising over a hundred individuals, have been found in South Africa, East Africa and the Tchad area.

At Olduvai Gorge in Tanzania, the most famous and certainly the most important early stone age site in the world, Dr and Mrs Leakey in 1959 excavated a magnificently preserved skull which they called *Zinjanthropus*, Man of Zinj, which is the name by which the East African coast was known in medieval times. Because of its excessively large crushing and grinding molars it was nicknamed 'The Nutcracker Man'. It has since been realised that this fossil belongs to the *australopithecines*.

The *australopithecines* had a small brain, around 450-550 cubic centimetres compared to our own of around 1,500 cubic centimetres. They were perhaps no taller than four feet, had no forehead but a ridge of bone along the skull and a marked bony brow. The lower jaw was massive, with particularly large molars, and in comparison small incisors and canines, which

Figure 7 Principal Stone Age sites in East Africa

suggest a predominantly vegetarian diet. These teeth demanded a heavy jaw and muscles to support that jaw and the thick skull bones provided support for those muscles. Altogether fragments of some ten individuals have been found at Olduvai and further ones near Lakes Natron and Eyasi. Potassium argon dating, an isotopic method in which the decay of the radioactivity of the argon in the deposit containing the fossils is measured, has been used at Olduvai to provide a date between $1\frac{1}{2}$ and $1\frac{3}{4}$ million years for the *australopithecines*.

Man, the Tool-maker

Contemporaneous with *Australopithecus* in East Africa, was another hominid called *Homo habilis*, 'the skilful man' who was the first systematic tool-maker and some authorities would say the direct ancestor of modern man. Six representatives of *Homo habilis* have been found at Olduvai. It was a creature with a rather bigger brain than *Australopithecus* and both hand and foot bones have been found belonging to it. Many palaeontologists however suggest that *Homo habilis* represents only a more developed *australopithecine* rather than a separate genus.

The significance of the *australopithecines* is that they have been found associated with the first true tools. There is at present no ideal way of demonstrating when an advanced hominid with erect posture walking on two feet can be called Man except by pointing to the regular manufacture of tools for a preconceived purpose. Language was once thought of as one of the criteria of Man but this is something on which the palaeontologists can never provide information. Language would seem to have a secondary importance; in itself it was a man-made tool for transmitting ideas. It has been suggested that as all the present peoples of the world use only a limited range of sound in their languages, and yet are capable of a wider range, that there was one single original centre of language and thus of mankind. The ability to make a wide range of sounds developed because of the greater flexibility allowed to the vocal chords when the angle between throat and mouth widened on the assumption of an erect posture. The size of brain was formerly also suggested as an indication of Man but the brain size of the *australopithecines* falls within the range of the great apes and not of modern man. Modern apes have been observed to use

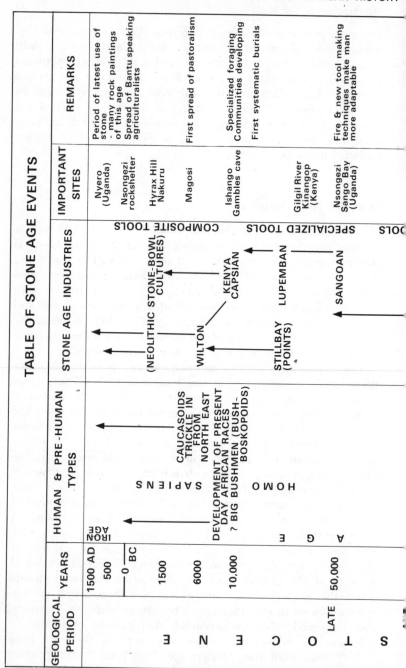

Figure 8 Table of Stone Age events

Epoch	Years B.P.	Hominids/Primates	Industries	Sites	Events
PLEISTOCENE (LATE)	300,000	HOMO ERECTUS (PITHECANTHROPUS)	ACHEULEAN (HAND-AXES etc.) STANDARDIZED	(Uganda) Olorgesailie (Kenya) Isimila & Olduvai (Tanzania)	hand axe industries Prehistoric fauna different from present
	750,000				First spread of man into Europe & Asia
PLEISTOCENE (EARLY)	1,500,000	AUSTRALOPITHECINES (& HOMO HABILIS)	OLDOWAN 'Chopping tools' FIRST TOOLS	Olduvai Peninj Garusi (fossils only)	← The Human Revolution →
PLIOCENE	3,000,000	RAMAPITHECUS (KENYAPITHECUS)		Fort Ternan	Period of probable development of bipedal primates
MIOCENE	15,000,000	DRYOPITHECUS (PROCONSUL)		Rusinga, Homa Mt., Napak Moroto	Partially bipedal primates emerging
	30,000,000				

and to make tools. We can only accept as proof of conceptual thought the regular process of making tools and using them to carry out preconceived purposes. It is almost certain that man first progressed from a tool-using to a tool-making stage. First he would find that a sharp stone was useful for sharpening a piece of wood or cutting a bough off a tree or taking meat from the bone of an already dead creature. Later, whenever he wanted to carry out a similar task he would look around for a sharp stone. It was only a relatively short cut to improving on nature and making one's own tools.

But, why, we might ask, should this have occurred to one group of the hominds. By around two million years ago in the relatively open environment of the Transvaal and the Eastern Rift Valley region of East Africa, the *australopithecines* had emerged as erect bipedal creatures. Their hands which were useless for defence were free to develop manipulative skills. Two of these skills which have been distinguished are the power grip, in which man tightly grips a stone, and the precision grip, when he uses his tools for delicate work by holding his tool between the thumb and forefinger. During the human revolution only the power grip was developed though during the earlier parts of the stone age the precision grip developed. Man at the beginning was not very dextrous. In the fairly open country he was vulnerable to attack and he needed to protect himself in different ways. One form of protection was to develop as a community and another was to pass from the tool-using to the tool-making stage. Both eventually became complementary features of the human revolution. Tools became extensions of the body and just as essential. Without tools to create weapons and the implements which would help procure a food supply, the *australopithecines* would have remained just another primate group, becoming specialised to an environment and ultimately becoming susceptible and vulnerable to ecological change. The human revolution essentially implies a change from susceptibility to adaptability.

The *australopithecines* were at first little better than scavengers competing for carrion with other scavengers like the jackal and the hyaena and making use of accessible edible fruits. One advantage may have been their bipedalism which allowed them to run away with stolen meat. Even scavenging would have needed group activity particularly when predators were around. Primate teeth are incapable of dealing quickly with tough raw meat and long bones and it was possible that in their camp sites, where bones would have accumulated, they first realised the value of the simple everyday raw materials and the usefulness of the sharp fractures in bone. Much of their food debris began to be utilised for the jobs at hand and occasionally for defensive and offensive weapons. But our only firm evidence comes from stone tools.

At Olduvai Gorge, archaeological and geological research has indicated a 300 foot thick sequence of lake deposits which have been exposed by the cutting of the gorge. The lake basin was somewhat tilted and the waters were shallow, so that creatures lived around the edge in what was a relatively dry area. The region is now noted for its extinct volcanoes but when the lake existed at the edge of the Serengeti plain they were still active. Deposition of the fine volcanic tuffs and unconsolidated material from the foot of the volcanoes was rapid and we have no reason to suppose that the vegetation was such as to afford more than the minimum stabilisation of the loose deposits. The lake persisted from before Pleistocene times (2 to 3 million B.C.) until 50 to 100 thousand B.C. All the time its waters fluctuated, leaving broad shore areas at times high and dry and at other times submerged by shallow waters. From the geological composition of the deposits five distinct beds have been differentiated, four of the age of the lake basin and the fifth being the infilling of the gorge cut through at the end of the mid-Pleistocene period. Earth movements were common in the area and largely explain why it disappeared, though it is probable that the infilling of several hundred thousand years was largely responsible for its disappearance. As the deposits include large amounts of fresh volcanic material, the K/A or Potassium Argon method of dating has been employed for dating the sequence.

The stones found in the lowest levels exhibited a regular pattern of intentional flaking which allows them to be identified as tools. This identification is supported by the fact that the lake deposits are comparatively stoneless so that any stones had to be brought into the area, presumably for the purpose of tool-making. The associated bones comprised large numbers of small creatures, juvenile pigs and antelope, frogs, tiny reptiles and birds. Catfish, which often survive in fairly seasonal lakes and swamps, also seem to have been caught quite easily by the *australopithecines* and even possibly by his predecessors. Of the long bones, the ends had been fractured in a way that clearly showed that the marrow had been extracted. It was significant that though many of the long bones bore signs of gnawing by carnivore teeth and all the bones were broken, the *Zinjanthropus* bones were intact, even the delicate facial bones, which would suggest that *Zinjanthropus* was not just another meal for a carnivore. Also from Bed I a windbreak of stones was found suggesting that these early 'men' built crude houses.

We can conclude, that man presumably first made tools when he began to realise the usefulness of naturally sharp bones and stones. From being a scavenger he developed into a systematic hunter, though at the beginning only of small creatures like frogs, birds, lizards and the more easily caught antelopes. No evidence from either South Africa or East Africa is conclusive enough to pin-point man's emergence in either locality, though the period was the Early Pleistocene and the creature who broke through the 'human barrier' probably an *australopithecine*. The earliest *pithecanthropine* remains, the only other contender for the title of being the first Man, from North Africa, Java and China, were contemporary with developed tools already recognisable as of the hand-axe tradition. The pithecanthropines were thus later in date than Bed I Olduvai or the Transvaal australopithecines. At Trinil in Java *pithecanthropine* remains have been dated by the Potassium Argon method to around 500,000 B.C.

Cultural Evolution

What is apparent is that the human revolution meant that rapid evolution took place. The brain, particularly the frontal lobes, expanded in response to the calls made upon it. An eminent anthropologist, Sir W. Le Gros Clark, has aptly said: 'It was the development of the distinctly human type of social organisation which demanded an accelerated development of those parts of the brain whereby emotional and instinctive impulses can be more effectively subordinated to the good of the community as a whole.' As hunting supplemented scavenging, a greater necessity for group consciousness took place. Hunting by primitive methods was a group activity particularly when larger animals were the prey. Ideas were shared and tools made in a regular intentional pattern. One important feature of humans and near humans is that the pelvic changes which resulted in bipedal movement led to the birth of their young in a more immature state, with a soft skull which has to mould itself through the small opening of the mother's pelvis at birth. Much of the development of the complicated brain had to take place after birth and the dependence of the young on their mothers allowed a greater opportunity for the transmission of ideas and habits. It also meant that the mother was withdrawn more and more from hunting so that man's social loyalties grew. A home-base at least for short periods became essential as man's range as a hunter became greater and mothers and babies were left behind. Hunting is often a long process and involves tracking and stalking and one difference between man and near-man is that his bipedalism was perfected by this constant use of his feet.

The growth of the brain was accompanied by a progressive reduction of the jaw and of the size of the teeth, particularly of the canines. The jaw was no longer a fighting mechanism and did not require such powerful muscular attachments. Selection was no longer a natural process but depended more on man's ability to transmit ideas, on his adaptability to different environments and on his success as a hunter using his tools and co-operating with others of his group. This process we call cultural evolution. In this sense man domesticated himself. Group activity and the transmission of ideas demanded language, particularly in a creature like man who was not equipped with the speed of a cheetah or the strength and power of the lion and had to substitute guile in the collective activity of hunting.

The Stone Age

The stone age in East Africa can be divided for convenience into three periods: an early period, down to 50,000 B.C., when the stone age societies were characterised largely by what the archaeologists call hand-axe industries and when our main evidence comes from the Rift Valley areas of Kenya and Tanzania and the Kagera river in Uganda; a middle period, from 50,000 B.C. to around 10,000 B.C., when man became more adaptable and more widely distributed because of his mastery of fire and of new stone tool-making techniques, and a late period when we are probably dealing with men similar to the present day races of Africa. This last period lasted until as recently as five or six hundred years ago.

The earlier Stone Age

An important feature of the earlier period is that physical and cultural evolution were closely interrelated. The more man used tools the less he used his jaws and the more he used his brain and so by the end of the period the human beings in East Africa probably had brains very much the same size as present-day people. The pace of change was slow. The first tools from Olduvai Gorge, which have given their name to the earliest stone age industry* in Africa, the Oldowan, were simple and made for the job in hand, such as chopping open bones and cutting branches off trees for spears. The waste flakes struck off in giving a pebble or splinter of stone a sharp edge were probably used for skinning animals, cutting difficult ligaments between bones and scraping skins and sharpening sticks. Soon after a million years ago Man discovered that tools with a sharp edge all round, and with a point formed by the convergence of two sharp edges, provided a highly practical all-purpose tool which the archaeologists call a hand-axe. It took another half million years before these hand-axes became fully refined. These industries are known to the archaeologists as Acheulean, after a place in France where identical hand-axes were first found over a hundred years ago. By the end of this earlier period, besides hand-axes, many other tools were being made, such as cleavers which had a straight cutting edge like a present-day axe, numerous scrapers and throwing stones, which may have been made into a throwing weapon called the bolus, and knives. Progress is measured as much by the complexity of tools, implying the number of jobs that could be done with them, as by the technological advancements in making tools.

Right throughout the stone age man was a parasite on the landscape. He lived by hunting and foodgathering. The stone age represents a progressive development of man as a hunter. At first he killed by driving animals into traps or muddy lake waters, or by outrunning and outwitting them. Except for scavenging large animals, which had died natural deaths or were caught unawares, he probably had to depend on smaller game. It was only by the end of the period that he could kill from afar with missile weapons. His social groups were probably small, perhaps no more than an ideal, easily fed hunting band of

*In this chapter the word *industry* is used rather than the more commonly used term *culture* as it is felt that it describes more closely the nature of our evidence.

twenty to thirty, and they constantly changed camp, largely keeping to lakes and rivers where animals came to drink. Man, who needs water almost daily, and who had few containers for water, was also tied to the same environments. But if comparisons with modern hunting peoples are valid it is almost certain that a greater part of his food supply came from collecting activities, digging up roots, eating berries and nuts, insects and various greens. Africa was probably then the most populous continent, though the total population perhaps rose from no more than 100,000 around half a million years ago to perhaps three or four million by the end of the stone age, the largest number a hunting economy could have supported.

When we link these population figures with the length of time involved in the stone age we can understand why remains of the early stone age are so abundant, particularly in East Africa where on sites like Olorgesailie in Kenya, Nsongezi in Uganda, Isimila (near Iringa) and Olduvai gorge in Tanzania, stone tools are numbered in tens of thousands. Stone tools are heavy, they easily lose their edges and must have been used on the spot for butchering-up animals rather than being carried around. It is reasonable to assume that each day many tools were made and abandoned. Multiply this process by the nearly two million years of the stone age and it is easy to see why stone tools are so numerous. Unfortunately none of the wooden tools that men made, and which were perhaps more important for hunting, have survived.

By around 750,000 B.C. the principal human type was *Homo erectus* (formerly called *Pithecanthropus erectus*) and had a brain size of 1,100 cubic centimetres. He may have been preceded by another creature intermediate between the australopithecines and himself, a few of the bones of which have been found in the Lake Baringo area. By this time man had spread from Africa into Asia and Europe. The process was probably a slow one with hunting groups moving north and eventually passing into the other continents. By half a million years ago early hand-axes and chopping tools occur in both southern Asia and western Europe.

It would appear that at that time the forests were too difficult to live in for these primitive hunter-foodgatherers. Most of the stone tools were made from fine grained rocks like quartz, quartzite and obsidian. Sites of the early stone age are normally discovered as the result of erosion in which present-day rivers have cut through old lake deposits or river gravels, as at Olduvai or Olorgesailie, and tools or fossils erode out of the deposits or become exposed so that the archaeologist knows exactly where to dig. Fishing, particularly for swamp fish, was probably also practised. The fossils of the animals which were the contemporaries of early man indicate varieties long extinct, like *Sivatherium* (a giraffe-like animal with horns), various large pigs and even tiger.

The middle Stone Age

By 50,000 B.C. fire was systematically in use. With its use man could drive out carnivores from rockshelters and keep himself warm in high altitudes, but most important of all it helped in hunting. He could make the gums of trees into glues for hafting shaped stones on to wooden shafts for lances, cook hitherto poisonous roots to make them edible, and extract and process the poisons of berries and insects which he then painted on his spears to make them deadly. Fire was also used for scaring animals from thickets and for felling trees. At the same time new tool-making techniques allowed him to make smaller tools by shaping the tool on the core of stone, from which he then struck off a thin almost ready-made implement. The large numbers of small tools of the period, and the distinct signs of their utilisation, suggests that the hunter had a mastery over skin and sinews and could almost certainly make suitable ropes and strings from animal products or bark. More efficient lances capable of leaving a blood spoor made hunting less hazardous. Tools became specialised and there were tools for working wood, pounding roots and working bone. Both fire and technological advances made man more adaptable and it is from this time that we find more evidence of man in the more heavily vegetated areas of western Uganda and in the thickly wooded mountain regions.

Two main cultural traditions from around 50,000 B.C. can be distinguished, one in the more wooded areas (Sangoan-Lupemban industries) where the tools are specialised for wood-working and digging up roots and include adzes and chisels; and a second (Stillbay industries) in the open country of the Rift Valley and Central Tanzania, the tools of which are smaller with leaf-like lance points being the most distinctive. The woodland peoples probably had a more vegetarian diet as their tools include large numbers of heavily abraded stones presumably for pounding roots.

The later Stone Age

By 10,000 B.C., or perhaps somewhat earlier, a new people entered East Africa, akin in physical appearance to the Caucasoid peoples of south-west Asia and North Africa. They brought with them new technological advances in stone tool-making. Instead of striking flakes from a core of rock by direct percussion, they had learnt to strike off thin blades of stone probably by using a punch between the hammer and the core. It was realised that more efficient tools could be made by using smaller sized points or cutting components. The invention of the techniques of blade manufacture allowed small, sharp stone tool-components to be produced, which could then be used in composite tools. Instead of a large number of specialised stone tools of assorted sizes, the new tools consisted of variously-shaped small sharp blades and bladelets which, when blunted along the edge or at the end, to avoid splitting the handle or shaft in which they were placed, could be hafted to form arrows with or without barbs, to make knives and bolts for small game. Though the scrapers of the middle period of the stone age continued in use, new varieties, small and haftable, appeared to have given a completely different appearance to the industries. The use of these tiny blades or microliths allowed man to exploit raw materials hitherto unused. Small pebbles of jasper, chalcedony, rock crystal and chert, unsuitable for a Stillbay point, could now provide a fine-grained raw material suitable for these smaller tools. Several microliths have been found mounted as barbs, and it is certain that the use of the barbed arrow and spear was one of the chief technological advances of the period. Barbs allowed the point to remain for a longer period in the animal and thus facilitated a more effective blood trail, and if the barb was poisoned it enabled the poison to invade the bloodstream. The bow and arrow was almost certainly in use, and the bow was also used for drilling holes in seeds and discs of ostrich eggshell to make beads.

Many of the sites of this late period are found under overhanging rocks, often commanding wide views of the countryside from which the hunter could spy out game. Occasionally the

rockshelter was near water, as at Nsongezi on the Kagera river
or Magosi in Karamoja in Uganda, in an area where natural
rock cisterns retain water through the dry season. In several
caves, particularly in Kenya, burials have been found. At
Gambles Cave near Elmenteita the skeletons were placed in a
contracted position, perhaps representing rebirth, covered in
ochre to represent blood. These burials are the first indication
of systematic religious practices. The burials are of Caucasoid
peoples. But these new peoples, whose industries have been
called Capsian after a site in North Africa, were never very
numerous. They passed their ideas to their neighbours to the
west and south and by 5,000 B.C. industries incorporating
microliths, for a long time known as the Wilton industries,
were common throughout East Africa. The most distinctive
microliths were less than an inch long and crescentic in shape
with the backing on the curved edge.

It is possible that the predominant population about this time
was composed of what the archaeologists call 'Big Bushmen,'
who in physical appearance were somewhat similar to the
present-day small Bushmen hunting peoples of south-western
Africa. Skeletal remains of similar men have been found in both
West Africa and the Nile Valley and it would appear that they
formed the basic stock of Africa from whom the present-day
African races of Negro and Bushmen have developed in the
last ten thousand years. During the late stone age, man spread
over the larger part of East Africa including parts of the East
African coast.

One of the main features of the later stone age was that
highly specialised and successful hunting societies developed.
Several of these societies, such as the groups around Lakes
Edward and Rudolph, were fishermen using barbed bone points
as fish spears and possibly even harpoons for catching Nile
perch and other fish. A date of around 6,000 B.C. has been
obtained for the fishing site of Ishango at the mouth of the
Semliki river on Lake Edward, where the fishing camps were
covered by the grey volcanic ash of the Katwe explosion craters
which were then active. Their diet included fish, fowl and game
as well as oysters of different kinds. A carved bone with sets
of parallel lines probably indicates that a simple calendrical or
numeration system was known. Other late stone age peoples
lived around Lake Victoria, subsisting on a diet of shells and
fish and leaving behind large middens of shells. In the more

forested areas, flaked stone axes were polished for tree felling, grinding stones were used for grinding seeds and heavy stones perforated, by laborious pecking away from both ends with another stone, and used as digging stick weights for the more systematic collection of roots. Probably towards the end of this period boats were made for going out to islands and to help with fishing. Some of the industries of Karamoja are similar to those described from Somalia and Ethiopia and indicate that contact from the north-east existed. In the Rift Valley area of Kenya between Nairobi and Eldoret, where the natural volcanic glass, obsidian, is found, the late stone age industries are characterised by the presence of particularly long knives which were easy to strike off from cores of obsidian and one of the latest industries is known as the Elmenteitan.

Rock Art

A large amount of our information about the more recent stone age hunters and food-gatherers comes from rock paintings. Rock paintings tell the archaeologist more about the spiritual and religious life of the hunters than ever can stone tools or even burials. The paintings of East Africa are all relatively recent; some are the work of Iron Age pastoral peoples. Those that survive are probably only a fraction of many that were painted, as a large number suffered from exposure to sun and rain. The paintings are largely on the underside of overhanging rocks, mostly on granites that weather, leaving numerous clefts and overhangs. Other pictures were probably painted on pieces of bone, skin, barkcloth and wood, but except for one decorated bone from Nyero in Uganda the rest have vanished. By the late stone age man was a skilful tool-maker and hunter. He had the technical ability to decorate, and his success as a hunter gave him both the time and the stimulus for art. As a hunter he had to observe the life of the animals he hunted. Much of his time was invariably spent in stalking prey, looking for it from raised viewpoints, and so he acquired a keen memory of the details of the animals he hunted. Why he painted is difficult to answer, but it is probable that he depicted animals sometimes to commemorate his successes and at other times hoping that by drawing the desired animal he would have luck in hunting. But the art probably formed part of his vivid folklore and it is difficult to disentangle what was considered magic and what was functional for the success of the hunt.

The paintings are dated by finding pieces of decorated rock in the deposits, at the foot of the painted overhangs, which are associated with stone tools dateable by other means. Occasionally the subject matter of the paintings, such as cows with long horns in a rockshelter on Mount Elgon near the Enderbess area, give a clue as to age. Very often one painting obscures another and it is possible to date the sequence of painting at a particular site. The paints were obtained by grinding down rotted ironstone (ochre) and mixing it with urine or fat when red was required, manganese or charcoal for black, and kaolin or guano for white. Fingers, splayed ends of sticks, and feathers were probably the most often used brushes.

The largest number of sites is in Tanzania where over a thousand are known, concentrated particularly in the Central Region in the Kondoa area though also around Singida and Lake Eyasi, where until recently the Hadza, the last present-day hunting and food-gathering groups, lived. In Kenya the only sites are on Mount Elgon and in Turkana and Masailand and the latter are very recent, whilst in Uganda sites are found amongst the granite inselbergs of eastern Uganda with a single site in Karamoja. The Tanzanian sites largely depict animals and a few humans. Many lively scenes occur, in some of which the people are masked. The very latest paintings are in white whilst the earlier ones are in various shades of red, brown and orange. The earlier paintings are more lively than the later ones and in style and subject matter have affinities to paintings in Zambia and Rhodesia. The Uganda paintings are largely of schematic designs such as concentric circles and dumb-bell shapes though canoes are found at two localities. Associated with some of the paintings in Uganda are rock gongs. These consist of slabs of rock, both upright and horizontal, which have weathered off the parent rock but are still gripped or wedged by supporting rocks at one end so that they vibrate when struck. It is probable that most rock gongs are of iron age date though the tradition of making them may have begun in the stone age. Rock engravings, common in South Africa and in the Sahara, are rare in East Africa and the two main ones in Uganda consist of schematic designs.

The Legacy of the Stone Age

By 1,000–1,500 B.C. a knowledge of agriculture and pastoralism was entering East Africa from the north. Many of the stone industries associated with the first food-producing pastoral societies are similar to the Capsian and Elmenteitan industries of the late stone age peoples, and like them their burials are of Caucasoid peoples. A knowledge of food production had probably been preceded by a knowledge of pottery in East Africa and in many rock-shelters late stone age industries are associated with pottery. At first the new societies, who were characterised by the use of stone bowls, probably lived by both hunting and agriculture or pastoralism. Until around A.D. 500 the impact of the pastoralists and agriculturalists was slight and confined to the eastern Rift Valley zone as far south as Lake Eyasi.

From around A.D. 500 as iron-using negro agricultural peoples began to expand, perhaps from the west and south, the hunting and food-gathering peoples steadily became less and less important as an element in East Africa's population and were restricted to the largely bush-covered lower rainfall areas like the Rift Valleys, or the thick forests. Slowly many hunters and food-gatherers acquired the use of metal for their arrows and some groups, realising the advantages of a settled life with assured food supply, were probably absorbed amongst their Bantu-speaking neighbours. The traditions of many East African tribes speak of the inhabitants they found on arrival in their present homelands as being small hunting peoples, possibly akin to the Bushmen of southern Africa.

Much of the final disappearance of the survivors of the stone age has taken place comparatively recently. In Uganda the Ateso found hunting peoples in Teso in the eighteenth century whilst in north-eastern Karamoja, a small group of Teuso peoples still try to live by hunting and food-gathering. In Kenya, the Wanderobo were still common in the late nineteenth century whilst in Tanzania the Hadza are only just settling into an agricultural existence. Many present-day populations probably retain an element of the original population in their physical make-up. Agriculture allowed populations to expand whilst the hunters were never numerous and their effect on the population, even on absorption, was probably slight. Besides the few present-day survivals of hunting and food-gathering peoples, the legacy of the stone age was small. Certain specialisations, like fishing, a little forest clearance, an extensive knowledge of the useful plants and medicines that nature had to offer and perhaps in some areas a tradition of rock painting, are all that have survived.

Further reading

CAMPBELL, B. C. *Human Evolution,* Edinburgh, 1966.

CLARK HOWELL, L. *Early Man,* Chicago, 1965.

COLE, S. *Prehistory of East Africa,* London, 1963.

LEAKEY, L. S. B. *Adam's Ancestors,* London, 1953.

LE GROS CLARK, SIR W. 1961 The Humanity of Man, *Nature* No. 4792, 1961.

PILBEAM, D. R. Man's Earliest Ancestors, *Science Journal* Volume 3, February 1967.

POSNANSKY, M. (Ed.) *Prelude to East African History,* Oxford, 1966.

WILLCOX, A. R. *The Rock Art of South Africa,* Johannesburg, 1963.

4

The Settlement of East Africa

J. E. G. Sutton

This chapter outlines the making, development and blending of East African society from peoples of varied stocks and origins. This means looking back, not just to the beginning of the iron age but beyond it to the first evidence of agricultural settlement and livestock husbandry in East Africa. The story is reconstructed mainly from archaeology, anthropology and linguistics.

The chapter is divided into three parts. The first discusses some general aspects of food-production in East Africa, both by cultivating crops and by keeping livestock, both with iron tools and without them. The second part explains how the peoples of East Africa are grouped and classified, especially by language. With this background, the third part is an historical reconstruction of the settlement and peopling of East Africa. Finally, for those who are perplexed by the non-mention of 'Hamites' and 'Nilo-Hamites', the appendix provides an apology.

The Production of Food

We have seen that the history of man as a tool-making animal goes back about two million years, according to the evidence from East Africa. For almost the whole of this period (about 99½ per cent of human history) men were directly dependent on

nature for their livelihood. Throughout the inhabited parts of
the world they lived off wild produce—the animals they could
ensnare or run down with wooden spears, clubs or stones, or
in the later periods of the stone age shoot with bow and arrow;
the fish they could spear or trap in streams, rivers, lakes or
floodwaters; the eggs they could filch from nests, and the wild
fruits and vegetables they could pick off trees and plants or
dig from the earth. These foods and other necessities of life
were prepared with tools of wood, skin, bone and stone, supplemented in time by the use of fire. Progress there was, but
extremely slow by modern standards, and imperceptible in any
man's lifetime. Then, during the course of the late stone age,
commencing about ten thousand years ago, man began in certain
parts of the world to assert himself over nature by producing
his own food—that is, by the cultivation of plants and the
taming of animals, bringing them under his control, making
them dependent on him, modifying their forms by cross-breeding
and selection, and adapting them to new environments. Some
writers have referred to this as the food-producing revolution:
perhaps it is more correct to regard it as an evolution, for the
first steps towards cultivation and domestication must have been
very gradual and largely unconscious. But, as the ideas of food-
production have gained momentum, as they have spread from
country to country and from people to people, their effects
have been truly revolutionary. More reliable food supplies
and man's greater regulation of them have encouraged larger
and more settled populations, specialisation in crafts, industries
and trade, and developments in social and political organisation.
After the beginnings of tool-making, food-production is doubtless
the most important development to have occurred in the history
of mankind.

Crops and Livestock

Only in a few places in the world has the evolution from gathering
and hunting to agriculture and herding been played out from
the first stages. For the first cultivation of any plant, the first
steps towards taming any animal, could have occurred only
where that plant or animal already existed in a wild state. For
instance, we know that taro and bananas were first cultivated
in the wet regions of south-eastern Asia, wheat and barley in
the hills of western Asia, and several of the millet crops in the

savannahs of Africa, that donkeys were first tamed in northern or north-eastern Africa and llamas in South America, because these are the places where the ancestors of these plants and animals grew or ran wild. Then, once successfully brought under human control and care, plants and seeds could be carried to new regions by means of trade, contact with neighbours or the migration of an expanding agricultural people. Alternatively, as herds increased or exhausted the grass, they would be led in search of new pastures. Often it would be found that particular crops or animals would not thrive in a new environment with a different climate and soil. But sometimes they might be adapted, by human perseverance and ingenuity in developing new strains of the animal or plant in question.

With the spread and increasing variation of crops and domestic animals, cultivators and herdsmen learnt by experience what would succeed and what would fail in particular environments. This is well illustrated by the widely varying methods of sub-sistence observable nowadays in Africa, and especially in East Africa. In the northern part of the continent the principal grain crops have been barley and wheat, but south of the Sahara various types of sorghum, millet and eleusine have been found more successful. In forested regions with heavier rainfall these grain crops are comparatively less important, and more reliance is placed on planted crops, notably in East Africa the banana. Most East African peoples combine their agriculture with live-stock-husbandry. This is truer of grain-cultivators than of banana-growers, whose dense populations and forest environ-ment leave little room for grazing. Whereas cattle, except in areas of tsetse fly, are valued primarily for their milk, sheep and goats are kept for meat. Certain tribes go to the extreme of disdaining agriculture and live predominantly or exclusively off their livestock. Some do this almost by choice, notably sections of the Masai whose fine plateau grasslands can produce enough milk for subsistence round the year. But in less favoured regions, such as the semi-desert of northern and eastern Kenya where crops will not grow, people are forced by circumstances to be nomadic pastoralists. Some of these latter regions are not suitable for cattle, and camels instead provide the mainstay of life. In most cases, exclusive pastoralism does not rule out the possibility or necessity of obtaining agricultural produce, by exchange with other tribes, for use at those times of the year when the milk yields are low. Some tribes, notably in northern Kenya, are themselves divided into interdependent pastoral and agricultural wings. The pastoral wing consists mainly of the young men who lead the herds to grazing over the plains, while the women, old folk and young children remain at home in the agricultural land, retaining just a few head of stock for family use. Pastoralists tend to occupy or roam over large areas in search of grazing and water round the year, but in fact those who live a purely or predominantly pastoral life are not very numerous. The prestige of the pastoralist is a high one and ownership of cattle has a social as well as an economic value; hence many people, who for their actual subsistence rely more on their fields than on their herds, maintain a strong cultural and emotional attachment to the latter. It is one thing to imagine oneself a pastoralist, another really to be one.

It is true that East Africa has not played an important role in the initial cultivation of crops from wild plants or in the first taming of animals from the wild. The staples of life in East Africa were probably all introduced from outside. The cultivation of millet and sorghum apparently spread from the Ethiopian highlands three to four thousand years ago, along with goats, sheep and cattle which had earlier been brought to Africa from western Asia. Bananas, as well as taro, rice and perhaps sweet potatoes, began to reach Africa about two thousand years ago along the trade and migration routes of the Indian Ocean. During the last five centuries maize and cassava have been introduced to Africa from the Americas, but few East African tribes used these on a large scale before the twentieth century. Recently, however, they have in many areas superseded the traditional millets as the principal crops. Nor should we consider only the main carbohydrate foods: equally important is the wide variety of pulses, green, stalk and ground vegetables grown in East Africa. These similarly are of diverse origins and antiquities. Food-production, therefore, did not suddenly arrive in East Africa from a single source: rather, different crops and different methods of husbandry have infiltrated from different directions at different times. Hence the complex economic pattern of modern East Africa.

Furthermore, in identifying these external origins, we are in danger of overlooking the no less important East African achievements in adapting crops and livestock to local conditions, and in creating viable economies throughout East Africa. Hardier varieties of millets, sorghum and eleusine have been developed, some of them by crossing introduced forms with indigenous wild grasses. Yet more impressive has been the region's contribution to the cultivation of bananas for cooking, brewing and eating raw: East Africa has more varieties than the rest of the world put together. Some are peculiar to particular areas, as can be seen by comparing those of Rungwe, Buganda and Kilimanjaro, where dense populations rely on bananas as the main staple.

Pastoralist and Agriculturalist

Equally significant progress has been made with livestock-husbandry in East Africa, in developing breeds of cattle and small stock able to thrive locally and to withstand droughts, diseases and other hazards. It is commonly said that East African herdsmen are idle and only interested in the quantity, not the quality, of their cattle. This view is basically false and derives from a misunderstanding of the principles and problems of livestock-husbandry in the varied regions of East Africa. To provide food for a family around the year, the management of the beasts and of their breeding and grazing demands very high standards of attention and experience.

Another common misconception about pastoralism is to regard it as historically separate from and essentially opposed to agriculture. There has been a tendency to imagine the history of East Africa (and indeed of northern and eastern Africa in general) as a continual feud between pastoralists and agriculturalists. The herdsman as a noble warrior has been contrasted with the cultivator as a servile labourer; or, to reverse the prejudices, the treacherous and aggressive raider and cattle-thief is pitted against the more industrious and progressive farmer. It is true that there is often a sharp division between the pastures and the arable land. This is very marked in some of the northern regions of East Africa, where open grazing stretches across the lowland plains away from the fields which are situated in the better-watered country, often around the hills and forests. Or occasionally, as in parts of Kenya and northern Tanzania, the finest pastures are the highland plateaus, whereas agricultural communities may inhabit fertile valleys and irrigated basins below the escarpments. These contrasts may lead to specialisation, but similarly they encourage co-operation. We have already observed how grain cultivation and livestock-husbandry are ideally complementary, how pastoralists and agriculturalists will exchange their respective products, and how some tribes divide into agricultural and pastoral wings as the most efficient way of utilising resources and supporting themselves. These divisions may be based on age and sex, cutting across the family. But there do arise circumstances in which tensions develop, or in which the pastoral wing, ranging further and further afield in search of grazing in the dry season, will eventually break entirely away from the agricultural nucleus to form a separate tribe living an exclusively pastoral life. It is then that pastoralism may become almost fanatical, a religion unto itself. But the uncertainties of drought, disease and cattle-theft and, most important, competition for grazing, mean that few people succeed as exclusive pastoralists. The case of the Masai is interesting. They are popularly regarded as pure pastoralists, but in fact the rich plateau grasslands of Masailand are sufficient for only a minority of the Masai-speakers. The rest have to supplement their milk and blood diet with grain foods or undertake intensive agriculture, as do the numerous Arusha Masai. Some have joined Bantu-speaking agricultural tribes. All this was essentially true even before the alienation of parts of Masailand by the British and Germans. As a very crude generalisation we might say that agriculture has accounted for the settlement of peoples and pastoralism for their dispersal, but in fact each very strongly influences the other.

Fertility and Erosion

There is a fair correlation between maps of rainfall and of population density in East Africa. In general, the more rain, the more intensive the agriculture and the more people each square mile can support. But the correlations are not always so close. Some of the best watered areas are not well exploited because of thickness of forest, unsuitability of soils, unattractive climate, tsetse fly or some other cause. There are, for instance, wide parts of southern and western Tanzania with fair rainfall but sparse populations.

Both fields and pastures can and do deteriorate. For agriculture and grazing place an unnatural burden on the land. Crops exhaust the fertility of the soil in a way that natural vegetation does not; cattle devour the grass and goats the browsing, sooner and more thoroughly than do wild animals. As the woods are cut or burnt to provide fields and as domestic animals swallow the young shoots and prevent the regeneration of bush cover, the rain runs off faster, the soil suffers and the land erodes. This may lead to further clearing of the forest or bush for new fields and the abandonment of old fields to pasture, while the former pastures deteriorate into semi-desert. East African peoples have for long been aware of this, of course. Herdsmen have to move from pasture to pasture; some manage to follow a fairly regular annual pattern of movements to provide their herds with sufficient grazing, others have to be more adaptable and resourceful year by year according to circumstances. Cultivators know how many years they can harvest a crop on a particular plot of land before it must be left to recover its fertility. Banana plantations in some regions will bear a sufficient food supply for very many years. But millet fields may yield only two or three crops. Hence in many of the mediocre or poorer regions a family may require a wide area to slash and burn, or for bush-fallowing, over the years. In certain favoured places irrigation may promote more intensive cultivation.

Tools and Food-production

The types of land that are cultivated, the range of crops grown and general efficiency in producing food are largely determined by the tools available. Metal tools, and especially iron, are more efficient than those of stone and wood for cutting bush or forest, for sowing, planting and reaping crops and for preparing food. In many parts of the world food-production began in the late stone age, before the discovery of how to work metals; and this was the case in much of Kenya and parts of northern Tanzania.* In other regions of East Africa the first food-production apparently began later, at the same time as iron-working.† Iron-working could never have been introduced before food-production, for hunter-gatherer communities are too unsettled, and lack the resources and incentives to develop such skills. For to smelt iron from sand or rock and to forge knives, axes,

*This food-production without the knowledge of metals is often referred to as 'neolithic'. As this term is sometimes used loosely and can confuse, we prefer to avoid it: instead of 'neolithic communities', we speak of 'late stone age food-producers'. This adequately distinguishes them from late stone age hunter-gatherers on the one hand, and iron age food-producers on the other.

†We might note that iron was the first metal to be used in East Africa: there was no copper or bronze age as in some parts of the world.

hoes and other tools is a highly specialised craft and a secret to be guarded. The smith, therefore, is generally respected or even feared. The dependence of an agricultural community upon his skills often assures him a high social rank or even political power. Many pastoral or semi-pastoral communities, however, notably Cushitic and certain Nilotic groups, tend to despise smiths and other craftsmen as servile castes. But their necessity is acknowledged and hence the need to maintain the iron-working clan or caste.

Though iron is not essential to food production, its coming greatly increased agricultural efficiency and encouraged the opening-up of new land which had earlier remained untouched except by hunters and gatherers. In particular, iron-working helped cultivators to tackle the regions of high rainfall and thick forests—those in which the banana has become so important as the staple of life for vast numbers of people. Iron, then, led to an increase and expansion of agricultural peoples, to a more intensive settlement of East Africa.

The Peoples of East Africa

The peoples of Africa belong to three main physical types— Negroid, Bushmanoid and Caucasoid. The last covers much of northern and north-eastern Africa, as well as western Asia, India and Europe. The Negroid and Bushmanoid races are exclusively African—or were before overseas slave-trades. As for pygmies, they probably do not constitute a race of their own, but a division of the Negroid specially adapted to forest conditions.

In East Africa the present peoples are almost entirely Negroid (excluding, of course, the small numbers of recent immigrants from overseas). An exception is north-eastern Kenya, where the Galla and Somali constitute representatives of the Caucasoid stock or fairly even balances of Negroid and Caucasoid. Many other peoples of Kenya, northern Tanzania and perhaps western Uganda, though definitely Negroid, do betray indications of some admixture of Caucasoid blood. This suggests that Caucasoid peoples were once more widespread in East Africa. The Swahili peoples of the coast, moreover, have combined some Caucasoid elements through intermarriage with Arabs. The Bushmanoid type can nowadays be found among the Sandawe and their neighbours in central Tanzania, but their distinct features are becoming rapidly blurred through Negroid expansion and absorption. The only pygmy negroes now in East Africa inhabit the forests above the western Rift Valley on the borders of Uganda, Rwanda and the Congo. It seems clear that Bushmanoid peoples, and perhaps pygmies as well, were more widespread in East Africa in the period before the introduction of food-production. Since then they have undergone gradual assimilation by Caucasoid and more particularly by Negroid peoples, expanding in larger numbers with agriculture, domestic herds and better tools. The unassimilated Bushmanoid and pygmy remnants have been forced into the least attractive types of country.

These physical differences are not very useful for classifying tribes or groups of tribes. The distinction between racial types is vague, and individuals vary enormously. We can only make very general observations on how the Hehe, for example, look different from the Acholi or the Kikuyu: we cannot attempt to define tribes in this way. A tribe is a tribe because it feels it is one. It must possess a common culture, and particularly a common language. It is not necessarily a highly organised political unit. Tribes, moreover, are fluid groupings: some members are lost, others are absorbed, through the continual processes of migration and interaction with neighbours. There is no such thing as a 'pure' tribe, derived from a single founding ancestor. Again, arbitrary division or merging of tribes, for administrative convenience or through the ignorance of government officials was not unknown in the colonial period.

Linguistic Classification

The most useful and objective method of classifying tribes and larger groupings is by language, as in the scheme on Fig. 10. This is based mainly on Greenberg's classification. Doubtless there are numerous modifications or refinements still to be made in the exact placing of certain groups and individual tribes. However, the general picture for East Africa should hold fairly well.*

The important groups that the student of East African history should note are those in big block capitals between the horizontal lines in Fig. 10—Bantu, Nilotic, Cushitic. The names of families and their main divisions (above the upper

*Thanks are due to Mr. Ehret for advice on linguistic relationships and nomenclature.

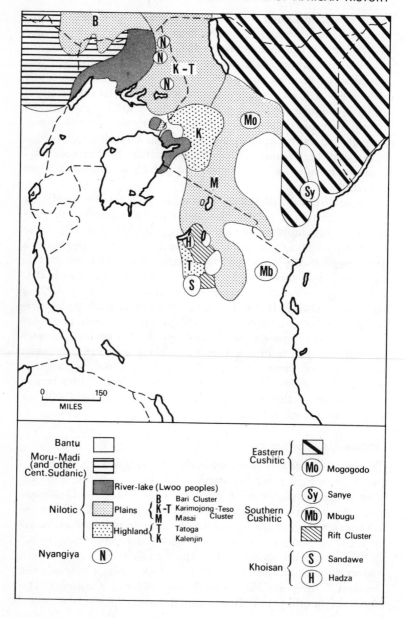

Figure 9 Peoples of East Africa: Linguistic Classification

horizontal line) are only important when relating the languages of East Africa to their general African context. Similarly the divisions of Bantu, Nilotic, etc., and the names of individual tribes are included mainly for reference. For simplicity's sake, Bantu prefixes have been omitted.

A few notes are required on the classification and relationships of languages. Greenberg divides African languages into four main families, each of which is represented in East Africa. (In fact, examples of all four can be found within the Kondoa district of central Tanzania—a phenomenon that occurs nowhere else in the continent.) Between these four families no relationships can be traced. Nilotic appears to be totally unrelated to either Bantu or Cushitic; but it is distantly related to Moru-Madi which stems from the same family. The divisions and sub-divisions which have occurred in each family are the result of long historical processes. Languages are never static: they are constantly changing or evolving. Hence, when a tribe speaking a single language splits into two or more parts, so will the language split, since each part will begin to evolve separately. Relationships and family-trees can be reconstructed by comparative studies of present-day languages. It is very difficult to work out when particular splits and changes occurred. But it is possible to date changes relatively. For instance, within Nilotic, the divisions between the three branches—River-lake, Plains, Highland—must have occurred at some time before the Plains branch divided into three further clusters. On the other hand, the ancestors of Nilotic must have separated from those of Moru-Madi at a much earlier period. By correlating this linguistic scheme with other historical considerations it may be possible to estimate the approximate time-depth of some of these developments. This is attempted in the latter part of this chapter.

While languages have been continually evolving and splitting, many have also been dying out. For when people of two separate stocks combine to form a single tribe, whether through conquest or through peaceful assimilation, one language eventually prevails, the other withers and dies. Though a few words of the discarded language may be borrowed by the surviving one, genuinely mixed or hybrid languages do not emerge. Sometimes it is the language of the majority that is adopted as the common tongue, sometimes that of the minority; sometimes that of the more powerful element, sometimes of the weaker. This depends on various social and political factors. Below we will trace

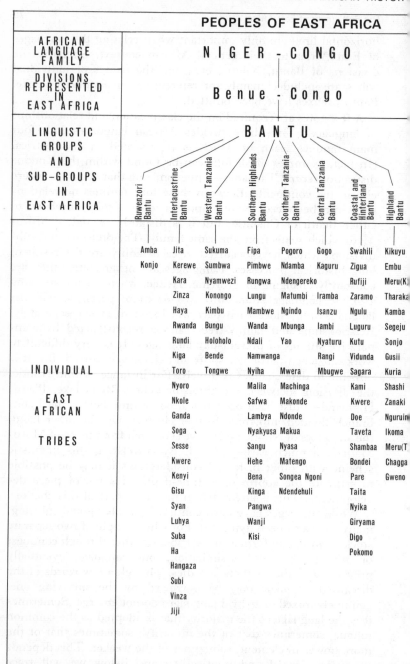

PEOPLES OF EAST AFRICA							
AFRICAN LANGUAGE FAMILY — NIGER - CONGO							
DIVISIONS REPRESENTED IN EAST AFRICA — Benue - Congo							
LINGUISTIC GROUPS AND SUB-GROUPS IN EAST AFRICA — BANTU							
Ruwenzori Bantu	Interlacustrine Bantu	Western Tanzania Bantu	Southern Highlands Bantu	Southern Tanzania Bantu	Central Tanzania Bantu	Coastal and Hinterland Bantu	Highland Bantu
Amba	Jita	Sukuma	Fipa	Pogoro	Gogo	Swahili	Kikuyu
Konjo	Kerewe	Sumbwa	Pimbwe	Ndamba	Kaguru	Zigua	Embu
	Kara	Nyamwezi	Rungwa	Ndengereko	Iramba	Rufiji	Meru(K)
	Zinza	Konongo	Lungu	Matumbi	Isanzu	Zaramo	Tharaka
	Haya	Kimbu	Mambwe	Ngindo	Iambi	Ngulu	Kamba
	Rwanda	Bungu	Wanda	Mbunga	Nyaturu	Luguru	Segeju
	Rundi	Holoholo	Ndali	Yao	Rangi	Kutu	Sonjo
	Kiga	Bende	Namwanga		Mbugwe	Vidunda	Gusii
	Toro	Tongwe	Nyiha	Mwera		Sagara	Kuria
	Nyoro		Malila	Machinga		Kami	Shashi
	Nkole		Safwa	Makonde		Kwere	Zanaki
	Ganda		Lambya	Ndonde		Doe	Nguruin
	Soga		Nyakyusa	Makua		Taveta	Ikoma
	Sesse		Sangu	Nyasa		Shambaa	Meru(T
	Kwere		Hehe	Matengo		Bondei	Chagga
	Kenyi		Bena	Songea Ngoni		Pare	Gweno
	Gisu		Kinga	Ndendehuli		Taita	
	Syan		Pangwa			Nyika	
	Luhya		Wanji			Giryama	
	Suba		Kisi			Digo	
	Ha					Pokomo	
	Hangaza						
	Subi						
	Vinza						
	Jiji						

(Row header for the tribe listing, left column: INDIVIDUAL EAST AFRICAN TRIBES)

Figure 10 Peoples of East Africa: Linguistic Classification

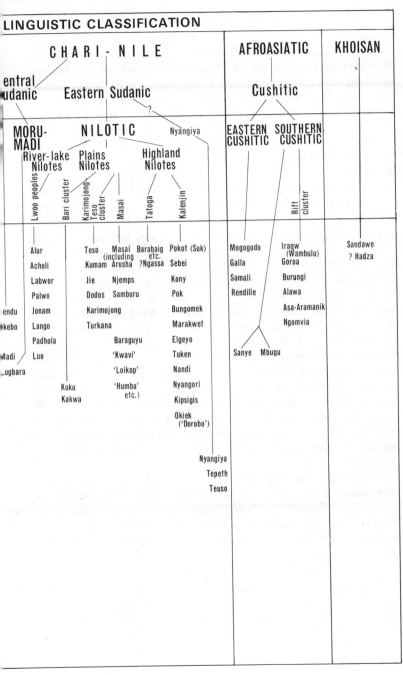

LINGUISTIC CLASSIFICATION

CHARI - NILE			AFROASIATIC	KHOISAN
Central Sudanic	Eastern Sudanic		Cushitic	
MORU-MADI	NILOTIC Nyangiya		EASTERN CUSHITIC SOUTHERN CUSHITIC	
River-lake Nilotes	Plains Nilotes	Highland Nilotes		
Lwoo peoples	Bari cluster Karimojong-Teso cluster Masai	Tatoga Kalenjin	Rift cluster	

	Alur	Teso	Masai (including Arusha)	Barabaig etc. ?Ngassa	Pokot (Suk)	Mogogodo	Iraqw (Wambulu)	Sandawe
	Acholi	Kumam			Sebei	Galla	Goroa	? Hadza
	Labwor	Jie	Njemps		Kony	Somali	Burungi	
	Palwo	Dodos	Samburu		Pok	Rendille	Alawa	
endu	Jonam	Karimojong			Bungomek		Asa-Aramanik	
kebo	Lango	Turkana			Marakwet		Ngomvia	
	Padhola		Baraguyu		Elgeyo			
Madi	Luo		'Kwavi'		Tuken	Sanye Mbugu		
ugbara			'Loikop'		Nandi			
		Kuku	'Humba' etc.)		Nyangori			
		Kakwa			Kipsigis			
					Okiek ('Dorobo')			
					Nyangiya			
					Tepeth			
					Teuso			

examples of Cushitic-speakers who have been absorbed by
Nilotic groups; and we shall see how peoples of various stocks
have been and still are being 'Bantuised'—absorbed into Bantu-
speaking tribes while forgetting their original non-Bantu speech.
This reinforces the point made above that no tribes are 'pure'
or derived from single ancestors. It also shows that we cannot
explain tribal or group history merely by reference to the
linguistic classification. The history of the Nilotes, for instance,
is not just the history of the Nilotic languages; it must consider
also the numerous interactions with various peoples originally
of non-Nilotic speech that have been absorbed into the Nilotes.
Nevertheless, this does not detract from the point that languages
and their classification remain very important historical factors.

To what extent do linguistic families and groups correlate
with physical types and with cultural features? Of Greenberg's
four language families, it will be observed that two, Niger-
Congo and Chari-Nile—represented in East Africa by Bantu,
Moru-Madi and Nilotic—are in general the languages of
Negroid peoples, that Afroasiatic includes most of the languages
of the Caucasoid and semi-Caucasoid peoples of Africa, and
Khoisan those of the Bushmanoid peoples. But these general
observations must be applied exceedingly cautiously. For the
Niger-Congo language family does include some Caucasoid
peoples, whereas there are also some Negroid peoples speaking
Afroasiatic languages, even of the Cushitic division. This
underlines the importance of not muddling the labels used for
physical types and linguistic groupings. We cannot talk of 'Negro
languages'; nor can we use the terms 'Bantu' or 'Afroasiatic' to
describe racial types.

On peoples' cultures, their economies and social and political
organisations, we can also make some useful observations. If
we compare Bantu and Nilotic-speakers, we notice that most
Nilotes attach more importance to cattle while Bantu on average
cultivate more. But there are some Bantu who keep large herds
and despise agriculture, whereas some Nilotes have no cattle
at all. Circumcision, to take another example, is commonly
regarded as a Cushitic trait, for it is virtually universal among
Cushitic-speakers. But when we find that a number of Bantu
and Nilotic-speaking tribes in Kenya and northern Tanzania
have adopted this custom, we cannot call them Cushites. They
remain Bantu and Nilotes, culturally influenced by Cushites,
perhaps.

One further point on the naming of linguistic groups. Many of the names are apparently geographical. 'Nilotic' for example originally meant 'of the river Nile.' But as a term for a group of related languages, 'Nilotic' does not include all the peoples living by the Nile. The Madi live on both sides of the Nile, but their language is not Nilotic. Conversely some of the Nilotic-speakers live a long distance from the river. So, as used here, the word 'Nilotic' has really nothing to do with the river Nile. Similarly linguistic divisions into 'western', 'eastern', etc. are not always geographically strict.

Before embarking on a general historical account of the peopling and settlement of East Africa, a few words must be said about each of the main linguistic groups.

Bantu languages

These cover the larger part of the Congo and of eastern and southern Africa. South of a line drawn from the Niger Delta to the southern Somali coast, almost all African languages are Bantu, except for the area of Khoisan speech in the south. There are some irregularities in the Bantu Line, most notably a wedge of various other languages in the highlands and Rift Valley of Kenya and northern Tanzania (as shown on Fig. 9). The Bantu languages number several hundred. They are, as groups of languages go, very closely related, indicating that their dispersal over a wide region began perhaps only two thousand years ago. But the details and directions of this spread, in East Africa and elsewhere, are only beginning to be worked out. By Greenberg's classification, Bantu is merely a sub-group of a branch of the Niger-Congo family. Other branches of Niger-Congo cover most of West Africa.

The inter-relationships of the various Bantu languages of East Africa have not been sufficiently studied. Therefore the groupings suggested on Fig. 10 are exceedingly arbitrary and based partly on geography. Some use has been made of Bryan's classification of Bantu languages.

Moru-Madi

Most of the languages of the Central Sudanic division of the Chari-Nile family are found in scattered blocks in the southern

Sudan, the north-eastern Congo and the Central African Republic. The so-called 'Moru-Madi group' extends into north-western Uganda. It was probably once more widely spread in this region.

The Nilotic Group

Much more extensive in East Africa is the Nilotic group, some sections of which have made fairly dramatic 'explosions' in a southward direction in the last thousand or two thousand years. We propose here a new classification of the Nilotes in three branches.* The Highland branch of the Nilotes consists of the Kalenjin cluster in the western Kenya highlands, with the Tatoga as well as small numbers of Okiek (or 'Dorobo') scattered further afield as far as central Tanzania. The Plains Nilotes fall into three main sub-groups: the Masai in Kenya and Tanzania; the Karimojong-Teso cluster of north-western Kenya and north-eastern Uganda with extensions into south-eastern Sudan; and the Bari cluster, mostly in southern Sudan, but in the case of the Kuku and Kakwa extending across the border of the West Nile district of Uganda. The River-lake Nilotes consist of the Dinka and Nuer of the Sudan, as well as the Lwoo-speaking peoples, who are divided into a number of tribes extending from the southern Sudan to northern Uganda and the lake-shore of western Kenya.

The Nyangiya Group

This consists of small numbers of scattered hill-cultivators and hunter-gatherers in north-eastern Uganda. It is not yet certain whether their languages belong to the Chari-Nile or the Afro-asiatic family. But clearly they are the unassimilated remnants of a pre-Nilotic population.

Cushitic Languages

The Afroasiatic family (also called 'Erythraic') has several divisions covering most of northern and north-eastern Africa as well as south-western Asia. (It includes Arabic and other Semitic tongues.) The Cushitic division is entirely African.

*See appendix re the designation 'Nilo-Hamites'.

It is centred in the Ethiopian highlands, and is divided into five main groups. Of these the Eastern Cushites extend from the southern highlands of Ethiopia across the Horn and over much of north-eastern Kenya, where they have expanded in relatively recent times—very recent in the case of the Somali. The Southern Cushites are confined to East Africa, and have been there much longer. They were once more widely spread in Kenya and in northern and central Tanzania. Several of these languages are dying out on account of absorption, mostly by Bantu. The Mbugu in Usambara, the Sanye of the lower Tana, and speakers of several of the languages of the 'Rift cluster' of north-central Tanzania are nearing the point of extinction. The Iraqw, however, are holding their own.

The Khoisan Family

The Khoisan (or 'Click') family comprises the languages of the Bushmen and Hottentots of the Kalahari and adjacent parts of southern Africa. The fact that Sandawe of central Tanzania belongs to this family is one of several indicators that these people were once more widespread in eastern and southern Africa. The position of the Hadza hunters near Lake Eyasi is less certain: Greenberg regards their language as Khoisan, but others suggest that it may be Afroasiatic. Like many other odd languages, it needs more careful study.

Peopling and settlement: historical reconstruction

When the first food-producing communities began settling in parts of East Africa in the late stone age, they would have found the country thinly populated by bands of hunters and gatherers. Many of these, especially in the more southerly regions, belonged to the Bushmanoid stock. This is indicated by skeletons of Bushmanoid type occasionally discovered in late stone age sites, and by certain other lines of evidence. Commonly the most distinctive finds from the camping and cooking sites of late stone age hunters and gatherers are minute stone tools of types known as Wilton (see Chapter 3). The Wilton extends from eastern to southern Africa, where it is connected with ancestors of the present-day Bushmen. The most usual camping-sites were under the shelter of overhanging rocks, which in central Tanzania are frequently painted with wild animals and hunting scenes. These rock-paintings also have their counterparts in southern Africa, where they are attributed to the Bushmen of earlier times. It is particularly significant that many of the Tanzanian paintings are in or next to the territory of the Sandawe, who are physically and linguistically related to the Bushmen of southern Africa, and who were until very recently living by hunting and gathering. The Sandawe, therefore, are the remnants of a Bushmanoid population with Khoisan speech that roamed more widely in the savannahs and woodlands of much of East Africa before the beginning of food-production. The Hadza are possibly another such remnant.

In some parts of East Africa there were probably hunter-gatherers of different stocks. In many of the highland regions of Kenya and northern Tanzania, stories are told of dwarfs that once lived or hid in the thick forests. The reliability of these stories is difficult to assess, but they may refer to the former presence of pygmies. Certainly the pygmies of the Congo, who extend right up to the Uganda border, descend from populations that have for long been adjusted to gathering and hunting in the forests.

More important is the evidence of advanced late stone age hunters and perhaps also fishermen in the highland savannahs of Kenya and northern Tanzania. These are known from finds of stone tools of the Capsian type (see Chapter 3), famous for blades, perhaps used as knives and spear-heads, made of the fine obsidian rock. These advances probably began reaching the Kenya highlands ten thousand years ago. They may have connections with the Middle Nile region or with Ethiopia. But their origin as well as the type of people responsible remain far from clear at the present stage of archaeological research.

The First Cultivators and Herdsmen

These advanced hunters lived in precisely those highland regions which, towards the close of the late stone age, experienced the first introductions of agriculture and domestic herds into East Africa. Dating by the radio-carbon method indicates that these developments had begun by 1,000 B.C. in the Kenya highlands. The newcomers were of the Caucasoid physical type: this is shown by skeletons excavated from a number of their burial sites. In fact, most of our knowledge of these earliest food-producers comes from burials, for very few living sites have been discovered. The burials are usually under cairns (stoné mounds). Large ones measure twelve feet in height and fifty feet in diameter, but many are much smaller. They can be found either singly or in groups, occasionally numbering a hundred or more. Their distribution extends from northern Kenya to central Tanzania, the whole length of the Rift Valley and the highlands on either side, as well as across the plains that stretch away to the east and north as far as Ethiopia. Often the burials contain offerings or some of the belongings of the dead man or woman. These include grindstones and pestles, earthenware pots and stone bowls which apparently contained food. From this we conclude that these people cultivated grain crops, presumably types of sorghum and millet. Animal bones show that they kept cattle, and probably goats and sheep. Nor was hunting despised; it continued to supplement the diet. It seems that there was considerable interbreeding between the newcomers and the indigenous hunters and gatherers of the highlands and adjoining plains.

A very famous communal burial site of this period is the Njoro River Cave in the elevated part of the Kenya Rift Valley. It was excavated by Dr and Mrs Leakey. They found that the bodies had been cremated—an unusual practice, but one which ensured that many grave-goods that would normally have rotted were carbonised and thus preserved. (They are now in the National Museum in Nairobi.) These include basketry, cords, gourds and a beautifully carved and decorated wooden vessel, presumably a milk container. Also famous from this site are the pendants and hundreds of beads belonging to necklaces. The beads were made from bone, ostrich eggshells, nuts, sedge-seeds, and various semi-precious stones, all obtainable locally.

The Njoro River Cave is only one of many burial sites of these late stone age cultivators and herdsmen, one which provides, however, an unusually rare insight into their material culture and economy. But, like the hunters and gatherers, they lacked all knowledge of metals. Their knives, scrapers and spears were made of stone, principally obsidian that provided beautifully sharp edges. Their axes would also have been of stone, their hoes of stone or wood. They preferred, therefore, the more open country with light soils, where fields could more easily be cleared and dug and where grazing was more available. Possibly it was in this pre-iron period that the first irrigation works were constructed for agriculture in the highlands. Many systems of irrigation channels exist in Kenya and Tanzania to this day, both in the hills themselves and, more valuable, at the base of escarpments where rivers flow into the drier plains. We do not know how old these complex feats of engineering may be; but it is certain that many of them are ancient, and their present users often attribute them to tribes that have now vanished or been absorbed. Of similar antiquity, perhaps, are the big dams in the plateau grasslands that doubtless provided reservoirs for watering cattle, and the deep rock-cut wells in the drier plains of north-eastern Tanzania and eastern and northern Kenya. Many of these wells are still used and enlarged by the present inhabitants of the plains, Masai, Galla and Somali. But the reservoirs have fallen into disuse. There is a fine series of these old reservoir dams at Ngorongoro, just above the crater.

The burials with their grave-goods, the red ochre with which the corpses were often adorned, and the special placing of skulls or jaw-bones, provide clear evidence of religious beliefs connected with cults of the dead. The burials are so numerous, both male and female, that it is difficult to believe that they represent important persons only. Quite probably, the societies of the highlands, then as now, were mostly chiefless.

Can we identify these late stone age food-producers more precisely? The Ethiopian highlands would have been the most likely direction from which seed-agriculture and domestic livestock would have diffused into the highland and Rift Valley regions of East Africa. The Caucasoid physical type also points to an Ethiopian origin: so do the methods of burial, for cairns are constructed in Ethiopia to this day by Cushitic-speaking peoples. The practice of circumcision as an initiation rite, and certain other social and cultural traits widespread among the present peoples of the Kenya and northern Tanzania highlands, also indicate earlier Cushitic influences in these regions. The Southern Cushites (see Fig. 9 and Fig. 10) provide the obvious answer. Only a few pockets survive, the largest tribe being the Iraqw; but it is clear on linguistic grounds that they are the remnants of a population that expanded from Ethiopia a few thousand years ago. Physically they should now be classified as Negroid, doubtless through intermarriage with other stocks in East Africa, but they still betray many Caucasoid features.

As far as we can trace it at present, this late stone age food-

production was confined to the highlands, Rift Valley and plains
of Kenya and northern Tanzania. But it would not be surprising
were we to discover that it extended into the southern highlands
of Tanzania, or were evidence to be produced of food-production
during the same period in northern Uganda. Neither region has
been well examined. Nevertheless, it seems fairly certain that
most of East Africa, including the Lake Victoria region and
western and southern Tanzania, remained the territory of
hunters and gatherers until the beginning of the iron age.

The Iron Age

It is still not clear just how and when iron-working first reached
East Africa. The commonly accepted view is that it was brought
from the north, on the presumption that it diffused through
sub-Saharan Africa from Meroe on the Middle Nile (north of
Khartoum) where there was a large iron-smelting industry two
thousand years ago. This view is clearly over-simplified, and
no convincing evidence has been produced for a line of diffusion
from Meroe to East Africa. The eventual answer will doubtless
be more complex, and it is now being suggested that iron-
working was introduced to East Africa from several directions—
the south-west, the Indian Ocean and the north—during the
first millennium A.D. This is supported by a few recently
obtained radio-carbon dates. One thing is certain: there was no
rapid or absolute change-over from a stone to an iron technology.
Some peoples, particularly those who adhered longest to
hunting and gathering, had no iron till very recently. And many
iron-using peoples, for long supplemented their tool-kit by
continuing to work stone. Throughout the iron age, iron tools
were never too plentiful.

  The most famous of early iron age sites in the East African
interior is Engaruka in the Rift Valley of northern Tanzania.
It has been described as a 'city' with a population of many
thousands. This is an exaggeration. It was an important and
concentrated agricultural settlement, dependent, in this area of
low rainfall, on the irrigation potentialities of the river that
rushes down the rift valley wall. Ancient field-systems stretch
away from the river on either side. Some are on the hillside,
where, naturally, they were constructed as narrow stone-
revetted terraces; those in the valley are laid out in grid-fashion,
often divided by stone lines. Remains of old irrigation channels

can be seen among some of the fields; but it is not certain that all were irrigated. Homesteads were mostly on the hillside, partly no doubt with a view to defence. They consist of platforms cut into the steep ground and enclosed by dry-stone revetting. These homestead-enclosures are very numerous, but they were not all in use at the same time. The preliminary excavations so far undertaken at Engaruka by the Tanzania Antiquities Department suggest that the occupation of the site may have spanned more than a thousand years, continuing until recent centuries. There may, of course, have been breaks in the occupation: for all we know the site may have been deserted and resettled on several occasions. At any one time the population would have numbered hundreds rather than thousands. Nevertheless, Engaruka remains an important archaeological site with much more to tell us yet. There are some similar but smaller sites in the same region.

We cannot yet say which group or groups of people inhabited Engaruka. At a guess they were Cushites, who were formerly more extensive in this region. Unlike the earlier Cushites discussed above, the inhabitants of Engaruka used iron tools. The art of iron-working may have been brought from Ethiopia by secondary Cushitic migrations or contacts. It could have come from the coast; but there is no good evidence of long-distance trade-routes linking the coast and interior in this period, nor of commercial activities at Engaruka. A few imported beads and cowrie-shells have been found there, however, showing that there was at least some indirect contact with the coast. Alternatively, the iron-working may have been brought to Engaruka by one of the new groups of peoples that began penetrating East Africa in the first millennium A.D.—the first Nilotes and Bantu.

Both Bantu and Nilotic-speakers are Negroid, but their histories are very distinct. The Nilotes entered East Africa from the north or north-west, from the southern Sudan and perhaps the western Ethiopian borderland; whereas Bantu migrations into East Africa were probably from the south, south-west and west. This is based on linguistic analyses and comparisons. It is important not to over-simplify the picture. Neither Nilotes nor Bantu arrived in East Africa all at one go. Instead, we should imagine numerous Bantu and Nilotic movements throughout the length of the iron age—a period of one to two thousand years from the present. Some of the more pastoral Nilotic immigrants may have sped across the northern plains and grasslands as conquering waves or as desperate splinter-groups in search of land or refuge: but more often migrations were slow and gradual, involving peaceful penetration and settlement. As populations increased and more land was required, so expansion and migration proceeded, and new territory was cleared from the wild, for homesteads and fields. If this was the normal case with the Nilotes, it was even truer of the Bantu, who settled in primarily agricultural regions.

This picture of early Bantu and Nilotic migration and settlement is reconstructed mainly from linguistic and anthropological evidence. There is no help from oral traditions, for the period is too remote. Nor is there much from archaeology as yet. Nevertheless, one important class of archaeological material may well be connected with the early spread of Bantu peoples. This is a distinctive type of pottery known as 'dimple-based' ware, found in a number of distantly-spaced parts of East Africa—the northern sides of Lake Victoria, Rwanda, central and north-eastern Tanzania, near the Kenya coast, and at Kalambo Falls at the southern end of Lake Tanganyika. Further archaeological exploration will probably fill some of the gaps in this distribution. Moreover, 'dimple-based' pottery is related to that known as 'channelled' ware obtained in a number of excavations in Zambia and Rhodesia. Both types date to the first and early second millennia A.D. It is not yet clear where it originated or how it spread, but a movement into East Africa from the direction of Zambia seems most likely. It is also noteworthy that in most regions where it occurs it appears to be the pottery of the first cultivating and first iron-using communities, so suggesting the early Bantu expansion.

This begs the question of how iron-working had already reached Zambia—whether from West Africa through or round the Congo forests, from the Indian Ocean up the Zambezi valley, or from East Africa? It was very possibly from this last direction that the cultivation of grain-crops (sorghum and millets) had spread to southern Africa, for as we have seen they were present in the East African highlands at a much earlier period.

But grain agriculture is not the only consideration. The distribution of 'dimple-based' pottery also shows the opening-up of forested and heavy rainfall regions, such as Rwanda and the shores of Lake Victoria. Here the banana has proved the most successful staple crop, able to support dense populations. Iron tools doubtless facilitated this primary opening-up of the banana country, but it was necessary in the first place to have banana suckers to plant. As we have seen, the banana originated in south-eastern Asia, and was brought to Africa by traders or immigrants about two thousand years ago. From studies of cultivated bananas, it seems likely that the first ones reached the lake regions of eastern Africa, not by being carried up-country directly from the coast, but by entry into the Zambezi region and expansion northwards.

So the distribution of 'dimple-based' and 'channelled' pottery seems to indicate more than just the spread of early Bantu and of the first agriculture and iron-working into the southern and western regions of East Africa. It also denotes the beginnings of agricultural specialisation: in the more open country greater emphasis would be placed on millet crops, in the wetter regions on bananas. Thus began the opening-up of the most fertile parts of East Africa. The Cushites, who from much earlier times had been settled in the highlands of Kenya and northern Tanzania, had been more restricted in their choice of land, since they had lacked both iron and bananas.

The early Bantu expansion was not enacted in a complete vacuum. The same applies to the early Nilotic movements from the north, which took place during roughly the same period. As already noted, there were populations of hunter-gatherers, who would have entered into relationships with the newcomers and exchanged products. Many were absorbed into the food-producing tribes; others maintained their independence by retreating into the forests and other types of country less favourable for crops and herds. There are to this day a number of groups or bands that live by hunting and gathering, and exchange with their agricultural and pastoral neighbours. These include the Sanye and others in the plains of eastern Kenya, and the bands called 'Dorobo' in the highland forests of Kenya and northern Tanzania. Not all these hunter-gatherers and forest-dwellers are in fact true descendants of the pre-food-producing inhabitants of East Africa. Some have reverted to this mode of life, for in hard times many people will take refuge in the forest or revert to a life dependent on nature. A cultivator whose crops fail, a herdsman whose cattle die or are stolen, people fleeing from wars or repudiated by their kinsmen, are liable to 'turn Dorobo', as the saying goes. Dorobo may be despised by pastoral and agricultural peoples, but the honey, game-meat and other products of the forest which they trade are appreciated. This interdependence is essential for their continued existence.

Intermingling and Assimilation of Peoples

More extensive processes of assimilation by Bantu and Nilotes have taken place in the highland regions of Kenya and northern Tanzania already occupied by the southern Cushitic-speaking food-producers. The first and most important Nilotic group in the highlands were the ancestors of the present Kalenjin tribes. Linguistic and archaeological studies show that at certain times in the past they have been more widespread in the highlands and Rift Valley than they are now (see Chapter 8). The Bantu approach to the highlands was from the opposite direction—the south and the coastal region. The Cushites were not simply overthrown by the successive waves of newcomers: there were some very long processes of intermingling. Though, as we have seen, the distribution of southern Cushitic languages is today very restricted, these people have left a deep mark on the customs, beliefs, economies and social and political organisations of the Bantu and Nilotes now inhabiting the highlands.

We should not envisage the history of the peopling of East Africa in the iron age merely as a process of Bantu and Nilotes absorbing the earlier Bushman-type hunter-gatherers and Southern Cushitic food-producers. There was also considerable interaction, both peaceful and hostile, between various Bantu and Nilotic groups. Through central Uganda there has been much friction and intermingling in the last five centuries since the Nilotic Lwoo peoples began pressing against the northern borders of the Bantu (see Chapter 7). The expansion of the Lwoo in north-western Uganda has also helped to reduce the areas of Moru-Madi-type languages, which may already have been pushed back by the more northerly Bantu. On the edges of the western Kenya highlands and southwards into Tanzania, Bantu sections have impinged upon older populations of Highland Nilotes, resulting in assimilation in both directions over many centuries. The Bantu who live in the highlands east of the Rift Valley (Kikuyu, Kamba, Chagga, etc.) and those at its southern end (Rangi, Nyaturu, Gogo, etc.) have absorbed many non-Bantu elements. These include, besides hunter-gatherers and

Southern Cushites, pastoralists of diverse origins—Highland Nilotes, Galla and other Eastern Cushitic groups, and in the last century or two Masai of the Plains branch of the Nilotes. Whereas Nilotes have tended to dominate the highland and Rift Valley grasslands, Eastern Cushites, expanding from Ethiopia and the Horn, have for several centuries roamed the dry plains of northern and eastern Kenya and perhaps north-eastern Tanzania, stretching from the highland edges right down to the coast. Pressure from Eastern Cushites was one of the factors that induced Kikuyu and other Bantu groups to move from the coastal regions and river valleys into the highlands. Surrounded by Nilotes and Eastern Cushites, both jealous for the grasslands, the highland Bantu have been mainly confined to the fertile forested hill-slopes where few cattle can be kept. But here they provide refuges for pastoralists who from time to time fall on evil days and lose their cattle or are driven by stronger rivals from the grasslands. For instance many of the highland Bantu, particularly those of Kilimanjaro and Mount Meru, have absorbed numbers of Masai, or in some cases have themselves been absorbed by the more agricultural of the Masai, such as the Arusha.

One further question of possible Cushitic influences needs discussion. This concerns western Uganda, north-western Tanzania, Rwanda and Burundi—what is commonly called the interlacustrine region. The peoples of this region are entirely Bantu-speaking; but a minority, which tends to form a pastoral aristocracy known as Hima or Tusi within these various Bantu tribes, possesses physical features suggesting that some of their ancestors may have been of the Caucasoid type. Certain writers have surmised that the region was invaded some centuries ago by Western Cushites from the south-western Ethiopian highlands, and that these invaders were responsible for the origins of the organised interlacustrine kingdoms that have persisted till this century. The presumed invaders have been associated not only with the ancestors of the present Hima and Tusi clans, but also with the legendary Bachwezi who are said to have ruled a large kingdom called Kitara centred in western Uganda some five hundred years ago (see Chapter 9). This theory of Western Cushitic migration remains problematical—unproven, but not impossible. Unfortunately, it has been bedevilled by association with more notorious theories of 'Hamitic' conquest and superiority (for which see the appendix to this chapter).

Lastly, Nilotes have absorbed Nilotes, and Bantu have absorbed Bantu. To take Nilotes first: from Lake Kyoga northwards there has been fusion of Lwoo-speakers and elements of the Karimojong-Teso cluster pressing from opposite directions in recent centuries. The Lango have come through this maintaining the Lwoo speech, whereas, among the Kumam and the Teso, Plains Nilotic languages have prevailed. In the highlands and Rift Valley, Masai have assimilated some of the previously far-ranging Kalenjin, while the Kalenjin have been constantly interacting among themselves and thus forming new tribes. Similarly, within the Moru-Madi group of peoples, the expanding Lugbara have in the last hundred years or more swallowed up part of the Madi tribe. For an interesting example of inter-Bantu fusion, we might observe the region to the east and south-east of Lake Victoria. Here Bantu who have come around or across the Lake have mixed with others who have crossed from the eastern highlands through the Nilotic zone of the Rift Valley. Elsewhere there have been constant and numerous inter-Bantu movements. Though, as we have seen, the main Bantu penetration into East Africa appears to have been from the south-west, this has not prevented secondary migrations in the opposite direction. Several tribes in central Tanzania claim to have originated through the fusion of a resident Bantu population with new arrivals, also Bantu, from the east or north-east. Some of these movements were connected with increasing populations and the need to open up more land for agriculture. Finally, the Ngoni movements, conquests and settlements in the nineteenth century (Chapter 12) demonstrate how new Bantu tribes were formed in what had long been Bantu territory. It is not surprising then, that although there have been Nilotes and Bantu in East Africa for one or two thousand years, the traditional histories of individual Nilotic and Bantu tribes usually go back only one, two or three hundred years, and never for more than six hundred.

Thus we see the complex nature of tribal origins and compositions. Though we may for convenience classify tribes by their languages as Bantu, Nilotic, Cushitic, etc., the more we examine them, the more mixed we find their ancestries to be. A tribe emerges not by maintaining the pure blood of its ancestors, not by sedulously avoiding contact with its neighbours, but by successfully assimilating its diverse elements. To survive, a tribe must continually adjust itself to surrounding circumstances.

This will be further borne out in the chapters that follow, covering the later histories of the main East African ethnic groups. The history of East Africa and of its component regions is not just a collection of histories of individual tribes or groups of tribes, but a story of fusion and interaction by which all tribes and groups have been constantly altered or even transformed. If we try to study tribes or groups in isolation, we will end up not with a history of East Africa, but with tribalist histories full of biases and antiquarianism.

Appendix: 'Hamites' and the Hamitic myth

In the foregoing account the reader will have noticed no mention of 'Hamites' or 'Hamitic influences'. Since these have figured prominently in other writings on the history of eastern Africa, some explanation is required. The term 'Hamitic' is highly confusing, and also hedged with racist overtones. It has been used in a variety of ways to denote linguistic, physical and cultural traits, and often more vaguely, reflecting European presumptions that light-skinned peoples are more intelligent than dark-skinned. For the 'Hamites' have commonly been envisaged as the 'more European-like' of Africans—in other words those peoples with lighter skins, thinner lips and straighter noses inhabiting most of northern and north-eastern Africa. To these 'Hamites' have been attributed any remarkable technological feat, any notable political organisation, any trace of 'civilisation' in black Africa. For instance, old irrigation systems and drystone walling in the East African highlands and rock-cut wells in the plains, the coming of iron-working and the origins of the interlacustrine kingdoms, have all been related to 'Hamitic' invasions or influences from the north. Hence were invented theories of vanished 'Hamitic civilisations' in certain regions, theories of 'conquest of inferior by superior peoples' (as Speke surmised in the Lake Victoria region), theories of interaction and intermarriage between 'Hamites' and Negroes by which the latter were raised from utter barbarism (as Seligman imagined), and theories of imitation by which Negroes tried to improve their lot by copying the example of the 'Hamites'. As Seligman put it, 'the civilisations of Africa are the civilisations of the Hamites'; the history of Africa, he believed, could only be written in terms of 'Hamites' and their influences. It is time that we reject such illogical and prejudiced views of Africa and her past.

It is odd, moreover, that the 'Hamites' as popularly conceived should include some of the least cultured or 'civilised' peoples in Africa. For the 'Hamitic problem' has been further confounded by its association with pastoralism. Large tracts of eastern and northern Africa are best suited to a herding life involving seasonal movements in search of pasture and water. This type of economy does not in general encourage the development of advanced material cultures or political systems. But the pastoralist, with his proud bearing as he watches his herds and commands the plains with his spear, and with his contempt for his agricultural neighbours, has won a romantic admiration from European observers. He has been hailed as innately superior, especially be he light-skinned. Clearly a definition of 'Hamite' on the basis of pastoralism or any other cultural consideration is subjective or unhelpful.

The use of 'Hamitic' to describe a physical (or racial) type can be avoided by adopting a more scientific terminology. The lighter-skinned inhabitants of northern and north-eastern Africa should properly be classified 'Caucasoid'. This description does not extend to East African pastoralists such as Masai, Karamojong, Turkana, Hima and Tusi, who have commonly been called 'Hamites' or 'semi-Hamites'. These peoples are decidedly Negroid, though they may have incorporated an admixture of Caucasoid blood in their ancestry.

Lastly, as a linguistic term, 'Hamitic' has been used in at least two main senses—for a large family of languages stretching from the Moroccan to the Somali coasts, and for a division within this family covering much of Ethiopia and the Horn with scattered outposts in Kenya and Tanzania (e.g. the Iraqw). To prevent confusion, it is strongly recommended that we use Greenberg's linguistic terminology avoiding the word 'Hamitic'. We should thus speak of the main family as 'Afro-asiatic', and the divisions as 'Cushitic' (as in Fig. 10).*

'Nilo-Hamites'

If 'Hamitic' is unacceptable, the same must apply to 'Nilo-Hamitic'. The peoples formerly designated 'Nilo-Hamites'

*One word of warning: Cushitic languages have no connection whatever with the Nubian and Middle Nile regions which the ancient Egyptians called Kush, and where the kingdom of Kush, based on the cities of Napata and Meroe, flourished some two thousand years ago.

belong to four main groupings—Kalenjin (with Tatoga), Masai, the Karamojong-Teso cluster and the Bari cluster. They were called 'Nilo-Hamites' because they were considered on both linguistic and cultural grounds to be mixtures of Nilotes and 'Hamites'. The 'Hamites' in this case were Cushitic-speakers. We would, however, strongly oppose any suggestion that the 'Nilo-Hamites' be reclassified 'Nilo-Cushites'. Recent studies of their languages show that they are basically Nilotic, and that any Cushitic word-borrowings are superficial. Some of them, notably Kalenjin and Masai, have assimilated numbers of Cushites and have also made cultural borrowings from them (as explained in this chapter), but this is irrelevant to a strictly linguistic classification which we insist on using here. Moreover, certain linguists believe that the so-called 'Nilo-Hamites' do not constitute a single branch within the Nilotes. Mr. Ehret argues that 'the Nilo-Hamitic hypothesis has made a unity of diversity'. The Nilotic languages should be divided into three main branches (as suggested above, and ref. Fig. 10). The River-lake branch comprises the peoples formerly called 'Nilotes' or 'Nilotes proper'; the Plains and Highland branches are those formerly called 'Nilo-Hamites'.

Further reading

Most of the literature relevant to the settlement of East Africa is outdated, controversial or too difficult for the student or, non-specialist. There are as yet no satisfactory general accounts. However, some of the following contributions to the subject may be of use.

MURDOCK, G. P. *Africa: Its Peoples and their Culture History,* McGraw-Hill, New York, 1959. (Introductory chapters and those on East Africa.)

GREENBERG, J. H. *Languages of Africa,* Indiana University and Mouton, The Hague, 1963. (For map and classification.)

Journal of African History, Volume III, No. 2, 1962, Cambridge University Press. (For discussion of food-crops and languages.)

WRIGLEY, C. Speculations on the Economic Prehistory of Africa, *Journal of African History,* Volume 1, No. 2, 1960, pp.

189-203. (Some stimulating ideas on food-production and iron.)

COLE, S. *The Prehistory of East Africa,* 2nd edition, New York, 1963; Weidenfeld and Nicholson, London, 1964.

OLIVER, R. and MATHEW, G. (Eds.) *History of East Africa* Volume I, Oxford University Press, 1963.

POSNANSKY, M. (Ed.) *Prelude to East African History,* Oxford University Press, 1966.

OGOT, B. A. The Movement of Peoples in East Africa, *East Africa, Past and Present,* Presence Africaine, Paris, 1964.

OLIVER, R. The Problem of Bantu Expansion, *Journal of African History,* Volume VII, No. 3, 1966 (pp. 361–376).

Azania, Journal of the British Institute of History and Archaeology in East Africa, Volume I, 1966, Oxford University Press. (Contains articles on recent work at Engaruka, the highlands of Kenya and northern Tanzania, early Iron Age pottery, etc.)

MCCALL, D. F. *Africa in Time-Perspective : A Discussion of Historical Reconstruction from Unwritten Sources,* Ghana and Boston University Presses, 1964. (A general discussion of historical reconstruction.)

5

The Coast Before the Arrival of the Portuguese

Neville Chittick

Our written historical records for the interior of Africa go back
only a century, and the oral traditions nowhere more than five
hundred years or so, and that only where conditions for their
being remembered are exceptional. For the history of the coast,
however, we have written accounts which profess to give a record
of events spanning the last two thousand years.

These historical sources fall into two groups; those written
by people living outside East Africa, and those set down by
chroniclers who lived on the coast itself. For the period before
the arrival of the Portuguese, the first group consists mainly
of the works of Arab geographers. These works, the product
of the most advanced civilisation of its age, are mostly descriptions of the world as it was then known, together with some
historical observations and anecdotes; others contain accounts
of travels. So far as East Africa is concerned, they are based
mostly on the reports brought back by merchants, but one or
two are written by persons who actually sailed to these shores
and so at least in part are based on what the authors saw. These
accounts are of the highest evidential value, since they describe
the state of affairs when they were set down and also events
which had happened only a short time before. Unfortunately,
however, many parts of these accounts are difficult to understand. The geographers believed that southern Africa curved

round in an easterly direction to join up with countries of the Far East, and this makes accounts of the southern regions and islands confusing: Waq-Waq, for example, is usually the name of some islands off eastern Asia, but also denotes an area of Africa. Many names are corrupt and difficult to interpret, for short vowels are not usually written in Arabic, and many of the consonants are distinguished from each other only by dots, so that the placing of a dot in the wrong place, or its omission, will change the pronunciation of the name. There is often imprecision in the use of terms, too: 'Zenj' is used both for black people in general, and for a particular negroid group. Moreover the geographers were not particularly interested in the history of the regions they were describing and neither they, nor most of their informants, understood the language of the native peoples of the region.

The historical sources from outside East Africa are thus of the highest value for what they do tell us; but this is not a great deal. The most important works are those of al-Mas'udi (first half of the tenth century) and Ibn Battuta, who describes things as he saw them in about 1331.

The second group of sources comprises those accounts which were set down on the East African coast. These are mostly chronicles of individual towns, giving the names of their rulers and some account of their doings. They were written in Arabic or in Swahili in Arabic script. The only one of these chronicles which is of any antiquity is that of Kilwa, which was written around 1530 and has come to us in two differing versions, one transmitted by the Portuguese historian, de Barros, who wrote in the mid-sixteenth century, and the other copied in Zanzibar in 1877. Most of the rest of the chronicles were set down only in recent times, and none can be traced back beyond the second half of the eighteenth century. These histories from our coast have much to tell of events before the arrival of the Portuguese; one of them even has quite a lot to say of happenings before the Hijra, the flight of the Prophet Muhammad from Mecca to Medina in A.D. 622, which marks the beginning of the Islamic era.* But an historical document can only set out facts remembered at the time when it was written, unless the author is relying on an earlier written source. To this extent they should

*Years of the Islamic era are indicated by the letters A.H. *(anno Hegirae)* before the date thus: A.H. 600 (=A.D. 1203–4).

be treated as we would oral traditions that have been committed
to writing. While all historians have appreciated that some of
the stories told in these chronicles are mythical or semi-mythical,
none of them has submitted these chronicles to a sufficiently
critical approach. Most historians of the coast have been trained
in the European tradition of recent historical scholarship in
fields where we have many sources; those trained in the traditions
of oral history have concentrated their attentions on the peoples
of the interior.

Application of the principles of criticism used with oral
traditions, together with other evidence with which we shall
deal later, is leading to some important amendments to facts
of the history of the coast as hitherto received. These new
theories have not yet been entirely accepted and it will be
found that in some respects the dating or account of events in
what follows differs from what will be found in older books;
where appropriate I have indicated the view previously taken
of certain matters.

We have just referred to another type of evidence. This is
that derived from archaeology, by which we mean not only the
evidence of objects and structures which have been dug out of
the ground, but also of inscriptions on graves and buildings,
and the style of architecture of the buildings themselves. There
is also the evidence provided by linguistics, by place-names,
by anthropology and ethnology, but these are of small importance in the study of the history of the coast as compared with
that of the interior, where other evidence is scanty.

Archaeological research in this region has only been undertaken on any significant scale in the last few years and we have
already learnt much from the discoveries. Substantial evidence
for the revision of aspects of coast history has come from
excavations, in particular from the coins which were minted
by certain of the sultans of Kilwa.

Before Islam

The original population of the coast probably consisted of
hunting peoples of which the Sanye and Boni, who live in the
hinterland of the southern Somali and northern Kenya coasts,
are survivors. We do not know precisely the ethnic group to
which they should be assigned, but some of these peoples were

probably allied to the Bushman and Hottentot peoples who live further south at the present day.* They were responsible for the 'microlithic' stone industries, with very small tools, typical of the late stone age. Such industries have been found near the coast from Kilwa in the south to Kilifi in the north.

Some historians have suggested that Egyptians, Phoenicians, Persians and others may have come to the East African coast centuries before the birth of Christ. There is, however, no real evidence that this was so; Herodotus gives a brief account of the circumnavigation of Africa by Phoenicians, who are supposed to have wintered on the continent, but this account is almost certainly spurious. The Egyptians, it is true, voyaged to a land they called Punt, but this was almost certainly west and north of Cape Guardafui.

The huge expansion of Rome early in the Christian era was not only a military conquest, but led also to a great increase in trade, especially in the Indian Ocean. Out of the need for a guide and pilot for traders came the *Periplus of the Erythraean Sea,* the anonymous work of a Greek merchant living in Egypt. This is the earliest document we have dealing with East Africa and the most informative before the tenth century. Nevertheless, it tells less about the East African coast than about most lands of the Indian Ocean (known to the Greeks and Romans as the Erythraean Sea) and, as unfortunately parts of it are apparently corrupt, it is difficult to identify most of the place-names. It has generally been thought to have been written in the latter part of the first century A.D., but it may be as much as 150 years later. What the *Periplus* tells us can be considered with the information in Ptolemy's *Geography,* of which the parts concerned are thought to date from the fifth century.

The East African coast was known as Azania to these writers, and as the Land of the Zenj to the Arabs. Its chief town was called Rhapta, so called from the word for 'sewn', in reference to the sewn boats which were a feature of that place and of the island of Menouthias (probably Mafia, standing for all the islands of the Zanzibar group). The site of Rhapta has never been found— nor has any other place of this period—but its most likely location was in the Rufiji Delta. Rhapta was the last settlement known to the south, as well as the most important, by the time

*The theory is currently advanced that these are not ethnically entirely distinct from the negroid peoples, as was thought hitherto.

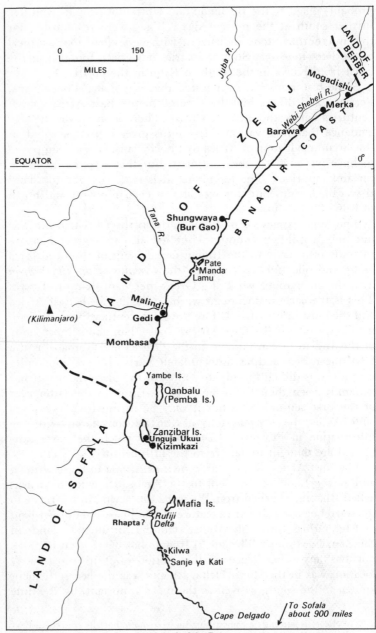

Figure 11 The Coast before the arrival of the Portuguese

of Ptolemy; we are told the names of numbers of other ports further north. Arab traders from south-west Arabia sailed to these ports on the north-east monsoon wind which blows from November until April, returning with the monsoon which blows in the reverse direction from June until October. Some of these Arabs knew the language of Azania, and intermarried with women of the people there. What these people were by race is not clear; the *Periplus* is more concerned with describing the goods which merchants should take with them, and what they might get in exchange, than it is with the inhabitants of the countries it describes. All that we are told is that the people were very tall, that they were pirates, and that they had a chief in each place; since they had boats we know that they were seafarers. As nothing is said of their colour, some historians have deduced that they were not negroid. This argument is weak, however, and in fact from the little we are told they could have been negro, even Bantu-speaking (though this seems unlikely in view of present theories of the spread of Bantu speech). They could equally well have been Cushitic, like the present-day Ethiopians, or even of Indonesian extraction. This last would indeed fit the facts best, except that Indonesians tend to be short in stature. We know that some time in the first millennium A.D. many Indonesians settled in Madagascar, bringing with them food crops, notably the banana, which were to become of great importance to Africa. It is possible, too, that they settled on the coast of what is now Kenya and Tanzania, although the time of the *Periplus* is rather earlier than it is thought this immigration took place. But the fact that Ptolemy speaks of man-eating Ethiopians in the southernmost part of this region indicates that the people were dark in colour, for this is the connotation of 'Ethiopian' in Greek.

The Azanian coast was under the suzerainty of Charibael, who was ruler of Himyar in south-west Arabia; we are told that it had long been under the domination of whichever was the most powerful state in Arabia. However, the people of Mouza (the port of Mocha in the Yemen) controlled the coast under the authority of Charibael, and it is from this port that most of the ships came.

The goods that they came to barter for were those typical of the exports of East Africa throughout history, primarily the products of the animals which were so exotic to the rest of the known world. First in importance was ivory; then turtle-shell and rhinoceros horn. In addition a little coconut oil was exported; this piece of information is important, because it shows that the coconut palm had already reached the coast from the east, and also that some people at least were living in permanent settlements. It is notable that slaves are not mentioned, though we are told that they were brought from the coasts of the Horn of Africa. From that northern region, the chief exports were aromatic gums and spices.

The main goods which the traders brought to exchange for these commodities were metal tools—hatchets and daggers and awls, and lances which were specially made for this trade at Mouza. These tools would mostly have been of iron, and indicate that the inhabitants of Azania had little or no knowledge of how to smelt this metal. The traders also brought glass vessels, and, to some places, a little wine and wheat as gifts to get the goodwill of the inhabitants.

For some four centuries after the time of Ptolemy we have no reliable information about the coast. It is probable that some trade continued with the Arab world, and that there was a trickle of Arab immigration. This may be at the root of unreliable traditions of colonisers being sent by Harun al-Rashid or others, but this is by no means certain. There is a tradition from Oman, of doubtful authenticity, of an emigration from that country to the land of Zenj in the seventh century. This is the story of the brothers Sulaiman and Sa'id, joint rulers of Oman, who are supposed to have left with their followers after being defeated by an 'Umayyad army. And de Barros tells of the coming of some heretic Muslim people he calls Emozaidij, by which he probably means followers of the Shi'a leader Zaid. This probably has some historical truth, and may incorporate memory of the arrival, in the eighth or ninth century, of some Zaidis on the Banadir coast, from which they were later displaced by orthodox immigrants, becoming largely absorbed in the interior by the pagan inhabitants. Such movements and trade were certainly on a very small scale, for no archaeological remains of settlements of this (or the earlier) period have yet been found.*

In the ninth and tenth centuries we find the first information

---

*A few finds of Greek and Roman coins have been reported from East Africa, but some are undocumented and the others have been found with later coins, and probably reached East Africa in a later period.

in Arabic sources, notably al-Mas'udi who died about A.D. 945; and it is from that period that the earliest identified town sites date. Most of the ships at that time came to the coast from the Persian Gulf, especially from the great port of Siraf, and from Oman. Al-Mas'udi himself made at least two journeys to the East African coast once from each place. In this and subsequent periods the coast was usually considered as divided into three parts: Berber, which extended down to the Webi Shebeli; the land of the Zenj proper, which extended thence down to the land of Sofala, whose northern limit was probably in the region of Pangani, opposite the island of Pemba, and extended for a thousand miles or so to the south. Beyond this is the shadowy, hardly-known land of Waq-Waq. Of the islands, only one is mentioned by name; this is Qanbalu which is probably to be identified with Pemba.

By this period, negroid Bantu speakers had already settled on the coast, and were even living as far north as the southern part of what is now Somalia, where lay, or was soon to come into being, their famous town of Shungwaya. They are referred to by Arabs as Zenj, and at least in the Sofala country and probably further north they had a quite highly organised society. They were governed by kings who could be elected and who maintained armies. It was a religiously-minded society; we are told more than once of men preaching to the people, and some of these priests probably advised the king. Al-Mas'udi tells us that they harnessed oxen like horses, and used them both for transport and for war. Their social organisation seems to have closely resembled that of the western lacustrine states, notably Rwanda, in recent centuries, where a cattle-keeping, pastoral aristocracy ruled over a settled peasant population.

Early Muslim Settlement

The number of Muslims who had so far settled on the coast must have been small; as late as about A.D. 1150 the towns of the mainland from Barawa south are described as pagan. This is according to al-Idrisi who, however, does not appear to be very reliable. We know from al-Mas'udi that in the tenth century the island of Qanbalu had a mixed population of Muslims and Zenj pagans; the former, presumably Arabs, had conquered it long enough earlier for the Muslims to have adopted the Zenj language. The ruling family was of the Muslim group. There are other indications of Arab immigration in this period; there was a colony of Muslims at Merka, probably dating from the tenth century, and also as we shall see at Manda near Lamu and at Unguja Ukuu in Zanzibar. Probably most of these immigrants came from the Persian Gulf; those at Merka came from the great port of Siraf, and de Barros tells us of the coming of a group of refugee people from Al-Ahsa near Bahrein on the opposite side of the Gulf, who are supposed to have founded Mogadishu and Barawa. This event, if historical, most likely occurred in the eleventh century. Traditions of the Zanzibar islands and the Mrima coast tell of people called Wadebuli trading and settling on the coast. These people probably came from Daybul, which was a great Muslim port in north-west India near the mouth of the Indus, until it was destroyed about A.D. 1250. These people were probably then sailing to the southern part of the coast too, though few seem to have settled and they were rapidly absorbed.

The earliest coastal settlements which have yet been discovered date from the ninth and tenth centuries, and we are able to supplement knowledge from historical sources with that from archaeology.

These trading towns, not only in the earliest period, but until quite recent times, were sited for preference on islands; failing this the favourite position was on a spit of land almost encircled by creeks and mangrove swamps. This was for security; with a stretch of water protecting their wealthy towns from the poorer inhabitants of the hinterland, they had no need of defensive walls, which in the earliest period are seldom found. They would cultivate on the mainland if it was close, crossing to their *shambas** in boats, but did not venture into the interior. A very similar pattern is still found in the Lamu archipelago, where all the main settlements are on islands. Indeed, in recent times of insecurity on the mainland, refugees have settled at the sites of old island towns which had been abandoned for centuries.

Though these towns looked out on the ocean for the wealth they derived from their commerce, they had to obtain from the mainland the goods to barter for their imports. These goods were brought to the coast by the people of the interior; there is

*Swahili; cultivated grounds.

hardly any evidence of expeditions inland until the nineteenth century. It is probable that goods which came from a long distance were bartered from tribe to tribe, rather than being carried by long distance caravans.

Two town-sites of this period have been partly excavated. The lowest levels at Kilwa date probably to the ninth century, but it was a poor, though quite extensive place. Most or all the inhabitants were pagan, but they were trading on a small scale to the Arab lands. Unguja Ukuu flourished at this period, but has not been dug; to judge by the amount of imported pottery and the finding of a hoard of gold dinars there many years ago it probably had a Muslim population. We know from a famous inscription dated the equivalent of A.D. 107, in a mosque at Kizimkazi in Zanzibar, that a Muslim town was there at that time.

The most important early town at which excavations have been carried out is Manda, near Lamu. Though work has been on a small scale, enough has been found to show that it was a very wealthy place. Some of the buildings were of coral stone set in mortar, though many were of mud and wattle; masonry walls built against the sea are of very large coral blocks, many weighing over a ton—a massive form of construction found nowhere else in sub-Saharan Africa. From the finds we can tell something of the goods which were imported. Probably cloth was as important as anything, but of the objects which have survived Islamic pottery, imported from the Persian Gulf, is the most important. This is found in very large quantities indeed; it is about seventy-five times commoner than at Kilwa in the same period. Some fragments of Chinese porcelain and stoneware show that trade had already begun with China, though (as in all subsequent periods also) this was not imported direct but transhipped in the Gulf and probably elsewhere earlier on its journey. Glass was also imported from the Arab countries in large quantities—much more than at any later period; it is worth remarking that glass was also mentioned in the *Periplus* as an import. Oddly enough, hardly any glass beads of this period have been found either at Manda or Kilwa, though beads of shell were made in large numbers. Coins are lacking too, so trade was by barter; at Kilwa, cowrie shells were used for trade. A remarkable industry was the smelting of iron (of which only very poor ores are available near the coast) at both places, and apparently on a large scale at Manda; so that there seems to be some truth in al-Idrisi's remarks about the iron mining and working (and export of iron) of the Malindi-Mombasa region.

We learn more of the exports from Arab authors. Most of them are the time-honoured natural products of which we have already read in the *Periplus*—ivory above all, which was sent as far as China, ambergris, leopard skins and turtle-shell. But a new commodity, gold, is mentioned for the first time in the tenth century. This was known to exist in the interior of the mysterious land of Waq-Waq, far to the south, and was mined in what is now Rhodesia. For export, it was carried down to the coast of the Sofala country, and shipped from there; this trade, however, does not seem to have developed until a later date. Subsequently, as we shall see, this was to become much the most important source of Kilwa's wealth. Slaves are only once mentioned, and then only as being shanghaied after an episode of legitimate trading; but we know that large numbers of slaves must have been exported—perhaps mostly from the Horn—since there were enough Zenj in Iraq to stage a long and largely successful revolt in the ninth century.

The Shirazi Dynasty

No archaeological work has been done on the Somali coast, but the towns of the Banadir were probably becoming places of importance in the eleventh and twelfth centuries. Several waves of immigrants came to this region, probably mostly from the Persian Gulf, but some from southern Arabia. These groups settled among the Bantu of the area,* each establishing a sort of alliance with the tribe with which they were closest in contact. The immigrants brought few if any women with them, so that most of their descendants must have increasingly intermarried with the Bantu.

Many of these groups of immigrants settled in Mogadishu, which by the thirteenth century was the most important town on the coast. It was a mercantile city, governed by a council of elders, and already controlled the gold trade with Sofala. Some of these immigrants came from Persia, as we know from two thirteenth-century inscriptions in Mogadishu. Of outstanding

---

*Few if any Somali had by this time reached the region south of Mogadishu.

importance was the group of people associated with the name Shirazi, though whether the immigrants were all or mainly Persian is doubtful—Shiraz was the capital of Fars, which controlled the eastern side of the Gulf where there were many Arabs too; and the name of the capital town is often given for that of the province.

Though there was at least one Shirazi family at Mogadishu, most of them seem to have settled further south, in the Shungwaya region, and at its main town of the same name near the modern Bur Gao (Port Durnford). Here there evolved a polity, more African in character than at Mogadishu, though apparently ruled by the Shirazi element. It was from this zone that all the great north-eastern group of Bantu tribes later dispersed under pressure from the Galla.

From this region of the Banadir coast the Shirazi, by then of somewhat mixed blood, began to migrate to places further south, probably in the second half of the twelfth century. They settled at various places, no doubt at various times, including probably Shanga (and Manda) in the Lamu islands, the Tanga area (Yambe Island), Pemba, Mafia, the Comoro Islands, and most important of all, Kilwa. With the arrival of the Shirazi at Kilwa, begins the period when the Kilwa Chronicle provides us with the first detailed knowledge of events and personalities. This is in a sketchy and inaccurate form, but nevertheless approaches what can be called History in the accepted sense.* The story of the sultans of Kilwa would be tedious and somewhat unprofitable to set out in detail but can be found in works listed at the end of this chapter.

At the start of the Shirazi dynasty, towards the end of the twelfth century, Kilwa seems to have been of little more importance than neighbouring places; indeed it is quite probable that the earliest sultans ruled from Mafia and not from Kilwa. The early coins are commoner there than at Kilwa; of these the very first to appear are minute pieces, some of silver, which bear the name of al-Hasan. The next in date have the name Ali ibn al-Hasan, probably his son and the founder of the dynasty

---

*This account, and much of what follows, sets out the author's own views on the origin and early history of the Shirazi and succeeding dynasty at Kilwa. These views (Chittick, 1965) have found wide acceptance, but it should be stated here that the hitherto received view is that the Shirazi came direct from the Gulf to Kilwa in the latter part of the tenth century, and established a dynasty which was still ruling when the Portuguese arrived.

as set out in the Chronicle. Succeeding sultans were much troubled by wars with the neighbouring island state of Shanga, on Sanje ya Kati, and they were twice deposed by usurpers from that place. However, by about A.D. 1230 Kilwa is of sufficient importance to be mentioned, along with Mogadishu, as a stage on the voyage to Madagascar. By the time of the death of the last of the dynasty, the grandson of the founder, near the end of the thirteenth century, Kilwa was a power to be reckoned with, second only to Mogadishu.

The throne was now seized by a man belonging to a family (Ahdali) which seems to have come from the Hadhramaut. Soon after the beginning of this dynasty there is a marked change in the archaeological record, notably in the style of architecture and in local pottery. This change is dramatically exemplified in the building of the great palace and trading emporium of Husuni Kubwa, covering over two acres and the largest single early building known in Africa south of the Sahara. These innovations were almost certainly associated with new immigrants, coming probably this time from South Arabia. They were Sunni Muslims of the Shafi'i persuasion, whereas their predecessors had been Kharijites.

It is probable at this time, too, that Kilwa gained entire control of Sofala (which name now denotes a specific town) and of other parts on the southern coast. Kilwa had earlier shared in the gold trade with Mogadishu but now had almost a monopoly. The gold was paid for mostly in cloth (much of which was manufactured at Kilwa) and glass beads, of which increasingly large numbers are found from deposits dating from about A.D. 1200 onwards. It was the huge profits of the gold trade that made it possible to carry out the great amount of building executed at this time. Previously stone houses had been rare; now they became common and, besides Husuni Kubwa, the Great Mosque was much extended at this time. Expensive Chinese porcelain, of which only tiny quantities had hitherto been imported, now became common.

Kilwa controlled Mafia and the ports of the Mozambique coast, but very little else. Zanzibar and Pemba were probably under her hegemony for a period, but in the fifteenth century Zanzibar was independent and minting its own coinage. But nevertheless much of the mercantile prosperity of the times rubbed off on other towns; it is from this period that many of the smaller ruined settlements that are scattered along the coast have their origin. Each of these was autonomous; some, like Gedi and other towns of the northern Kenya coast, were quite large, with many houses of stone. The dwellings in many others were of mud and wattle, like the houses of the coastal villages at the present day; only the main mosque and the tombs, which are often large, were of stone.

In the second half of the fifteenth century Kilwa suffered from severe dynastic intrigues, and it is probable that the rate of profit to be had from the gold trade was much reduced. She was thus already in decline when the Portuguese appeared on the scene, and was easily overcome by them. In this period, for reasons that are not clear, the focus of power and prosperity, which had first moved southwards from the Banadir coast to the Kilwa region, began to move back again, now to the northern part of the Kenya coast. This process was much accelerated after the establishment of Portuguese suzerainty; in the sixteenth century Kilwa and other places declined with extreme rapidity while those in the north suffered less, or even increased in prosperity.

Mombasa was rising in importance in the fifteenth century and, further north, Pate was becoming a substantial town. This place has established for itself an unjustifiably important place in the early history of the coast, as a result of an over-hasty acceptance of the story told in the unreliable Pate Chronicle. It was in fact non-existent or insignificant before the fourteenth century, and rose to importance only in the sixteenth and later centuries, with which period we are not here concerned.

The Fourteenth-century Scene

We can form a fair idea of the aspect of the towns of the coast, their inhabitants and the way of life in the fourteenth and fifteenth centuries from the evidence of excavations, supplemented by the eye-witness accounts of Ibn Battuta and the Portuguese.

The inhabitants can be considered as falling into three classes in most of the important settlements. The ruling class (except where a recently arrived immigrant group had succeeded in making itself dominant) was of mixed Arab and African ancestry, brown in colour, well read in the faith of Islam. Such would probably be also the landowners, the skilled artisans, and most of the religious functionaries, and merchants. Inferior to them (in many cases in a state of slavery) were the pure-blooded Africans, some of them recently arrived, who performed the menial tasks, and tilled the fields. Apart from both were the transient or recently settled Arabs, still incompletely assimilated into the society.

Of occupations, that of merchant was the most prominent; also many were engaged in crewing the ships in which the merchants also sailed. Apart from agriculture (including, no doubt, the growing of cotton), the weaving of cloth seems to have been the biggest industry. Other crafts include the striking of coins and other work in copper, the carving of bone and ivory, and the working of semi-precious stones. Many must have been employed as stone masons and carvers, the standard achieved in the latter (especially in some inscriptions) being very high.

The towns must have looked much like the older places on the coast, such as Lamu, at the present day. The houses were built very close to one another, often sharing a party wall and sometimes linked together, suggesting a family relationship between the occupiers. The blocks of buildings were separated by very narrow lanes, though often there were gardens behind. They were of one storey, except in the largest towns, up to three being found at Kilwa. Roofs were flat, built of stone laid on mangrove poles which were usually squared; the weight of these massive roofs and the strength of the timbers restricted the width of the rooms, which is eight feet or a little less. The houses followed a fairly uniform plan. They were entered by a doorway leading to a sunken courtyard. Facing on to this was usually a reception room or verandah, with the main living room behind, and bedrooms to the rear of this; such a basic arrangement was often much elaborated by the addition of other rooms. The main entrances into the courtyard of the larger houses were impressive, and in the Kilwa area ornamented with borders of recessed cut stone, sometimes with herring-bone ornament, the commonest decorative motif at this period. At least one latrine, well constructed in cut stone was included in each house, with an adjoining 'bidet' for ablutions. Houses at Gedi were also provided with a special compartment for cooling water jars.

There were usually no windows, except in the facade facing the courtyard, so the inner rooms must have been dark, but their ceilings and thick walls would have been cool. The walls were plastered and never painted. Decoration of any sort was sparing. Ornamental niches in cut stone were sometimes set in walls or on either side of doorways, which were often beautifully assembled of cut coral. Some of the main rooms were decorated with hangings, probably carpets, and carved wooden friezes, as is attested by rows of holes for suspension pegs. In the fourteenth century decorative motifs in cut stone are found; in the succeeding century their place, in the Kilwa region, was to some extent taken by glazed bowls of Persian and Chinese wares which were inset in vaulted roofs of buildings.

Cooking was commonly done over a portable earthenware stove, with three horns on which the cooking vessel was placed, with charcoal beneath. A sort of bread was baked of rice or millet flour in an oven set in the floor (*gai ya mkate mofa*).

The upper classes ate off imported glazed Islamic ware, or Chinese porcelain; by the fifteenth century even the poorer people seem to have had their food served in an eating-bowl rather than straight from the cooking-pot. At Kilwa, at least, those who could not afford glazed imported bowls had individual bowls to eat from.

We can supplement this picture by eye-witness accounts. Ibn Battuta early in the early fourteenth century describes Mogadishu as a town of enormous size living by trade, with many rich merchants. He writes of a curious system under which one of these men would entertain any visiting merchant, who could only buy and sell through his host. The town was famous for its woven fabrics, which were exported widely. A highly developed court life revolved round the sheikh, as the ruler was entitled. When Ibn Battuta went to the mosque in his presence, he was brought special clothes to wear. The sheikh walked through the town with a four-tiered canopy or parasol of silk carried over him, and accompanied by a band of drums, trumpets and pipes. The people were obese, from eating to excess. He describes a meal brought to him from the sheikh: rice cooked in ghee with a seasoned sauce of meat and vegetables, and side dishes of bananas cooked in fresh milk and ginger, peppers, and mangoes in sour milk.

Kilwa sounds from Ibn Battuta's description to have been rather smaller than Mogadishu. He is most struck by the piety of the sultan, who was being visited by numbers of ships from Hejaz. These descendants of the Prophet Muhammad were being maintained by the sultan out of booty taken in raiding expeditions against the pagan Zenj of the interior. The Zenj, at least those of Kilwa itself, tattooed their faces, as do the Makua and Makonde at the present day; though it seems unlikely that these tribes were in the area of Kilwa at the time.

At the beginning of the sixteenth century, the Portuguese were considerably impressed with what they found in the towns of the coast. They were most struck with the luxury of the adornment of the upper classes. Clothes were of rich silk as well as cotton, though slaves wore only a loin cloth; we read of much gold and silver jewellery, earrings and bangles for both arms and legs, none of which have come down to us. We learn more of their agriculture; millet and rice were the grain crops, and we know from another source that rice was actually exported to Aden, and so must have been obtained in quantity from the mainland. Oranges, lemons, pomegranates and Indian figs as well as onions and other vegetables were grown in gardens watered from wells. Fat-tailed sheep, goats, cattle and hens were raised; of course fish also formed a large part of the diet. Bees were kept in cylindrical hives hanging from trees, much as on the mainland at the present day. The boats of the coast ran up to about fifty tons, built with planks sewn with coir cords and with matting sails. These vessels were evidently of the *mtepe* type in use until recently, whose ancestry goes back to the time of the *Periplus*.

An Islamic Society

In conclusion, we should try to set in perspective this society which flourished on the eastern coast before A.D. 1500.

There is little doubt that this civilisation was the highest which existed at the time in Africa south of the Sahara. To what extent it was an 'African' society has been much argued, often in a muddled way, for to think of a cultural unity related to the continent as a whole is only confusing.

Culturally Africa falls into three or four divisions. The northern part, all that north of the Sahara, with fingers as it were, extending across the desert and up the Nile into the Sudanese belt, belongs to the Mediterranean world; Ethiopia too belongs partly to that sphere, and links more closely with the Arabian sub-continent on the other side of the Red Sea. The eastern coast and Madagascar belong to the world of the Indian Ocean. All these regions have closer links with lands overseas than with the rest of the African cultural unity. To people who have ships, the sea is a road, not a barrier: it is the land, especially waterless land and thick forest, which divides.

These cities of the coast look out over the ocean; their society was primarily Islamic, and their way of life mercantile. This does not mean to say that it was Arab; the immigrants were probably few in number, and intermarrying with African women and those already of mixed blood, their stock was rapidly integrated with the local people. Probably by the second or third generation they would have abandoned their spoken language for Swahili or the local language, though retaining Arabic for writing. Some elements of the African culture survived and were incorporated in the whole but were always secondary to the Islamic framework.

At the same time, the impact of this civilisation on much of the mainland coast was slight, and inland non-existent. It is unlikely that any Moslems went into the interior, save on an occasional war-like raid, dignified by Ibn Battuta as *jihad,* a holy war. Their religion never penetrated beyond the shore of the mainland, nor did their impressive skills in building have any influence in the hinterland. Buildings in stone and the burning of lime for mortar were unknown even five miles from the coast.

We should picture this civilisation as a remote outpost of Islam, looking for its spiritual inspiration to the homeland of its religion, but hardly contributing to the advancement of science or of learning. Scornful of their pagan neighbours, but willing to compromise with them in the interest of profit, the citizens of these towns built up a society and culture that had much that was individual to itself, but which contributed little to the heart of Africa.

Further reading

As explained in the introduction, the account set out above differs from the hitherto received history in certain respects. The arguments supporting these differences are set out in two articles by the author, and other earlier works should be read bearing these arguments and conclusions in mind. The two articles are:

CHITTICK, N. The 'Shirazi' Colonisation of East Africa, *Journal of African History,* Volume VI, No. 3 (1965) (pp. 275-294).

CHITTICK, N. Kilwa, a Preliminary Report, *Azania,* Volume I (pp. 1-36).

Other reference books include:

FREEMAN-GRENVILLE, G. S. P. *The East African Coast: Select Documents from the First to the Earlier Nineteenth Century,* Oxford University Press, 1962. (A convenient source-book which gives translations of most of the important documents.)

FREEMAN-GRENVILLE, G. S. P. *Medieval History of the Coast of Tanganyika* (Sets out and analyses the versions of the Kilwa Chronicle. The archaeological sections of this work are somewhat unreliable even where they are not out of date.)

OLIVER, R. and MATHEW, G. (Eds.) *History of East Africa Volume I* (G. Mathew, The East African Coast until the Coming of the Portuguese), Oxford University Press, 1963. Reprinted with other early chapters as *History of East Africa: The Early Period,* Nairobi, 1967.

GRAY, SIR J. *A History of Zanzibar,* London, 1962. (A standard work, but follows the old chronology.)

GARLAKE, P. S. *The Early Islamic Architecture of the East African Coast,* Oxford University Press, 1966. (An exhaustive and well-illustrated account of the subject.)

CERULLI, E. *Somalia, Scritti vari editi ed inediti,* 3 volumes, Roma, 1957, 1959 and 1964. (Contains a wealth of information, in Italian with Arabic texts.)

KIRKMAN, J. S. *Men and Monuments of the East African Coast,* Lutterworth Press, London, 1966. (Gives a popular account of the sites in their historical setting, with emphasis on Kenya. The same author's archaeological reports on Gedi and other sites may also be consulted.)

6

The Coast from the Portuguese Invasion to the Rise of the Zanzibar Sultanate

F. J. Berg

Until the beginning of the nineteenth century the East African coastal belt belonged to the rest of the continent only in a geographical sense. Before A.D. 1800 events at the coast passed almost unnoticed in the interior, while people living along the coast were rarely touched by what happened upcountry. But in the long run the destiny of the coast became indissolubly linked to that of the entire region. From our present perspective, the most significant development on the coast during the period 1500 to 1850 was the growth of long distance trade between coastal and upcountry Africans.* Yet, as will be seen, the origin of this caravan trade was in comparatively recent times. It seems less a logical outgrowth of past experience than a radical break with tradition, and it marked a new departure in the relationship between coast and hinterland.

Throughout most of the years prior to 1850 inhabitants of the coast were preoccupied either with their own local affairs or with successive intrusions by Portuguese and by Omani Arabs. The dominant interest of their time was not the opening of the interior to commerce, but a series of intermittent wars against foreign invaders. It may be no coincidence that the peace

*Some long-term, even indirect, consequences of the caravan trade are discussed in Chapters 11 and 16, which deal with the Arab impact on East Africa and with pre-Independence economic and social developments.

which the Zanzibar Sultanate brought to the coast was accompanied by a vigorous expansion of trade inland. After 1850 the future of the coast was shaped, not by local wars, but by its association with the interior. The pivot of its history, once situated in the Middle East or Europe, slowly swung inland to the uplands and plateaus of East and Central Africa.

The years 1500 to 1850, therefore, were only a prelude to what may be regarded as the modern history of the coast—its affiliation to the rest of East Africa. Essentially they belong to the self-contained, pre-modern period of coastal history, the period of warring city states whose fortunes rose and fell on the currents of international trade and politics. The coast's encounter with the interior, crucial as it was for East African history, began almost as an afterthought at the very end of this period.

Our knowledge of the commercial and political rivalries of the coastal towns and of the extent to which their people were affected by the intervention of Portuguese and Omani empire builders is often fragmentary and incomplete. Nevertheless, a broad pattern emerges from the surviving Portuguese, Arab, and Swahili sources.

It is clear that the coast settlements were, at the time the Portuguese became aware of their existence, largely independent of one another and of foreign control. Their struggle to preserve their independence against the Portuguese and later against the Arabs of Oman is the first of two great themes which run through the coast's post-Portuguese history until the middle nineteenth century. This is the theme which most directly concerned the Portuguese and about which most information survives. Swahili and Portuguese chroniclers alike gave it a prominent part in their histories.

The other theme, though perhaps equally important, was less well understood by the writers of the day and is consequently less familiar. It concerns the continual ebb and flow of preliterate peoples up and down the coast in the vicinity of the northern Swahili towns. These migrations of clans and small tribes appear to have begun soon after Portuguese fleets became established in East African waters, perhaps by the middle of the sixteenth century. Along the coast of Kenya and northern Tanzania the movement was mostly from north to south, following the ranges of hills fringing the coast. Tribal traditions are substantially agreed that the homeland of the immigrant

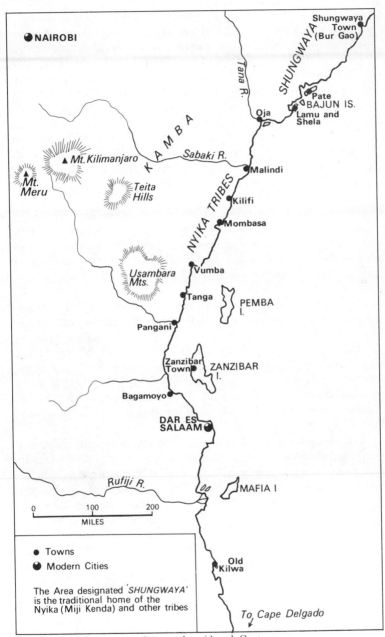

Figure 12 The East African Coast to the mid-19th Century

peoples was an area known as Shungwaya, located approximately between the Tana and Juba river valleys.* Much less is known about tribal movements in the immediate hinterland south of Tanga, no doubt because the central Tanzanian coast was more sparsely settled by Swahili townsmen than the area to the north. Relocations and adjustments among the coastal peoples seem to have been largely complete by 1700, though conflicts between the newly settled Bantu groups and the last wave of Galla invaders from the north-west kept the Kenya coast in turmoil for another century. The migrations' overall effect was to intensify the disruptive impact of the Portuguese on Swahili society. Many settlements, under attack by sea and by land, disappeared completely.

Against the background of these two long-term trends in coast history—the Swahili townsmen's struggle to maintain their independence and efforts by immigrant clans and tribes to find shelter in the neighbouring hills and valleys—it is possible to discern three periods into which the years 1500 to 1850 may conveniently be divided.

The first of these lasted approximately a century, from 1500 to 1600, and can be described as the Late Shirazi Period. During this time the Swahili towns remained generally independent of Portuguese control and under the government of their own traditional Shirazi ruling families. Portuguese fleets did some of the towns considerable damage, but Portugal had little effective territorial control over them till the end of the sixteenth century. Earlier, Portugal was more an interventionist in disputes between towns than their real overlord.

The second period, that of the Portuguese Ascendancy, also extended over a century, from 1600 to 1700. Portuguese garrisons occupied several points in the area and Portuguese officials deposed local princes at will. This century of Portuguese supremacy was preceded, or in some cases accompanied by, the final downfall of the leading Shirazi dynasties. The most notable of these, in Mombasa, fell victim not to the Portuguese but to one of the immigrant tribes which had begun to occupy the coast lowlands and hills. During this phase most of the coastal Bantu groups came to rest in the area they presently

---

*The exact location of Shungwaya will probably be open to discussion for many years to come. It has been described as a city and as a region; very likely it was both.

occupy. Similar advances into the coastal zone by non-Bantu Galla and later by Masai proved to be temporary, though distressing to Swahili and more recently arrived Bantu alike.

The third period witnessed the explusion of the Portuguese from East Africa and lasted from about 1700 to 1850. Joint action by local Swahili and allies called in from Oman terminated Portuguese rule. Since the Imams of Oman were recognised as sovereigns of the coast in return for their aid, and since a local Omani dynasty at Mombasa emerged for a time as the leading power on the coast, this final phase of pre-modern coastal history can best be termed the Omani Arab period. Its last decades merge almost imperceptibly with the Sultanate of Zanzibar's ascendancy, during which the caravan trade with the interior reached its greatest extent. And it is with the caravan trade that the East African coast and interior enter the modern world together.

The Shirazi States and the Portuguese, 1500 to 1600

In their dealings with the Shirazi sheikhs the Portuguese possessed a number of decisive advantages. Two were theirs the moment Vasco da Gama anchored off Kilwa in 1498: an advanced naval and military technology and sufficient resources to concentrate greater power on any given part of the coast than a single Swahili city state could assemble. A third, perhaps as important as either of the others, they soon acquired. This was a strategic vision that embraced the entire Indian Ocean, transcending local East African trade rivalries and dynastic hatreds. Unlike their Shirazi opponents, the Portuguese approached political and economic problems in the Indian Ocean basin with a unity of purpose that maximised available resources. Within the first two decades of the sixteenth century they had seized or been given bases beside most of the commercial crossroads between East Africa and the Indies. To the Portuguese, East Africa was only a subsidiary part of the global picture, an important one perhaps, but by no means their primary concern. For years it was sufficient, from the Portuguese point of view, to play one coastal state against another without going to the trouble of crushing or occupying every one of them.

The Shirazi field of vision was much more restricted*. Though the Swahili settlements' prosperity rested upon the same Indian Ocean commercial system that the Portuguese had only recently discovered, the limited resources at their sheikhs' disposal restricted each state's political activity to the East African coast. The Shirazi political tradition, therefore, was limited to local interstate rivalries with no hope of controlling international trade and little fear of international enemies. The sudden appearance of Portuguese fleets constituted an economic and political revolution for which they were completely unprepared. Not surprisingly, the Portuguese found it possible to profit from divisions among the small coastal powers and were rarely confronted with united or co-ordinated opposition.

At the time of Vasco da Gama's arrival there were numerous Swahili states scattered along the coast, of which four—Kilwa, Mombasa, Malindi, and Pate—were predominant. Zanzibar and Pemba seem often to have been partitioned among several rulers, and when ruled by a single island-wide prince, as Portuguese records suggest happened occasionally, no important consequences resulted.

Kilwa, most geographically extended of the states, proved to be the most vulnerable. Its sheikh agreed to pay tribute to Portugal in 1502. Three years later the Portuguese detached Sofala and the Sofala-Mozambique gold trade from their new subject's dominions. Portuguese interference in domestic politics and the presence of a Portuguese garrison in Kilwa from 1505 to 1512 hastened its rapid decline. Thereafter little is heard of it; Kilwa's possessions to the south passed permanently to Portugal, and the city itself entered a period of stagnation that ended in a massacre of the population in 1587 by the notorious Zimba.†

*Most but not all ruling dynasties of the Swahili city states were 'Shirazi'. The Nabahani clan of Pate was of Omani origin, and the Nabahani had representatives on Pemba as well. Other Pemba notables were Shirazi, as were some on Zanzibar. Shirazi families, mostly related by ties of blood or marriage, governed Kilwa, Mombasa, Malindi, and numerous less famous settlements such as Kilifi and Oja (Ozi or Ungwana).

†The Zimba were a warrior band which first appeared in the Zambezi valley and later marched as far north as Malindi before being defeated and dispersed in 1589 by Swahili, Portuguese, and Segeju. Their origin and the cause of their irruption into East Africa have yet to be satisfactorily explained, though numerous theories have been advanced. Though their appearance coincides with the coast's 'time of troubles', during which Segeju and other Bantu tribes moved south from Shungwaya, it had no connection with this much greater migration.

With the exception of Malindi, which at once made a firm alliance with the Portuguese, the northern tier of states and the islands proved more resistant. Malindi long supplied Portugal with the territorial foothold it desired in the area and supplemented the somewhat unsatisfactory base the Portuguese established in the far south at Mozambique in 1507. Other towns, including Mombasa and Pate, were slower to submit. Mombasa, a particularly irreconcilable foe, was three times attacked and plundered by the Portuguese (in 1505, 1528, and 1589) before losing its independence. This steadfast resistance suggests that Mombasa had by 1500 emerged as the leading town on the coast, which in turn accounts for Malindi's willingness to make common cause with Portugal.

As the major northern Swahili power, Mombasa had most to lose by accepting Portuguese overlordship and, at the same time, most to fear from possible results of a coalition between Portugal and envious local rivals. Its position, however, was a strong one. Portuguese descriptions of its wealth and its proven ability to recover repeatedly from devastation suggest that it tapped a considerable part of the triangular trade between the East African ports, the Middle East, and India. Moreover, though nominally an island state, it functioned as a mainland power. Its Shirazi sheikhs were kin to rulers of smaller mainland states nearby and seem to have had access to military aid from the non-Swahili people who lived in the hills behind Mombasa Island. Such was Mombasa's resilience that an unusual combination of circumstances was necessary to bring about its overthrow.

One of these came in the guise of an ally. Two Turkish expeditions to the coast, in 1585 and 1587, caused the Portuguese to feel the security of their position in the Indian Ocean severely threatened. Far from strengthening the Sheikh of Mombasa, the second Turkish expedition provoked a major Portuguese counterstroke against the Mombasans and their new allies. Coincidentally a warband of Zimba appeared outside Mombasa while the Portuguese fleet was blockading it. An informal division of labour between Zimba and Portuguese enabled the Zimba to occupy the city, which was then pillaged for the third time in a century. Yet the destructive power of the Zimba, as well as their cannibalistic appetite, seems to have been greatly exaggerated by Portuguese and later historians. Two years later Mombasa had sufficiently recovered to mount a major land

expedition of its own against Malindi. This, however, culminated in disaster and enabled the Portuguese to seize control
at last. The Mombasan army was surprised and routed at an
encampment on the road to Malindi by the Segeju, a newly
arrived tribe allied to the Sheikh of Malindi. The Segeju then
occupied Mombasa Island, shortly afterward surrendering it
to the Sheikh of Malindi and the Portuguese.

For Portugal, possession of Mombasa was the turning point
in its involvement with East Africa. At a single blow the Portuguese eliminated their most important enemy and converted
his stronghold into the mainstay of their authority upon the
coast. In 1593, a year after the island had fallen into their hands,
they acknowledged their ally, Sheikh Ahmad of Malindi, as
ruler of Mombasa (the last sheikh of the old dynasty had been
killed by the Segeju), garrisoned the island, and built the famous
Fort Jesus. Hereafter Mombasa was headquarters for Portuguese
governors on the coast and chief port of call for vessels sailing
between Goa and East Africa. Mombasa's strategic location,
combined with Portuguese fears of further Turkish raids from
the Red Sea, persuaded Portugal to convert a system of alliances
and casual collection of tribute into something more nearly
resembling an East African empire. Fort Jesus, the point from
which it was administered, soon became regarded as the principal
embodiment of Portuguese power and the main objective of its
antagonists.

The Portuguese Ascendancy, 1600 to 1700

Mombasa's transformation into a dependent ally garrisoned by
Portuguese soldiers removed the last challenge to Portugal's
paramountcy on the coast. For nearly a hundred years afterward
her sovereignty was acknowledged by the Swahili towns. The
century was hardly a peaceful one, being punctuated by frequent
uprisings, but until the end Portuguese supremacy was reasserted as frequently as it was resisted. This does not mean that
Portuguese officials exercised day-to-day supervision over the
coastal states, but simply that their rulers acquiesced in paying
tribute to the King of Portugal through his representative, the
Captain of Mombasa.* Failure to do so could and often did

*Kilwa and its remaining possessions, notably the Island of Mafia, were
considered for a short time to be outside the jurisdiction of the Captain of
Mombasa. By 1600 the city had shrunk to such unimportance that this scarcely
mattered; it had drifted out of the mainstream of coastal events.

result in dethronement, possibly death. In addition to keeping a close watch on the 'kingdom' of Mombasa-Malindi and collecting customs there, the Portuguese maintained a customs house at Pate and intermittently kept up small communities and religious establishments in the larger towns. Generally life on the coast was not hazardous for individual Portuguese traders or adventurers, who often enjoyed excellent personal relations with the ruler and people of the communities in which they settled. This was true to such an extent that official efforts were sometimes made to restrict the activities of unapproved settlers and to concentrate them at Mombasa. Toward the end of the century greater frequency of anti-Portuguese risings dissipated much of this friendly atmosphere.

Portuguese success in overcoming opposition by the Shirazi princes, however, was counterbalanced by steady deterioration in her position elsewhere in the Indian Ocean. Dutch and English commercial competition grew more intense every year, while Persia and Oman had by 1650 ousted the Portuguese from their fortresses on the Persian Gulf. Re-emergence of strong oriental powers to the north, coupled with a drop in revenue from Indian Ocean trade and attacks on Portuguese settlements, cast a long shadow on Portuguese influence at the coast. Unaided, divided, and overawed by a locally entrenched Great Power, the Swahili towns could do little but submit. But against a weakened oppressor and with help from Arabia they had reason to hope that rebellion might pay. It was against a background of mounting Portuguese incapacity and increasing outside encouragement that the revolts of the last half of the century took place.

Another factor, as yet little understood, but perhaps nearly as important as the long-term decline in Portugal's imperial fortunes, was immigration by various tribes into the coastal zone. This may actually have strengthened the Portuguese position on the coast and compensated partly for decreasing assistance from Portugal and Goa to the Captains of Mombasa. One earlier by-product of the migrations had been the defeat of the formerly hostile Shirazi state of Mombasa by the Segeju, and continuing unrest outside the coast towns probably hurt the Swahili more than the Portuguese. Portugal was not concerned with the defence of every town and island. That was the concern of the townsmen. For the Captain of Mombasa it was enough to be sure of the security of Mombasa Island, to collect customs and tribute, and see to it that no town or sheikh made good an attempt to defy his authority. All available evidence suggests that the Portuguese took little interest in tribal movements within their sphere of influence. References to Segeju, Galla, a group behind Mombasa described as 'Mozungullos', and, at the end of the period, to the Nyika, occur in Portuguese records; but these references rarely tell much about the people to whom they apply. The Segeju and 'Mozungullos' are exceptional in this respect, as the one group was for a while closely associated with the allied state of Malindi and the other with the Portuguese establishment at Mombasa.

However uninteresting or incomprehensible seventeenth-century folk-wanderings along the coast hills may have seemed to contemporary Portuguese officials, they were of the greatest importance to the Swahili and, of course, to the migrant peoples themselves. Nyika and Swahili traditions identify as Galla the aggressors who forced the Shungwaya tribes out of their home-land and pursued them down the coast as far as Mombasa. The traditions are so much agreed on this point, and so much substantiated by early nineteenth-century European observers, that there can be no doubt the Galla were a major disruptive factor on the coast. Nevertheless, it is known that immigrant groups fought one another as well as Galla and must have displaced the clans or tribes which preceded them. It is also possible that the original emigration from Shungwaya was more due to gradual dessication of the area between the Tana and the Juba than to Galla or even Somali pressure. In this case Galla, as the most recent and most aggressive group to press down the coast, would have been blamed retrospectively for the entire series of migrations.

Ultimately the Nyika or *Miji Kenda* tribes* reached defensible havens in the hills from which they were able to repel Galla attacks. By 1700, perhaps earlier, they were established in approximately the same areas they presently occupy (though the Giriama have since expanded to the north) and had begun to attract Portuguese attention. Whether the 'Mozungullos' mentioned earlier by the Portuguese were absorbed by the Nyika, driven away, or were an earlier migration of Nyika is uncertain. The Segeju remained in the vicinity of Malindi

*These tribes now prefer to be known simply as the Miji Kenda or Nine Tribes. They include the Chonyi, Digo, Duruma, Giriama, Jibana, Kambe, Rabai and Ribe.

about three decades after its sheikhs abandoned the town in favour of Mombasa. Then, some time after 1635, they pushed further south and settled near the coast on either side of what is now the Kenya-Tanzania border. During the last half of the century, and throughout the century following, Galla raids kept the Swahili and their neighbours in a state of constant alarm.

Because of widespread insecurity on the mainland the seventeenth century was also a time of resettlement and migration for townsmen. Inhabitants of Swahili settlements on the north coast fled south, sometimes accompanied by Nyika. Pemba, the Bajun Islands, and Mombasa absorbed some of the refugees. Most of the Twelve Tribes which comprise the present Swahili population of Mombasa occupied the island in this period, including those which formed the *Thalatha Taifa*, larger of the two Swahili federations which reconstituted the old Shirazi city state. And it is possible that many of the little Swahili towns along the *Mrima** of Tanzania were founded as part of the same shift of population. In an environment of deserted mainland plantations and towns, southward and island-ward migration by Swahili, and confusion in the immediate hinter-· land, the Portuguese were well able to maintain themselves. Absorbed as they were in maritime trade and without much interest in events outside the larger ports and sheikhdoms, the problems besetting seventeenth-century coastal society seem hardly to have attracted their attention.

The Decline of Portuguese Power

The only major Portuguese commitment was to Mombasa and to the great fortress which dominated it. As long as Fort Jesus and Mombasa harbour were secure, the African side of the Indian Ocean commercial system was in Portugal's grip. This, far more than tribute from small Swahili communities, was what mattered to Portugal. Under these circumstances, Portuguese interest in domestic politics and even in the course of day-to-day affairs at Mombasa was inevitable.

Seen from this point of view, Sheikh Ahmad of Malindi's decision to occupy Mombasa and place himself under Portuguese supervision was unwise. But considering the city's strategic position, its comparative security and past fame, and the

*Swahili: the coastland of East Africa.

disordered state of affairs outside Malindi, it was also understandable. During his lifetime, partnership between his dynasty
and the Portuguese worked well. Probably with Portuguese
aid, and certainly with Portuguese approval, Sheikh Ahmad
added Pemba to his dominions, sending forth a new wave of
Shirazi settlers to guarantee future loyalty. These colonists
may have come from the area around Malindi, which seems
to have declined greatly in importance when the sheikh shifted
his court to Mombasa. Malindi, moreover, had already been
attacked by Zimba and was then surrounded by Segeju. It may
have seemed no more attractive to its inhabitants than to their
ruler.

Soon after Sheikh Ahmad's death in 1609 there began a
series of disputes between Sheikhs and Captains of Mombasa
which ended in a royal revolt in 1631. Tactless behaviour by
the Captains, whose actions were impossible to supervise either
from Lisbon or Goa, were mostly at fault. Portuguese accounts
admit that great injustices were done to the sheikhly family.
The incumbent sheikh, Yusuf bin Hasan, succeeded in surprising
and destroying the Portuguese garrison. A year later he fled
the city after withstanding one Portuguese siege. Yusuf's
apparently voluntary departure made possible a prompt Portuguese reoccupation.

So great a blow to their prestige seems to have done the
Portuguese little immediate harm, for they continued to collect
the accustomed tribute from subject states and kept their
customs house at Pate. Zanzibar, whose sheikh enjoyed the
privileged status of non-tributary ally, likewise remained loyal.
Yusuf bin Hasan's later visits to the coast stirred up a short-
lived rebellion on Pate in 1637 which was put down with
aid from neighbouring towns. This was Yusuf's last serious
attempt to injure Portuguese interests; the next year he was
reported to have died at Jiddah on the Red Sea. He was not
replaced by another sheikh, and the Captain of Mombasa was
thereafter directly responsible for governing the city.

Resistance to Portuguese rule eventually centred on the
Nabahani state of Pate. Different members of the Nabahani
dynasty had for a time alternated between loyalty and rebellion,
but later sheikhs decided on resolute opposition. Pate's futile
revolt of 1637 proved the forerunner of more serious attempts
in 1660, 1678, 1686, and 1687. All were suppressed, though
with increasing difficulty. On each occasion the Imam of Oman

supplied aid to Pate, and on the first his troops besieged Fort
Jesus for several months and plundered Mombasa. Omani
intervention completely upset the old balance of power; it
reinvigorated local resistance at the very time Portuguese
strength was ebbing. The end came in 1698 when, after a
three year siege, Mombasa fell to an army from Oman and
Pate. A few years later Zanzibar, sole surviving Portuguese
ally, was occupied by Omani troops. Excepting a brief, almost
accidental reconquest of Mombasa in 1728–9, Portugal's
ascendancy in East Africa did not survive the century.

The Omani Arab Period, 1700 to 1850

Expulsion of the Portuguese from Mombasa was not the
beginning of a corresponding Omani ascendancy. The fortunes
of war in the Persian Gulf alone were sufficient to prevent this;
a few decades later Oman was almost entirely overrun by
Persia. As a result the Yarubi dynasty, which had been
responsible for Oman's emergence as a maritime power and
an active Omani policy in East Africa, fell into disrepute and
out of power. Though the BuSaidi successors to the Yarubi
never renounced claims to the East African coastal towns they
inherited from them, they were unable to enforce these claims
before the early decades of the nineteenth century. Oman's
liberation of the coast was thus of little benefit to the Omani
Imamate.

For this the East Africans were partly to blame. Each Swahili
town prized its own freedom above all else and none was eager
to see the Imam of Oman's governors step into the boots of the
former Captains of Mombasa. Struggles with the Portuguese
had not been essentially a matter of Muslim against Christian,
but of small states trying to break free of a domineering larger
one. Mere community of religion with the Arabs was not
sufficient to make forceful Omani government any more
acceptable than the Portuguese regime had been. The Omani
tried at first to post garrisons at strategic points along the
coast, with a concentration of force at Mombasa. Though
the system began to break down almost as soon as it was initiated,
to a great extent because of insubordination and strife between
rival garrisons, it was nonetheless galling to the local sheikhs.

Their resentment produced an embassy to Portuguese
officials in Goa inviting Portugal to dispatch a fleet to East

Africa and resume her old position there. Individuals from various parts of the coast had previously urged this, but in 1727 the Sheikh of Pate himself authorised a treaty of alliance with the Viceroy of the Indies at Goa. Soon after, a joint Patan-Portuguese fleet appeared off Mombasa during an outbreak of fighting between townspeople and garrison. It easily got possession of both city and fortress. The following year the Mombasans found Portuguese rule as intolerable as ever and ousted the garrison without outside help. The significance of this brief Portuguese interlude (1728–9) lies entirely in the demonstration it offers of the coast towns' determination to resist control from abroad. So long as the Imam of Oman confined his sovereignty to assistance against foreign enemies the towns were pleased to acknowledge it, but imposition of garrisons or more than nominal tribute soon set them to plotting with the Portuguese.

The revolt of 1727–8 set the seal on Oman's failure to replace Portugal as Great Power on the coast. Civil wars and Persian invasions kept the Imams occupied for nearly a century, and the Swahili towns were again free to forge their own destiny.

Nevertheless, Oman's unsuccessful bid to occupy Portugal's position led to a continuing involvement with East Africa. Reverses on the coast and temporary anarchy at home did not close channels which the wars against Portugal had reopened. Individual Arabs and whole Arab families remained in the coast towns after the Imam's authority had lapsed. They were sometimes reinforced by additional emigration from south-eastern and southern Arabia. It is difficult to weigh the importance of their presence in the early eighteenth century, but by the end of the century a process of re-Arabisation seems to have begun on the coast, in which Arab kinship, values, and some elements of material culture gained prestige at the expense of Swahili culture. In the long run Swahili society was considerably modified by this process, a process that gained impetus after Omani authority was reasserted in the 1820's and 1830's. The Omani Arab period thus ranks with the era of Shirazi colonisation as one in which the impact of the Middle East upon the coast was highly significant.

Mombasan Supremacy under the Mazrui

Omani political influence of a local kind was not absent even during the century-long gap between the frustration of Yarubi hopes and the creation of a BuSaidi realm centred on Zanzibar. The Mazrui, a clan of Omani Arabs in the service of the Yarubi Imams, established themselves as hereditary rulers of Mombasa soon after the brief Portuguese reoccupation and presided over yet another revival of this famous old city state. Under Mazrui rule Mombasa's power reached its zenith, outstripping that of the Shirazi and Malindi dynasties. For many years, Pemba and the mainland from Tanga past Malindi owed allegiance to Mombasa. Even Pate passed briefly under Mombasan influence, first as an ally and later as a virtual protectorate. The political history of the coast from 1750 to 1840 can in fact be read mainly as a struggle between two Omani dynasties, the Mombasa-based Mazrui and the Muscat-based BuSaidi, with all but the very last victories going to the Mazrui.

Yet it would be a mistake to regard the Mazrui simply as successors of the Shirazi and Malindi sheikhs. The structure of the Mombasa polity, indeed, grew more complex with each change of dynasty and each accretion of new population. What evidently had been a rather simple sheikhdom under the Shirazi evolved into an uneasy Portuguese-Malindian condominium during the Portuguese ascendancy and, finally, under the Mazrui, into an amalgam composed of two hostile groups of Swahili tribes which acknowledged members of an Omani family as heads of state because of the impossibility of coming to an agreement among themselves. Though this combination had potential for great instability, it served Mombasa well enough to dominate most of the northern coast for several decades after 1750.

The way in which various elements in the coastal political system realigned themselves between 1700 and 1750 helps to explain why this was possible. For the first time in more than two hundred years foreign powers capable of decisive intervention in local rivalries had retreated from the coast. Those Swahili states which survived the dislocations of the previous century consolidated their position. In the far south, Kilwa clung stubbornly to existence as a quiet non-participant in political affairs; its revival as chief mainland port for the East African slave trade had not yet begun. Zanzibar and Pemba, which as yet lacked a tradition of being co-ordinated polities in their own right, were content to acknowledge nominal Omani sovereignty and enjoy *de facto* independence. The mainland opposite these islands was divided among groups of small

Swahili chieftaincies focused around Bagamoyo, Pangani, Tanga, and Vumba. The Vumba group had close ties with the northern states, while the groups along the Tanzanian *Mrima* did not.

Further up the coast states were fewer but larger. Several old settlements, including Malindi and those between it and Mombasa, had disappeared altogether. The number of mainland towns near Pate and the Bajun Islands had likewise dwindled, most having been abandoned during the earlier time of troubles. Mombasa thus enjoyed a considerable field for expansion, there being no substantial rivals between Vumba and the Bajun Islands. Pate, predominant among the northern island states, had to reckon on the presence of well-established neighbours, of which Lamu was the most important. Still further north lay a string of settlements along the Somali coast which played as little part in events to the south as they had done during the Portuguese period.

Of the non-Swahili tribes occupying the coast those most important to the city states were the Segeju, allied to the *Diwans** of Vumba; the nine Nyika tribes, associated in various ways with the Swahili of Mombasa and, to a lesser extent, with Vumba; and the Galla, who continued to menace Nyika and Swahili mainlanders alike until the 1840's. Other inland peoples occasionally appeared at the coast but seem to have had no lasting political impact upon the towns. The situation behind the *Mrima* coast is, however, not well known, largely because coastal settlements there neither preserved much in the way of traditions or chronicles of their own nor attracted much outside notice.

The general picture, therefore, is of a collection of small states occupying a freer, less turbulent, and poorer environment than formerly. Foreign powers had disappeared and mainland upheavals subsided, but international trade across the Indian Ocean had gone dry after two centuries of war. Among the coastal states only two were outstanding: Pate and Mombasa. Pate expended its vigour on civil wars over possession of the sheikhship. Mombasa alone conducted an active foreign policy. The Mazrui, by solving the riddle of who should govern Mombasa, bridged the gap between the city's Swahili factions and directed its energy beyond its own borders.

*A Swahili term meaning magnates.

Mombasa, however, was fortunate in more than simply enjoying three generations of government by able Mazrui *liwalis* (governors). It also benefited from being an important refuge for townsmen from all over the coast during the seventeenth century. Clans and families from places as far distant as Kilwa and Barawa in Somalia had gradually drifted into Mombasa after the fall of the Shirazi dynasty.* Their presence in the city, as much as its excellent harbours and the security afforded by Fort Jesus, made it unofficial capital of the northern Swahili. When the Mazrui first arrived, native and immigrant Swahili had sorted themselves out into two antagonistic federations. One—the larger, though comprising only three tribes, the *Thalatha Taifa*—had its headquarters at Kilindini Town on the western side of Mombasa and occupied a few villages on the mainland. The smaller group—made up of nine tribes, the *Tisa Taifa*—was identified with the oldest and most recent Swahili population and lived mostly at Mombasa Town or Mvita. The first task of the Mazrui was to make peace between the federations, something they achieved while still representing the Imam of Oman. By 1746 they asserted and successfully defended their independence from Oman and were acknowledged by the Swahili as heads of state at Mombasa. Though often strained, the unity of the Mombasan polity never broke down under their rule. Quarrels among *Thalatha Taifa* and *Tisa Taifa* and succession disputes between rival Mazrui claimants sometimes flared, but never so long or so divisively as the civil wars of Pate.

Mombasa derived one more benefit from consolidation under the Mazrui: a complete set of Nyika alliances. All nine Nyika groups, excepting the southern Digo near Vumba, looked upon certain leaders of the Swahili tribes of Mombasa as their intermediaries with the outer world. Once it was certain that these Swahili notables all owed allegiance to a single state it was possible for that state to use Nyika manpower in war and obtain the major share of Nyika trade in peace. Thus Mombasa, alone among the coastal states of the eighteenth and early nineteenth centuries, could consistently tap the resources of a significant non-Muslim, non-urban tribal area.

---

*Most of these immigrants came from places north of Mombasa. Though cases are known of individuals coming from the southern coast, all clan and tribal names of the Mombasa Swahili are of northern origin.

In 1746 *Liwali* Ali bin Athman al-Mazrui definitively established independence of Oman by overcoming an Omani force
that had assassinated his brother Muhammad, the first Mazrui
liwali to disown the BuSaidi dynasty. Mombasa then moved
from strength to yet greater strength. Under Ali the city detached Pemba from Oman and nearly overran Zanzibar. Ali's
successor, Masoud bin Nasir, seems to have been the first liwali
to initiate an alliance with the Nabahani of Pate by acknow-
ledging their claim to a share of the government of Pemba.
Mombasa in return was able to keep a garrison in Pate. Though
the agreement was soon repudiated after one of Pate's many civil
upheavals (1776), the two states continued to co-operate as
partners, with Mombasa enjoying precedence. The *Diwans* of
Vumba also acknowledged Mombasa's supremacy, perhaps
because of internal breakdowns in the Vumba polity in 1792 and
1824. Whatever the cause, they assisted the Mazrui in maintaining a sort of diplomatic suzerainty over Tanga and the
southern Digo.

Mombasan Decline and Rise of Zanzibar

Not until 1810 or 1812 (the date, an important one, is disputed)
did Mombasa's fortunes begin to decline. The immediate cause
was a proverbially disastrous defeat at Shela inflicted by Lamu
upon an army dispatched by Mombasa and Pate. The battle of
Shela clearly established Lamu's independence of Pate, ended
Pate's career as dominant state in the Bajun Islands, and under-
cut Mombasa's position as senior power on the entire coast.
It also opened the door to a revival of direct Omani influence
from Muscat, which was probably its most important long-term
consequence.

Sayyid* Said bin Sultan had held power in Oman for only a
few years at this time, but did not hesitate to reassert his
dynasty's claim to govern the East African coast. The people
at Lamu, perhaps astonished and a little frightened by their
success at Shela, at once appealed to him to send them a
governor and garrison as protection against further attacks.
Said complied with Lamu's request. This was the origin of
the Omani reconquest, which Sayyid Said came near to completing in his own lifetime.

*The title 'Imam' had by this time lapsed in Oman.

Several circumstances favoured him. Sayyid Said himself was a shrewd, determined, and—very important—long-lived ruler. He had the foresight and good fortune to make a very useful alliance with Great Britain. This proved helpful in strengthening his control of Oman and in winning British approval of his objectives in East Africa. Oman, though neither rich nor easy to govern, ranked as a Great Power by East African standards and could, with a second-hand naval technology borrowed from Britain, command East African waters with little difficulty. Further, several coastal states had begun to fear Mombasa more than Oman. Others, like Kilwa, had become too weak or indifferent to offer opposition to either Oman or Mombasa, and Oman had the greater resources.

Lamu's submission in 1813 gave the Sayyid a base off the northern coast. Before 1813 he held little more than Zanzibar and strategically insignificant acknowledgement of his interests by Kilwa and the *Mrima* towns. Then, in 1823, a dynastic quarrel at Pate gave him the opportunity of terminating Mazrui influence there. A successful campaign in the Bajun Islands encouraged the Omani forces to sail to Pemba, where Said's commander was again victorious, partly because of Pemba Shirazi discontent with Mazrui government. Though loss of Pemba (1823) isolated Mombasa, the Mazrui soon after produced an extraordinarily able *liwali,* Salim bin Ahmad, who was able to stave off defeat till his death in 1835. But this was only a temporary respite. There followed a succession dispute between Mazrui factions which alienated the more influential Mazrui supporters among the Swahili. In 1837, Sayyid Said's attack on the city, his fourth, gained its objective. Fort Jesus was then garrisoned by a mercenary detachment. A year later the leading Mazrui were either deported or driven from the city and local authority divided between leaders of the two Swahili federations and a non-Mazrui Arab *liwali.* This was Sayyid Said's major political achievement on the coast and symbolises the end of an era far better than his son Majid's later conquest of Pate. Said, meanwhile, transferred his capital from Muscat to Zanzibar Town in 1832, thereby giving his possessions an East African rather than an Arabian orientation.

The Omani Arab phase of coastal history can thus be regarded as shading off imperceptibly into a Zanzibari phase during the decade 1830 to 1840. Sayyid Said's creation of the Zanzibar

Sultanate brought renewed prosperity to the coast. The southern region from Cape Delgado to Tanga rapidly developed a flourishing caravan trade in ivory and slaves with the far interior. The islands of Zanzibar and Pemba, drawing on slaves exported from Kilwa and the *Mrima* towns, turned into plantation societies specialising in the production of cloves. Zanzibar Town itself became an important international port. To the north there was a primary development of grain and coconut plantations—which also relied on slave labour, procured through Zanzibar—and a secondary but nonetheless important ivory trade with the interior. The entire pattern of economic growth was underwritten by Indian capitalists at Zanzibar and co-ordinated, as far as it could be, by the Sayyid's government. In some respects it can be compared to the coast's participation in the pre-Portuguese Indian Ocean commercial system; in other respects it prepared the way for East Africa's entry into the modern world. Probably no tendency in this last direction was more important than accelerated growth of the caravan trade through Zanzibari encouragement.

Origins of the Caravan Trade, 1800 to 1850

The question of how and where the Swahili towns got the goods which were their contribution to the Indian Ocean trade has long been one of the great uncertainties of coast history. Much has been made of the Kilwa gold trade, and it has been suggested that it was gold from south-central Africa which somehow nourished much of the coast in the days before the Portuguese. Ivory has also been singled out as a major item in the coast's external commerce, and a miscellaneous collection of relatively uncommon products ranging from ambergris to hippopotamus teeth has similarly found its way into commercial itemisations. Yet there is little indication before 1800 of the means by which the Swahili obtained goods—like ivory—with an upcountry origin, or even of there being a large enough commerce in them to support the Swahili towns.

After 1800, however, it is possible to piece together a picture of the commercial life of the coast. Quite likely the situation at the beginning of the nineteenth century resembled that of the preceding centuries in their less prosperous phases. At least what is known of this period* is not inconsistent with the scraps of evidence which survive from earlier times.

In the opening years of the century most coastal towns do not seem to have enjoyed a flourishing commerce. Ordinary citizens appear often to have lived by cultivating *shambas* near their city, frequently on the mainland if the town were on an island. Settlements on Pemba and the Kenya coast traded extensively in grain with southern Arabia. By volume this was easily the most important international commercial activity at the coast. There was also a moderate seasonal grain trade up and down the coast between towns, islands, and the Nyika. Galla raids on mainland *shambas* were the greatest obstacle to it. Some communities levied a grain tax to purchase peace from the Galla.

Indirect trade with the interior supplemented agriculture and grain shipping. The middlemen seem traditionally to have been the Nyika and their 'Mozungullo' predecessors along the northern coast; the situation along the southern coast is not known until 1840. Nyika traders bought ivory in small lots from the Kamba and a few other inland tribes, and carried it back through their own country for sale at the ports. The trade they carried on was essentially a short-range operation and seems not to have involved large numbers of people. Once at the coast the ivory was purchased by Swahili, Arab, or Indian Muslim and Hindu merchants.† Probably this had been the pattern of trade for centuries; certainly there is no record of anything more extensive before the nineteenth century.

Then, in the third and fourth decades of the century, the emphasis began to shift. At first initiative remained with the people of the interior. Changes reflect simply the greater number of tribes and people involved. The first recorded appearance of a Kamba caravan at Mombasa was in 1825, and this may actually be one of the earliest Kamba ventures. On the Tanzanian coast opposite Zanzibar, the earliest recorded Nyamwezi caravan appeared in 1839; possibly direct Nyamwezi contact with the coast began a decade or two sooner. Whether

---

*Most of the evidence for the pre-caravan period comes from detailed observations made by British visitors to Mombasa in 1824–5, supplemented by what is known from traditions and other sources.

†There were small Indian communities in the larger towns during the earliest years of the nineteenth century, considerably in advance of the influx of Indians after establishment of the Zanzibar Sultanate.

there had been middlemen similar to the Nyika operating between the Nyamwezi and the coast is as yet impossible to say.

In any case Swahili and Arabs soon began sending their own caravans into the interior, inspired by the commercial upturn encouraged by Sayyid Said's activity at Zanzibar. The Sayyid himself financed caravans from Zanzibar as early as 1837. Privately organised expeditions began to go up-country from Pangani, other *Mrima* ports, and Mombasa at approximately the same time. This did not discourage the Nyamwezi, who continued to organise caravans during most of the century. The Kamba, however, seem to have given up their part in the trade some time in the decade 1850 to 1860, possibly because the Masai closed the northern routes at times. Swahili and Arabs, with access to the resources of Indian merchants and money-lenders, were better able to contend with such difficulties.

Though later development of the caravan trade belongs more to the Zanzibar Sultanate than to the Omani Period, its origins lie in the hazy transition between the two. What prompted the Kamba and Nyamwezi to begin taking their ivory direct to the coast is still unknown. But the break with tradition of coast traders themselves organising caravans into the interior is less difficult to explain: Sayyid Said's economic revival made it worthwhile. In this way, the Zanzibar Sultanate helped launch the first prolonged encounter between coast and interior, pointing to the direction the future would take.

Further reading

BOXER, C. and AZEVEDO, C. *Fort Jesus and the Portuguese in Mombasa,* 1593–1729, London, 1960.

CHITTICK, H. N. The Shirazi Colonisation of East Africa, *Journal of African History,* Volume VI, No. 3, 1965.

FREEMAN-GRENVILLE, G. S. P. *The East African Coast : Select Documents,* Oxford, 1962.

FREEMAN-GRENVILLE, G. S. P. *Medieval History of the Tanganyika Coast,* London, 1962.

GRAY, J. M. *The British at Mombasa, 1824–26,* London, 1957.

GRAY, J. M. *History of Zanzibar from the Middle Ages to 1856,* London, 1962.

GUILLAIN, M. *Documents sur l'histoire, la géographie et le commerce de l'Afrique Orientale,* 3 volumes, Paris, 1856–58.

KIRKMAN, J. S. Historical Archaeology in Kenya, 1948–56, *Antiquaries Journal* (1957), XXXVII, 1–2.

KIRKMAN, J. S. *Men and Monuments of the East African Coast,* London, 1964.

PRINS, A. H. J. *The Swahili-Speaking Peoples of Zanzibar and the East African Coast* (International African Institute Ethnographic Survey), London, 1961.

STRANDES, J. (translated by J. Wallwork) *The Portuguese Period in East Africa,* Nairobi, 1961.

TRIMINGHAM, J. S. *Islam in East Africa,* Oxford, 1964.

7

The River-Lake Nilotes from the Fifteenth to the Nineteenth Century

D. W. Cohen

Up to the fifteenth century, all River-Lake Nilotes lived just south of the point where the River Bahr-el Ghazal meets the Nile in the southern Sudan. Their descendants moved and settled all through the southern Sudan, along the Sudan border in Ethiopia, into the Congo, across northern Uganda, and as far as the coasts of Lake Victoria in Kenya and Tanzania. In the Sudan, the groups of River-Lake Nilotes found today are the Dinka, the Nuer, the Jur, the Shilluk, the Anuak and some few others. The Anuak are also in Ethiopia. In the Congo near Lake Albert are the Alur. In the northern part of Uganda are found the Acholi and the Paluo and certain families of the Lango who have historical and not just linguistic ties with the original River-Lake Nilotes. In eastern Uganda are the Padhola, and along the eastern side of Lake Victoria are the Luo of Nyanza. All through the Bantu-speaking world to the north and west of Lake Victoria are found River-Lake Nilotic clans, now speaking Bantu languages. In some cases, they are the ruling families of their predominantly Bantu areas. All these peoples are grouped together in this book as one great family called the 'River-Lake Nilotes'.*

The term 'River-Lake Nilotes' can be used in different ways

*See chapter 4 Appendix: 'Hamites' and the Hamitic Myth.

by different people. The linguist or language expert uses the term to group together peoples with languages of one type. There are many other ways to group peoples together, such as common physical characteristics, type of economy, or type of government. Each system of classification will produce a different result. In the study of history, the historical ties among people are the most important to consider, and so here, the term 'River-Lake Nilotic' is used to group peoples who are historically related by blood to the first Nilotes.

The original group of River-Lake Nilotes who lived along the Nile in southern Sudan consisted of three families. This place of origin has often been referred to as the 'cradleland of the Nilotes'. They were the *Naadh* (now called the Nuer), the *Jiaan* (now called the Dinka), and the Lwoo. The Lwoo lived somewhat south of the first two groups. The Naadh and the Jiaan were closely related, and the Lwoo have since the fifteenth century migrated the most extensively. Today we find the Naadh and the Jiaan still near their place of origin, while the Lwoo have migrated all over the north-west corner of East Africa. When we speak then of River-Lake Nilotic migrations we mean the migrations of the Lwoo.

The way of life of the early River-Lake Nilotes was greatly influenced by the climate and the geography of the region in which they lived. In this region the year is divided into two climatic seasons, a very dry one and an extremely wet one. During the dry season, the green savannah grasslands turn brown. It is so dry that the people must migrate to permanent swamps and rivers. During the wet season, the rivers of the Nile river system flood, and the flat savannah becomes a vast swampland. Only where hills were very near the rivers could people live safely in one place for both seasons of the year. For those who did not live on such hills near permanent water, the change in season meant a change in residence. As the dry season began, families would gather their possessions and livestock and move great distances to where they could be sure of the availability of water. This necessary seasonal movement is called *transhumance*.

These transhumant people would arrive at riverside camps at the beginning of the dry season. There they would find people from many different hills together in one camp. These were people whom they would never meet during the wet season because of isolation caused by the swamps. This transhumance had a great effect on the way they organised themselves. In fact,

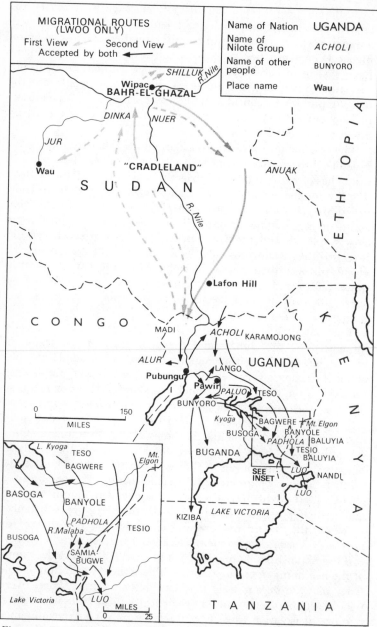

Figure 13 The Migrations of the River-Lake Nilotes

they had two different types of social organisation in the year: (i) in the wet season on the hilltops, each father ruled his own family; (ii) in the dry season when many families came together, one strong family would rule the others or they might all live together in peace by mutual co-operation.

A wet season, hilltop village usually consisted of just one large family of a man, his wives and daughters, his sons and his sons' families. On this small hill the father was the chief, ruling his family as any father would. When the family grew too big for one hill, a son would move to another hill with his family and would be the leader of this hill. Because of the swamps, the father's hill and the son's hill would be completely separated during the wet season. At one time in the past, perhaps the families of a clan were distributed on different hills in the same area and would meet together in one camp. The head of the clan was then the leader of the camp. But as the family was the only unit of organisation for half the year, no political organisation could develop.

But it is quite possible that the Lwoo, though in the same cradleland region as the other River-Lake Nilotes, had a somewhat different environment and adjusted differently to it. The Lwoo settled on ridges close to permanent waterways and so were not forced to move their homes during the dry season. Rather, they could just send their children down the ridges to the permanent rivers to get water and to herd cattle during the drought. These riverside ridges were much larger and so could hold more people than the hills occupied by Naadh and Jiaan.

Settlement of the ridge usually began with one small family building on only one small part of the ridge. Other families and clans would come later and ask for permission to settle. In return for permission to live on the ridge, they would treat the first family as their rulers. The head of the first family would rule all the different families of the ridge. He was a political chief, for he ruled not only his own family or clan, but people from other clans and families as well. Moreover, he ruled throughout the year. His title was *jago*. Every ridge, like every clan, had a name, and it was usually named after the leading family of the ridge.

During the dry season when communication between ridges was possible, certain ridges would associate together more than others, and in times of trouble they would join together in war or in defence. These associations often arose from the

fact that one clan had members settling, and even leading, a
number of neighbouring ridges. These associations of ridges
grew into tribes* and were identified by a special name, again
perhaps the name of the leading family or clan in the area.

A second aspect of Lwoo political organisation developed
from a political idea of the very earliest Lwoo. The Lwoo who
still live near the cradleland and some Lwoo who have migrated
speak much about Nyikang (or Nyikango) whom they call the
founder of their people and the original hero of their culture.
Nyikang was given a title, *reth* or *rwot*, which can be translated
as 'king'. This kingship was passed down through Nyikang's
male descendants to the present day. Nyikang is said to have
distributed the first people on their ridges. His descendants
formed a royal clan. This royal clan eventually took control
of many ridges. Around this privileged clan grew three other
groups. The first group was the *Ororo*. They were a clan made
up of people originating from the royal clan. They performed
important duties for the king. The second group was the *Bang
Reth*. They were the servants of the king. Some were slaves,
some were refugees from other peoples, some were merely
faithful Lwoo servants. Their descendants formed an important
community at the king's capital. The third group were the
common Lwoo clans. Each clan consisted of the descendants of
the founder who could trace their descent through males,
and was usually named after the founder. In most cases a man
could not marry a woman of his own clan. Sometimes these
clans split into two or more clans. The common Lwoo clans, by
service to the kings, and by their constant loyalty, were rewarded
with ridge chiefships. The king stood at the centre of the whole
organisation and symbolised the unity of the Lwoo people. His
prestige came less from his political duties, which were mainly
the confirmation of ridge chief appointments, than from his
ritual duties and powers. The king was thought of as a divine
or supernatural king. He carried out special sacrifices for rain,
for victories in war, and for good harvests, and was said to be

---

*The word 'tribe' is often used without general agreement on a proper definition.
For this chapter the word 'tribe' refers to a group of people who recognise a
common unity against other similar groups. The idea of generally common
origin is also meant. The 'tribe' is usually too large, and often too old as well,
for people to be certain just how they are all related as members of one group. A
'clan' is usually smaller than a tribe and refers to a group in which the members
can be more definite about the ties that bind them together as one family.

able to communicate directly with the first Nyikang and with Jok, the most important spirit worshipped by these early Lwoo This generally is a picture of the political and social developments of the Lwoo in their cradleland, particularly of the Shilluk people. But important elements of this kingship and social system were widely distributed by the migrating Lwoo.

In the River-Lake Nilotic cradleland, we have discussed two quite different developments in social and political organisation. In the first case, transhumant people relied foremost on family rule to keep order among the people. In the second case, with the Lwoo, the large, rather permanent settlements allowed for the growth of larger and stronger political and social units: (i) the ridge with its many different families subordinate to a dominant family chief; (ii) the stronger tribes composed of different clans living on a number of neighbouring ridges; (iii) the kingship, supported by the people's belief in a divine king. The king encouraged their loyalty by giving ridge chiefships to clans and the large royal clan was at the king's service, always interested in the strengthening of the kingship, because any increase in the powers of the king could mean that their own privileges and prestige would increase. The River-Lake Nilotes who migrated far and wide in East Africa were not those whose organisation was limited to the family, but rather those organised on a broader, political basis.

Let us look at certain other aspects of traditional River-Lake Nilotic life. In some cases these characteristics have survived the great migrations and mixing of peoples; in other cases they have been lost or considerably altered. The most outstanding characteristic of ancient River-Lake Nilotic people (and of many River-Lake Nilotic groups today) was the great importance of cattle in all spheres of life, economic, social, and religious. The cow provided the largest part of the diet. River-Lake Nilotes drank milk as a major source of food, and milk made into cheese and milk products also made up a large part of the diet. The blood of the cow was used as a sauce for porridge or was eaten in dried form. Meat was eaten only on religious or ritual occasions.

Skins were used as bedding, for bags, and for making all sorts of things like shields and pipes. Bones were made into every sort of simple tool. Dung was used for plastering walls and floors, and also as fuel. Urine was used in making milk products, and for bathing.

Cattle also had social importance. Friendships were made

through the borrowing and lending of cows. Marriage was made legal (in the traditional sense) when the bridegroom's family gave cattle to the family of the bride. Cows were given to settle claims for compensation after murder or injury. Nicknames were given to a man according to the characteristics of his favourite cows. Wars and raiding were carried out only to seize or to defend cattle. People without cattle were always scorned; the ownership of many fine cows gave a man considerable prestige. Cows were frequently sacrificed to spirits, and when a man wished to communicate with spirits and with ghosts, cattle played an important part in the ritual.

It was because of cattle that the River-Lake Nilotes needed to be near plentiful supplies of water. Wherever they went in their migrations, the River-Lake Nilotes sought an environment like the one they had left in the cradleland—savannah grasslands or savannah woodlands near the banks of year-round rivers, an environment ideally suited to a cattle-keeping people. But even the most dedicated cattle-keepers would grow some crops. In the cradleland area these were mainly millets, but as they migrated, the River-Lake Nilotes learned of other crops and cultivated them as well. Some River-Lake Nilotes even gave up cattle-keeping for cultivation but this was usually because they found themselves in an area unhealthy for cattle.

Hunting was not important among the cradleland River-Lake Nilotes, and is not important among most River-Lake Nilotes today. But fishing was very important and fish formed a good part of the diet, especially during the early part of the rainy season when the grain from the previous harvest had run out and the next crop was not yet ready. As they travelled down rivers, the River-Lake Nilotes depended a great deal on fish for their food.

There are some simple characteristics that stand out concerning the dress and appearance of the River-Lake Nilotes. First, most River-Lake Nilotic men disliked clothing, although among some peoples fathers wore skins. Second, most River-Lake Nilotic peoples had a fondness for ornaments—ivory and wooden bracelets, lip plugs, ear rings, decorative markings, and elaborate hair styles. Also, the River-Lake Nilotes removed two, four, or six lower incisor teeth.

Generalisations about the religious beliefs of these River-Lake Nilotes are difficult to make. It can be said though that most believed in the spirit or spirits called Jok (or Djok, or Juok). For some Jok was the creator of all things and was consulted by the kings. Among other River-Lake Nilotes, Jok represented the spirits of rivers, hills, and trees, spirits usually friendly and helpful to people but which could cause them trouble. Ancestors were regarded as intermediaries between the living and the dead by most River-Lake Nilotes; usually a family leader made a sacrifice to an ancestor in times of sickness or difficulty.

Witchdoctors were generally important and were able to communicate with the Jok spirits. The witchdoctors cured patients, gave others protection in times of war or when travelling, and, if successful, enjoyed great prestige. There were also sorcerers who would use herbs to kill or to cast spells over people, in contrast to the good works of the witchdoctor. A sorcerer would be killed if caught in the act of sorcery. Although the above are general aspects of religion and belief among River-Lake Nilotes, any two River-Lake Nilotic tribes have some differences in ritual or religion; of particular importance is the role of the kings in ritual and religion.

Early Lwoo Migrations

During the fifteenth century, the Lwoo, probably through pressure by peoples from the East, began to leave their cradleland. There are two different views about how this migration occurred. The older opinion is that the main group of Lwoo moved north up the Nile, turned east, and then south. This movement is said to account for the present position of the Shilluk and Anuak peoples north and east of the original cradleland. According to this view, the northwards moving Lwoo were led by Nyikang and they settled in present-day Shilluk country. After they had settled, Giilo, Nyikang's brother, tried to take away the reth-ship from Nyikang. Giilo's side won but Giilo decided to move away anyway. They moved eastwards, some of them stopping and settling in Anuakland, which now lies on both sides of the border between Ethiopia and Sudan. Some pressed ahead in their travels, this time south-west. They passed Lafon Hill in the Sudan where another split occurred, some staying, some moving on, the main group eventually reaching northern Uganda.

According to the contrary account, the Lwoo moved southwards from their cradleland to the Nile valley lands of northern Uganda, and there divided into two groups. One group, under

the leadership of Dimo and Nyikango, moved north to a place
called Wipac on the Bahr-el Ghazal. At Wipac, there was another
split, this time between Nyikango's group and Dimo's. Dimo's
group moved to and settled in Wau, and Nyikango's group
moved to and settled in present-day Shilluk country, reaching
there between 1500 and 1600. In this view, the Anuak are also
thought to have broken off from the main body at Wipac,
moving under Giilo to settle in their present homeland along
the Sudan-Ethiopia border.

According to both views, the migrating Lwoo were probably
not in one vast group. Rather, a number of small groups,
culturally and linguistically similar, moved along at intervals
perhaps twenty-five to fifty years apart. But although geographically separate, groups may have kept allegiance to the
same reth. The great prestige of the reth probably induced many
non-Lwoo people to join the Lwoo travellers, eventually being
absorbed as Lwoo.

Both accounts of the Lwoo migrations through the Sudan
agree that the main group arrived in northern Uganda, at a
place called Pubungu, on the Nile. It is likely that the first
arrivals at Pubungu were at the end of the fifteenth century.
Pubungu was just the sort of place that many of the travellers
were looking for, to settle after such a long journey. But many
were not satisfied with Pubungu and wished to continue the
migrations still further.

Oluum was a very important man in discussions of this
problem. He had a number of sons including Labongo (or
Nyabongo), Gipiir (or Nyipiir), and Tifool, each with his
own party of supporters.

The two sons, Gipiir and Tifool, eventually left Pubungu,
moved westwards into the Congo, and established themselves
as chiefs of the Alur. Today there are many of these independent Alur chieftainships. Prior to the arrival of the Lwoo,
the Alur had no chiefs and spoke a Sudanic-type* language.
When the Lwoo arrived, they won respect as chiefs. Gradually
the Alur gave up their language for that of the Lwoo, and the
two groups intermarried and became one people, though the
old Lwoo clans were royal and the previous Alur clans were
commoners.

*See Chapter 4.

Oluum's son Labongo, with his party, moved to the north-east into present-day Acholiland. From this point, the evolution of the present-day Acholi and Lango peoples is extremely complicated. Before Labongo's Lwoo group moved north-east from Pubungu, there were already in northern Uganda two important and different groups: (i) The Madi, a Sudanic-speaking people, in the western part of the area; and (ii) The Lango, then pastoralists, speaking a Highland and Plains Nilotic language and now thought to have come from the east and north some nine centuries earlier. These Lango were related to the present Karamojong and Teso peoples.

The Lwoo who first arrived in the area joined the Madi in defence against the Lango, and today the Lwoo language has won out over the Sudanic language and the two groups have completely intermarried to form one Acholi tribe. In the seventeenth century, in the North, this combination pushed the Lango people southwards towards Lake Kyoga, where the Lango gradually gave up pastoralism for settled agriculture. The Lango absorbed some Lwoo people and they lived close to Lwoo peoples, and it was perhaps because of this that the Lango slowly gave up their old Highland and Plains Nilotic language and began speaking a Lwoo language.

This whole area was further complicated by the movements of individual families back and forth among the peoples of northern Uganda, and also by the later arrivals in Acholiland of Anuak-Lwoo from the Sudan-Ethiopia borderland. The Lango are a good example of a people who are River-Lake Nilotic in language but not in actual historical fact.

When they arrived in Acholi country at different times, the Lwoo were typically divided into smaller tribal groups made up of a number of commoner families under a 'rwot' or king, and his royal family. As they settled on the land, the rwot confirmed the appointments of chiefs. These village chiefs were called, as in the cradleland, 'jago'. The Madi who were there earlier than the Lwoo were absorbed as commoners.

The Lwoo clans broke up at a very early date and members moved into different tribal areas of Acholiland. The chiefs became stronger because the families they ruled were weakened by separation and division. In the past, there was a great deal of warfare between villages and between tribes. But the villages recognised a wider tribal unity, maintained by the rwotship (kingship). The Acholi maintained a strong interest in cattle

while also concentrating on cultivation. Unlike the cradleland
River-Lake Nilotes, the Acholi (and also the Alur) were en-
thusiastic hunters.

Bunyoro

In the late fifteenth century, the main group of Lwoo left
Pubungu and moved southwards, settling on the northern edges
of Lake Kyoga, and also settling across the Nile in the bend of
the Nile between Lake Kyoga and Lake Albert. This area is
called Pawir or Chope. South of these Lwoo settlements were
Bantu-speaking peoples, then probably ruled by the Bachwezi
kings, who had achieved great fame and power in a rather short
period, and who were considered superhuman. These Bachwezi
had built a large, though not solid, empire between the great
lakes of Uganda. Some historians say that they were early Lwoo
travellers who won great respect among the people of western
Uganda; others say they were Madi; and still others say that
they were originally Cushitic-speaking. But the important thing
to consider here is that these Bachwezi, after ruling for about
two or three generations, began to lose their Bantu supporters,
and this at a time when the main Lwoo group was arriving at the
northern edge of the Bachwezi kingdom. The Bachwezi fled
southwards, giving up their kingdom. It was the Lwoo who
assumed kingship over the remnants of the Bachwezi empire,
called Kitara. Some stories tell us that the Lwoo were invited to
take over as rulers by the Bachwezi before they ran away. The
number of Lwoo who went over into Kitara must have been few,
for they soon gave up their Lwoo language for the language of the
Bantu-speaking peoples they ruled. They began a dynasty of
kings (each called mukama) that has lasted some eighteen
generations, perhaps four or five centuries. This dynasty is called
the Bito dynasty because the founders were of the Jo-Bito clan
of the Lwoo. Their kingdom came to be called Bunyoro, and
while the Bito family gave up speaking the Lwoo language, it did
introduce many Lwoo customs, words, and clans into the Bantu-
speaking parts of Uganda. Bito families established themselves
as dynasties or sub-dynasties as far as Kiziba in the south near
the border of Tanzania and western Uganda, across the northern
and eastern parts of Busoga District, in Bugwere in Bukedi
District of eastern Uganda, and in Buganda where the founder
of the royal dynasty, Kimera, is said to be the twin brother of

Isingoma Mpuga Rukidi, the founder of the Bito dynasty in Bunyoro. In every one of these Bito-dominated kingdoms, the Lwoo influence is present to varying extents.

Going back to the figures Oluum, Gipiir, Tifool, and Labongo, we must be careful in crediting these stories, as they might only just represent how large families were related and how they split and moved off. Gipiir, Tifool, and Labongo were perhaps major leaders in the very large group at Pubungu, who are today symbolically remembered as brothers.

The Padhola

About four and a half or five centuries ago, some Lwoo families started moving east, away from Chope or Pawir in North Bunyoro along the northern shores of Lake Kyoga. Other groups, particularly that of Adhola, began moving south from Acholiland. Moving in small groups, they reached Kaberamaido, a peninsula which juts south-westwards into Lake Kyoga. There they joined other Lwoo people and, after a short time, began moving east, south-east, and then south around the fingers of Lake Kyoga.

The Teso, a 'Plains Nilotic'-speaking people related to the Karamojong and the early Lango, began arriving along this migrational route (now in Teso District) just after the passage of these Lwoo people.

Adhola became one of the leaders of this new Lwoo migration and many of the clans involved in the migration tried to claim a blood relationship with him. These clans first settled along the eastern edge of Busoga at Budola, arriving there perhaps between 1500 and 1550. After staying there for perhaps two generations, they moved back to West Budama, which they had crossed on their trek south. The settlements in West Budama began in about 1625. These first clans in Budama found no one in the country when they arrived, but they did have to fight off cattle-raiding Masai coming from the East. These attacks forced them towards the western part of the area, and, to clear the thick forests there for settlement, Lwoo on the Masai side of these first settlements built in tight villages surrounded by steep trenches as a measure of defence. These Padhola also had to fight off the Banyole who tried to encroach from the north. By about 1700, the worst of these battles were over and the Padhola could open and expand in new areas. The Padhola had chosen a thickly-forested area, and it took great efforts and great commitment to clear this frontier for cultivation. More clans arrived—some Lwoo, some from Busoga, and some from Bugwere. Most clans claimed relationship with Adhola and unified around the memory of the important founder-figure Adhola. They co-operated in opening up villages, and there was little or no fighting between clans over land, for land rights came from the first occupation of the wooded and uninhabited country. As the population grew, a unified Padhola society and a unique Padhola culture emerged from this collection of clans with various origins. The Padhola were somewhat influenced by their Basoga, Bagwere, and Teso neighbours, but they played an influential role in respect to neighbouring peoples.

The Luo of Nyanza

Some groups continued migrating still further, eventually into the Nyanza region of Kenya. But the migrations and settlements of the Luo of Nyanza present us with a more complex problem than other Lwoo peoples, for the clans that now make up the Luo of Nyanza came from various places, by numerous routes, and at different times. Simply speaking, there are four major migrational divisions among the Luo of Nyanza, but it must be remembered that these are rough, general groupings while, in fact, people moved at different times in quite small groups.

The first major division was the Joka-Jok. They travelled from Acholiland in the same era as the Adhola group, and they reached and settled in Nyanza about the same time as the first Padhola clans reached Busoga, that is about 1500 to 1550.

The second major division was the Jok'Owiny. They were perhaps closely related, if only in migrational history, with the Adhola group. They appear to have moved along the western face of Mount Elgon, passing Mbale and Tororo, then turning west through Budama. Finding this part of Budama dangerous and unprotected from Masai raids, they crossed the River Malaba into the safer areas on the eastern edges of present Busoga District. This area was then relatively isolated from numbers of Bantu-speaking Basoga, but the Luo groups there did influence the Basoga. These Luo stayed at places like Budola and Bulugui for perhaps fifty years before moving on between about 1600 and 1625. They passed through Samia-Bugwe, some staying in Samia, to Alego in Kenya. There they found a number of Bantu-speaking groups, and the Jok'Owiny defeated them. Some Bantu-speakers were absorbed into the Luo of Alego, while others were driven off to Samia and Bunyala.

The third major division was the Jok'Omolo, who apparently travelled a more direct route, south of Lake Kyoga and through Busoga to Ibanda, arriving between 1540 and 1600. They had come from North Bunyoro. Ibanda is on the eastern edge of Busoga south of Budola. Occasionally they visited the islands of Lake Victoria. Some stayed in Busoga permanently, but most moved on to Samia and to Nyanza after staying at Ibanda for some fifty years.

The fourth major division were a very mixed group of peoples jointly called the Abasuba. This group had no true unity but included many refugees from Buganda, Busoga, the islands of the lake, and from Tanzania, as well as from other places. They were mostly non-Luo people who took up the culture of the Luo of Nyanza and settled mainly in south Nyanza.

What must be remembered about the peoples of all four of these divisions of the Nyanza Luo is that they did not come as tribes (like those tribes of the Nilotic cradleland), but rather as small groups of people, and these groups generally recognised no units larger than the clan, when they were travelling to and settling in Nyanza. Their first lakeshore settlements were isolated, and they practised transhumance.

With the first settlements there was a great deal of inter-clan warfare. The people then began the change from a primarily pastoral life of cattle-keeping to a primarily agricultural existence. We can only speculate on the possible reasons for this change. One possibility was that large areas of Nyanza proved to be unhealthy for cattle-keeping. Perhaps, also, population growth led to gradual Luo expansion to higher lands very suitable for agriculture. The mixing of peoples in Nyanza may have dampened the traditional Lwoo attachment to cattle-keeping, particularly in their conquest of earlier Nyanza peoples who perhaps cultivated and placed great value on land. Whatever the reasons, agriculture, and thus rights to land, became very important to the Luo. Land questions resulted in still more inter-clan feuding.

This increasing importance of land was a big factor in the eventual organisation of diverse families into a Luo Nyanza nation. The first clans on the land were recognised by latecomers as dominant in the area. Distribution of land was in some cases actually in the hands of the dominant family. Gradually co-operation grew among the many families in one area, and feelings of loyalty developed towards the dominant family. They made war together, combined to defend their lands, so that tribal feeling grew, and often the tribe took the name of the dominant lineage. In this way there developed a number of strong tribes in the northern and central Nyanza areas in the years between about 1550 and 1750. Within these tribes, individuals, especially of the dominant lineage, gained respect for their leadership in war and were looked to for decision-making concerning the whole tribe.

But the population in central Nyanza became too large and warfare among clans more frequent. Between 1750 and 1800, many clans broke up, with some members crossing the Kavirondo Gulf to south Nyanza. This weakened the clans, and the people began to look more and more for protection and rule not to their clan heads, but to the head of the dominant family in the tribe. A form of chiefship was indeed emerging.

Throughout this early period, and even later, wars with Masai, Nandi, and Baluyia groups gave the Luo tribes of Nyanza a feeling of unity against all other peoples. They continued to expand and conquer along their borderlands up to 1900. The arrival of the Plains Nilotic-speaking Tesio (a branch of the Teso) cut the Luo off from their Padhola neighbours and contributed to a feeling of stronger Luo unity. As peace developed within the country, and as clans began to break up geographically, there was a good deal of individual movement which resulted in extensive intermarriage and in a growing unity of society and culture. From many separate pieces, a people conscious of their unity emerged.

Summary

The foregoing account may be summarised as below.
1. The cradleland of River-Lake Nilotic peoples was along the Nile in the southern Sudan.
2. In the cradleland, two types of social organisation developed, much according to the environment: (a) a family organisation; (b) a political or centralised organisation.

3. The centralised organisation and the River-Lake Nilotic migrations involved mainly the Lwoo group rather than the other two groups of River-Lake Nilotes.

4. On the migrations, the Lwoo travellers absorbed many people of different origins.

5. The Lwoo did not travel in one mass but in many small groups, each moving at its own pace.

6. Along the way, the Lwoo split, some settling in a particular place, some moving on.

7. The Lwoo influenced other peoples in two principal ways: (a) by becoming their chiefs and (b) by causing them to change their language.

8. The Lwoo settled differently and met different people in each area, resulting in different types of historical development.

Further reading

BERE, R. M. An Outline of Acholi History, *Uganda Journal,* II, i, 1947, (pp. 1-8).

BUTT, A. J. *The Nilotes of the Sudan and Uganda,* Ethnographic Survey of Africa, London, 1952.

CRAZZOLARA, J. P. *The Lwoo,* parts I (1950), II (1951), and III (1954), Verona, Italy.

OGOT, B. A. *A History of the southern Luo Peoples, 1500-1900,* Volume I, Nairobi, 1967.

OLIVER, R. and MATHEW, G. *History of East Africa,* Volume I, Oxford, 1963 (pp. 169-211).

SOUTHALL, A. W. *Alur Society,* Cambridge, 1956.

8

Cushites and the Highland and Plains Nilotes

Christopher Ehret

It is fitting that the histories of the Cushitic-speaking peoples in East Africa and of the more easterly Nilotic peoples should be considered together. Their courses have so often impinged, not only in the north of East Africa along the edge of the Ethiopian highlands, but as far south as central Tanzania. Some aspects of these contacts have long been recognised, though often misinterpreted; other equally important aspects have, however, gone entirely unnoticed. Of the various Cushites of north-eastern and eastern Africa, only two groups, the Eastern and Southern Cushitic peoples, seem from present evidence to have played significant roles in the history of East Africa. Those Nilotes who have had particularly close relations with the Eastern and Southern Cushites speak languages belonging to the Highland and Plains branches of the Nilotic language group. The Highland group of peoples has had an especially complex history of Cushitic contacts.*

It should already be evident that the naming of peoples in this chapter is based on language criteria. A people is called Cushitic because as a people they speak a Cushitic language; or they are called a Kalenjin people because their speech belongs

*For a classification of these groups and a listing of the East African peoples belonging to each, the reader should refer to Chapter 4.

to the Kalenjin group of languages. Neither features of culture nor physical types are meant to be implied by the names.

The Nilo-Hamitic Hypothesis

The older view of the contacts between the Highland and Plains Nilotes and the Cushites may be characterised as the 'Nilo-Hamitic' hypothesis. By 'Hamitic' was implied the Cushites, among others. Behind the hypothesis lay recognition of a series of contacts between Nilotic and Cushitic peoples, contacts evidenced in both the cultures and languages of the peoples involved.

But the Nilo-Hamitic viewpoint did historians the great disservice of making a unity of diversity. Only too often the Nilo-Hamites became in the eyes of their proponents a single people created in one era of history, a true amalgam of Nilotes and Hamites distinct from either Nilotes or Hamites alone. Moreover, the hypothesis, almost without exception, took the form that the Hamites were the creative and dominant force in the amalgam. The truth seems to be that influences flowed not only from the Cushites to the Nilotes, but in the opposite direction as well; that Cushitic influences were exerted in far greater quantity and in different ways on the Highland Nilotic peoples than on the Plains Nilotic peoples; and that cultural influences, even ultimately deriving from Cushitic-speaking peoples on occasion, were borrowed by Nilotes from other Nilotic peoples, and not directly from Cushites at all.

While the Nilo-Hamitic hypothesis thus greatly oversimplified the history of Cushitic and Nilotic contacts, it also focused attention on the very prominent Galla and Somali and related Eastern Cushitic peoples as the sources of the 'Hamitic' element in 'Nilo-Hamitic'. As a result it led attention away from the investigation of evidence for still other and wider contacts of the Highland and Plains Nilotic peoples. In particular, the extremely important place of Southern Cushites in the history of the Highland Nilotic group has gone entirely unrecognised.

A yet greater disability of the Nilo-Hamitic hypothesis was its integral participation in the still more ambitious oversimplification of African history, the Hamitic hypothesis. The fallacies and weaknesses of this viewpoint have previously been discussed in Chapter 4. The term Nilo-Hamite has thus not been used here. Other designations for the Plains and Highland

Nilotic peoples, such as 'Paranilote', which try to get around the Hamitic pitfall but still imply a special linguistic or historical community between the two groups, should similarly be avoided.

Historical Evidence and Migrational Tendencies

Both the preceding criticism of past approaches and much of the following re-evaluation of Cushitic and easterly Nilotic history in East Africa depend primarily on linguistic and cultural evidence. Some of the ways in which historians find clues to the past in the forms of modern cultures and languages will become apparent from these discussions. Archaeology will eventually also play an important part in this sort of historical reconstruction, because it can far better define the locations of early cultures, describe their materials and economies, and date their beginnings, developments, and ends. But the effective correlation of cultures discovered by archaeologists with cultures revealed by language and social evidence will in many cases require a more detailed archaeological knowledge of East Africa's past than has yet been obtained. Nevertheless, some tentative correlations of this kind will be suggested. Oral tradition, of course, provides historical evidence for only the last few centuries, and written documents are of value for a still much shorter period.

For most of the areas of East Africa and periods of history in which the easterly Nilotes and the Eastern and Southern Cushites figure, not only the investigation of archaeology, but also the collection of tradition and the analysis of linguistic and social evidence are each just beginning. The present chapter cannot therefore be more itself than a beginning. Without a doubt, most of its statements will be greatly elaborated and expanded as knowledge grows, many amended, and others changed.

Three further considerations should be kept in mind in understanding the following discussions. The first is that migration is a common feature of human existence. People move because of lack of land, because of lack of status in their own communities, because of the disruptions of war, and for numerous lesser reasons. They move as groups and as individuals. Migration which brings language or culture changes is only a special case of a more general pattern. For every movement in East

Africa that triggered change there must have been several occasions when migrants were quietly absorbed into pre-existing communities.

The second consideration is that migration is generally a very short-distance affair. People move from one village or valley to the next. The great Ngoni movements of the nineteenth century are notable only because they are such exceptions. More often than not the expansion of a people in East African history is best understood as the accumulation of many small movements of people over a period of generations.

The third point is that extermination or expulsion of a previous population by immigrant invaders is the rare exception, and interaction and assimilation of peoples the rule. If one says, 'The Q people spread south,' it must not be taken to mean that the previous inhabitants to the south disappeared. Rather, certain Q people moved southward, interacted with the previous Z people and for some reason the Zs assimilated to the Qs and adopted the Q language. Assimilation occurs, not only because it is difficult to kill or drive away large numbers of people, but for the better reason that a 'tribe' or 'people' is a fluid grouping. It grows and changes by adoption and amalgamation, and declines by attrition and schism.

Southern Cushitic Locations and Influences

The earliest Nilotic- or Cushitic-speaking people in East Africa, so far revealed in the available evidence, were Southern Cushites. The extensive differences existing among modern Southern Cushitic languages suggest that their presence in East Africa dates from a very early period, perhaps as much as 3,000-4,000 years ago or more. Other language data suggests that the ancestral Southern Cushitic community was formed by the assimilation of an indigenous and previously non-Cushitic-speaking population to a much smaller group of Cushites. The Cushitic elements brought with them their language and the knowledge of pastoral pursuits. Presumably the proto-Southern Cushitic community had some acquaintance also with agriculture, and probably lived somewhere in southern Kenya.

This much is suggested by present linguistic evidence. The culture thus described has notable similarities with the first archaeologically attested food-producing communities of East

Africa described by Dr Sutton in Chapter 4. There seems to be no present reason for questioning his attribution of the culture to Cushitic-speaking agriculturists, coming ultimately from Ethiopia. Dating, location, and type of material culture all agree with the possibility that the bearers of the cultures were, or included among their numbers, the ancestral Southern Cushites.

By some time in the first millenium B.C. the original community had evolved into at least three successor Southern Cushitic-speaking groups—one probably in south-eastern Kenya, another in north-eastern Tanzania, and still another further into the East African interior. Perhaps south-western Kenya is a good guess as to this last group's location, since languages descended from the speech of this third people were certainly spoken in this part of Kenya in later periods. The three groups will be referred to here respectively as Dahaloan, Mbuguan, and Rift Cushitic. Dahalo and Mbugu are the only languages still spoken belonging to their respective groups; the Rift group has been so named because its modern representatives—Iraqw, Burungi, Gorowa, and Alagwa of Mbulu and Kondoa districts, and Asa-Aramanik and Ngomvia to the north and south of them respectively—are all spoken in or near the Rift Valley country of north-central Tanzania. Very possibly there were still other Southern Cushitic groups living in East Africa during the last thousand years before the Christian era, but they have left no linguistic descendants among the modern languages.

The Mbuguan and most of the Rift Cushites were and have remained agriculturists and cattle-keepers, but the Dahalo, Ngomvia, and Asa-Aramanik present another problem. All three groups are, or have in the past been, hunters and gatherers in economy. Several explanations are possible. These Southern Cushitic food-collecting communities may descend from non-Cushitic hunting peoples, who at different times and places took over the Cushitic languages of their dominant agricultural neighbours, or their ancestors may have been formerly farmers and herders who turned for one reason or another to hunting and gathering pursuits. Another interesting possibility may be that the early Southern Cushites combined food-collecting and food-producing activities to such an extent that the option was always open to their descendants, either to become more fully agricultural in economy or to give up farming and herding altogether. Some descendant groups then might have chosen the one course, and some the other, depending on the particular geographical and historical situations each group encountered.

Of the three known Southern Cushitic groups of the first millenium B.C., the Rift Cushitic peoples were historically the most significant. By the early or middle centuries of the first millenium A.D., languages of the Rift group were spread from the western highlands of Kenya through large areas of central and southern Tanzania (Fig. 16). In the latter region, Rift Cushites became a major element in the formation of the later Bantu-speaking populations of much of East Africa. The heaviest concentration of these Cushites would seem to have been in the southern highlands of Tanzania and adjoining regions to the north, but Rift peoples must also have been dominant in a much broader surrounding area. Probably there were already dialect differences among the eastern Bantu who assimilated the indigenous Cushites; however, the evidence also suggests that these Bantu formed a fairly closely associated group of communities. While cattle-keeping and grain cultivation had been introduced into southern Africa by other peoples, the Rift Cushites may have been responsible for the introduction of cattle-milking to the Bantu.

Most of the immediately preceding conclusions follow directly from linguistic evidence. In particular, available data indicate that a goodly number of loan-words from Southern Cushitic languages occur in a majority of the Bantu languages of Tanzania and Kenya. These loans appear not only in portions of the vocabulary where word-borrowing is normally common, such as those dealing with material culture or wild animals, but in areas of vocabulary where loan-words are rare, such as in the nomenclature of the body. Such deep penetration of Rift Cushitic loans into Bantu vocabularies would require a strong Rift influence in the formation of many eastern Bantu peoples. That heaviest word-borrowing occurred in the Hehe group of languages and in Gogo suggests their regions as the former centres of Rift Cushitic population.

Early Nilotic and Eastern Cushitic Contacts

The ancestral Nilotic people probably inhabited an area along the southern fringe of the Ethiopian highlands near the Lake Rudolph region. Evidence of culture and language contacts with other peoples requires a homeland in these regions, and present distributions of Nilotic languages fit in well with such an origin. About the time the ancestral Southern Cushitic community was coming into being, the original Nilotic people was already differentiating into several successor communities. These were at least three in number, speaking dialects ancestral to the modern (i) River-Lake Nilotic, (ii) the Plains Nilotic, and (iii) the Highland Nilotic languages.

These successor peoples probably for a while carried on much of the culture inherited from their Nilotic origins. They no doubt kept cattle, possibly drank their blood, and if they did not yet know of milking, they must soon have learned. They extracted incisor teeth, perhaps as an initiatory rite, and they had some type of linear age-set organisation. In this period, Nilotic culture seems to have been a dominant influence along the edge of the Ethiopian highlands. In particular, the influence seems to have been felt by early Eastern Cushitic peoples, who may have borrowed the idea of age-sets and habits of more intensive cattle-keeping from Nilotes.

In later periods, the histories of the three groups of Nilotic peoples began to diverge sharply. The River-Lake Nilotes spread west to the Nile River region and dropped out of touch with events along the southern Ethiopian fringe—and thus out of the considerations of this chapter—even as the Eastern Cushitic peoples began to attain a new prominence in those events. Although the Plains Nilotes may have come into being near the Abyssinian Highlands, modern Plains cultures and languages do not suggest any especially intensive Cushitic contacts during these eras. But while these two groups had, if any, only limited contacts with Eastern Cushites, the early Highland Nilotic people seem to have come under exceptionally strong Cushitic influences: they adopted a Cushitic prohibition against eating fish, began to circumcise as their chief initiatory observance, and borrowed the idea of a cyclical age-set system.

In addition, the Kalenjin and Tatog languages contain numerous word-borrowings from Eastern Cushitic; some occur even in portions of vocabulary where borrowings are rare. Together, the borrowed features indicate that the particular Eastern Cushites who influenced the Highland Nilotes were closer both culturally and linguistically to the Galla and related peoples, such as the Konso, than to other Eastern Cushites, such as the Somali, Afar, and Sidamo. The simplest hypothesis

Figure 14 Modern locations of Southern Cushites, Kalenjin-Tatog and Nilo-Steppe peoples

seems to be that these contacts occurred in the north along the
Ethiopian highland fringes, before the spread of Highland
Nilotic-speakers southward into Kenya, and prior to their
coming under the influence of still other Cushitic peoples, this
time Southern Cushitic-speaking.

It may be worthwhile here to indicate why a trait has here
been taken as suggesting 'Cushitic' or 'Nilotic' influence or the
like. As an example, age-set systems of various kinds occur
among nearly all Nilotes today, but among the Cushites only
in a limited number of groups centred in the southern Ethiopian
highlands. The same Cushitic groups, however, have age-set
systems of a particular cyclical type which occurs among only
a very few neighbouring Nilotic peoples. By distribution, age-
sets *in general* appear to be old among Nilotes but more recent
among Cushites, therefore have Nilotic origins and indicate
Nilotic influence on Cushites. By the same criterion, *cyclical*
age-sets seem to be of Cushitic source and, where they occur
among Nilotes, to indicate Cushitic cultural influence.

Developments to A.D. 1000

The Proto-Highland Nilotic language, the ancestor of the
modern Kalenjin and Tatog languages, was probably already
spoken in East Africa during the early years of the Christian
era. The ancestor Highland Nilotes both kept livestock and
practised grain agriculture, though cattle-herding was probably
of more importance than cultivation. They also knew of iron
and iron-working. The evidence of loan-words clearly indicates
the dominance of Southern Cushites at this period in East
Africa, although it is not clear whether the particular people
who influenced the Highland Nilotic community belonged to
the Mbuguan, Rift, or other Southern Cushitic group. It is still
less clear where the ancestral Highland people might have lived.
In view of the importance of cattle to them, perhaps a place
especially suited to cattle-keeping might be suggested, such as
the areas about the Rift Valley in central and southern Kenya.

Between the birth of Christ and about A.D. 1000 no particularly significant role in East African history can as yet be
ascribed to the various Highland peoples. Fairly early in the
Christian era, the ancestral Tatog probably already formed a
separate community. Presumably their home area was somewhere in northern Tanzania, but they do not seem to have

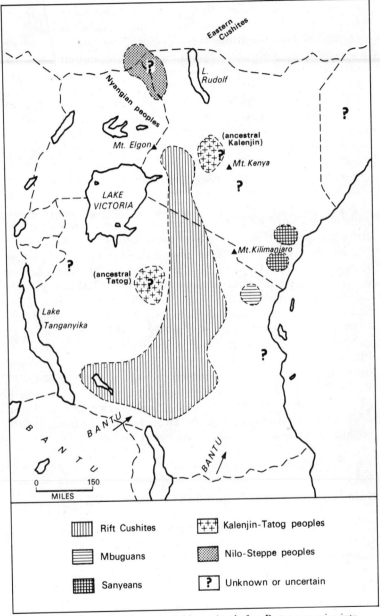

Figure 15 Southern Cushites and neighbours just before Bantu expansion into East Africa

had any notable contacts with Southern Cushites until recent centuries; both are problems to be investigated. Speakers of ancestral Kalenjin continued, however, to live close to important and culturally dominant Southern Cushitic communities. In particular, these Southern Cushites apparently spoke a language of the Rift group.

Nevertheless, the predominant theme in East African history during the first thousand years after Christ was the retreat of the Southern Cushitic languages, especially before the northward advance of the Bantu languages. The countervailing expansion of later Kalenjin peoples and of Masai lay several centuries ahead. By A.D. 1000 there may have been only three Rift Cushitic groups left—one from which the Ngomvia and Asa-Aramanik languages descend, probably living in the Masai steppe area, another in the country of the modern Iraqw and Burungi, and a third in south-western Kenya. The inhabitants of eastern Kenya must have included, in addition to a few Bantu, an Eastern Cushitic people whose linguistic descendants are the Mogogodo, and remnant Southern Cushitic groups. In the far north of Kenya, early Rendile-Somali communities had probably already spread from Lake Rudolph to the Indian Ocean, into territory previously mostly inhabited by hunters.

North-westward, where Kenya, Sudan, and Uganda meet, Plains Nilotes must already have divided into a number of quite distinct groups, and expansions which were to carry speakers of Plains Nilotic languages into their present territories were probably under way. The ancestral Masai, perhaps, were to the south of Lake Rudolph, and the ancestral Bari-Lotuko already farther west toward the Nile in southern Sudan.

Kalenjin and Masai Expansions to A.D. 1600

The history of the Plains Nilotes, Highland Nilotes, and Cushitic-speaking peoples in East Africa between about A.D. 1000 and the close of the eighteenth century was by no means a simple unfolding of trends already evident in the tenth century. Areas Southern Cushitic in speech continued to recede, but not in every case. And the ancestral Somali groups made no deeper incursions into East Africa but instead soon spread northward through the Horn of Africa. The Kalenjin speech area, moreover, underwent vast expansion and equally remarkable contraction within perhaps two or three centuries during this period.

In central Tanzania, in the areas just west of the Masai steppe, complex interactions between Tatog, Rift Cushites, and Bantu must have been taking place during the period following A.D. 1000. Within the region today are found speakers of all three groups of languages, along with Hadza and Sandawe who each speak a language descended from the pre-Southern Cushitic speeches of East Africa. Knowledge of the traditions of most of these peoples is regrettably small, but from other evidence certain general conclusions may be hazarded. To the early centuries of the present millenium probably belong the initial expansion and differentiation of the western Rift Cushites into the ancestral communities of the modern Burungi, Alagwa, and Iraqw. Later developments apparently led to the linguistic separation of the Gorowa from the Iraqw; and more recently still, the Iraqw seem to have been expanding southward into former Tatog territory. At the same time, the advance into the region of Bantu peoples, such as the Irangi and Iramba, was going ahead. Linguistically, the Bantu and Cushitic languages seem all to have borrowed words from each other; the Tatog, too, seem to have participated in the general interchange across language boundaries. But while the Bantu groups, and, among the Cushites, the Iraqw at least have gained territory in recent centuries, the Tatog seem to have been losing ground and declining in importance. It has been suggested that Iramba and Nyaturu country especially includes areas formerly Tatog-speaking.

Northward in Kenya, the later proto-Kalenjin community of about A.D. 1000 may have had its home in the country east and north-east of Mt. Elgon. The present distribution of Kalenjin dialects favours this origin, and tradition also points to the early importance of the Elgon region. The differentiation of this community, into the ancestors of the Pokot on the one hand and of the Nandi, Kony, Tugen, and closely related peoples on the other hand, probably belongs to the early centuries of the present millenium. The Pokot group seems to have formed in the lower country to the north. In this area they later came under the influence of Karamojong-related peoples, borrowed numerous words from them, and became assimilated in many outward respects to the cultures of their northern neighbours.

The ancestral community of the Nandi-related peoples meanwhile spread southward, perhaps encountering and absorbing Rift-speaking Southern Cushites: at least the loan-word evidence suggests this may have occurred. Still other Kalenjin dialects came to be spoken in the present Luhyia and Luo countries south of Elgon.

The greatest Kalenjin expansion, however, originated in the regions just east of the present Nandi and Pokot territories. Loan-word and ethnological evidence present a consistent picture. The expansion involved the imposition of a Nandi-related dialect and a culture in many respects identical with modern pastoral Masai culture, across a territory reaching from central Kenya as far south as the Gogo region of Tanzania (Fig. 16). In short, it must have been remarkably similar to the subsequent, better known Masai expansion. In Tanzania, the advancing Kalenjin people seem to have assimilated an earlier Rift Cushitic population, of which the Asa and Aramanik speakers living among the Tanzania Masai are the last unassimilated remnants. Elsewhere, the movement had noticeable impact on the surrounding Bantu languages and cultures, particularly in central Tanzania and in parts of eastern Kenya.

The expansion would likely not have begun much before 1500. Since the expansion group seems to have spoken a dialect with identifiable affinities to certain modern Kalenjin dialects, sufficient time has to be allowed, firstly for the development of two distinct ancestor dialects, Pokot and Nandi-related, within Kalenjin, secondly for distinct dialects to form within the Nandi-related ancestor language also. This process would hardly have taken less than four or five centuries, so that it would not have been far advanced before perhaps 1400 or 1500, if separation between the Nandi and Pokot groups is taken as beginning early in the present millenium. Perhaps by 1700 the great Kalenjin expansion was over. In the north, the Masai were already beginning to move southward to impose their own language on their Kalenjin-speaking predecessors.

The Masai expansion was certainly as rapid as the preceding Kalenjin advance. At mid-millennium, the Masai must have been an obscure people of north-central Kenya with a culture little different from that of their later relatives, speaking Karamojong and Turkana. By the beginning of the 1800's, the Masai-speaking peoples could already be found as far south as Gogo

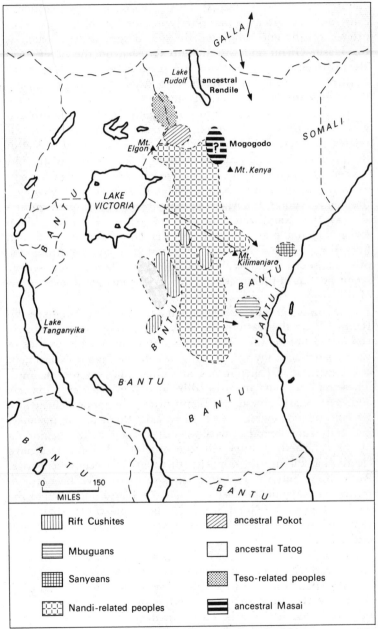

Figure 16 Southern Cushites, Kalenjin-Tatog peoples and neighbours c. 1500 A.D.

country in central Tanzania. Their division into two economically distinct groups—the purely pastoral tribes, the Masai
proper, on the one hand, and the mixed agriculturists, such as
the Uasin Gishu and the modern Arusha, on the other—was
already well established; and the earliest of the wars which
were to characterise the relations between the two groups in
the nineteenth century were beginning.

Whereas the great Kalenjin expansion seems to have brought
with it a culture similar, even in details, to that of the Nandi-
related peoples, the Masai may have taken over a great deal of
the previous Kalenjin culture, adding relatively few distinctive
elements of their own. The Masai vocabulary contains extensive
word-borrowing from a Nandi-related dialect, and, alone among
the Plains Nilotes, the Masai in many respects assimilate culturally to the Nandi-related group of tribes. Probably Masai
expansion should be seen as the movement of a minority, which
first disrupted and then took the initiative in re-forming the
previous society, and as the new formative element imposed its
language, but in the process often used the ideas and institutions
of the majority people.

The more gradual replacement of Kalenjin language by
Bantu along the eastern Lake Victoria shore was probably
completed before A.D. 1500. The subsequent inland advance of
Bantu languages toward Mt. Elgon and the Nandi escarpment
at the expense of Kalenjin has continued into very recent times.
These replacements are attested by loan-words in Bantu dialects
and, particularly among the Bantu nearer the modern Kalenjin,
by cultural borrowings. The Tiriki and Bukusu, for instance,
had fully functioning cyclical age-set systems at the beginning
of the twentieth century. On the other hand, influences have
clearly passed in the opposite direction in recent centuries.
Agricultural innovations, especially, seem to have been transmitted to Kalenjin peoples through the Bantu and Luo to the
west of them. The Nandi words for both maize and potato, for
example, are borrowed from languages of the Kavirondo gulf
regions.

By the 1600's oral tradition begins to offer a useful tool for a
closer reconstruction of events within the wider group of
Kalenjin peoples. The big difficulty is that Kalenjin traditions
dealing with the seventeenth and eighteenth centuries have
been collected in only the barest manner. The Nandi seem to
have come into being in the early seventeenth century along the

southern Nandi escarpment. They gradually expanded north-ward by absorbing people of various other Kalenjin groups into their community. Their major preoccupation from sometime in the eighteenth century on into the nineteenth was coping with their militarily stronger neighbours to the east, the Uasin Gishu Masai. For the plains Pokot, further north, there are traditions suggesting conflicts during the same period with Masai and Turkana for possession of the Kerio Valley area. Elsewhere among Kalenjin peoples, available traditional evidence is still more scanty. The thorough collection of such traditions remains an extremely important task for historians of Africa.

Movements in the Kenya-Uganda and eastern Kenya-Tanzania Borderlands

There remain to be considered two other areas of East Africa where Cushitic or easterly Nilotic presence obtained during the last thousand years. One is the lands on both sides of the Uganda-Kenya border north from Mt. Elgon, and the other is the region of south-eastern Kenya and the neighbouring far north-eastern corner of Tanzania. For neither has evidence relating to the earlier periods been effectively collected and analysed.

For the Kenya-Uganda border regions, only Plains Nilotes speaking Teso-related languages seem to have contributed much to recent history. Teso-related peoples probably still inhabited a rather restricted territory as late as the 1500's. Collation of traditions suggests a homeland in the areas surrounding Mt. Moroto along the middle Kenya-Uganda boundary. The ancestral Teso may have lived to the south-west of Moroto, the Karamojong to the north, the Toposa perhaps further north, and the Turkana to the north-east of Moroto along the edges of the escarpment. In eastern Uganda, at least, the Teso and their relatives were certainly preceded by the Nyangiya peoples. Remnant groups of these are the Nyangiya of far northern Uganda, the Teuso of the same general area, and the Tepeth of the Moroto and Amudat areas of Uganda. The earlier home of the ancestors of the Teso-speaking group may have been slightly to the eastward in Kenya, but this at present is only a matter of conjecture.

The movements to which tradition ascribes the present distribution of Teso-related peoples probably all fall within the last three to four centuries. The expansion of Teso-related languages no doubt often coincided with these movements; but dialect differences in some cases would seem to have existed before the movements accentuated them. The Teso themselves seem to derive from a westward expansion from the old home-land into the area between Mt. Nepak and Lake Salisbury in Uganda. Teso-speakers were well established there by the beginning of the nineteenth century, and from this second homeland were later to spread southward into the larger terri-tories they now inhabit. But even as the original Teso speech area was being expanded westward toward Lake Salisbury, the Karamojong were beginning a southward expansion which was to end with the complete assimilation of the Teso remaining in the east. The Jie and Dodos peoples to the north seem, on the other hand, to derive from northward expansions from Karamo-jong areas. At about the same time as the other movements, the Turkana began to expand north-eastward, then later to the south-east, where, in the later 1700's, they apparently came into conflict with the Samburu. The Toposo of the far south-eastern Sudan speak a Teso-related language and certainly owe their existence in part to people spreading from the same general region as the Teso-related groups, but these events occurred in the nineteenth century and are not properly the concern of this chapter.

Nor would these examples seem to exhaust the movements of peoples traceable from Uganda-Kenya border areas. In particular, one element in the formation of the Luo-speaking Lango may have been a people who originally spread westward from Karamoja. A very interesting question for future historical studies will be why so many movements of peoples should have emanated from one particular area within the space of only a century or two.

As for north-eastern Tanzania and south-eastern Kenya, Southern Cushites, Eastern Cushites, and Highland Nilotic groups may all have had parts in the developments of the past thousand years. The Southern Cushitic role is not yet well understood. It would seem, though, that people speaking a language with Mbuguan affinities preceded the Shambala and Zigula in portions of their present territories, and that people speaking a Dahaloan language may still have been an important population element in parts of the immediate hinterland of the southern Kenya coast until not too many centuries ago. The presence of the last remaining Mbuguan- and Dahaloan-

speaking groups near those respective areas today makes these
possibilities all the more likely.

Early Eastern Cushitic or Kalenjin populations in south-
eastern Kenya are indicated by the widespread occurrence of
circumcision and of age-grade and age-set systems among the
Bantu peoples of the area. The forms of the age-grade systems
especially suggest Eastern Cushitic influence. But these influences seem attributable not to such late movements as either
the great Kalenjin expansion of mid-millenium or the Galla
incursions into eastern Kenya of the sixteenth or seventeenth
centuries, but to an earlier Eastern Cushite group in East
Africa, the ancestors of the Mogogodo. For the present, however,
there is no evidence for deciding one way or the other.

The last notable Cushitic or Nilotic contribution to the
shape of events in eastern Kenya was the Galla invasions
mentioned just above. The East African movement was only
one phase of much wider Galla expansion, beginning in the
early 1500's, by the end of the century affecting the major part
of the Ethiopian highlands, and in effect transforming the
Galla from an insignificant tribe of the south-eastern edge of
the highlands into one of the dominant Ethiopian peoples. In
Kenya, the Galla Boran pushed first southward between the
Rendile and the Somali, then into the dry country on both
sides of the Tana River. Here they particularly influenced the
Bantu Pokomo, some of whose clans claim Boran origin and
whose language and culture contain many borrowings from
the Galla. The Galla reached their height in the seventeenth
century when their raids extended probably into parts even of
far north-eastern Tanzania. Since then their power has declined,
especially through the resurgent Somali strength north of the
Tana.

Further reading

The bibliography for this chapter can only be a very short
one. Few articles and books deal specifically with the periods
covered by the chapter, and fewer still are easily accessible
to the general reader. Most of these few are concerned with
only a certain series of events, namely those producing the
'Nilo-Hamites', and their viewpoints are generally hopelessly
at odds with the views expressed here. For a good deal of

the rest of the chapter, nothing at all has previously been published.

Instead of noting the few unsatisfactory works in the bibliography, an attempt has been made to put the reader on to some of the basic evidence used here for historical reconstruction. Listed below are several survey works which summarise much of the available ethnographic material on the peoples whose histories are discussed in the chapter— ethnology having provided an important element of the evidence. These survey works in turn contain bibliographies of more detailed and specialised works on the peoples dealt with, to which the reader may further refer. Unfortunately, most of the linguistic evidence for the chapter is taken from the unpublished research of the writer.

CERULLI, E. *Peoples of South-West Ethiopia and Its Borderland,* London: International African Institute, 1956.

GULLIVER, P. and P. H. *The Central Nilo-Hamites,* London: International African Institute, 1953.

HUNTINGFORD, G. W. B. *The Northern Nilo-Hamites,* London: International African Institute, 1953.

HUNTINGFORD, G. W. B. *The Southern Nilo-Hamites,* London: International African Institute, 1953.

MURDOCK, G. P. *Africa : Its Peoples and Their Culture History,* New York: McGraw-Hill Book Company, Inc., 1959. (Chap. 24, 25, 42, 43.)

PRINS, A. H. J. *The Coastal Tribes of the North-Eastern Bantu,* London: International African Institute, 1952.

9

The Western Bantu Peoples from A.D. 1300 to 1800

Gideon S. Were

As used here, the term 'the Western Bantu' refers to the Bantu-speaking communities of East Africa to the west of the Rift Valley. In Uganda this group comprises the Banyoro, Banyankole, Batoro, Baganda, Basoga, Banyole (Banyuli) and the Bagishu. Further east in western Kenya live the Abaluyia to the north of the Kavirondo Gulf and the Abagusii to the south of the Gulf. In Tanzania the group is represented by the Bahaya, Bakuria, Wasukuma and Wanyamwezi.

For some time now, the history of this region has largely been limited to the study of the various ruling dynasties. This is particularly so in the case of the interlacustrine kingdoms of Bunyoro, Toro, Ankole, Buganda, Karagwe, etc.* In these territories, there is much more information about the various royal clans and dynasties than about the rest of the communities. Apart from the Abaluyia, Basoga, Baganda, and, to a limited extent, the Bagishu, the history of this region is still incomplete. A great deal of work remains to be done before we can have a fairly comprehensive history of the whole region.

It is customary to start the 'modern' history of the interlacustrine region with the period immediately preceding the coming of the Abachwezi. Very little is known or remembered about this remote period, and that little is so fragmentary that it does not make the historian's task lighter.

*Note that all the kingdoms and ruling dynasties discussed in this chapter are now defunct.

In Bunyoro and Ankole the pre-Abachwezi period is actually associated with the time of creation. During this period, Ruhanga (the 'Creator') is said to have created the world and all that is in it. In Bunyoro in particular, this period of the gods and creation is associated with the reign of the Abatembuzi. The Abatembuzi dynasty, founded by Ruhanga from heaven, lasted for about four or five reigns. The dynasty was founded by Ruhanga (God, Creator) and his brother Nkya. Nkya was succeeded by his son, Kakama Twale, and he in turn by his son, Baba. Baba was succeeded by his son Ngonzaki, and he by his son Isaza. Since they were gods, the Abatembuzi are said never to have died; they simply disappeared or ascended into heaven.

As we move from the remote and vague period of the dynasty of the Abatembuzi to that of the Abachwezi, the picture becomes a great deal clearer. Much has been said and written about the mysterious Abachwezi, their material culture and identity. Taking note of the relics of the culture of the Abachwezi and also of the oral traditions relating to them, some writers have hastily concluded that their ancestors must have been Egyptians. Yet others have concluded that the ancestors of these mysterious people must have been Greeks of Ethiopian (Cushitic) origin. Much of this, however, is still sheer speculation and the 'Hamitic myth' as an explanation for the existence of any material cultural development or civilisation in black Africa must equally be rejected. The correct identity of the Abachwezi and their original homeland have yet to be discovered.

Throughout Bunyoro, Ankole, Toro, Rwanda, Burundi, and the Bukoba District of mainland Tanzania, there are local traditions of a strange people variously called Bachwezi (Abachwezi), Batutsi, Bahuma or Bahima, and Bahinda. Traditions throughout the above territories are agreed that the newcomers were great pastoralists who kept long-horned cattle as distinct from the indigenous short-horned humpless ones. Again, the strange immigrants are said to have been great hunters and magicians, who wore cow-hide sandals and built grass houses. Legends further suggest that they were 'brilliant', perhaps light-skinned. They would appear to have come from the north or north-east and settled in the country without any significant resistance by the local people. Their descendants can still be identified throughout the region especially in Bunyoro, Ankole, Rwanda, Burundi, and Karagwe, where, until recently, they formed the ruling aristocracy (except in Bunyoro).

The Bachwezi dynasty is linked by tradition to their predecessors, the Abatembuzi. As a result, some writers regard the two as belonging to the same racial stock. This appears to be supported by some local accounts which state that the Bachwezi were 'like the Bahima, but more brilliant'. Yet other accounts suggest that the Bachwezi were Bahima. The two did not markedly differ in race.

Be that as it may, tradition asserts that long ago, the Bachwezi succeeded the Abatembuzi as the rulers of Bunyoro-Kitara, a kingdom at that time presumably a great deal bigger than it is today. Its centre was to the south of modern Bunyoro, in the downlands which include part of present-day Ankole, Toro, and part of Buganda and Karagwe. It is uncertain whether at that time this great empire was effectively governed as one administrative unit or was rather a congeries of semi-independent sister states. Nevertheless, tradition relates that Ndahura (Karubumbi), the founder of the Bachwezi dynasty, was the paternal grandson of Isaza, the last ruler of the Abatembuzi. He was succeeded by his son, Wamara, the last of the Bachwezi rulers. Altogether, the Bachwezi would appear to have been in the country for only a generation or two.

We know almost nothing about the indigenous peoples who became the subjects of the pastoral newcomers. It is generally agreed that they were Bantu and that they were primarily cultivators. Some of them, however, kept short-horned humpless cattle. They appear to have been organised on a clan basis, both socially and politically. Before the coming of the pastoral Bahima, Bunyoro is said to have been partly occupied by the Bantu Basita, Karagwe by the Bantu Banyambo, Rwanda by the pygmoid Batwa and Bantu Bahutu, and Ankole by the Bantu Bairu. It is quite obvious that there were many more communities but memory of them is now dim.

The Bachwezi seem to have been one of the last bands of the pastoral Bahima who entered Uganda from the north-east and appear to have brought in a better material culture than that of their predecessors. They are credited with the reconquest and reorganisation of the Kitara empire after the departure of their Abatembuzi predecessors, and are associated with the introduction of barkcloth manufacture, coffee cultivation, iron working, earthwork fortifications, and reed palaces. To the Bachwezi is also attributed the introduction of a centralised monarchy and a hierarchy of officials both in the palace and in the provinces. As there is evidence to suggest that the pre-Bachwezi (or pre-Bahima) communities were organised on a clan basis, perhaps it is justifiable to associate the introduction of a centralised monarchy and larger political or administrative units with the Bahima. However, it is not certain whether they actually imported this institution into Uganda, although in Bukoba this was certainly the case. It seems quite probable that in western Uganda this political system evolved from the encounter of the pastoral immigrants and the indigenous communities. In that case, the system must have been significantly influenced by the native culture and the Bahima rituals which the Bahima introduced.

The Bachwezi left behind their regalia—ancient crowns, royal drums, spears, arrows, stools, etc., and also the institutions of slave artisans, palace women, and of administrative officials ruling small areas in the provinces and districts as the representatives of a centralised monarchy.

Archaeological evidence in western Uganda gives support to the belief that at one time there was an extensive pastoral kingdom. A careful examination of relics at the important cultural sites at Bigo, Mubende, Kibengo, Kagogo, Kasonko, and Ntusi revealed this valuable information. The principal features of this ancient culture are pottery forms consisting of spherical bowls, jars, shallow basins and footed dishes, decorated with roulette patterns. Another outstanding feature is large earthworks which seem to have been generally situated in undulating country, usually located by a river.

At Bigo, the largest of these cultural sites, there was a ditch system of over six and a half miles. As the ditch system is known to have included good grazing in the meadows of a Katonga tributary, the makers of the site at Bigo would seem to have intended it partly for defensive purposes and also to protect large herds of cattle. This is further proof that there was a pastoral state in the area. The pastoral Bachwezi, or a similar people, may, therefore, safely be associated with the Bigo culture.

An ancient enclosure bank at Bigo, which has been interpreted as a royal enclosure *(orirembo)* is similar to those which survived in Karagwe, Ankole and Rwanda till late in the nineteenth century. This, together with finds of large quantities of cattle bones, is a clear indication that Bigo was the capital of a pastoral state in western Uganda. In that case, the other territories, e.g. Ankole, Karagwe, and Rwanda must have been ruled by subordinate chiefs. However, the Bachwezi reign was short. They were in the country for only one or two generations. Oral tradition and archaeological evidence suggest that the Bachwezi culture flourished between about A.D. 1350 and 1500.

The Impact of Lwoo Invasions—Bunyoro and Buganda

About the beginning of the sixteenth century or a little earlier, the Lwoo migrated southwards from the south-east corner of the present Sudan Republic. In Bantu Bunyoro, the Nilotic immigrants adopted the local language, further north in modern Acholiland, Alurland, and the Lango country, they retained their native language and culture. In Bunyoro, the Nilotic invaders founded a new dynasty called the Babito. To this day the Babito dynasty still flourishes in Bunyoro. The local ruler is known as Omukama.

Traditional evidence in western Uganda, notably Bunyoro, suggests that the Babito came in peacefully. This occurred during the reign of Wamara, the second and last of the Bachwezi rulers. It is further suggested that Isingoma Mpuga Rukidi, the founder of the Babito dynasty, was the son of Kyomya, the half-brother of Ndahura, the founder of the Bachwezi dynasty. Rukidi is said to have come from a district vaguely called Bukedi, not necessarily the present Bukedi. It must, however, be added that the Bachwezi culture just described was superior to the much less sophisticated culture of the Lwoo newcomers. Rukidi himself had to be trained in the Bachwezi rituals of kingship and other affairs of state by the local people. It does seem, therefore, that the Bachwezi were not related to the Lwoo Babito, who must be regarded as invaders of the pastoral Bachwezi kingdom of Bunyoro-Kitara which was already in the process of disintegration.

The factors responsible for the disintegration of the once extensive pastoral state are not clear. Traditional evidence suggests that the Bachwezi voluntarily left the country because they were weary of constant strife, insubordination, and increasing misfortunes. The mysterious death of Bihogo, the darling cow of one of the princes, and the unfavourable interpretation of the incident by a soothsayer from Bukedi is said to have been the last straw. It is, however, quite probable that there were other factors. The Bachwezi power may have been undermined by natural calamities such as smallpox and cattle disease. To a pastoral community, like the Bachwezi, the latter would be particularly fatal. Local revolts and even civil war may further have weakened the central government. Whatever the case, the collapse of the Bachwezi state must have been accentuated by the contemporary Lwoo invasion.

The coming of the Lwoo had a tremendous impact on the history of this region. First, the disintegration of the Bachwezi state was completed. There now arose a number of separate states such as Bunyoro, Ankole, Buganda and Karagwe. The foundation of a Bahima (Abamuhima) state at Imanga (the nucleus of the later Kingdom of Wanga) which was dominated by the Bahima immigrants from western Uganda, may also be associated with these developments. The Nilotic newcomers founded a number of related dynasties in Uganda, of which the Babito of Bunyoro was the most important. Babito sub-dynasties were subsequently founded in Bukoli, Bugwere, Bulamogi and Bugabula in Busoga, and in Kiziba in the Bukoba District of Tanganyika. All this happened between nine and seventeen generations ago, around A.D. 1490 to 1733. A separate Babito dynasty was established in Toro in the nineteenth century. Apart from ritual connections, there is no reason to believe that these principalities were actually tributary to Bunyoro.

Further east in Buganda, similar developments were also taking place. Bunyoro accounts suggest that dynasties in Buganda and Bunyoro were founded respectively by Lwoo twin brothers, Kimera and Rukidi. The Lwoo origin of the former ruling dynasty of Buganda has been accepted by many writers. On the other hand, there is ample evidence to support the contrary theory that Kimera belonged to the Bachwezi and, therefore, to the pre-Lwoo inhabitants of Bunyoro. The coming of Kimera and his followers to Buganda may have been caused by the appearance of the Lwoo in Bunyoro.

At first, Buganda was a small state, presumably on the same scale as some of the principalities of Busoga. Busiro-Mawokota was probably the home of the earliest inhabitants, who seem to have been Bantu. The area of first occupation may have included present-day Kyadondo. By the 18th century, however, many more immigrants had arrived and the state gradually expanded as more settlers came in from Bunyoro, the

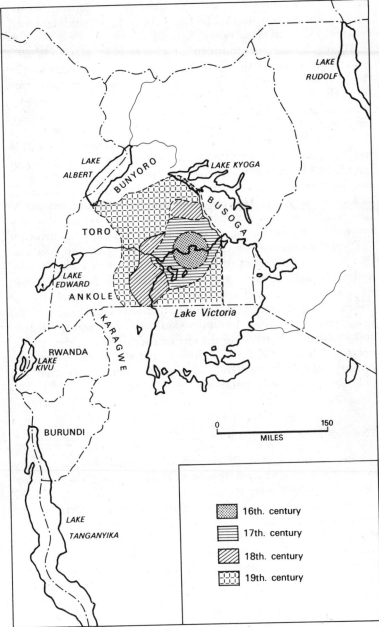

Figure 17 The growth of Buganda 16th-19th Centuries

Mount Elgon direction and the Sese Island. After Kabaka Junju's annexation of Buddu from Bunyoro in the eighteenth century, the local clans joined Baganda clans.

About thirteen or fourteen of the present clans claim to have come with Kintu, the Baganda hero who is credited with the centralisation of the state. He is said to have originally come from the Mount Elgon region via either Bunyoro or Bugishu, Budama and Busoga. On the other hand, six clans claim to have come with Kimera, founder of the Buganda dynasty.

Up till the middle of the seventeenth century, Buganda, like many neighbouring states, was at the mercy of the powerful kingdom of Bunyoro. About this time Bunyoro was busy raiding Ankole, Rwanda, the principalities of Busoga, Buganda, and even Karagwe. However, the process was reversed in the late seventeenth and eighteenth centuries, when Buganda more than doubled its size, largely at the expense of Bunyoro.

By the nineteenth century, Buganda had grown so powerful that it was raiding all over the region. It absorbed Koki, Buddu, and Mawogola (Bwera) and most of the Basoga principalities were tributary to it. This strong position was attained by the creation of a strong royal bodyguard, the strengthening of the royal power through centralisation and appointing district and sub-district chiefs, and the virtual suppression of the original clans and traditional heads. Thus by the end of the eighteenth century, seven of the ten county chiefs were appointive and only three were still hereditary.

The Bahinda of Ankole

As already noted, Ankole was one of the small successor states to the defunct Bachwezi kingdom. Here the pastoral Bachwezi held their own. Under Ruhinda, son of Wamara, the last of the Bachwezi kings, Ankole maintained its independence. The dynasty of the Abahinda which still survives in Ankole was founded by Ruhinda. Sometime towards the end of the sixteenth century, Ruhinda and his followers moved into Karagwe in the Bukoba District of mainland Tanzania. He then deposed the local ruler, Nono, son of Malija, and became ruler himself. Subsequently, he sent out his sons, each with a royal drum, to found the Bahinda sub-dynasties of Gisaka, Kyamtwara, Ihangiro, Buzinza, Busubi, Ukerewe, and Nasa. Ruhinda is also credited with the establishment of the contemporary dynasty of Burundi. On Ruhinda's death, these principalities became independent. Like Ankole, they were characterised by a pastoral aristocracy and an agricultural lower class.

Many of the clans of the Bahaya (i.e. the inhabitants of Bukoba District) claim that their ancestors came from Bunyoro where the histories and traditions of such clans usually begin. Many of the clans would thus seem to be sub-clans *(mahiga)*, of clans in Bunyoro. This may partly explain the close relationship of the Lunyoro and Luhaya languages. It also supports the theory that the Karagwe region of Tanzania was part of the wider cultural area of western Uganda. Banyankole sources in fact suggest that the territories south of the Kagera River were part of the domain of the Bahinda of Ankole even before Ruhinda transferred his headquarters there.

The immigrants from Bunyoro seem to have come in small family bands, each under its own leader. Apparently, they settled without much resistance as, apart from minor skirmishes, no major military encounter is reported. Before this immigration, the district was primarily agricultural although a few of the inhabitants kept short-horned humpless cattle. Thus from their native Bunyoro and Ankole, the pastoral immigrants brought with them their famous long-horned cattle and the institution of a centralised monarchy. However, the pastoral Bahinda allowed the existing clan and sub-clan organisation to continue at the local level. Their major administrative reorganisation entailed the regrouping of the independent clans together into bigger administrative units, the chiefdoms. There were eight such chiefdoms—Kianja, Bukara, Kiamtwara, Kiziba, Bugabo, Ihangiro, Misenyi, and Karagwe.

The Bahinda would seem to have been accepted as rulers because of their mental and physical qualities. Being unbiased judges and arbitrators, they were welcome and preferred to their predecessors. Furthermore, the Bahinda newcomers were rich in the all-important commodity of cattle with which they could reward and assist their subjects. And the fact that people believed in their divine origin (see the Abatembuzi and Bachwezi above) and associated them with the supreme deities of the Bahaya world of gods was of no less significance.

In Karagwe, this initial stage of settlement and reorganisation was followed by a fairly uneventful period. In fact, nothing is related about the next seven rulers after Ruhinda. However, in the 1770's, the Banyoro invaded the country. At that time the young Ntare VI was in power. His mother fled with him across the Kagera to Buha leaving his brother Luzenga to act as regent. The Banyoro killed Luzenga, overran the country, and ruled it for about six years. Then, after they had been decimated and weakened by a certain disease, Ntare VI returned from Buha and drove them back to Bunyoro. Hence his nickname Kitabanyoro, 'the slayer of the Banyoro'.

Further south and south-east live the Wanyamwezi and Wasukuma. They seem to belong to the same group as the Bantu of western Uganda and the Lake region of Tanganyika. Unfortunately, information on the early history of these two communities is extremely thin and fragmentary. Their later history, particularly from the second half of the nineteenth century to the early years of the present century, is however, much more complete.

Assuming their institution of chiefship was imported by immigrants from southern or western Uganda, this must have occurred previous to the coming of the pastoral Bahima and the Lwoo. Otherwise it would have been influenced by the later political organisation of the Bahima and the Lwoo already described. On the other hand, traditional evidence indicates that the present lake area of Usukuma was previously occupied by the pastoral Bahima who were subsequently driven out by the Wasukuma from the south. It is, therefore, quite probable that the institution of chiefship was indigenous but that its structure was subsequently influenced by later contacts with the pastoral Bahima. For the time being, the early history of these people—their migrations, settlement and evolution— must be regarded as disappointingly incomplete.

Bagishu and Basoga

The history of the eastern half of the region is largely that of the origins and migrational movements of the ancestors of the local communities, and their development as cultural and political units. Included in this group are the Basoga, Bagishu, Abaluyia and the Abagusii.

The more closely we examine the past of these peoples, the more we become convinced that, between about nine and twenty generations ago, therefore around A.D. 1382 to 1706,

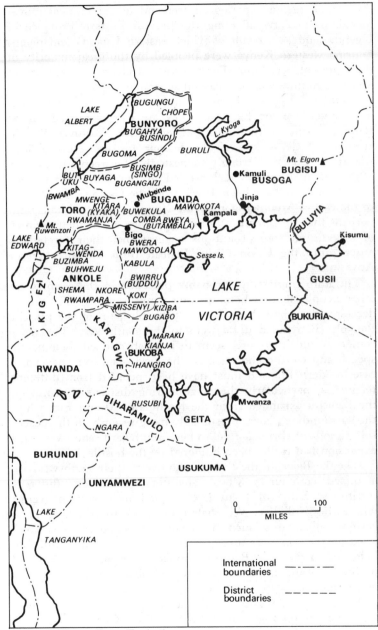

Figure 18 Western Bantu Territories

this whole region experienced tremendous migrational movements, particularly affecting the present Eastern Province of
Uganda, and as a result of which eastern Uganda and neighbouring western Kenya were peopled by the great majority of
their present occupants. For the sake of clarity, the history of
each community will be analysed separately.

To the north-east of Lake Victoria in the Mount Elgon region
of Uganda live the Bagishu. They are closely related to the
Babukusu, the northernmost section of the Abaluyia. So far,
relatively little is known about their history. Nevertheless,
traditional evidence strongly suggests that between A.D. 1517 to
1652, the first settlers had arrived in Bugishu. Earlier, they
would appear to have been driven from the Uasin Gishu Plateau
to the east of Mount Elgon by the Nandi, Masai, Turkana, and
perhaps the Abyssinians. Nothing is known about their country
of origin, but some traditions suggest that their forefathers
moved into the Uasin Gishu Plateau from the direction of
Abyssinia.

The immigrants were probably preceded in the country by
other people about whom we now know nothing. Their predecessors may have been Bantu, probably akin to the present
Banyole (Banyuli) and Bagwere to the south-west. The newcomers would, therefore, seem to have abandoned their native
speech and culture and adopted the local ones. Whichever the
case, modern Bugishu must have been peopled from different
territories, particularly the neighbouring districts. Eventually,
the Bagishu expanded from the foothills of Mount Elgon into
the surrounding plains, presumably more recently in the peaceful period of British rule. Their southward and westward
expansion had earlier been hindered by the hostile Teso.

Like the Bagishu, the Basoga who live to their south-west are
a mixed community whose ancestors came from different
territories. Some of them later moved into western Kenya
where they still live. We shall come back to this later. The
earliest inhabitants such as Nanyumba's people (Banyole)
lived on the lakeshore areas of modern Bukoli. They probably
belonged to the same Bantu group as the original communities
of Bunyoro and Buganda already described. By about twenty
generations ago, between A.D. 1382 and 1409, the first settlers
had already arrived and, some time later, were joined by others
from the Mount Elgon area, led by either Kintu or Mukama,
who eventually crossed over into Bunyoro. Some of their

descendants live in the south-west and north-east of Busoga. In due course, more people came from the neighbouring territories of Budama, western Kenya, Kigulu (Sigulu) Island in the Kavirondo Gulf, and Bugwere. By this time too the Lwoo had also arrived in Bukoli and the northern districts of Busoga on their way from the southern Sudan. All this happened between about thirteen and fifteen generations ago, between 1517 and 1598. The great majority of the Lwoo later crossed over into western Kenya. By about twelve generations ago, A.D. 1598 and 1625, more settlers had arrived, this time from Bunyoro; many of them settled in Bugabula and Bulamogi.

Thus by about nine generations ago, A.D. 1679 to 1706, Busoga was already peopled from different territories. Among the settlers in the southern districts were the ancestors of some of the major clans of the Abaluyia. Notable among these are the Abashitsetse of Wanga, Abafofoyo of Marachi, Abaguri of Bukhayo, and the Abakhekhe of Samia locations. On the other hand, as has been noted, some of the immigrants came from Bugishu, the immediate homeland of the Babukusu. It is therefore evident that between about nine and twenty generations ago, 1382 to 1706, modern Busoga and Bugishu as also Buluyia in western Kenya were partly settled by people of the same stock.

As already noted, as a result of the establishment of the Lwoo Babito dynasty in Bunyoro, a number of related sub-dynasties were founded in Busoga. They ruled in Bukoli, Bugwere, Bulamogi, Bukono, Bugabula, and Bugweri. Whereas the first two were contemporary with the Babito dynasty of Bunyoro, the rest were founded between about 1598 and 1733. At first they were virtually independent and formed separate alliances from those of the Banyoro.

By the nineteenth century there were about fifteen such principalities, most of them very small. In the northern district where there were Banyoro migrants, the Baisengobi (bushbuck) clan provided the rulers for seven of the northern and eastern principalities. Much of the north was under Bunyoro domination in the nineteenth century. In fact, by 1862 when Speke visited Bunyoro, the north was paying tribute to the *mukama* (ruler) of Bunyoro. On the other hand, the south seems to have been ruled by dynasties of either an eastern or a Lake Victoria islands' origin. The southern principalities were generally smaller than the northern ones.

The Abaluyia and Abagusii

About the same time (i.e. A.D. 1382 to 1706) that the Bantu of eastern Uganda were settling there, similar developments were taking place further east in Buluyia. The Abaluyia also are a hybrid community founded by people of different origins and cultures. The earliest settlers in the northern half of Buluyia were of Kalenjin origin. By the beginning of the seventeenth century, the ancestors of the Kalenjin had migrated from their original homes and settled on Mount Elgon.

Some time later, the migrants staged a second dispersal which ultimately gave rise to the present Kalenjin septs—the Nandi, Kipsigis, Tugen, Suk, Marakwet, and the Elgeyo. Those who remained behind in the Elgon area became the ancestors of the present Kony, Bongomek, and Bok or Sebeyi of the same district. They still retain their original language and culture. On the other hand, a few of them were completely Bantuised. They include the present Abatachoni, Abashieni of South Marama, and Abamulembo, Abanashieni and Abatobe of Wanga. Thus by about A.D. 1598 to 1625, northern Buluyia was already inhabited by people of Kalenjin origin. On the other hand, the south was largely unoccupied except for isolated Bantu communities in four of the locations. Traditional evidence suggests that many of the clans of the Abaluyia were founded by people from a country vaguely called *Misri* (Egypt). The only district which fits the description is the Lake Rudolf area. They subsequently settled in eastern Uganda.

The period between about eight and twelve generations ago, A.D. 1598 to 1733, saw large-scale immigration from the Bantu areas of eastern Uganda and Buganda. The ancestors of the majority of the present occupants of the locations of Tiriki, Wanga, Bukhayo, Samia, Marama, and Bunyore, parts of Kabras, Butsotso, Maragoli and Marachi arrived about this time. By about ten generations ago, A.D. 1652 to 1679, the migration from southern Busoga, Bunyole, and parts of southern Bugishu was virtually over. Some of the migrants settled in central Nyanza from where they moved further north on the appearance of the Luo. The migration from eastern Uganda seems to have been caused by dynastic and domestic disputes, overcrowding, tsetse flies and sleeping sickness, and the desire for a better country.

Between about eleven and thirteen generations ago, A.D.

1571 to 1652, a small column of Masai or Nandi came from the eastern direction and settled in Idakho. They were later Bantuised and lost their original language and culture. Their descendants (variously called Abashimuli, Abamuli, Abashisa and Abashirotsa) today live in Idakho, Kisa, Bunyore, Gem and Tiriki locations. Some of the Abamani and Abakhobole of Gem and Kisa belong to this group. By about eight generations ago, 1706 to 1733, the southern half of the country had been settled. Some of the immigrants came from Ankole (e.g. Abamuyima of Wanga) and the Mount Elgon area (i.e. those of Kalenjin origin). A few others, especially in the Port Victoria area, were of Luo origin. The earliest immigrants arrived between about 1463 and 1625.

As already seen, by the beginning of the seventeenth century, the ancestors of the Bagishu, Bamasaba and Babukusu had settled in Bugishu and the Tororo district. They were living as a single united community. However, between about six and eight generations ago, A.D. 1706 to 1787, the Teso invaded their settlements in eastern Uganda and dispersed them. The majority of them moved farther north and joined their kinsmen in modern Bugishu. Others scattered all over western Kenya—Samia, Bunyala, Marachi, Bukhayo, Isukha and Buholo. A few others went to Ebwayi, Amukura hill and to Bukusu hill. Nevertheless, it was not until four or six generations ago, around 1760 to 1841, that the Teso greatly increased in population (they were joined by others from Kumi and Soroti), expanded into the border territories of Amukura and Ebwayi, and forced the great majority of the Babukusu into their present settlements in Buluyia.

It was also due to the Teso invasion that the ancestors of the Abanyala (Navakholo) left their homes in Buyemba (then occupied by the Bagishu, Babukusu, etc.) and settled in present-day Bunyala (Navakholo). Some of the Abanyala are of Masai origin. Thus by the second half of the nineteenth century, the long process of immigration into Buluyia was virtually complete.

About this time too, the present country of the Abagusii and related peoples to the south of the Kavirondo Gulf was being settled. The history of this district is still uncertain because incomplete. This particularly applies to the migrations of the Abagusii before their settlement in their present country. Nevertheless, according to linguistic evidence, the Abagusii have their closest affinities with the Abalogoli section of the

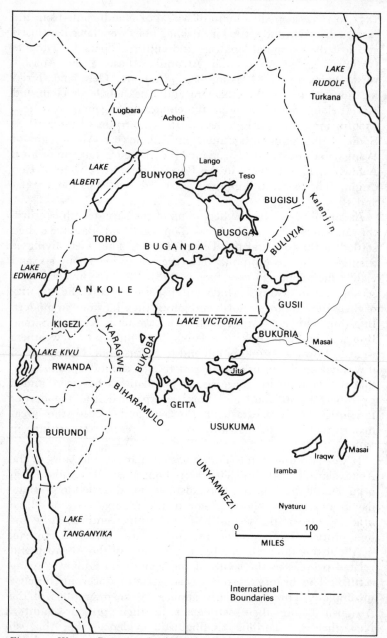

Figure 19 Western Bantu peoples and their neighbours

Abaluyia, the Bakuria (Batende), and the Kikuyu. Traditional evidence indicates that at least some of the clans of the Abagusii and the Abalogoli are related. The traditions of the Abalogoli suggest that their ancestors immediately came from the southern part of Uganda. This was after their supposed migration from the mysterious '*Misri*' to the Congo. On reaching Rusinga Island, some of the migrants travelled northwards, crossed the Kavirondo Gulf, and settled in the present Luo locations of Kisumu and Seme. They became the ancestors of the Abalogoli. The second group settled to the south of the Kavirondo Gulf and became the ancestors of the Abagusii. On the other hand, Abagusii traditions indicate that their ancestors moved from Mount Elgon to the Nandi Hills. While the Abalogoli remained here, the Abagusii subsequently moved farther south into the Kano Plains.

The earliest settlers seem to have arrived between about A.D. 1463 and 1571 and settled in the Kano Plains. Due to famine and pressure from the Masai and the Luo, they left the Kano Plains about 1760 and settled in Gelegele. Thus by about the end of the eighteenth century, the Abagusii had settled in their present country. Some time between about 1790 and 1820, the Abagusii sections of Kitutu, South Mugirango, Wanjari, Bassi, and Majoge fled to the north of the Kavirondo Gulf under separate leaders. The flight was presumably caused by mounting pressure from their Masai neighbours. After about thirty years, they all recrossed the gulf, again individually. As a result of these movements, intermarriage, and the arrival of new immigrants of diverse origins such as the Masai, Kipsigis and the Luo, people became very much mixed. Furthermore, in the first half of the eighteenth century, more settlers arrived from southern Buganda and Busoga and settled on Mfangano and Rusinga Islands. Later, however, they moved to Gwassi on the mainland where they became the ancestors of some of the Abasuba community.

Western Bantu Religious Beliefs and Political Organisation

Although religion played an important role in the day-to-day life of the Western Bantu peoples, it was generally at the family level. This form of religion, which has been called 'ancestor worship', is still active to this day in many areas. The whole basis of this religion was a strong belief in the continuity of human life—life after death. It was this belief which gave rise to the idea that though a man might die physically, he would, all the same, continue to protect and care for his family, relatives and even friends. The deceased thus became the guardian angel of the living, particularly of the family. He was supposed to see to their welfare and to protect them against the evil actions and intentions of their enemies. Such enemies, or supposed evil-doers, might themselves be dead or alive.

The very fact that the dead could still protect or harm the living necessitated the latter's taking appropriate measures. They resorted to sacrifices of all sorts and for diverse purposes. In many areas each clan or village had a leading sacrificial priest. Similarly, each family had an elder who performed sacrificial duties at the family level. Periodically sacrifices were offered to good spirits as a gesture of gratitude and an expression of good-will. In contrast, evil spirits were usually expiated, again through sacrifices. The latter was particularly the case where the people concerned had a reason to believe that their calamity, mis-fortune, or ill health was the work of the evil spirit of a particular person. Again, the good spirit of one of the ancestors might be appealed to for intercession should some evil spirits be suspected of malicious and harmful intentions or acts.

It would, however, appear that the ancestral spirits were primarily regarded as influential and authoritative agents or media. In other words, despite their supposed ability to give help or harm, their powers were actually limited. For, through-out this whole region, there was a vague belief in the power of the omnipotent Creator who was in complete control of all life and the elements. The sun, the moon, a river, a mountain, or even a hill might personify such a being. Again, throughout the region, there was a general belief in minor gods—the god of the river, the god of the lake, etc. However, all these gods were vague, remote and impersonal, unlike the guardian spirits of the ancestors. Ancestor worship was, therefore, a religion whose twin aims were the satisfaction of the spiritual and physical needs of a particular family, clan, or village. It was founded on practical and more immediate considerations—fear of the un-known, a desire to protect the lives and the welfare of the people, and a genuine belief in the continuity of life without which ancestor worship would have been needless and irrelevant.

Broadly speaking, the political world of the Western Bantu

was characterised by two types of government. In the interlacustrine region, as we have noted, there were centralised
states and principalities. Elsewhere in Buluyia (except the
Wanga Kingdom), Gusii, and Bugishu, the clan was the effective
unit of government. In Buluyia, for example, the Abaluyia
consist of about eighteen major sub-tribes, each of several
clans. In pre-colonial days, the clan was an effective political,
social and economic unit: it chose its own allies or enemies,
fought its wars, sometimes with the aid of its allies, and legislated
for its people. Clan elders appointed a leading, influential, wise,
and impartial elder to take charge of the affairs of the clan,
variously called *omwami, omukali, omukhulundu, omukasa,
weng'oma,* etc. While the office was hereditary in some areas,
in others it was elective. Again, this clan leader might be subject
to deposition in one area while in another he was not.

The functions of the *omwami* were numerous. He had to
protect the people, maintain law, order and peace, and generally
attend to the welfare of his people. In many areas he also settled
cases and received the fees. Throughout, however, he had the
help of a council of elders. The council advised him on all
important matters such as land disputes, inheritance, the interpretation of customary law, and the settlement of criminal and
civil cases. In return the *omwami* received payment, usually
in kind, e.g. meat, grain, and beer. Thus though a society of
this kind did not attain to a centralised state transcending family
or clan ties, it had its own government and laws.

By far the best example of the second type of political organisation, i.e. the centralised state, was Buganda. In Buganda as
in the rest of the interlacustrine states, the king (*kabaka*) was
the effective ruler. Among other things, the royal insignia
consisted of drums, stools, and spears. As the state was composed of clans of diverse origins, it was bound together by
allegiance to the ruler and, through him, to the state. Despite
the dynastic civil wars at the end of each reign, the office of
kabaka was hereditary.

The *kabaka* ruled with the help and advice of the *lukiko*
(legislative council). In the provinces and districts he was
represented by his agents. The *katikiro* (chief minister) was the
most important commoner in the state. He was directly responsible to the king. Under the *katikiro* was a complex chain of
officials graded in importance, among them court officials,
county chiefs, county agents, court servants, pages and messen-

gers. By the close of the eighteenth century the majority of the
county chiefs and agents were appointive rather than hereditary.
This was a source of great strength and influence to the monarchy
for the ruler had virtual control over the appointment and dis-
missal of leading servants.

Unlike the first category of political organisation, the
centralised states were generally much bigger. This does not
apply to several principalities of Busoga, some of which equalled
the clan in size. Due to the size of the centralised states which
necessitated an efficient machinery of government, the kingdom
had to be sub-divided into counties and sub-counties. This was
particularly the case with Buganda. The counties and sub-
counties were directly ruled by appointed chiefs and the entire
kingdom legislated for by a common *lukiko*. The administration
which resulted from this complex organisation was highly
efficient, if rather ruthless and autocratic.

Further reading

ROSCOE, J. *The Northern Bantu,* Cambridge, 1915.

ROSCOE, J. *The Bagesu,* Cambridge, 1924.

ROSCOE, J. *The Baganda,* London, 1911.

ROSCOE, J. *The Bakitara,* Cambridge, 1923.

BEATTIE, J. *Bunyoro, An African Kingdom,* Oxford, 1960.

DUNBAR, A. R. *A History of Bunyoro—Kitara,* Oxford, 1965.

MORRIS, H. F. *A History of Ankole,* Nairobi, 1962.

CORY, H. *Historia ya Wilaya Bukoba (History of the Bukoba
District),* Mwanza.

CORY, H. *The Ntemi, Traditional Rites of a Sukuma Chief
in Tanganyika,* London, 1951.

LUBOGO, Y. K. *A History of Busoga,* Kampala, 1960.

RICHARDS, A. I. (Ed.), *East African Chiefs,* London, 1960.

FALLERS, L. A. *Bantu Bureaucracy,* Cambridge, 1956.

LA FONTAINE, J. S. *The Gisu of Uganda,* Ethnographic Survey
of Africa, East Central Africa, Part X, London, 1959.

ROBERTSON, D. W. *The Historical Considerations Contributing to the Soga System of Land Tenure*, Kampala, 1940.

BARKER, E. E. *A Short History of Nyanza*, Nairobi, 1958.

WHITELEY, W. H. *The Tense System of the Gusii*, East African Linguistic Studies, No. 4, 1960.

MAYER, P. *The Lineage Principle in Gusii Society*, London, 1949.

WAGNER, G. *The Bantu of North Kavirondo*, London, 1949.

OSOGO, J. *A History of the Baluyia*, Oxford, 1966.

GOLDTHORPE, J. E. and WILSON, F. B. *Tribal Maps of East Africa and Zanzibar*, Kampala, 1960.

WERE, G. S. *A History of the Abaluyia of Western Kenya c. 1500-1930*, Nairobi, 1967.

WERE, G. S. *Western Kenya Historical Texts*, Nairobi, 1967.

WERE, G. S. and WILSON, D. A. *East Africa through a Thousand Years*, London, 1968.

10

The Eastern Bantu Peoples

B. G. McIntosh

The peoples of eastern Kenya and north-eastern Tanzania who speak Bantu languages are the subject of this chapter. As major groups, they comprise the Kikuyu, Meru, Kamba, Pokomo, Bajun, Nyika, Taita, Pare, Shambaa and Chagga. The evidence for their history is disparate and often conflicting. Linguistic analysis has provided a degree of insight into the distant past, but archaeologists have yet to provide sufficient radiocarbon dates for the Bantu period in the eastern interior of East Africa. Oral traditions are therefore the main source of evidence for the period covered by this chapter, but both in quantity and quality they are unevenly distributed and present serious problems of interpretation. Hence, in the attempt to reconstruct the history of the Eastern Bantu peoples to the beginning of the nineteenth century, and for the purposes of communication and clarity, certain basic themes have been accepted and emphasised. These are: that the Eastern Bantu, like all Bantu-speaking peoples, are descended from an ancient Bantu nucleus situated in northern Katanga; that from this area their ancestors expanded in force to occupy the East African coast between Lamu and the River Juba; and finally that from the thirteenth century A.D. their more immediate ancestors began to migrate out of this northern coastal settlement area into lower coastal regions and into the interior.

The Eastern Bantu Background

To place the Eastern Bantu peoples in historical perspective, it is necessary to begin by examining in brief the wider problem of the Bantu expansion. A theory of expansion in four stages has been suggested* which is based upon a preference for Malcolm Guthrie's linguistic scheme, but which accommodates that of J. H. Greenberg in modified form as concerning the initial stage of the expansion. The four stages are as follows:

1. At some period towards the end of the first millenium B.C., a small group of 'pre-Bantu' speakers migrated from an area in the central Cameroons. They travelled by canoe along the Ubangi River to the Middle Congo and then up the River Kasai until they came to the light woodlands south of the Congo forest. Here they found an environment which corresponded ecologically to the area from which they had come. There was good rainfall, plentiful fishing and hunting, hardy cereals for cultivation, and rich deposits of iron ore.

2. The second stage extended in the first millenium A.D., and is referred to as the 'proto-Bantu' period. It was here, in the Bantu nucleus in Northern Katanga that the parent Bantu language was formed and the first rapid expansion of population took place. The eleusine millets and sorghums which had been introduced into the area at an earlier stage by Cushitic-speaking peoples were cultivated, and iron was fashioned into tools and weapons. The result of expansion within the nucleus was a movement of peoples west to the Atlantic coast and east to the Indian Ocean coast.

3. Between about A.D. 400 and 1000, the proto-Bantu expanded from the broad coast-to-coast belt occupied during the second stage into high-rainfall areas such as the inter-lacustrine regions of East Africa, the Shona area of south-central Africa, and the humid East African coastal belt. The dynamic force behind this new stage of expansion was an unprecedented rate of population growth based upon a food-producing revolution. The proto-Bantu in this stage had acquired south-east Asian food plants, especially the banana and the Asian yams. These had been introduced on the East African coast following the Indonesian colonisation of Madagascar in the early Christian centuries and had spread to the Bantu area along the line of the

---

*ROLAND OLIVER, 'The Problem of the Bantu Expansion', *Journal of African History*, VII (1966).

Zambesi valley. Cultivated in areas of high rainfall, these food plants were capable of supporting dense populations. Conquest by the iron spear undoubtedly played a part in this expansion, but it was the superior rate of population increase which permitted the proto-Bantu to occupy new and wider territories. In the east, impelled by the food-producing revolution, and in possession of iron weapons and the Indonesian outrigger canoe, the ancestors of the Eastern Bantu peoples had penetrated the coastal belt as far north as the Juba River by the tenth century. References to the *Zanji* in Al Mas'udi (about A.D. 915) are the earliest documentary evidence of proto-Bantu presence on the northern coast. The main area of settlement lay between Lamu and the Juba; this was once a fertile area but became semi-desert as a result of more recent occupation by pastoralists.

4. The fourth and final stage of the Bantu expansion belongs to the present millennium. Broadly speaking, the surplus populations created in the areas occupied during the third stage moved into the remaining areas of modern Bantu Africa. Such areas were the dry centres of east, central, south and south-west Africa, and the extremely humid regions of the equatorial forest — areas which were less well-suited to the cultivation of Bantu food plants. In these areas the rate of occupation was much slower and the absorption of established inhabitants was less complete. It is at this stage that, for the purposes of this chapter, the history of the Eastern Bantu peoples begins.

The Shungwaya Settlement Area

Most of the Eastern Bantu peoples have traditions of migration from an area north of the Tana River, and in this context the name, Shungwaya, frequently occurs. Under a variety of spellings, Shungwaya appears on a few old maps: J. H. Van Linschoten (1596), Willem Blaeu (1662), de la Feuille (1700), Ogilby (1700), Rebmann (1850) and Rebmann and Erhardt (1856). The pre-1700 maps plot it as a coastal town, but the later ones show it as an area-name. All locate it roughly in the vicinity of the present Port Durnford Bay. Shungwaya, however, is a Bantu word meaning 'to be driven a long way', and is therefore a secondary name for an earlier homeland. Thus, the early cartographers were mistaken in showing it as a single town. It seems much more reasonable to suppose that Shungwaya was a general settlement area, and that its peoples had connections with a number of towns along the coast.

Fragments of information about the coastal peoples of the Shungwaya area may be gleaned from early written accounts of the East African coast. The *Chronicle of Kilwa* records the story of al-Hasan ibn Ali Sultan of Shiraz in Persia who came to the East African coast with six sons and a band of followers to found settlements, and whose son, Ali, became the first ruler of Kilwa in A.D. 956. This legend is deservedly treated with scepticism by archaeologists and coastal historians as having been acquired by certain peoples for its status value. At the same time, it may be regarded as a mythical representation of genuine Persian (Shirazi) settlements on the East African coast—Shungwaya being one of the areas to receive Persian immigrants at an early stage of its development. Al Mas'udi, writing in the tenth century, describes the negroid *Zanji* as worshippers of many kinds of totem, and of ancestral spirits, but who believed in a god called *Maliknajlu*. There was in addition, he notes, a ruler whom the *Zanji* believed to be the son of their god. In the twelfth-century writings of Al Idrisi, the coast still appears to have been predominantly non-Muslim; he mentions, for example, that pillars are worshipped in Brava. Unfortunately, none of the early geographers has any clear information on the peoples of the hinterland.

From these written accounts, from oral traditions, and from inference, it is possible to speculate on the general nature of the Shungwaya culture. This culture—*Kishuru* in its ancient appellation—probably flourished between the twelfth and the fifteenth centuries. It was derived from the intermixing of a proto-Bantu majority with Persian, Arab and possibly Indian immigrants, and with Cushitic-speaking pastoralists from the Horn of Africa. The proto-Bantu were mainly agriculturalists and may have been organised in a confederacy with local leaders and possibly a single paramount chief. The Digo say that at the time of the exodus from Shungwaya all tribes were ruled by a *mfalme* or king who later went with a body of warriors to occupy the slopes of Kilimanjaro. Similarly, the Segeju say that in Shungwaya a single chief ruled them with the Bajun, Somali, Galla and Barawa. Nearer the coast, the proto-Bantu fell within the political and commercial influence of the towns. This may have been an earlier pattern of the system which prevailed in post-Shungwaya days when political ties bound the Segeju to Vanga, the Giriama to Mombasa, and the Rabai to Malindi and Jomvu. The development of trade (Mas'udi lays his emphasis on ivory, Idrisi on iron) resulted in a vigorous commercial life amongst the proto-Bantu at the coast, and their contact with foreign immigrants in turn produced the urban commercial sector of the Shungwaya population. In addition to the farmers and townsmen, there was a section of herdsmen which was descended from proto-Somali immigrants from the north.

In ethnic terms, two main stages of formation may be said to have taken place. First, with the arrival of Persian immigrants and their absorption into the proto-Bantu living between the Juba and the Pokomoni Creek opposite Lamu, the formation began of populations of townsmen and of farmers and fishermen. The proto-Digo may have been amongst those most influenced by the Persians, whilst the rural peoples comprised the ancestors of the Lower Pokomo, Taita, Bajun, Kamba and Northern Nyika. The peoples least affected by Persian influences were the ancestors of the Kikuyu. The second stage of ethnic formation began with the arrival from the north of the proto-Somali pastoralists, and the result of their contact with the Shungwaya peoples was the emergence of the ancestors of the Segeju, Meru and Tharaka. By this time, however, the proto-Pokomo, Kikuyu, and Kamba had already departed from Shungwaya.

It is possible that some Galla groups had co-existed peacefully with the Shungwaya peoples. But with the arrival of the proto-Somali and the spread of cattle-keeping in the area, the traditional enmity between the two Cushitic-speaking peoples resulted in civil war and Galla attacks of increasing intensity. By the sixteenth century, if not earlier, Shungwaya was subjected to full-scale Galla invasion, and in the early seventeenth century the Galla raided as far south as the Kilifi Creek. This was the setting for the migrations from Shungwaya. A chain reaction of displacement took place with a general movement of peoples to the coast south of the Tana, and from the coast into the interior. If one may argue a connection between secondary Shirazi traditions of the Swahili coast and the Shungwaya traditions, it is possible that the so-called Shirazi were the upper classes of the Shungwaya towns who migrated further south by sea at the same time as the ancestors of the modern Eastern Bantu peoples were migrating by land.

The Traditions of Migration

In this section, the various traditions relating to migration are reviewed. The traditions of certain peoples have been investigated fairly thoroughly in the past, whilst those of others have as yet been examined very lightly or not at all. It is, however, impossible in the space of one chapter to give more than the main outline of the traditions, but an attempt is made to co-ordinate them into a reasonable historical framework. The theme of a common origin for all peoples in the Shungwaya area is maintained throughout although future co-operative research may result in certain modifications of this theme.

1. The Peoples of the North-eastern Highlands

It was suggested earlier that the proto-Kamba and proto-Kikuyu had left the Shungwaya settlement area before the arrival of the proto-Somali and before the start of the Galla invasions. Kamba traditions, it is true, do not mention Shungwaya. The peoples of eastern Ukamba say that their ancestors came across the River Athi from Ulu, while the peoples in the west around Ulu say that their ancestors came from Kilimanjaro. Meantime it is maintained by the peoples in the south around Kikumbuliu that they originally came from Taita, while the peoples in the north around Mumoni claim that they originally came from Giriama country. The idea that the proto-Kamba moved into their part of the eastern highlands directly from the south may be discounted. It is more consistent with Eastern Bantu traditions as a whole to argue that the proto-Kamba came down the coast from north of the Tana, one section entering modern Ukamba directly from the coast above the River Sabaki, and the others arriving via Taita and Kilimanjaro. After their arrival, the peoples of the north-west mixed with proto-Kikuyu and proto-Tharaka, and there may be an admixture of proto-Segeju in the Kamba peoples dating from the time when the former were temporarily settled in *Dhaicho*—an old name for north-eastern Ukamba.

Similarly, amongst the Kikuyu peoples there are no traditional references to Shungwaya. It has been suggested that their ancestors too entered the highlands from the south by following the line of the River Athi. But a popular legend of creation points to a dispersal area nearer to Mount Kenya at *Mũkũrwe wa*

Gathanga in the Nyeri district. More specifically, it was apparent to travellers in the nineteenth century that the Kikuyu peoples were in the final stages of their expansion through the forest from the north. Hence it is not unreasonable to suppose that the proto-Kikuyu were the descendants of early Shungwaya peoples who moved up the Tana, settling initially in Mbere country south-east of Mount Kenya. H. E. Lambert has tentatively dated their arrival in the north at about A.D. 1400 and in the Kiambu area about 1800. In their expansion south-wards, the proto-Kikuyu absorbed Dorobo hunters but com-pensated them for the loss of their lands. Another pre-existing people to be absorbed were the Gumba—the most ancient inhabitants of the Mount Kenya forest. The Gumba seem to have pursued a sedentary way of life, and they are recalled in Kikuyu traditions as clever dwarfs who lived in underground tunnels.

The proto-Meru arrived in the Mount Kenya region con-siderably later than the proto-Kikuyu peoples. The likelihood that they were descended from contact in the Shungwaya area between proto-Bantu and proto-Somali has already been stated, and their occupation of the country north-east of Mount Kenya is estimated as having occurred about A.D. 1750. It appears that they departed from Shungwaya in the company of a number of other peoples, for example the proto-Digo and Segeju. In Meru traditions, reference is made to a period when the ancestors lived as subjects of a fair-skinned people near to 'the great water' south-east of Meru country, the name of the place being given as *Mbwa*. From here they migrated in response to attacks by the *Nguntuni* and settled for a period at *Urumba* or *Ugairo*. The latter name may correspond to the *Kirao* resettlement area which is mentioned in the traditions of the Digo, Segeju and Kilindini. In this area, between Lamu and the Lower Tana, the proto-Meru branched off from the proto-Digo and Segeju and com-menced their migration further into the interior. Mention is made of the crossing of a wide river (obviously the Tana) in two parties. One crossed at dawn and the other in full daylight, the time of crossing giving rise to the description of the clans of one party as 'red' and those of the other as 'white'. After the crossing, the proto-Meru divided into several groups. One, the Tharaka, remained close to the Tana, and the others, the Mwimbi, Imenti, Tigania and Igembe moved into the present Meru country. Absorption took place of Dorobo (or *Athi* as they are sometimes called) and clashes occurred between the immigrants and a cattle-keeping people who were probably Borana Galla and whom the Meru call *Mwoko*.

Tharaka traditions are very similar to those of the Meru peoples. The ancestors once lived at *Mbwa* near the sea and arrived in Tharaka country from *Ugairo*. One part of the proto-Tharaka came from Meru, and the other at a later date from *Ugairo*, possibly as an offshoot of the proto-Pokomo. The original inhabitants of Tharaka were the *Njuwe*, who correspond to the *Mwoko* of the Meru, and who were absorbed through intermarriage.

In Chuka traditions there are only vague references to migrations by some families up the Tana. The proto-Chuka are believed to have absorbed Gumba forest-dwellers and to have intermarried with proto-Tharaka and the Mwimbi group of the proto-Meru. Embu traditions, likewise, give no clear information about early migrations. The proto-Embu may have been an offshoot of the proto-Kikuyu column of migrants who settled in Embu country about A.D. 1425. But the only migrations recalled with certainty are those by Kikuyu, Meru and other surrounding peoples into Embuland—usually times of famine—in the nineteenth century.

2. The Coastal Peoples

The proto-Bajun emerged in the Shungwaya area during the early stages of ethnic formation as a rural people whose main pursuits were agriculture and fishing. At a later stage, a pastoralist element was added as a result of contact between proto-Bajun and proto-Somali. Shungwaya traditions are very clear and numerous amongst the Bajun, but no mention is made of *Kirao*. This is reasonable since the Bajun today still live north of Lamu, and clearly in the period of migration the advance of the proto-Bajun stopped short of *Kirao*. It would seem, therefore, that the proto-Bajun were more successful than other Shungwaya peoples in withstanding Galla attacks. This may have been so because of the absorption of an Arab group which reinforced their strength. The modern Bajun thus comprise three elements: the descendants of the original proto-Bajun; the Katwa who are akin to the Somali; and those who are of more recent Arab descent.

Amongst the Pokomo, only the Buu peoples have a tradition actually naming Shungwaya as an earlier dwelling place. It is said that their ancestor, Sango Vere, had settled in the Tana district long before the arrival of the Galla. But the Pokomo as a whole have traditions of migration from the north towards the bed of an old river. This old river may have been a tributary of the Tana which flowed into the Pokomoni Creek opposite Lamu. After settling in the area between the Pokomoni Creek and the lower reaches of the Tana, the proto-Pokomo were joined by the advance sections of the proto-Segeju. This caused them to move further south to the Ozi-Tana delta. One section of the proto-Pokomo apparently continued in the company of the proto-Rabai to Kilimanjaro but returned to the Tana later. The main body of the proto-Pokomo proceeded to occupy the banks of the Tana as far upriver as point 39° east. In the Lower Tana region the proto-Pokomo intermarried with Swahili, and further north Sanye hunters were absorbed and intermarriage took place with sedentary Galla.

According to Digo traditions, the proto-Digo fled from Shungwaya at the same time as the proto-Segeju. This may have been in the late fifteenth or early sixteenth century. In a manner similar to that of the other displaced peoples, a resettlement was made at *Kirao*. With renewed Galla pressure, the migrations continued. Some of the *Kirao* peoples remained behind at the Tana, others went to Kilimanjaro, whilst others again went to the Mombasa area where they built two strongholds. From here the proto-Digo moved to the modern Digo area where they were joined by a section of proto-Rabai in the eighteenth century.

After leaving Shungwaya and settling temporarily at *Kirao*, the proto-Segeju migrated to Mangea Hill near Malindi. At this point they are recorded in Portuguese writings as a fast-moving, cattle-keeping, warlike people who finally checked the advance from the south of the fearsome Zimba warriors by defeating them at the siege of Malindi in the closing years of the sixteenth century. Under pressure once more from the Galla, the Segeju ancestors dispersed into a wide area known as *Dhaicho*, thought to comprise north-eastern Ukamba and the bend of the Upper Tana. Here also they clashed with the enemy and were forced to split into three groups: one was absorbed amongst the Kamba; another migrated to Bwiti in Southern Usambara; and the final group went down the Tana and followed the coast until they arrived in their present area where they intermarried with Digo and Swahili.

The history of the Swahili, with all of its foreign connections, lies outside the scope of this chapter. Nevertheless, the Kilindini, who together with the Mvita, form the original stock of the Mombasa Swahili, have Shungwaya traditions similar to those of the Digo and Segeju. The Kilindini claim that in the exodus from Shungwaya the Digo and Segeju were their subjects. They settled first at *Kirao* and then moved to Mombasa, apparently before the Portuguese occupied the island. This is rather unlikely since the proto-Segeju were at Malindi only in the 1580's, and since the Kilindini themselves admit that they were vassals of the Portuguese when they built their walled town on Mombasa. In later years the Kilindini were joined by other *Kirao* peoples, for example sections of the proto-Duruma.

The original Duruma left Shungwaya and arrived in their present habitat via Malindi. They claim to have occupied Gedi for a period and to have lost most of their fighting men in a Galla attack upon that town. From Gedi a forced march was made to the present Duruma country behind Mombasa. Inter-mixing took place with an earlier Sanye people, known as *Ndigiri,* with *Makua* (African soldiers attached to Portuguese garrisons) in the Port Reitz area, and with Kamba, some of whom became unassimilated settlers in Duruma country.

The proto-Rabai were a part of the peoples who migrated from Shungwaya, and in the early seventeenth century, a people called the *Rabai* are mentioned in Portuguese records as living in the hinterland north of Mombasa. The Rabai claim, however, that their ancestors went first to Kilimanjaro and returned from there to their present country during the first half of the seventeenth century. It is possible, therefore, that the section of the proto-Digo who reached Kilimanjaro may have been the ancestors of the Rabai who rejoined their own people at the coast. After the reunion, three groups emerged: one joined the Digo, another the Pokomo, and the third became the Rabai proper. In later stages of development, the Rabai absorbed much foreign blood owing to the position of Rabai Kaya as a famous market.

Ribe, Kauma, Kambe, Chonyi and Jibana are all closely interrelated, and are mixed also with Rabai, Digo and Duruma. They all have Shungwaya traditions, but claims and counter-claims are made as to order of precedence in the sequence of migrations. The Kambe, for example, whose tradition of previous age-classes suggests a departure around 1550, claim that at the time of the exodus they were already a separate tribe and not part of a larger group of peoples. The Kauma say that they arrived south of the Sabaki after the Segeju but before the Rabai and Duruma. Of all the smaller Nyika tribes, it may be said, therefore, that their ancestors were included amongst the larger columns of peoples migrating from Shungwaya in the sixteenth century.

The ancestors of the Giriama, together with the proto-Taita, are believed to have been the last to depart from Shungwaya. According to genealogical evidence, this may have been in the early seventeenth century. The proto-Giriama migrated to the Taita Hills, but returned later to occupy Mangea Hill near Malindi. The Galla forced them to retreat to Ribe country, but by the nineteenth century the Giriama had moved back to Mangea and were slowly expanding into the area between the Sabaki and Tana rivers. In this process they had absorbed Sanye hunters and intermarried with other Nyika peoples and even Galla.

3. The Peoples of the South-eastern Highlands

Taita traditions make no specific reference to Shungwaya, but in the mid-nineteenth century the German missionary and explorer, Johann Rebmann, was informed by the Taita peoples that their ancestors came from thirty days' journey north beyond the Tana River. From a comparison of the traditions of the Taita and Giriama peoples, it appears that the ancestors of both travelled down the coast together. However it is not clear whether the arrivals of the proto-Taita and proto-Giriama in the Taita Hills coincided. The proto-Taita are said to have divided into three sections after being forced to leave Mangea during a period of renewed Galla attacks. The three sections arrived in the Taita Hills about two hundred years ago, but from different directions. Towards the end of the eighteenth century, groups of Taita peoples moved to the Taveta forest and thus became the main stock of the modern Taveta. Earlier Dorobo-like inhabitants called *Mbisha* were absorbed and settlers came in from Kamba and Masai countries.

During the eighteenth century, there was an onward migration

of proto-Taita into the areas now inhabited by the Chagga, Pare
and Shambaa peoples. There were earlier inhabitants to be
absorbed, and it is possible that amongst these may be counted
the remnant peoples left by those sections of the proto-Kamba,
Pokomo, Rabai, Digo, Giriama and Segeju who are said to have
visited the Kilimanjaro area before the occupation by proto-
Taita groups. In more recent times, the Chagga, Pare and
Shambaa areas attracted Kamba and Masai-speaking settlers,
and others from areas such as the Usambara Mountains, the
Ngu Hills, and Unyamwezi.

From this review of the various traditions of migration, it is
possible to suggest that the order of departure from Shungwaya
of the ancestors of the Eastern Bantu peoples was as follows:
first, at an early stage, the Pokomo, Kamba and Kikuyu; then,
during the period of the Galla invasions, the Digo, Segeju and
Meru, followed by the Giriama and Taita. It would be too
simple, however, to assume that the migrations from Shungwaya
took place in close succession, or that the migrants moved
swiftly through empty lands. The departures from Shungwaya
of the proto-Pokomo, Kamba and Kikuyu may be said to belong
to the thirteenth and fourteenth and those of the Nyika, Meru
and Taita to the fifteenth and sixteenth centuries. In the course
of the migrations several temporary resettlements were made at
Kirao and at other places, and many peoples took circuitous
routes and retraced their steps before settling permanently. And
finally, although the Eastern Bantu were multiplying in numbers
more rapidly than any other peoples, the process of absorption
of pre-existing peoples and of expansion into their modern
habitats was far from complete at the start of the nineteenth
century.

Developments to the Beginning of the Nineteenth Century

Having reviewed the traditions of migration amongst the Eastern
Bantu peoples, we turn to the developments which stemmed
from their penetration and settlement of the coastal and inland
areas. One of the first developments (discussed more fully in
Chapters 3 and 4 above) was the establishment of large, well-
organised, iron-using, and cultivating populations where none
had existed on such a scale before. The earlier inhabitants were

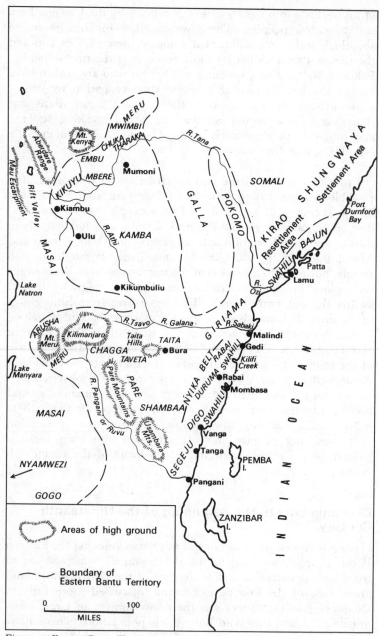

Figure 20 Eastern Bantu Territory c. 1800

absorbed or relegated to the status of insignificant minorities by peoples who were both exploiting and altering their environment. Only a few survivors of the earlier inhabitants of East Africa remain today, for example the Dorobo and Sanye in Kenya, and the Hadzapi and Sandawe near Lake Eyasi in Tanzania.

Further developments, particularly with regard to social and political organisation, resulted from contact and interaction between the settled agriculturalists and pastoralists such as the Galla and the Masai-speaking peoples. (The map which accompanies this chapter shows a Galla penetration between the territories of the Pokomo and the Kamba peoples, and a long strip of Masai territory lying adjacent to that of the peoples of the north-eastern and south-eastern highlands.) In the interlacustrine regions to the north-west, interaction between Bantu agriculturalists and immigrant pastoralists was of a very high degree of intensity, and a main result of this interaction was the formation of states. East of the Rift Valley, the interaction was of a lower intensity, and the results were of a different nature.*

Broadly speaking, the Eastern Bantu peoples adopted in varying degrees from the pastoralists their systems of age-sets and age-grades, their ideas on descent and inheritance (patrilinearity—calculated through the father's side of the family), their initiation rites, and some of their weapons, ornaments and hairstyles. The pastoralists maintained their own way of life to a large extent, but some of them exchanged it for the Bantu sedentary existence and changed to agriculture. The Arusha peoples to the west of Mount Meru, for example, are Masai-speaking but both in economy and in culture they closely resemble their Bantu-speaking neighbours.

No states were formed east of the Rift Valley. The Eastern Bantu peoples retained and developed the original Bantu characteristic of a well-ordered system of authority not through rule by chiefs or kings but based upon territorial allegiances and operated by councils of elders. Amongst the elders, an individual distinguished by wealth, wisdom, and probably a record of military achievement, could rise to a position of prominence

---

*The theory of important developments resulting from the interaction between agriculturalists and pastoralists is used here to express a general tendency rather than an absolute or sharply-defined process. For fuller treatment of this subject, see Chapter 4 above.

and leadership. It would appear, however, that such a person was not more than 'first amongst equals' with regard to his fellow elders.

Exceptions to this general rule were to be found amongst the Chagga and Shambaa peoples. It has been suggested that in their cases ruling houses emerged as a result of external influences. A ritual form of kingship, originating in the northern interlacustrine region as early as the 15th Century, was carried southwards to the Western Bantu peoples of modern Tanzania. From their homelands, diluted into the form of *Ntemi* chieftainships, the political institution was carried eastwards to the Chagga and Shambaa in the 18th Century, either as a result of a population expansion amongst the Nyamwezi, or by Nyamwezi trading chiefs on their journeys to the east coast. Recent research has, however, indicated that the Nyamwezi did not trade with the coast until after 1800. And the results of further recent research amongst the Sukuma and Pare tend to disprove the older 'diffusionist' theories, and to lay greater stress upon internal developments within a society as factors making for change and development. Furthermore, whilst the institution of chieftainship is recognised as being very diverse in origin, a clear distinction is now being made between the spread of ideas and institutions, and the movement of peoples.

It was mentioned earlier that there are traditional references to paramount chiefs or kings who ruled in the Shungwaya area. One wonders, therefore, why there were no such rulers amongst the Eastern Bantu peoples in post-Shungwaya days. The only possible answer is that the Galla invasions destroyed whatever political confederacy might have existed, and in general terms, that the Shungwaya culture was strained out or diluted as it was carried through different ecological backgrounds during the migrations, new features being added and old ones discarded in response to the needs of varying regional situations.

By 1800 a considerable inter-tribal and long-distance trade network existed amongst the Eastern Bantu peoples. The Kikuyu peoples, for example, augmented their livestock by supplying food to the Masai, and iron implements to the Embu and Kamba. The Pokomo, likewise, as purveyors of agricultural produce, obtained ivory from the Galla, axes and hoes from the Swahili, and bows and arrows from the Boni hunters. Inter-tribal markets could be either open or 'discrete'. In the latter case, usually between mutually hostile peoples, the exchange of goods was made in such a fashion that the groups involved never actually came face-to-face. Of the open markets, Rabai Kaya near Mombasa was probably the largest and most famous. Here, foodstuffs, livestock, hoes, baskets and cotton goods were bought and sold, and caravans of Kamba, Taita, Swahili, Dahalo and Langulu (Sanye peoples), Nyika, and even Galla, were frequent visitors. In the relations between the Nyika peoples and the Swahili towns, however, the system which prevailed was one of tribute rather than of trade. That is to say, the towns expected to be supplied with food and livestock by the surrounding peoples. Ivory and produce such as gum copal were the only items paid for in salt, iron, cloth and other goods.

In the long-distance trade, the chief carriers and middlemen between the interior and the coast were the Kamba. The Kamba operated as ivory hunters as far north as Samburu, and sold their ivory to Arab and Swahili merchants at the coast, either directly, or through Duruma and Digo agents. Commercial agreements existed between the Kamba and such peoples as the Nyika, Taita and Kikuyu which ensured the former safe passage and provisions on their journeys to and from the coast. In the nineteenth century, foreign traders found that the Kamba exercised a monopoly over the long-distance carrying trade, and were forced to employ Kamba guides before they could begin to trade with the peoples of the interior.

South of Kamba country, Kilimanjaro lay as a main provisioning point for caravans coming from Mombasa and from other towns to the south. One route led to the mountain via Taita and Taveta, and another via Southern Usambara and up the River Ruvu. From Kilimanjaro, other routes led to Lake Tanganyika and Lake Victoria. It is not unlikely, therefore, that Kilimanjaro and its peoples played a major part in the development of the inland trade upon which towns between old Malindi and Pangani flourished before the nineteenth century.

African control of trade extended into the era of firearms and foreign penetration in the nineteenth century. In the 1840's, large Kamba ivory caravans were arriving at the coast every week, and a prominent trader called Kivoi was a well-known figure in Arab circles in Mombasa. The story of trade in the nineteenth century belongs to a later chapter, but in closing, it should be noted that the trade routes followed by Arabs and Swahili had been in existence for a very long time.

Further reading

Books

BEIDELMAN, T. O. *The Matrilineal Peoples of Eastern Tanzania,*
Ethnographic Survey of Africa, London, 1967.

GREENBERG, J. H. *Studies in African Linguistic Classification,*
New Haven, 1955.

KIMAMBO, I. N. *A Political History Of the Pare,* (East Africa
Publishing House), Nairobi, 1968.

KIMAMBO, I. N. and TEMU, A. (Eds.), *History of Tanzania,*
(East Africa Publishing House), Nairobi, 1968.

LAMBERT, H. E. *Systems of Land Tenure in the Kikuyu Land
Unit, Part 1. History of the Tribal Occupation of the Land,*
Cape Town, 1950.

LINDBLOM, G. *The Akamba in British East Africa,* Uppsala,
1920.

MURDOCK, G. P. *Africa : Its Peoples and their Culture History,*
New York, 1959.

OLIVER, R. and MATHEW, G. (Eds.), *History of East Africa*
Volume I, Oxford, 1963.

PRINS, A. H. J. *The Coastal Tribes of the North-eastern Bantu,*
Ethnographic Survey of Africa, London, 1952.

STAHL, K. M. *History of the Chagga People of Kilimanjaro,*
London, 1964.

Conference Papers

HAMILTON, R. A. (Ed.), *History and Archaeology in Africa,*
School of Oriental and African Studies, London, July 1957.

PRINS, A. H. J. 'Problems of traditional history and cultural
likeness in Bantu North-east Africa', Conference on East
Africa and the Orient, British Institute of History and
Archaeology in East Africa, held at the University College
Nairobi, April 1967.

Articles in *Journal of African History*
FORBES-MUNRO, J. Migrations of the Bantu-speaking peoples
of the Eastern Kenya highlands: a reappraisal, VIII, 1967.

GUTHRIE, M. Some developments in the prehistory of the Bantu languages, III, 1962.

OLIVER, R. The problem of the Bantu expansion, VII, 1966.

SABERWAL, S. C. Historical notes on the Embu of Central Kenya, VIII, 1967.

WRIGLEY, C. C. Speculations on the economic prehistory of Africa, I, 1960.

11

The Arab Impact

Norman R. Bennett

By the latter part of the eighteenth century the peoples of the East African interior had developed political organisations that made it possible for Arabs* to travel inland with profit in search of the two commodities of the interior—ivory and slaves—that could survive the heavy costs of transportation to the coast. The initial stimulus for this movement came from Africans of the interior, especially the Nyamwezi, Bisa, Yao and Kamba, who opened trade routes that Arabs later followed. As early as the mid-eighteenth century, there are reports of trade goods reaching distant Buganda, probably through African traders, and by the beginning of the nineteenth century, a regular trade carried on by Africans with the coast was on in full force. Three general routes of penetration developed as the century went on. On the southern Tanzanian coast, centring on such ports as Kilwa Kivinje, Mkindani, and Lindi, trade routes crossed the sparsely populated southern region of Tanzania, the areas inhabited by such peoples as the Makonde, Makua, and Yao, to reach the more populated, and thus more profitable, area around and beyond Lake Nyasa. By the middle of the nineteenth century, the trade along this route was primarily in slaves, with the Yao playing a major role in securing them. There was little

*The term 'Arab' in this chapter is used for both Arabs and the Afro-Arabs of East Africa.

lasting Arab impact along these trading routes, however, since the Arabs founded their principal bases outside of present-day Tanzania.

The principal penetration route for the coastal traders began opposite Zanzibar, from such ports as Bagamoyo and Sadani, and passed through the areas of many peoples—the Zaramo, Kami, Sagara, Luguru and Gogo, among others—before reaching the land of the Nyamwezi. From there the traders followed routes to Ujiji and across Lake Tanganyika into the Congo, to Karagwe and northwards to Buganda and beyond, and to the south-west to the area north and west of Lake Nyasa. Some slave raiding and trading did occur throughout these regions, especially in the earlier years of the nineteenth century, but the main concern of traders was the securing of ivory.

The third general route of penetration began on the northern Tanzanian and southern Kenyan coasts, from such ports as Pangani, Tanga, and Mombasa. Various roads led to the Chagga around Mount Kilimanjaro, and beyond through the territory of the Masai to the eastern shores of Lake Victoria. Other routes led north from Kilimanjaro passing the fringes of Kikuyu territory, eventually reaching even the distant regions around Lakes Baringo and Rudolf. There was no strong Arab impact throughout this region. The coastal traders did come to dominate use of the routes and to displace the earlier successful Kamba traders but they did not found any major Arab centres. The caravans, because of the dangers present, did not attract the leading coastal traders. Rather they were made up of co-operative groups of traders, each with moderate amounts of capital to invest in trade goods. After leaving the Kilimanjaro region the caravans tended to proceed to minor centres along the route from which smaller groups could leave the caravan to search for the limited amounts of available ivory. Very little slave raiding went on since the goodwill, or at least the toleration, of local African groups—such as the Masai, Nandi, and Kikuyu—was necessary, because of the harsh nature of the land through which the traders passed, for the survival of the caravans. It also was virtually impossible to recruit new porters to replace men lost in battle. There were exceptions to this general pattern, however, since some traders did join in raids in the Kavirondo region, inhabited by the Luo and Luyia, especially with the Wanga Luyia. Thus although there developed a steady trade in the exchange of cloth, wire, beads, and some firearms for ivory

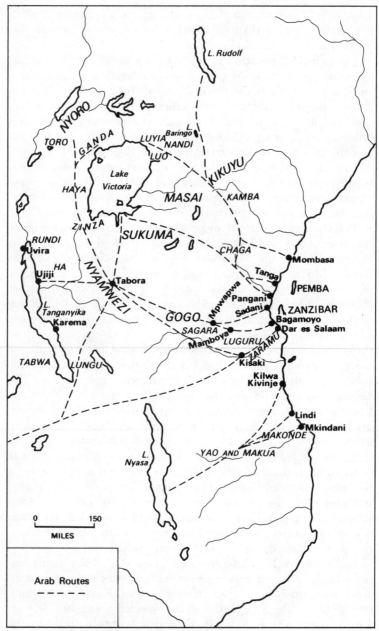

Figure 21 The Arab impact in East Africa

(it was estimated that about 20 per cent of the ivory coming to the coast came from this route), the African predominance ensured that no strong coastal influence would flourish.

In all areas the nature of the Arab impact directly reflected the realities of African political power and of African control over the supplies of food and water necessary to long-distance traders. The Arabs did have a certain superiority because of their possession of firearms, but this advantage was not absolute. They, with their African followers, were not numerous, and given the often primitive nature of their firearms and the lack of training of the men who used them, they had little chance in the long run of success in battle against a well-organised and resolute African society. The main concern of the traders was naturally a profitable trade and thus outright conflict had to be avoided unless there was no doubt of an Arab victory which would contribute to their aims.

The Arabs of Unyanyembe

One way to study the Arab impact is to examine the nature of the contact between the coastal visitors and selected African groups along the routes of penetration. The Nyamwezi are one of the most important African peoples for this type of examination. In the early years of the nineteenth century most of the trade along the important central routes was carried on by Nyamwezi caravans. Groups of Nyamwezi, after the planting season, would organise to visit the coast. As they neared the trading settlements, agents of Indian firms based in Zanzibar would attempt to induce them to trade at a particular port. The whole resulting process of bargaining was a long one, and one that had to change as the demand in Zanzibar for ivory and slaves increased.

Under the able leadership of Said bin Sultan, ruler of Zanzibar and Muscat from 1804 to 1856, began developments from the late 1820's that ensured the island port city a pre-eminence that endured until the days of European rule. Said bin Sultan developed the clove industry of Zanzibar and Pemba, thus making the import of slaves for working the crop a constant necessity. He also made contacts with Indian, American, and European traders who bought the products of his island and of the interior. With these regular trade channels established it was essential to regularise the penetration of the interior to ensure a constant movement of slaves and ivory into Zanzibar.

The Nyamwezi and other Africans could not ensure this regularity and thus a more systematic penetration of the interior began, stimulated by Said bin Sultan with the vital aid of other Arabs and of Indian merchants residing in Zanzibar. The Indians quickly became the most important individuals in this process. Said bin Sultan left the principal direction of his economic affairs to an Indian official, the Customs Master of Zanzibar, who, for the payment of a yearly sum, had virtual control over the economic life of the island. The Customs Master, with the collaboration of the Indian community, advanced to caravan leaders the funds which made their inland ventures possible. The risks being great, the Indians charged heavily for these advances. Despite the failure of many individual caravans, profits were ensured by very high rates of interest, in addition to the excessive prices charged by the Indians for the merchandise and porters which they supplied for the caravans.

The impetus to an ever-deeper inland penetration came as the ivory-producing regions near the coast were denuded of elephants to supply the ever-demanding markets of India, America, and Europe. With this penetration a need developed for Arab centres along the central routes to serve as collection points for ivory and slaves, and as provisioning depots for the increasing number of caravans. An early centre was founded at Zungomero (near present-day Kisaki) in the territory of the Khutu, but bases farther inland were soon required.

The principal Arab settlement of East Africa developed among the Nyamwezi who continued to be the chief providers of caravan porters, and who also continued to send their own caravans to the coast. The Nyamwezi were divided into many independent chiefdoms—there were 31 in 1959—which were often at odds with each other. This lack of political unity, plus ever-present political quarrels over succession to the office of ruler, or *ntemi*, allowed the Arabs to maintain an influential presence among some of the Nyamwezi until the European conquest. The Arabs first established a camp at Msene to the west of Tabora, but Tabora itself, then a midpoint in the Unyanyembe chiefdom, eventually became their main centre.

On the road to Unyanyembe, caravans leaving the coast were able to obtain provisions and water, often from small stations established by Arabs, as they passed through the territories of such peoples as the Zaramo, Sagara, and Luguru. The Gogo provided the first significant difficulty to the traders. Their territory lacked easily available resources for travellers and the Gogo, although not politically united, were a strong people who could prove a major hindrance because of their power to cut off supplies. Gogo prices for these essentials were often high but the Arabs generally accepted them from necessity. However, despite their long years of contact with the Arabs, the Gogo were never significantly influenced by their coastal visitors. Once past the Gogo, the traders entered Nyamwezi territory, a prosperous agricultural region, where they could secure provisions and replacement porters.

The Nyamwezi of Unyanyembe were fully aware of the benefits of trade to be gained from an Arab settlement, and recognised the potential political and military support the Arabs could offer against rival Nyamwezi states. Thus an Arab establishment was not opposed; marriages soon occurred between the daughters of Nyamwezi leaders and important Arabs to help insure a permanent alliance. Unyanyembe had Arab, and Indian, resident agents from the early 1820's. These coastal men were without any significant control from the authorities in Zanzibar, and in their small community, which varied in size as traders and their followers arrived and left, direction for settling disputes and other problems gravitated into the hands of leaders accepted by the consent of the trading community. The African population had little direct contact with most of these visitors except for the needs of trade. The Nyamwezi lived in scattered clusters—what we now call Tabora was a series of these clusters. The Arabs had their own area of residence where their efforts were concentrated and, in distinction from Muslim traders in many other parts of Africa, they showed little inclination to spread their religion. They did not, of course, discourage those Africans who wished to accept Islam, but their main concern was clearly concentrated on business affairs.

But the growing needs of the Zanzibar market led to an effort from Zanzibar for a greater control of the Arabs in the interior. In the 1860's the Indian Customs Master appointed an agent, Said bin Salim—a former companion of Burton and Speke—as head of the Tabora community. He was given little means to enforce his will but the need for most Arabs to return to the coast at one time or another inevitably gave Said bin Salim a position of some strength.

The permanent Arab establishment inevitably led to their continuous involvement in the political life of the Nyamwezi of Unyanyembe. It has been suggested that, previous to the death of the Unyanyembe chief Ifundikira in the late 1850's, an agreement between Arabs and Nyamwezi was concluded whereby the Africans freed the Arab traders from taxes on their trade. The return to the Nyamwezi was the benefit of an Arab establishment in their centre rather than in one of the rival Nyamwezi chiefdoms. But when Ifundikira was succeeded by Mnywa Sere the power the Arabs could exercise became apparent. Mnywa Sere was challenged for the rule by a half-brother, Mkasiwa (or Kiyungi). The father of the later famous Tippu Tip, Muhammad bin Juma, who had married a daughter of Ifundikira, intervened to rout Mkasiwa. Stable political rule was of course vital to the Arabs because of their trading needs.

Despite this Arab support, Mnywa Sere, dissatisfied with his share of the profits of trade through Unyanyembe, increased the Nyamwezi share, a policy that was accepted for a time but which eventually turned the Arabs against him. The Arabs then joined with Mkasiwa and drove Mnywa Sere from his capital. Mkasiwa became *ntemi* but, being a man of weak character who clearly owed his position to the Arabs, remained their puppet throughout his career.

The change of rule led to difficulties. The result demonstrated the limitations of Arab strength when faced with a determined African military challenge. Mnywa Sere, until killed fighting the Arabs in 1865, was able to rally enough Nyamwezi to his side to carry on a war against Mkasiwa and his protectors. This war seriously affected Arab trade and no doubt was one of the principal reasons for the appointment of Said bin Salim as the representative of Zanzibar in Unyanyembe.

The Arab Impact on the Nyamwezi

The Arabs soon found that their support of Mkasiwa would not in itself secure them a position of unquestioned dominance among the Nyamwezi. Mirambo, originally ruler of the nearby small Nyamwezi state of Uyowa, came forward to contest the predominant position of the Unyanyembe Nyamwezi with the Arabs after 1871. The Arabs maintained their support of

Mkasiwa, and despite victories in battle by Mirambo that interrupted Arab trade, they gave no serious thought to supporting any other Nyamwezi but those of Unyanyembe. The war convincingly demonstrated the fundamental weaknesses of the Arabs of central Tanzania. They were a community geared to trade, loosely directed by a leader, Said bin Salim, whose purpose was not to win battles but to settle the problems that arose within the Arab community. Arab trade, however, supplied firearms to dynamic African leaders such as Mirambo and helped to make him an enemy they could not control. And the Arabs in the face of such a threat would not show a united front. Without powerful centralised control some Arabs continued to trade with Mirambo during the hostilities. An additional proof of Arab weakness was demonstrated when Sayyid Barghash of Zanzibar attempted to end the losses to his trading revenues by despatching a large force to Unyanyembe in 1873. The new army proved itself useless since the Arabs resident at Unyanyembe resented this outside intrusion and by quarrels over the leadership of the force blocked all military action.

During the course of the struggle with Mirambo, Mkasiwa died (around 1878); he was succeeded by his son, Isike, who had Arab backing. There were rivals for the chieftainship as usual, with Isike gaining his office only through Arab military strength. Isike—threatened both by his defeated rivals and by Mirambo—offers a good example of how an African ruler could deal with a potentially dangerous Arab resident community. Isike appeared in two widely different roles—one in the earlier and one in the later years of his rule. European visitors at first described him as a generally worthless individual who was merely a puppet in the hands of his Arab masters. But later in his career Isike was known as a fierce and resolute leader of his people and a determined enemy of both Arab and European. Since the change in character occurred when the Arabs became of little use to Isike, it is apparent that the Nyamwezi leader was playing a waiting game. Isike gave the Arabs the obedience they required in return for their support against his enemies, dropping this distasteful role when it no longer suited his interests.

The fact that Isike could maintain such attitudes illustrates the limited nature of the Arab impact among the Nyamwezi, the people of the interior with the most intimate contact with Arabs.

The Arabs always remained a foreign group at Unyanyembe. They lived in their own centres, surrounded by their followers, while the Nyamwezi remained apart in their own clusters. Isike, like most Nyamwezi rulers—Mirambo was a great exception—generally did not leave his own residence, his *ikulu ;* he was not a leader of warriors and he did not participate in campaigns as did Mirambo. Thus, except when specific Arab demands required his presence, Isike could remain supreme in his own Nyamwezi sphere where he acted as a traditional ruler. Both Isike and his people profited from the general prosperity the Arabs brought to Unyanyembe and by the supplies of gunpowder and muskets that alliance with the Arabs brought. In view of the potentially dangerous situation that could at any time threaten Isike through a combination of his Nyamwezi dynastic rivals and the Arabs, Isike's apparent subservience to the Arabs is understandable.

The most important individual to Isike was the forceful Arab raider and trader, Abdulla bin Nasibu. When Isike came to power Said bin Salim still held office as the leading Arab of Unyanyembe, but the dissensions caused by the unsuccessful war against Mirambo led to the expelling of Said bin Salim by a faction grouped around Abdulla bin Nasibu. Isike's Nyamwezi carried out the actual expulsion for the Arabs. Said bin Salim was held to be close to Mirambo, Isike's rival, while Abdulla bin Nasibu was a strong opponent of Mirambo. Therefore the expulsion was not the act of an Arab puppet but rather that of an interested ruler.

Abdulla bin Nasibu was in many ways typical of the leading Arab figures of the interior; he resembled the far more important Tippu Tip who rose through war to a prominent position in the Congo. Abdulla bin Nasibu originally came from the coastal region. He gained his reputation by successful raiding campaigns among the Zaramu and Sagara and from his generous distribution of booty to those who served under him. He had enough power of his own to keep the Arabs of Unyanyembe in order, and with the able aid of his brother, Sheikh bin Nasibu, Abdulla bin Nasibu soon became the most powerful Arab yet resident among the Nyamwezi.

In face of this Arab leader, Isike had to be all the more openly subservient, especially since Mirambo and other rivals remained actively plotting against him. This situation must cause reconsideration of such interpretations as that made recently by Trimingham in his *Islam in East Africa* (p. 24) where he asserts that the Arabs of the interior existed on the 'sufferance' of the local population. If the local population had been united behind a ruler, this might have been true, but in this case it was Isike who maintained his rule on 'sufferance'. Trimingham also feels that the Arabs feared involvement in local quarrels since this might hinder trade, but in Unyanyembe the Arabs involved themselves in a manner that ensured their local ascendancy; by giving vital support to Isike, the Arabs were assured of local dominance and thus of control of trade.

A secure local base was essential for Arab control of trade and was not necessarily antagonistic to African interests. An example of how African and Arab interests could coincide came in 1881 when a European trader, Segère, attempted to establish a centre in Unyanyembe for the purchase of ivory. Segère naturally antagonised the Arabs since he challenged their control of the ivory market; he at the same time roused the opposition of Isike by sending, or at least planning to send, gunpowder to Mirambo. Thus Isike and the Arabs combined to force Segère to flee Unyanyembe to save his life. To outsiders then reporting on Isike he was again acting as a puppet supporting Arab interests whereas he had to act to ensure that Mirambo did not become too strong.

The Segère affair had major repercussions for the Arab community and for the Nyamwezi. On his enforced return to Zanzibar, Segère protested to Sayyid Barghash and the French consul about his treatment. As a consequence, although there were other matters involved, Abdulla bin Nasibu was recalled to Zanzibar in the latter part of 1881. There he was imprisoned and later died, allegedly through poison administered on Barghash's orders. Abdulla bin Nasibu's brother, Sheikh bin Nasibu, had carried on as governor in Unyanyembe but he died in 1882, also supposedly from poison administered by an agent of Barghash. The Arab community never recovered from this double loss. No replacement was sent from Zanzibar for the Nasibus because, said Sayyid Barghash, he feared any new agent would fail to carry out orders and thus cause trouble with the increasing number of European visitors to central Tanzania. The remaining Arabs in Unyanyembe proved incapable of nominating a successor and there was consequent degeneration into factional strife.

Isike was placed in a dangerous situation with this loss of firm

Arab support against his rivals and, had he been a mere puppet, would have been driven from power. Instead, Isike reacted successfully to make himself the undisputed ruler of Unyanyembe, and even to expand his influence over many of the neighbouring Nyamwezi states. Finally, the death of Mirambo in 1884 cleared Isike's way of all obstacles. The Arabs now, lacking effective leadership, had to suffer his exactions upon their trade and the high costs he charged for recruiting porters. This situation remained essentially unchanged until Isike met death fighting the German invaders in 1893.

Thus the Arab influence in their most important inland East African base was very tenuous. Drawn there by trade, a small group of Arabs settled and proceeded to run their own affairs with little control from Zanzibar. They were sufficient in number to make them an important factor in the fluid power struggle within that Nyamwezi state. With able leadership the Arabs could and did profit from this situation, as did the Nyamwezi who allied with them. But with their main concern limited to commercial ends, the Arabs really had little influence upon the life and future of the Nyamwezi. New ideas and techniques were no doubt introduced along with trade goods from the coast. This process, however, would have gone on without the Arabs, although in a slower fashion, since the Nyamwezi kept their role as the main caravan men of East Africa throughout the nineteenth century.

The Arabs of Ujiji

Arab traders had pushed beyond Unyanyembe to reach Lake Tanganyika before 1830. Here an important Arab settlement developed at the port town of Ujiji in Bujiji, one of the six independent chiefdoms of the Ha people. Bujiji stretched along Lake Tanganyika's shores from the Luiche River to the frontiers of Burundi, with an inland extent of about twenty miles. Only those Ha living around Ujiji, usually called the Jiji, had commercial relations with the Arabs; the Ha to the east remained isolated, with a reputation for unfriendliness to visitors—to the explorer Henry M. Stanley they were 'the most extortionate tribute-takers in Africa'.

The Jiji shared in this reputation, but the area around Ujiji was an important one to the Arabs. Ujiji had a useful harbour, and the nearby region provided the necessary agricultural resources for a permanent trading base. And, despite their reputation, the Jiji proved willing to receive resident Arab merchants and to give them the security necessary for their operations. The political organisation of a Ha state centred around the chief, called the *abami* whose subordinate chiefs, the *abatware banini* (singular, *umutware munini*) administered their districts in the name of their superior. Ujiji port was included in the districts of Ugoy and Kawele, each ruled by a separate *umutware munini*. The *abami* himself had little military strength and he generally left the details of government to his subordinates who were often the hereditary rulers of their districts. They collected revenues, forwarding part to their *abami* after securing a share of their own. This loose system gave the necessary stability for the establishment of a community of coast merchants.

When the Arabs reached Lake Tanganyika in search of ivory they needed a port for the penetration of the territory to the west and south-west of the lake. Ujiji filled this need. By the 1840's the lake had been crossed; by the 1860's reports from Zanzibar indicated that the great bulk of the ivory reaching the island came by the route from Ujiji through Unyanyembe to the coast. Our first clear information about the role of Ujiji dates from the late 1850's when European visitors reported a small and unhealthy settlement with only a few Arabs present. Its principal use was as an outlying base for the Unyanyembe traders who sent caravans there to pick up ivory and to return to the Arab centre among the Nyamwezi as soon as possible.

Ujiji soon became more important due to its strategic location and to the rise to power of an important Arab, Mwinyi Kheri. He originally came from the coast opposite Zanzibar, probably arriving in the Lake Tanganyika region in the 1840's. Mwinyi Kheri became head of the Arab community by 1872 due to his long years in the country and the wealth and influence gained thereby. He also had firearms enough for his followers, a significant asset since reports indicate that the Ujiji Arabs were able to prevent the Jiji from acquiring these weapons as the Nyamwezi had. But the real source of Mwinyi Kheri's power came rather from the relationships which he worked out with the rulers of Ujiji. The *abami* lived inland and never visited Ujiji; he was satisfied with an Arab settlement because it drew trade to his chiefdom and allowed him to profit from visiting caravans.

Thus, left alone by the *abami*, Mwinyi Kheri easily controlled the *abatware banini* of Kawele and Ugoy, who also profited from the visiting traders, and he sealed this system by his marriage to one of the daughters of an *umutware munini*.

Thus again Arabs and Africans came together in a manner that brought the greatest mutual benefit to both. Since the local African power structure was different from that of the Nyamwezi, a different arrangement resulted. At Unyanyembe the Arabs gained their aims by using their power in the intergroup struggles of a potentially powerful people; at Ujiji Arab aims were gained by a virtual incorporation into the Ha political structure. Mwinyi Kheri took advantage of the Ha organisation to become in reality a part of the Ha state. Since the Ujiji Arabs lived in an outlying and consequently weaker section of an African state, their position was stronger than the Arabs of Unyanyembe living at the capital. The political and commercial arrangement was in many ways the most satisfactory worked out between Arab and African in East Central Africa. The Arabs received a secure base, with ample provisions for passing caravans; the Ha received duties on these operations and were left virtually in control of all aspects of their daily life. There was none of the friction here that was common between Arab and Nyamwezi in Unyanyembe. An indication of the established Arab position at Ujiji is the fact that once when a new *abami* of Bujiji had to be chosen, an Arab supervised the election of the ruler.

Prosperity came to Ujiji; it became a busy market town for all the peoples of the Lake Tanganyika region through two types of commercial activity. The Arab rush into the Congo, dating from the late 1860's, gave the Ujiji Arab and African residents the chance to profit from selling needed supplies. The resident Arabs left the Congo ivory traffic to other Arabs and, under the direction of Mwinyi Kheri, used Ujiji as the main base for their expeditions after slaves and ivory along the regions bordering Lake Tanganyika. Areas of especial concern were those of the politically weak Lungu and Tabwa (or Marungu) on the southern and eastern shores of the lake, and the well-organised Rundi to the north. The profits were no doubt less than those gained by other Arabs in raiding the peoples of the Congo, but they were sufficient for Mwinyi Kheri and his followers.

The Ujiji Arab settlement gave no formal recognition during its formative years to the authorities in Zanzibar. The Ujiji Arabs were on their own, a fact that did not greatly concern

Zanzibar since the trade of the lake eventually found its way to the coast. In this situation of isolation, Arab and African at Ujiji usually managed to settle their disputes in peace. For minor differences between individuals of each group, the aggrieved parties went either to Mwinyi Kheri or to the *umutware munini*. For major difficulties, the Jiji and Arab elders met jointly and made a settlement to prevent any disruption of the course of trade.

Mwinyi Kheri's position in Ujiji was so secure that he could devote much of his time to activities in the northern regions of the lake, where he was one of the pioneer Arab visitors. This region was a very difficult one for the Arabs. The state of Burundi was a powerful African entity, despite its frequent internal difficulties, and the Rundi opposed allowing Arab traders into their country. The Arabs had to content themselves with bases at the port town of Uzige and in nearby Uvira. Mwinyi Kheri recognised the Rundi strength and generally remained content with this sphere of operations. Later Arab leaders, notably Muhammad bin Khalfan (or Rumaliza) went beyond Mwinyi Kheri's cautious policies but their forces were decisively defeated when they attempted to move inland.

Mwinyi Kheri came formally into the Zanzibar orbit in 1881 when, due to difficulties stemming from the increasing European visitors, he finally recognised Sayyid Barghash's authority and hoisted the flag of Zanzibar. The recognition did nothing to alter the realities of the local power system and Mwinyi Kheri remained the effective head of the Ujiji community until his death in 1885.

In Ujiji therefore a very stable and mutually profitable relationship grew between Arab and African. The Arabs, by a careful policy, entered into the loose political fabric of the Ha state of Bujiji and both sides were satisfied with the result. Many other Africans of the Lake Tanganyika region suffered from Arab raids, but not the Jiji who remained allies of the Arabs.

The Arabs in Buganda

In distinction to the establishment of a balance of interests between Arab and African in Ujiji, or to the Arab involvement in the politics of the Nyamwezi, was the relationship of the Arabs to the powerful and united state of the Ganda. Arab traders moving northwards from Unyanyembe reached Buganda in the 1840's where the *Kabaka,* Suna, welcomed them. Not many Arabs, however, had made this long trip by the 1860's and no large Arab trading centre developed on this route. The Arabs followed a route that took them through many small Nyamwezi and Sukuma chiefdoms, through the troublesome Zinza, and then through the several Haya states to the west of Lake Victoria. The southern regions of the lake shore were relatively little visited, due to African internal instability providing unsatisfactory conditions for an Arab centre. Thus there was a late development of a regular dhow traffic across Lake Victoria to replace the long overland trip. One minor centre flourished for a time to the west of the lake, among the Haya of Karagwe, during the period when Rumanika ruled. The disorder following his death in 1878 ensured the ruin of this settlement.

Suna of Buganda died in 1856, and his successor Mutesa I, after some delay, allowed the return of Arab traders who had been prohibited from visiting Buganda for some years. The Egyptian authorities were then trying to extend their control southwards, and Mutesa particularly sought firearms and ammunition from the Zanzibari visitors. Slaves and ivory were, as usual, what the Arabs traded for, but the trade was carried on entirely under conditions imposed by the Ganda. Arab traders entered the Ganda state only with the permission of the Kabaka's officials. The Arabs sent gifts of considerable value to the Kabaka to ensure their reception, and were conducted to the Ganda capital where they remained until the terms of the Kabaka's trade were arranged. Only when this royal trade— in which the Kabaka had a monopoly of the firearms sold— was completed could the Arabs exchange their remaining merchandise with other Ganda.

The slaves and ivory traded to the Arabs were gathered by the Ganda through raids on their neighbours, or from tribute paid them, and the Arab traders were confined to the process of bargaining in the capital. They were also prevented from proceeding beyond Buganda, especially to the Nyoro rivals of the Ganda. This was ensured in the 1880's by the Ganda domination of the Karagwe, Zinza, and Toro territories that led to Bunyoro. A few Arab traders reached the Nyoro during the reign of Kabarega (about 1870 to 1899), but they never developed an important position there. Despite the restrictions imposed by the Ganda, this 'wholesale trade', as Stanley described it, was a profitable one for the Arabs, important enough to lead the ruler of Zanzibar to send an official representative to Buganda in 1869.

Even with the inequality of power between the small Arab community and the Ganda state, the Arabs had a greater measure of success in conversions to Islam than in any other East African area. Efforts were made to spread Islam from the early years of contact, especially by the Arab, Ahmed bin Ibrahim, who first arrived in Buganda in 1844. Islam had not been accepted by significant numbers of Ganda by the time of the arrival of Christian missionaries in the late 1870's, but some success had been achieved. Mosques were built in the 1860's, while Mutesa observed the rituals of Ramadan from 1867 to 1877 and also followed the Muslim calendar. Islam did not secure a similar success in any other state of this region, and even in Buganda the Muslim gains did not prove decisive. The representatives of the superior technical cultures of Europe soon achieved greater success, perhaps aided by the work already accomplished by the Muslim visitors. The resulting problems will be discussed below.

Arabs, Africans, and Europeans

Into the balance of interests between Arab and African came European intruders. The early explorers had little impact; the Arabs usually welcomed them, sold them needed goods, and then let them go on their way. The first significant intruders were missionaries. There was little missionary endeavour in East Africa until the 1870's when the exploits of Livingstone and others stimulated a new movement and most of the Arab centres soon had missionary visitors.

The British Church Missionary Society (CMS) organised a mission party for Karagwe or Buganda in 1876. Stations along the route inland were planned to support the venture; one location chosen was Mpwapwa in Ugogo. Mpwapwa was located on the main caravan route to Unyanyembe, and although it did not have a major Arab settlement, Mpwapwa nevertheless was a vital provisioning place for Arab traders entering or leaving Ugogo. The African ruler at Mpwapwa gave permission in 1876 for a CMS settlement, and the principal resident Arab

caused no undue difficulties. But once the settlement was
organised the missionaries raised problems by acting against the
slave trade. Slaves escaping from passing caravans were given
asylum by the missionaries, who refused to return refugees who
wished to remain. The Arabs could have reacted by using force,
but no doubt fearing the inevitable difficulties that would face
them in Zanzibar if coercion was used, they accepted the situation
with bad grace. The Arabs, to solve the problem, rerouted their
caravans to bypass the mission, an expedient that avoided
serious difficulties in the period before the European occupation
of East Africa.

Another British group, the London Missionary Society
(LMS), in 1878 reached Ujiji where they were welcomed by the
Africans, but not by the Arab community. The Arabs were
fully aware of the dangers the European missionaries might
cause to the Arab relationship with the Ha, but again managed
to avoid outright hostilities. Delaying tactics were used to
prevent an effective settlement in order to avoid a major crisis.
Mwinyi Kheri's Arabs left the missionaries free to proselytise;
at the same time Arab influence was strong enough to ensure
that no special ties were formed with the Ha power structure.
The LMS finally left Ujiji in frustration in 1883.

The White Fathers, a French Roman Catholic group, arrived
in East Africa in 1878 to found interior missions. One party of
White Fathers came to Ujiji in 1879 where they very quickly
observed that Arab influence would be a lasting hindrance to
their work. But the Frenchmen saw the need to act with the
Arabs, and, with the co-operation of Mwinyi Kheri, they
attempted operations on the shores of Burundi. There, one
White Fathers' mission was destroyed by Africans, following a
quarrel over slaves purchased by the missionaries from slave
traders. Some have blamed the resulting missionary deaths on
the Arabs, but there appears no foundation for the charge.
Mwinyi Kheri had nothing to gain from involvement in an
action countering his policy of peaceful containment of the
Europeans resident in his territories. In most later instances he
aided the White Fathers—often at a price—to found stations on
the lake shores.

The White Fathers in 1881 also set up a station in Unyany-
embe. Their main concern was a school for the education of
African boys. They attempted little local conversions, and both
Isike and the Arabs tolerated the newcomers. The mission was

forced out of Unyanyembe in 1889, but this was due to the exactions of Isike and not to the Arabs.

European missionaries in Tanzania were joined by representatives of the International African Association (IAA), a society founded in 1876 through the efforts of Leopold II of Belgium as part of his policy to secure a foothold in Africa. The IAA planned to establish what it called centres of civilisation; they would serve as places for supplying European travellers and for pacifying the neighbouring regions. This mainly Belgian organisation set up depots at Unyanyembe and at Karema on Lake Tanganyika. In general, the Arabs aided the IAA in East Africa and the IAA station at Unyanyembe lived at peace with the Arabs throughout its existence (1879 to 1881). The French and Germans also sent expeditions under the auspices of the IAA, the French with an establishment in Usagara and the Germans among the Nyamwezi of Uganda. Neither group had significant problems with the Arabs.

But if missionaries and IAA members were left alone by the Arabs since they did not greatly upset the Arab-African balance, one other class of European was not left in peace. European traders began to come inland from the early 1870's. We have already commented on the fate of the trader Segère at Unyanyembe, driven away for trying to interfere with the Arab-controlled ivory market. German traders, attempting to succeed where Segère had failed, opened in 1885 and 1886 a trading station in Unyanyembe where the Arabs and Africans did all possible to block the Europeans' business. When this did not entirely succeed, one of the Germans was killed by an Arab. This ended European inland trading ventures in the days before European occupation, except for the Irish trader, Charles Stokes, who succeeded by allying himself with the Nyamwezi of Usongo and by staying clear of Arab-dominated centres.

The Arab reaction to European non-governmental intruders amply demonstrates the nature of the Arab presence in East Africa. These Europeans were in the long run devoted to the ending of the slave trade, but as long as they took no direct measures the Arabs were content to leave them in peace. Conversion efforts were of little concern to the Arabs, and the spreading of Christianity would not be an issue causing friction. But when Europeans became commercial rivals, the Arabs had to react. European competition could displace the Arab traders, and thus threats and even violence were used to protect their established commercial positions.

This generally tolerant attitude changed with European attempts to assert political control in East Africa. A German society was given a charter for the area behind the northern Tanzanian coast in 1885, a control that was later extended to most of present-day Tanzania by an Anglo-German treaty of 1886. The Germans claimed that the Arab government in Zanzibar had no rights to the interior. They justified this by asserting that the Arabs had merely commercial and not political centres, a claim that was essentially true. The only inland Zanzibari garrison was at Mamboya, near Mpwapwa, which had been occupied since 1880. Mamboya was not a significant base, however, and Sayyid Barghash secured no recognition of political control from it.

Barghash did try to increase his control on the coast and in the interior in the face of German claims, but the threat of German force put an end to his efforts in August 1885. But this agreement had little effect in the interior where we have seen that it was a local Arab-African agreement that ruled affairs, and not any decision of the Arab ruler of Zanzibar.

German mismanagement on the Tanzanian coast led to war (1888 to 1890) ending the Arab power there. The German victory, however, had sealed the fate of the Arabs of the interior, since the outlets for Arab trade to the Indian Ocean ports were in German hands, while at roughly the same time the authorities of the Congo Independent State were turning the ivory trade of the Congo towards the Atlantic and away from the Ujiji route. Many of the important Arabs therefore left inland East Africa, either for the East African coast, or more commonly, for the Arab-dominated regions of the eastern Congo which remained independent of Congo Independent State control until the defeat of the Arabs (1892 to 1894).

The Germans moved inland in 1890, signing agreements with the small Arab settlements on the route to Unyanyembe with little difficulty because of the overwhelming German military might. The Arabs of Unyanyembe readily accepted a treaty, actually welcoming the Germans because of the heavy exactions of Isike. Most of the Unyanyembe Arabs remained loyal German allies in the forthcoming hostilities against Isike.

The situation at Ujiji was different. Muhammad bin Khalfan had succeeded Mwinyi Kheri and had attempted to extend Arab control over all the coasts of Lake Tanganyika. Most of his raiding, however, went on in areas of the present-day Congo and not in Tanzania, thus allowing the Jiji to continue profiting from the Arab presence. The Germans, too busy elsewhere to do anything significant about this Arab centre, did not occupy Ujiji until 1896. By this time Muhammad bin Khalfan had been defeated by forces of the Congo Independent State during the 1892 to 1894 Arab war and had fled to Zanzibar. The once powerful Arab community melted away following this defeat of Rumaliza and the Germans found in 1896 only a very few Arabs, who were fully disposed to recognise their new rulers' authority.

The Arabs of Buganda lost power in a very different way. There the successful conversion efforts of Muslims and Christians led to the rise of a class of young men who were no longer willing to accept the values of traditional Ganda society. Faced with threats from the kabaka, Mwanga, the Muslim and Christian groups combined in 1888 to depose him. This co-operation did not long endure, and soon the Muslim Ganda, aided by the few remaining Arab traders, expelled their Christian rivals. This success lasted only a short time. The Christian Ganda rallied to defeat the Muslim forces; in the hostilities the Arab community of Buganda was completely broken. The Ganda Muslims would later gain a place in a Buganda under British control, one in which the Arabs would have no role.

Conclusion

The story was much the same in other areas of East Africa. The Arabs of the interior usually did not oppose the European invaders because they had little hope of victory. They could not count on African support since their local agreements had been marriages of convenience, usually limited to largely commercial aims. The Arab penetration of East Africa had been a movement of individuals, supported and stimulated by the Arab ruler of Zanzibar and his Indian officials, which led to the creation of numerous trading centres throughout East Africa. In these communities, organised by the resident Arabs and little influenced from Zanzibar, the Arabs had come to terms in one way or another with their African neighbours. Where slave-raiding occurred, the areas of Arab establishment were left alone, while their African allies usually joined in the raiding to make Arab victories possible. Only among the Ganda had successful Muslim conversion taken place, but with little hope of long run success due to the even more successful efforts of Christian missionaries; without conversion there was little hope of really gaining African loyalty and support. The Africans were willing to accept the profits of the trade the Arabs stimulated, but accepted little else.

Thus when the Europeans arrived the Africans did not support the Arabs. Those who resisted were defeated and the fragile Arab community of the interior, little over a half-century in age, crumbled. What influences remained after this defeat? The Arabs had helped to open the interior by developing the routes initiated by Africans which later became the main avenues of commerce for the new European colonies. Perhaps their most important contribution to East Africa, and especially to Tanzania, was the spread of the Swahili language to the farthest corners of East Africa. As a whole, however, these few beneficial influences appear small when contrasted to the devastation that the Arabs and their African allies brought to the many regions affected by the slave trade and its aftermath of famine and disease.

The Arabs had built a domination that outwardly appeared powerful to nineteenth-century observers, but there were no germs for successful development within it. They remained a small and often alien group, using their successful commercial position to keep Africans, who were inherently more powerful, had they been united, under Arab influence. When the Europeans interfered with this influence, Arab weakness soon became apparent and their domination quickly passed away.

Further reading

BENNETT, N. R. (Ed.), *Leadership in East Africa. Six Political Biographies,* Boston University Press, Boston, 1968.

BENNETT, N. R. *Studies in East African History,* Boston University Press, Boston, 1963.

GEE, T. W. A Century of Mohammadan Influence in Buganda, 1852-1951, *Uganda Journal,* 22, 1958, (pp. 139-150).

GRAY, J. Ahmed bin Ibrahim—The First Arab to Reach Buganda, *Uganda Journal,* 11, 1947, (pp. 80-97).

GRAY, J. Trading Expeditions from the Coast to Lakes Tanganyika and Victoria before 1857, *Tanganyika Notes and Records,* 49, 1957, (pp. 226-246).

HARRIES, L. (Ed.) *Swahili Prose Texts,* Oxford University Press, London and Nairobi, 1965.

KABEYA, J. B. *Mtemi Mirambo,* East African Literature Bureau, Nairobi, Dar es Salaam, and Kampala, 1966.

LEWIS, I. M. (Ed.) *Islam in Tropical Africa,* Published for the International African Institute, Oxford University Press, London, 1966.

KATUMBA, A. and WELBOURN, F. B. Muslim Martyrs of Buganda, *Uganda Journal,* 28, 1964, (pp. 151-163).

OLIVER, R. and MATHEW, G. (Eds.) *History of East Africa* Volume I, Oxford, 1963.

TRIMINGHAM, J. S. *Islam in East Africa,* Clarendon Press, Oxford, 1964.

(Tippu Tip), *Maisha ya Hamed bin Muhammed el Murjebi yaani Tippu Tip,* Supplement to the East African Swahili Committee Journals, No. 28/2, July 1958 and No. 29/1, Jan. 1959.

12

The Nineteenth Century: Prelude to Colonialism

Edward A. Alpers

East Africa at the Beginning of the Nineteenth Century

By 1800 East Africa was poised on the brink of a new era. Until then there had been only limited contacts between the coast and the interior. These were most intensive along the trade routes running from Lake Nyasa to the Kilwa coast, which were dominated by the Yao of northern Mozambique. By the last quarter of the eighteenth century a few adventurous Swahili had also traded inland along these routes. Besides the Yao, the people who were most affected by these contacts were the Tumbuka and the Ngonde of northern Malawi. In central Tanzania the Nyamwezi had probably been journeying to the coast opposite Zanzibar since early in the 1700's. In the previous chapter we saw that a sprinkling of foreign trade goods had already reached the royal court of Buganda by the late decades of that century, but direct trade links between the coast and Uganda remained limited for about another sixty years. Beyond these, there were as yet no other significant routes joining the coast with the interior of East Africa.

New ideas did not, however, enter only from the coast. Nyamwezi and Fipa traders frequented the court of the Eastern Lunda paramount chief, Mwata Kazembe, on the Luapula River in Zambia, while the numerous peoples of the corridor between Lakes Nyasa and Tanganyika were regularly absorbing immigrants, and their ideas of political organisation, from northeastern Zambia. But these contacts with peoples living outside

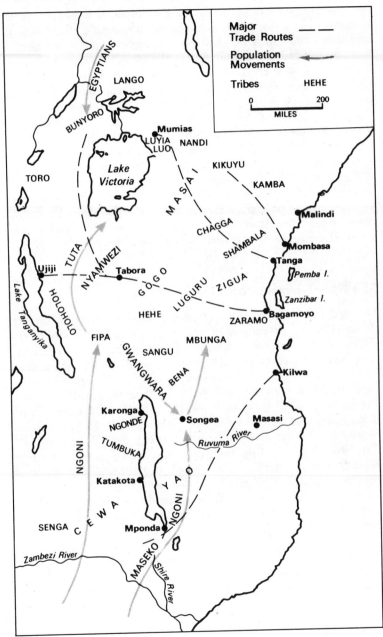

Figure 22 Prelude to Colonialism

the modern borders of the three East African territories were minimal. Their importance cannot be compared to the political and social changes which had been brought about in the north-west by the Nilotic invasions over the previous three centuries. East Africa was certainly not stagnant: changes were taking place within many societies; people were still moving into the agriculturally less attractive areas of central and south-eastern Tanzania; Luo and Masai influences, among others, were still being assimilated by their neighbours. Except in the immediate coastal hinterland of Tanzania and on Zanzibar and Pemba Islands, where the evil effects of the slave trade were already taking their toll, this internal process of change continued largely undisturbed until the early 1840's. At that time two separate invasions of East Africa began to take place. From the coast entered the Arabs, whose impact we have just read about. From the interior of southern Africa came the Ngoni.

The Ngoni Invasion of Southern Tanzania

On 19 November 1835, a day remembered in tradition for the occurrence of an eclipse of the sun, the great Ngoni chief Zwangendaba led his people north across the Zambezi River. The Ngoni traced their origin back to South Africa, where they had been one of the Nguni-speaking peoples of northern Zulu-land. In about 1820 they had fled from their homeland to escape the rising power of Shaka Zulu. During the next fifteen years Zwangendaba's army wandered through southern Mozam-bique and further inland before turning towards the middle Zambezi. After fording the river, the Ngoni continued their relentless march northwards through Malawi and Zambia until they reached the Fipa plateau in the early 1840's.

Over the years, many different people had been assimilated into the Ngoni nation—Thonga from Mozambique, Shona from Rhodesia, Senga, Cewa, and Tumbuka from north of the Zambezi. Zwangendaba's success in capturing so many non-Nguni speakers, who actually outnumbered the true Ngoni, and in fully integrating them into the Ngoni social and political system may be traced to his adoption of the revolutionary Zulu military techniques designed by Shaka. These innovations included the substitution of a short, stabbing spear for the traditional long, throwing spear. The new weapon was employed by warriors who were protected by massive cow-hide shields which left only a man's face exposed to the enemy. The warriors fought in organised age-regiments and their usual deployment in battle was in the shape of a bull's horns, the idea being to encircle the enemy and then to crush him. These regiments were maintained for long periods so that there was always a standing army ready for battle. Men who were captured from other tribes took their place in these regiments, while women and children fell to the married Ngoni men. There was practically no stigma attached to being from a conquered people, and a man of ability could quickly rise to a position of importance.

Zwangendaba's peculiar genius was the ability to keep his nation united, but on his death in about 1848, factionalism triumphed. Eventually, the nation split into five kingdoms, only two of which were established in Tanzania, while the others took root in Malawi and Zambia. The first Tanzanian group to break away from the main Ngoni body struck north from Ufipa. These Ngoni became known as the Tuta. Raiding all the while, they encountered the Holoholo living on the eastern shores of Lake Tanganyika. But the Holoholo successfully repelled the Tuta, having profited by their experience of an earlier defeat at the hands of the Ngoni in the Holoholo homeland to the south-west of the lake. Many Holoholo had fled east across the lake, settled in Tanzania, and adopted the impressive Ngoni military methods. Thus when the Tuta attacked them some years later, the Holoholo were able to pay them in kind. Here we have the first of several important Tanzanian examples of people who cast aside their traditional means of defence and took up Ngoni military tactics to preserve themselves from falling victim to the Ngoni. The Holoholo are a good example of a society who adopted radical new techniques in order to preserve the basis, indeed the very existence, of the society.

Recovering from this temporary setback, during the 1850's the Tuta harassed the Nyamwezi and upset the Arab trade route between Tabora and Ujiji. They eventually settled north-west of Tabora and raided as far as the southern shores of Lake Victoria. Many Nyamwezi were captured, the most important of whom was Mirambo, who later incorporated refugees from Tuta raids when organising his own forces, called *rugaruga,* against the Arabs. Clearly, the Tuta were an important element in unsettling a vast area of central Tanzania, but they also contributed to its stability by enabling Mirambo to build up a stronger Nyamwezi chiefdom than otherwise might have been possible.

This same contradictory pattern recurs in southern Tanzania, where the Ngoni were a much more important factor than the Tuta in Unyamwezi. This second Tanzanian Ngoni group, the Gwangwara, was led east from Ufipa to Songea by Zulu-Gama. But here they found yet another Ngoni kingdom already established, the Maseko Ngoni, who had never been a part of Zwangendaba's nation. They had come from southern Mozambique, had crossed the Zambezi nearer to its confluence with the Shire River than had Zwangendaba, continuing their march to the east of Lake Nyasa until they reached Songea, probably early in the 1840's. Led by Maputo, the Maseko Ngoni were more powerful than the Gwangara, but various intrigues weakened their superiority and in about 1860 the Maseko were driven back across the Ruvuma River, eventually to settle in south-western Malawi. It was not too long, however, before old rivalries split the always precarious Gwangara union into a northern and a southern kingdom.

From their centres in Songea, the Gwangara raided extensively throughout the area between Lake Nyasa and the coast, right until the imposition of German colonial rule. Southern Tanzania lived in constant fear of raids by the Songea Ngoni, who were always eager to build up their numbers by incorporating captives into their society. Furthermore, unprincipled bands of brigands, usually known as *maviti,* or *mafiti,* mimicked the external trappings of the Ngoni and terrorised the neighbourhoods in which they operated. These robber bands were considerably more destructive than the Ngoni; not being concerned with building a stable society in which their captives became members, they were more interested in gaining immediate profit from raids and usually sold captives into slavery. The Ngoni chiefs were not above dealing with slavers on occasion, but in general this was not the point of their expeditions.

In some very important cases, however, the Ngoni example had a constructive influence in southern Tanzania, just as it had for the Holoholo. This was so in Usangu, bordering Ufipa on the east, which had been badly ravaged by the Ngoni in the 1840's. During this period Mwahawangu, one of the many small Sangu chiefs, had withdrawn north-east to Uhehe. Returning after Zwangendaba's death, Mwahawangu conquered the other

Sangu chiefdoms and created a united Sangu state. He was succeeded in about 1860 by his grandson, Merere, who dominated much of the southern highlands from his base at Utengule into the early 1870's. Thereafter, the Sangu were overshadowed by the Hehe, whose more than thirty independent chiefdoms had been united under the leadership of Muyugumba during the previous two decades. Instrumental in Hehe unification was the adoption of Ngoni-influenced military regiments, weaponry, and field tactics. A crushing defeat of the Bena, who had also only recently begun to unite, was delivered by the Hehe in about 1874-1875; and Merere lost most of Usangu to Muyugumba in 1877. Not surprisingly, the Hehe soon came to blows with the Gwangara. Wars were fought in 1878 and 1881, but as no clear victory was won by either side a truce was concluded by the great Mkwawa, who had succeeded his father Muyugumba as chief in 1879. Together with the Songea Ngoni, the Hehe remained the most powerful state in southern Tanzania until effective German rule was established in the interior.

A final new power was established from the broken remnants of the Maseko Ngoni by the Ndendeuli. Using Ngoni organisational methods they rapidly gained force until they were routed by the Gwangara in about 1862. Fleeing north across the Kilombero valley, they settled south of Morogoro, where they continued their raiding and became known as the Mbunga. The impact which they made on their neighbours may be judged by the fact that the first clearly remembered period of pre-German history among the Luguru, who live around Morogoro, is called *wakati wa Wambunga,* the period of the Mbunga raids.

It is clear that the Ngoni invasion was a major factor in shaping the history of southern East Africa. The most challenging historical problem which faces us when we consider their impact is whether it was primarily destructive or constructive. Was it, as Professor Omer-Cooper suggests, 'a terrible disaster for the peoples of East Central Africa'? Or was it, as Professor Oliver writes, 'a kind of inoculation against what was to follow', against the Arab invasion and the worst atrocities of the slave trade? Within the dominions of the various Ngoni and Ngoni-inspired kingdoms, life was relatively secure, whereas the raids carried on by the Ngoni and by Ngoni-influenced bands of renegades exposed many defenceless peoples to the depredations of the slave traders. In view of the slave trade, we can see that the forcible integration of many weaker peoples into the Ngoni kingdoms was ultimately to the advantage of those weaker peoples. But it is more difficult to show that the Ngoni invasion paved the way for the slave trade and made it worse than it would have been had there been no Ngoni invasion. For the period of the Ngoni and Maviti raids did not come before the height of the slave trade, but coincided with it.

The Slave Trade

Although slaves had been taken from East Africa for many centuries, the slave trade was not really very important until after the middle of the eighteenth century. Only with the growth of a plantation economy on the French-dominated islands of Mauritius and Réunion, far to the east of Madagascar, was there a steady call for large numbers of slaves from East Africa. The French slavers favoured the Mozambique coast, but the high death rate of labourers on the rapidly expanding sugar plantations produced an insatiable demand that sent them looking for new sources of supply. Soon they were dealing in human lives at Kilwa and Zanzibar. At about the same time, there was a parallel growth in the Omani Arab demand for slaves, who were largely supplied by the Kilwa market. From the very beginning, then, the slave trade was focused on the southern interior of East Africa, and it remained so throughout the nineteenth century. By about 1810 at least 6,000, and perhaps as many as 10,000, slaves were being sold annually at Kilwa and Zanzibar town to the Arabs and the French. Thereafter the Arab slave trade became increasingly dominant, while the French colonial demand for slaves very slowly subsided in the face of British and metropolitan pressure to abolish both the trade and the institution of slavery.

In the following decade the pace of the Arab trade grew slowly, but it shot up from the late 1820's, as Sayyid Said bin Sultan of Muscat began to take a more active interest in his East African domain and to encourage his Arab subjects to settle in Zanzibar and Pemba. Many of these Arab settlers established plantations for growing cloves, which had been introduced in about 1818, and copra, on a considerable scale. Consequently, for the first time there was a big internal demand for slaves on both Zanzibar and Pemba. In 1839 a British observer estimated that some

40,000 to 45,000 slaves were sold annually in the Zanzibar market. Only about half of these people seem to have supplied the largely Arab demand abroad, while the remainder were purchased by Arab plantation owners on the two islands. In the 1860's a contemporary estimate suggests that as many as 70,000 souls may have been sold each year in the Zanzibar slave market. These figures are very general, and may well be exaggerated, but they give some idea of the scale of the slave trade in East Africa during the mid-nineteenth century. As the result of an Anglo-Zanzibar treaty signed in 1873 and two proclamations issued by Seyyid Bargash bin Said of Zanzibar in 1876, the export slave trade from the mainland of East Africa was rapidly reduced to a trickle. But this did not signal the end of slaving within East Africa. Rather, slaving actually increased; and the suppression of the export slave trade inadvertently encouraged a final period of unprecedented outrage, during which the value of human life was pitiably cheapened.

Although it was the Arabs and the French who had created and sustained the demand for slaves, and who thus bore the ultimate responsibility for the East African slave trade, it cannot be argued that they were equally accountable for its operation in the interior. The French never were involved in this aspect of the trade, the Arabs clearly were, but the exact role which they played inland varied according to the area in which they operated. We have already noted that the principal source of slaves was the southern interior, in particular the Kilwa hinterland and the Lake Nyasa region. Here, except for isolated pockets like Kota Kota and Karonga, in Malawi, the Arabs were never in control of the trade, but were generally the clients of powerful Yao chiefs like Mpanda, Makanjila, Mataka, Mtalika, and Machemba. The commercial and political base of these Yao chiefs was simply too strong to be challenged by the Arabs who moved inland from Kilwa. Writing in 1866, Livingstone noted that 'the caravan leaders from Kilwa arrive at a Waiyau village, show the goods they have brought, are treated liberally by the elders, and told to wait and enjoy themselves, slaves enough to purchase all will be procured: then a foray is made . . .' Side by side with this sort of activity, the Yao chiefs continued to send large caravans of slaves and ivory to the coast on their own account. This commitment to the slave trade was to make the Yao chiefs strong opponents to the imposition of colonial rule.

The situation in central Tanzania was considerably different. Unyamwezi and beyond was the focus of Arab activity in continental East Africa. Slaving in this quarter was almost exclusively in the hands of the Arabs, and the responsibility for the turmoil which resulted from it was largely theirs. Furthermore, the terrible brutality which is generally associated with the slave trade was more pronounced in this central region than it was elsewhere. Slaves were always secondary to the ivory trade here and the principal concern of the Arabs was to get their ivory to the coast, regardless of the human life which might be lost in so doing. Thus, particularly after the suppression of the export trade in slaves, it is along this central route that slave porterage was most frequently used and abused. We should recognise, however, that an easy supply of dispossessed people encouraged the accumulation of large slave holdings by prosperous Nyamwezi and Gogo ivory traders.

In the south, by contrast, trading profits from slaves were every bit as important as those from ivory, so that more care was taken in seeing that slaves reached the coast ready for sale. But the degradation of human life there was just as severe. Indeed, where Africans were enslaving each other for sale, as they were throughout the southern interior, it was worse. In these circumstances the mass of Africans were not being preyed upon by foreign scavengers, but by those elements in African society who had yielded to the temptation of personal profit without any consideration of the consequences for society as a whole. Once this process had begun, it sometimes took on the nature of a simple struggle for survival, stripping its participants of all dignity and shattering society. This is what happened around the south end of Lake Nyasa and in the Kilwa hinterland at the end of the nineteenth century.

There is, however, another aspect of the slave trade; not only did it uproot people, it also encouraged the growth of larger political units. Before the slave trade, people were attracted to the towns of the great ivory trading chiefs by the prospect of gaining greater wealth, as people are today attracted from the rural areas to the towns of modern Africa. Then, as life became increasingly dangerous in outlying villages because of the possibility of being raided by slave traders, people moved to these big towns for their own protection. So the slave trade, like the Ngoni invasion, was not simply a completely destructive force in East Africa. It also intensified that growth of larger political, economic, and social units which had always been a necessary part of long distance trade in Africa. In this respect the slave trade, like so many other nineteenth-century changes, set the stage for developments which were to be continued under colonial rule.

The Opening up of the North-eastern Interior

Beyond the reach of the Ngoni invasion and much less affected by the slave trade than the southern interior, the experience of the peoples of the north-eastern interior was considerably different from that of those in the south. External contacts came later and were both less widespread and less intensive here. Most of the more important tribal groups of the north-east remained aloof from, or were actually hostile to, traders coming from the coast. The most important peoples in this category were the Kamba, Kikuyu, Masai, and Nandi.

The Kamba were the northern counterparts of the Yao and the Nyamwezi. Living in the dry, famine-prone highlands between Kikuyuland and the coast, they were often forced to move great distances in search of food. By 1836 at the very latest a group was established at Rabai, in the neighbourhood of Mombasa. Kamba even penetrated into Zigua and Zaramo country, in Tanzania. The desire of the Kamba to maintain contacts amongst themselves and their response to the Arab demand for ivory at the coast led to the creation of a Kamba trading network in the north-east. Kamba trading superiority was at its height in the 1850's, but in the following decade they began to lose their markets to Arab traders. By the 1880's the Kamba route had become an Arab route. While maintaining trade links with the Arabs, the Kamba did not allow them to wander beyond the markets where they did their business. Unlike the Yao and the Nyamwezi, the Kamba did not affect coastal ways, but their trade and influence was on the upswing when the British came on the scene, and their early relations with the British were dominated by this revival.

Although the Kikuyu had been trading with the Kamba on the fringes of the forest for some time, and were willing to continue this business with the coastal operators, they resolutely refused to permit the Arabs to enter their homeland. Kikuyuland was prosperous, and a regular market system enabled goods to circulate freely within it. Indeed, the greatest problem facing the Kikuyu was their very prosperity. The nineteenth century witnessed a relentless growth of the Kikuyu population, with little extension of their tribal territory. On the eve of the colonial period Kikuyuland was bursting its seams. A crisis was in the making.

The territorial circumstances of the Masai were not unlike those of the Kikuyu during this period. By 1800 the Masai had already seen their greatest days of power. Expansion during the nineteenth century was minimal, and a precarious state of balance was struck with their neighbours. Thus thwarted, the Masai turned their aggressiveness inward. The struggle for grazing rights and chronic cattle raiding now took place among themselves in a long series of civil wars. The basic division in these Masai wars was between the pastoral and the agricultural Masai, who are often called 'Kwavi'. Within the pastoral grouping there was also a struggle for leadership waged by the Purko sub-tribe. On another level, there was the rivalry for the largest personal following between the various laibons, the priestly rain-makers who increasingly came to exercise secular power among the Masai. Of these the most outstanding were the Purko laibons, Subet who died in about 1866, and his son Mbatian, who was unrivalled by 1884. Despite the civil wars, the Masai were still masters of the plains, where they terrorised the Arab caravans which finally pushed into Masailand late in the 1860's. But, in the waning years of the pre-colonial era, a rapid succession of epidemic diseases, affecting both the Masai and their cattle, made their dominance more precarious than it had ever been before.

The rise of the Nandi owes much to the Masai. Nandi unity was focused on the orkoiyot, whose office was an adaptation of the Masai laibon. The way for their seizure of power between the Rift Valley and Lake Victoria in the 1870's was paved by the crushing defeat of the Uasin Gishu by an alliance of pastoral Masai. The Nandi were doing well enough on their own to see no need for dealings with the coastal strangers who were pushing their way north at this time. This defiant Nandi attitude applied equally to the British when they came along.

Not all the peoples of the northern interior were quite as reluctant to deal with the Arabs as were these four. In particular, the Arabs found willing partners and allies in the Pangani Valley. One of the most important of these was Kimweri, king of the Shambala, who ruled the Usambara Mountains from his capital at Vugha during the middle decades of the century. After his death in about 1869 the Shambala suffered a period of civil strife which endured until the imposition of German rule, but by then the coastmen were well established farther up the valley on the slopes of Mount Kilimanjaro, where the Chagga lived. The most powerful and extensive Chagga chiefdom was that of Kibosho, which reached its peak under Mangi Sina in about 1870. Sina actively encouraged Arab traders to come to his fortress at Maua, for he profited by their trade in ivory. Sina was supreme in the 1880's, but to the east, Mangi Rindi of Moshi had been bidding to eclipse Kibosho since he took power in about 1860. Temporarily dispossessed by Sina's father, Rindi returned to power by enlisting Arusha military assistance, then concentrated on enticing the Arabs to make their mountain headquarters at Moshi. Rindi's diplomatic game was aimed at the destruction of Kibosho and he ultimately turned to the Germans to achieve his aims. This style of Chagga chiefly politics persisted into the colonial era.

Another figure who saw that it could be to his advantage to ally himself with these new outside forces was Nabongo Shiundu of the Wanga, the most important Luyia sub-tribe. The Luyia, like their neighbours the Luo, were a loosely organised people; but unlike the Luo they had a tradition of kingship in the Wanga chiefship, which had reached its zenith in the previous century. During his reign, however, Shiundu was so hard pressed to maintain Wanga sovereignty that he sought outside military assistance. He first turned to the Uasin Gishu Masai who had settled in Wanga after they were driven from their homeland in the 1870's. Soon he was attracting Arab traders to his town so that he could receive a steady supply of arms and ammunition. Shiundu's success was only partial, but his tactics were continued after his death in the early 'eighties by his famous son Mumia, whose triumph was based on his early alliance with the British. It is often said that the colonial period marks a sharp break with the past in Africa. But here, as elsewhere in East Africa, the colonial period shows a continuation of nineteenth-century developments.

Uganda and the European Advance

If the changes brought about by outside pressures were less

obviously violent in Uganda than they were in southern and central Tanzania, they were even more revolutionary. Acknowledgement of these changes is fundamental to an understanding of a colonial and independent Uganda. The key to Uganda lay in the kingdom of Buganda, both from its bitter rivalry with the kingdom of Bunyoro and from the peculiar composition of Ganda society. In chapter nine we saw how Buganda grew from a small sub-kingdom of Bunyoro until, by the beginning of the nineteenth century, it was more powerful and aggressive than Bunyoro. The struggle against Bunyoro dominated all external policies of Buganda in the second half of the nineteenth century. Within Ganda society, allegiances of the people both as clansmen and as chiefs' clients was owed to the *kabaka,* who stood at the top of the hierarchies of the clan heads *(bataka)* and the territorial chiefs *(bakungu).* This factor, plus progressive centralisation and bureaucratisation, which meant that all chiefs were appointed by the kabaka, enabled the kabaka personally to dominate the Kingdom of Buganda. But the office demanded a ruthless and skilful politician who could eliminate his rivals and then balance all the competing forces within the system. Kabaka Suna, who reigned until 1856, and his son Mutesa, who ruled until 1884, both possessed these qualities.

During the first half of the century Buganda had little to fear from Bunyoro, whose weakness was highlighted by the loss of Toro to a royal usurper in the 1830's. Kabaka Suna was relatively free to cultivate his commercial relations with the Arab traders coming from Tabora. Under *Mukama* Kamurasi, however, Bunyoro experienced a notable revival. Kamurasi gained the throne through an alliance with the Lango, and then successfully beat off a Ganda attack. He also extended Bunyoro's trading connections so that he was not only competing with Buganda for the Zanzibar trade to the south, but was also dealing with Arab traders from Khartoum. For six years after he became kabaka, Mutesa was too preoccupied with disposing of his rivals to stand in the way of Bunyoro's revival. By the time he felt reasonably secure on his throne, Bunyoro was already a serious threat to Ganda domination of the region around the lakes. Kamurasi died in 1869, but his successor as mukama, Kabarega, immediately proved to be a leader of even greater stature. Meanwhile both sides were busy equipping themselves with firearms. Mutesa sought closer ties with Zanzibar, and the assurance of a steady supply of muskets to supplement the traditionally armed Ganda raiding parties, which brought in the trade goods which Buganda did not produce herself. Kabarega organised new military regiments, equipped with firearms, and employed men from Khartoum to help lead them. Into this explosive situation came the first agent of foreign imperialism in Uganda.

Sir Samuel Baker entered Bunyoro in April, 1872, as the representative of Egypt. Kabarega's main concern was to prevent a rival claimant to the mukamaship, Rionga, from following his lead in getting military aid from the Sudanese. Baker's demand that Bunyoro become an Egyptian protectorate as the price for aiding Kabarega against Rionga destroyed any chance of co-operation between Egypt and Bunyoro. When Baker threw his support behind Rionga, he was driven out of Bunyoro by Kabarega's army. As Baker's successor, General Charles Gordon focused Egyptian efforts on Buganda. Had Mutesa felt that he could join forces with Egypt to crush Bunyoro without sacrificing Buganda's independence, he undoubtedly would have done so. But he, too, saw that this was impossible, and Gordon described him in 1875 as 'fearing Egypt immensely and capable of anything to avoid annexation.' Mutesa even held an Egyptian column hostage at his capital for some months in 1876, but they were released unharmed. Gordon recognised Buganda's independence, and in 1880 Egypt retired permanently from northern Uganda. While the balance of power between Bunyoro and Buganda was unchanged by this Egyptian interlude, their bitter hostility was further aggravated. Moreover, the aftermath of Egypt's imperial ambitions in northern Uganda was very costly to Bunyoro, whose open clash with Baker permanently stamped her as being hostile to the advances of 'civilised' nations. This liability was eventually made worse by the fact that the European doorway to Uganda was through Buganda, so that the British came to see Bunyoro through the eyes of the Ganda hierarchy, that is, as an implacable enemy. The consequences were to be a dominant issue in Uganda politics right through the colonial period and into independence.

Meanwhile, within Buganda itself the basis of even more fundamental twentieth-century issues was being laid. Alert to the possibility of foreign threats to Buganda's sovereignty, Mutesa was nevertheless willing to tolerate outsiders in his kingdom so long as he felt that they could be useful to him and remained within his control. The position of the Arabs in

Buganda is a case in point*. So it was that Christian missionaries were tolerated on their arrival at his capital of Rubaga in June 1877. Mutesa had hoped that these Europeans would render him military help, such as the explorer Henry Stanley had given during his second visit in 1875. Mutesa was disappointed when they refused, but he decided that they might, after all, be able to offer him something. Thus the Church Missionary Society was allowed to begin its work at Rubega, under the watchful eye of Mutesa.

The conditions for missionary work were unique in Buganda, and the results were to be unique as well. Early missionary efforts elsewhere in East Africa were being thwarted wherever they were directed at tribal society. The only successes were being registered amongst the detribalised freed slave communities at Rabai, Masasi, and particularly at Zanzibar. Two factors made Ganda society unusually receptive to missionary ideas, both Christian and Muslim. In the first place, it was an open society in which ability and loyalty to the kabaka could earn one a high position in the power structure. Ambitious young men were eager to acquire new skills, both secular and religious, which would help them on their way. In the second place, there was no powerful Ganda religious hierarchy to oppose the spread of new religious ideas. The kabaka was not a religious leader; there were no clan-based ancestor cults; and the priests of the *lubaale* cult were out of favour and largely at the mercy of the kabaka. Two years later the Anglicans were joined at Rubaga by the French Catholic White Fathers. Their differences with the CMS were as apparent as those between Christianity and Islam, and Mutesa practiced his old art of playing one off against the other in the religious discussions which were held at court. Still, the missionaries were not bothered in their daily affairs. Working amongst the pages who were attached to Mutesa's court, both the CMS and the White Fathers soon won small but dedicated congregations. By 1884 each faith had over one hundred converts. It was to be of unrivalled significance for the later history of Uganda that these young men were taken from the lower ranks of the Ganda political hierarchy. When Mutesa died in October 1884, to be succeeded by his erratic son Mwanga, the foundations had already been laid for the 'Christian Revolution' in Buganda.

*See Chapter 11.

Conclusion

The nineteenth century was one of momentous change in East Africa. The key to this revolution was the growth of contacts with the outside world, and the way in which different East African peoples responded to this process. During the century a number of factors contributed to bring about change, foremost among them being the Ngoni invasion, the expansion of long distance trade and of the slave trade in particular and the coming of European missionaries. But we must not forget that the internal workings of the many East African societies were at least as important in defining their reactions to these external forces as was the nature of these new forces themselves. In other words, these outside influences were not simply acting upon a passive population, but were calling forth a very positive response from the people with whom they came in contact. In some cases, this response led to the formation of new political units. In others, it led to the adoption of new military techniques, or to basic changes within a particular society. Finally, we must remember that there were important independent changes taking place within many East African societies in the nineteenth century, and that there were some groups who remained notably isolated from many of the more outstanding external factors which were coming into play. These circumstances, as well as those resulting from interaction with the invaders of East Africa, were vitally important in preparing East Africans for the harsh realities of colonial rule.

Further reading

OLIVER, R. and MATHEW, G. (Eds.) *History of East Africa,* Volume I, Clarendon Press, Oxford, 1963. (The relevant parts of Oliver's chapter, and the chapters by A. Smith and D. A. Low are essential reading for the nineteenth century.)

OMER-COOPER, J. D. *The Zulu Aftermath : A Nineteenth-Century Revolution in Bantu Africa,* Longmans, London, 1966. (Especially chapters 1, 2, 5, 12. The most recent and best account of the rise of the Zulu and the Ngoni invasions.)

ALPERS, E. A. *The East African Slave Trade,* The Historical Association of Tanzania, Paper No. 3. East African Publishing House, Nairobi, 1967. (A more detailed look at the slave trade.)

COUPLAND, R. *The Exploitation of East Africa, 1856-1890.* Clarendon Press, Oxford, 1939. (A classic, detailed history by a British colonial historian.)

ABDALLAH BIN HEMEDI 'LAJJEMY, *The Kilindi* (Ed. J. W. T. Allen and W. Kimweri), East African Literature Bureau, in association with the African Studies Programme, Boston University, Nairobi, 1963. (The traditional history of the royal family of the Shambala. Also available in original Kiswahili as *Habari za Wakilindi.*)

STAHL, M. Outline of Chagga History, *Tanganyika Notes and Records,* Dar es Salaam, No. 64, 1965, (pp. 35-49). (A brief, clear account of the style of Chagga chiefly politics.)

OSOGO, J. *Nabongo Mumia of the Baluyia.* East African Literature, Nairobi, 1966. (A popular biography tracing Mumia's career as chief of the Wanga.)

GRAY, J. M. Mutesa of Buganda, *Uganda Journal,* Volume I, No. 1 1934 (pp. 2–39). (Still the best introduction to Mutesa and his policies.)

DUNBAR, A. R. *A History of Bunyoro-Kitara.* Oxford University Press, for East African Institute of Social Research, Nairobi, 1965. (An informative account of Bunyoro during the last four decades of the nineteenth century.)

OLIVER, R. *The Missionary Factor in East Africa* (2nd edition). Longmans, London, 1965. (The standard history of missionary activity in East Africa.)

TAYLOR, J. V. *The Growth of the Church in Buganda.* SCM Press, London, 1958 (Chs. 1 and 2 give an excellent account of why Christianity took root in Buganda and the effect it had on Ganda society).

LOW, D. A. *Religion and Society in Buganda, 1875-1900,* East African Institute of Social Research, Paper No. 8, Kampala, 1957. (A major piece of historical writing dealing with the same problems as the previous reading.)

13

Kenya Under the British, 1895 to 1963

Bethwell A. Ogot

Kenya as a Consular District, July 1895-April 1905

The declaration on 1 July 1895, of a protectorate over the small area between Mombasa and the Rift Valley came as a by-product of British involvement and activities in Zanzibar and Uganda. To the British Government, the East Africa Protectorate, to give it its official name, appeared in itself to be of little economic or strategic significance. But since Zanzibar and the coast formed a necessary base for British operations in East Africa and in the Indian Ocean complex, the Protectorate, a kind of Zanzibar backyard, had to be made safe. In the same way, the security of the East Africa Protectorate was regarded by the British as an essential part of the major strategic consideration for retaining control of Uganda and the Nile Valley.

The Protectorate was to be administered from Zanzibar by career diplomats. Indeed, the first Commissioner of the Protectorate, Mr (later Sir) A. H. Hardinge, was also Agent and Consul-General in Zanzibar. This system of dual responsibility continued until 1904, when, because of changed circumstances which we shall examine later, Sir Donald Stewart was appointed only to the position of Commissioner and Commander-in-Chief of the East Africa Protectorate.

This dual responsibility had other implications in the administrative field. Britain deliberately maintained the fiction which was already operating in Zanzibar, that the new Protectorate would exercise an important degree of control over its internal affairs. The British officials would be consuls supervising a local administration. The Commissioner had, therefore, to be a diplomat and the affairs of the Protectorate had to be conducted through the Foreign Office. Such arrangements usually operate only between two sovereign states. And even in the case of Zanzibar, Britain soon gave up the pretence, transferred the control over Zanzibar Affairs from the Foreign Office to the Colonial Office, and replaced the position of Consul-General with that of Resident.

In the East Africa Protectorate, the consular theory of administration was even more meaningless. Hardinge had inherited no definite system of administration from the Imperial British East Africa Company which had been trying to administer and develop the British sphere since 1888. With a capital of just under £250,000, its affairs being mismanaged, and the cost of military actions, especially in Uganda, soaring higher and higher, it was evident that the company was unlikely to prove equal to such a pioneering enterprise.

When, therefore, the Foreign Office took over the running of this area in 1895, a system of administration had still to be worked out. It is true that the company had succeeded in establishing its presence at the coast and in Buganda, as well as along the caravan route linking these two areas. But this did not produce an administrative system, nor was there any proper machinery of government. And to attempt to administer the East Africa Protectorate, which at that time was nothing but a geographical expression, on the basis of the consular theory, was really to attempt the impossible.

Hardinge's first task was to establish the British overrule in the Protectorate. He soon discovered that the local people were opposed to any form of foreign rule, and were prepared to fight for their rights.

In February 1895, four months before Hardinge was appointed, a serious rebellion had broken out at Takaungu, the northern headquarters of the Mazrui dynasty, over a disputed succession. On the death of Salim-bin-Hamis el-Mazrui, his son Rashid was selected by the IBEA Company's representative at Malindi, K. Macdougall, to succeed him. There was another claimant, a younger Mbaruk, who according to Muslim law, had a better right to the Governorship, but as he was not well disposed towards the British, his claim was disregarded. He thereupon withdrew to the elder Mbaruk's camp at Gonjoro and threatened armed resistance.

It was while affairs were in this unsettled condition that the rule of the Company came to an end. The Mazrui who had recognised neither the Sultan of Zanzibar's overlordship nor the Company rule were angered to hear that Hardinge was taking over the administration of the region in the name of the British Government. They decided to revolt against the new rulers.

In August the elder branch of the Mazrui decided to throw in their lot with their kinsmen, and the rebel forces were swelled by the inhabitants of most of the coast towns from Kipini in the north to Vanga in the South. Some of the coastal tribes, especially the Giriama, under their leader Ngonyo, also supported the Mazrui in their fight against the intruders. The rebels successfully attacked Freretown and Malindi. The Foreign Office could no longer leave matters to the Commissioner, because British prestige was at stake. Troops were sent from India to aid Hardinge's local force. The rebels were defeated. Mbaruk and his followers escaped to German East Africa. There was thus a general opposition to the imposition of British rule at the coast and it took over nine months of active fighting to establish political control of the area.

Further north in Jubaland, the Ogaden Somalis refused to recognise British overrule. And despite their defeat by Protectorate forces, again aided by Indian troops, in the middle of 1898, Government control was never really established in the area up to 1925, when Jubaland was ceded to Italy.

As far as the interior was concerned, the major concern of the Foreign Office between 1895 and 1901 was not so much the establishment of effective control over the different peoples, or the evolution of a suitable administrative system: their main interest was the construction of the Uganda railway. For strategic and economic reasons, it was desirable for the line to be built with the utmost speed, and this could only be done if peace was maintained with the surrounding peoples. Peace could not have been maintained if the Government had tried to extend its authority beyond the vicinity of the proposed railway line. Nor would it have been politic to employ outsiders such as the Arab or Swahili people (who were used extensively in German East Africa) in this delicate task of enlisting the support of the local people for railway construction. Hardinge was therefore forced to fall back on the only people who had some experience in dealing with the local people—the former servants of the Imperial British East Africa Company. He particularly relied on John Ainsworth the Sub-Commissioner at Machakos and Francis Hall who had been working at Kikuyu since 1893. Apart from their peace-keeping responsibilities, their main duty was to recruit local labour and to find food for the railway parties. Railway construction had thus to precede the establishment of political control. As far as administration was concerned, *ad hoc* arrangements were made by representatives of the Protectorate government to suit local situations.

The completion of the construction of the railway in 1901 brought many problems in its wake: Indian traders who had been moving inland as the railway progressed, were now established at several key points between Mombasa and Kisumu. The other group of newcomers whose numbers steadily increased after 1901 were the Europeans, comprising adventurers, traders, missionaries and settlers. Both the Indians and the Europeans were not content with operating within the administered districts: many of them pressed on into the uncontrolled areas. Since the Government was responsible for their safety, the jurisdictions of several administrators had to be extended every now and then to include all the areas in which the newcomers were operating. Instead of being regarded simply as a 'barren country' through which one had, of necessity, to pass on the way to Uganda, the Protectorate was beginning to acquire a character of its own. In the words of Sir Charles Eliot, Commissioner and Consul-General of the East Africa Protectorate (1900 to 1904), the country had 'unconsciously grown from a Consular District into a Colony.'

The new Commissioner not only wanted to introduce a Crown-Colony type of administration which he argued would be more suitable, he also insisted that new sources of revenue must be found to make the railway pay. In particular, he recommended the introduction of a Hut Tax—already introduced in Uganda and German East Africa—and colonisation of the highlands of Kenya by Europeans. The Africans so far had remained passive spectators, and had tended to regard the European administrators in the same way as they had looked upon the Swahili and Arab traders, viz., as temporary birds of passage. Indeed, with the Foreign Office policy of non-involvement, nothing had so far happened that could make the Africans think otherwise. But the implementation of Eliot's recommendations, which were accepted by the Foreign Office, was soon to awaken the African to the fact that the European had come to stay—and to stay as a ruler.

The emergence of the East Africa Protectorate as a distinctive territory was further hastened by the decision of the Foreign Office on 5 March 1902, to transfer the Eastern Province of Uganda to it. Not only was a large area added to the Protectorate, but much of this land was suitable for European settlement. And this had been one of the motivating factors in the Foreign Office decision. Moreover, the former Eastern Province of Uganda included one of the most densely populated regions in East Africa, and this meant that by a stroke of a pen, the African population in the Protectorate was more than doubled. Could the enlarged Protectorate continue to be governed from Zanzibar by career diplomats?

The answer to this question was obviously in the negative. Eliot therefore set about to create a more suitable type of administration. He also wanted the headquarters of the Protectorate moved from Mombasa to the more central new town of Nairobi. His immediate problem was that most of the African peoples had never accepted European rule. To obtain their acquiescence, it became necessary for the Government, between 1900 and 1908, to organise a series of military expeditions against recalcitrant tribes: expeditions against the Nandi in 1901, 1905 and 1906; against the Embu in 1904 and 1906; against the Gusii in 1904 and 1908; against the Kipsigis in 1905; and against the Bagusu and Kabras in 1907. And even in those areas to which no military expeditions were sent, force was used in the majority of cases to establish British rule.

But force alone would not have succeeded so quickly, if the Africans had been united. The British officials exploited the divisions that were inherent in most African societies to weaken resistance against their rule. They also easily found people like Mumia in Nyanza, Lenana and Kinyanjui in central Kenya, who for their own selfish motives, were keen to co-operate with the new rulers. These collaborators were propped up and inflated by the new masters. This was the beginning of a process that was soon to turn the chief into a mere instrument of the British government. In the words of a Kenya Government circular to Chiefs issued in 1941, their main activity was now 'to maintain a spirit of loyalty to the British Crown, and to inculcate such spirit . . .' They were no longer the custodians of their people's laws and customs.

Kenya as a Settlement Colony, 1905 to 1923

European settlers had been arriving in the country since 1896. But it was during the tenure of Charles Eliot as Commissioner that the first official encouragement was given to white settlement. From about 1904 settlers began to arrive from South Africa. This was the first of several government-sponsored European settlement schemes that were to be a marked feature of Kenya history. They were soon followed by other immigrants from Britain, Australia, New Zealand and Canada who, on the whole, brought more capital than their predecessors.

The new colonists were inspired by a dream. Since most of Asia, America and Africa was already explored, the highlands of Kenya appeared to be the only suitable area left for European colonisation. Kenya was to be the last of the typically British settlements established overseas, after U.S.A., Australia, Canada, New Zealand and South Africa. To quote the words of one of these early colonists, 'the goal of this generation is the establishment in East Africa of a new, loyal, white Dominion, securely founded in the principles of British tradition and Western civilisation.' It was assumed by Eliot and the settler leaders that this settlement was being carried out in a vacuum, and that their duty was to create an entirely new society and polity.

Any attempt to turn this European Dream into a reality was bound to run into several difficulties. To begin with, in Kenya, unlike in other settlement colonies, colonisation, in terms of the settlement of a white community, was preceded by the establishment of a form of Crown Colony Government. In all other countries, the pioneer settlers had preceded the establishment of any government. Moreover, almost for the first time in the British Empire, the Crown Colony system which had been specially designed for the government of so-called 'backward races', was now extended, from April 1905 when the Protectorate was transferred from the Foreign to the Colonial Office, to include, not only the Africans and Asians, but comparatively well-educated and politically articulate Europeans. It was an interesting constitutional experiment, but one which was fraught with difficulties right from the beginning. The Colonists' Association was soon formed to demand 'the ancient liberties' of every British person. And although the settlers were still very few, the British Government yielded to their pressure and agreed in 1906 to introduce a Legislative Council.

The system could not function smoothly. The most politically dominant element in the Protectorate was given the maximum chance for criticism and no opportunity for exercising responsibility, while the other communities were denied the same opportunity. The result was that politics among the Europeans assumed an unreal and irresponsible character, with much agitation and acrimony. European politics soon set a pattern first for Indian and later for African politics.

The other point which had not been taken into consideration was that Europeans who felt superior to the Africans, were unlikely to agree to do manual work in a country inhabited largely by Africans. The natural role of most of them working on the land, they felt, should be that of supervisors of African labour. Conscious of their status, they hoped that a poor white residuum would not appear, as had happened in South Africa. A class of poor whites, they feared, would pave the way to miscegenation, which in return would result in a debasement of racial standards. When many undesirable and penniless European characters swarmed into Nairobi from South Africa, the government quickly dealt with them under the Distressed British Subject's Act. If they failed to satisfy the Court as to their financial resources or past record, they were committed to prison at Fort Jesus in Mombasa for six months, followed by deportation to Bombay. This policy is perhaps responsible for there being very little miscegenation in Kenya, compared with South Africa, for instance. There is no separate population of 'coloureds' in Kenya. What is important, however, is that the policy of relying on black labour in what was intended to be a 'White Man's Country' was bound to pose difficult racial problems.

But the most serious challenge to the concept of a settlement colony came from the Indians in Kenya. They, too, had a dream. Their influence, which for over fifty years had been strong at the coast, with the building of the Uganda Railway extended up-country. Large numbers of coolies (as many as 13,000 were employed in December 1898) were brought in from India to build the line. Indian traders, as we have already seen, followed in the wake of the railway, pioneering retail trade inland. Indian troops were called in every now and then to help with the suppression of revolts. Much of the legislation in the infant Protectorate was based on Indian precedents and the currency was Indian rupees and annas. So by 1905 there was already a strong Indian influence in the territory.

Even with settlement, it was not clear initially whether this was not going to be a joint enterprise between the Europeans and the Indians. Sir Harry Johnston when he was Special Commissioner for Uganda had stated that 'East Africa is, and should be, from every point of view, the America of the Hindu.' But he also conceded that the Kenya Highlands were 'admirably suited for a white man's country.' Eliot, at least up to 1902, was prepared to encourage both Indian and European settlement. It was increased pressure from the European pioneer settlers that forced him to the conclusion that the Kenya Highlands must be reserved for the White colonists only.

It should, however, be emphasised that the Indians in Kenya were not the helpless and innocent victims of British Imperialism, as many writers would want us to believe. Mr Benarsidas Chaturvedi, a leader of the Greater India Movement, wrote in one of his letters of the Indian Dream:

'If there is any man in India who has got a true perception of this vision and who has worked incessantly for its realisation it is Mr Andrews and none else. In fact he has been living in Greater India for the last fourteen years and his mind has wandered from Borobuder, the famous temple of Java, the Yava Dwip of Greater India of ancient times to the Khoja Jamat Khana—the great mosque at Nairobi. He realises that India had her cultural colonies in the distant past and she may have them again in the near future. Mr Andrew's Greater India will not belong to an Imperial system, it will be definitely cultural . . . What Mr Andrews sees in his imagination and what we cannot see is the Greater India of A.D. 2000. The fact is that many of our leaders have not been abroad. It is said that some of our Indian *Sadhus* in olden times had a sort of miraculous power by which they could fly away to any part of the world. I wish some *Sadhu* like that could send a good number of our leaders to the colonies in the twinkling of an eye. Let them be sent to Mombasa or Dar-es-Salaam. Let them see that Mombasa is just like any town of Gujerat. Sir John Kirk, the British Agent at Zanzibar used to refer to East Africa as India's

America. Let some of our leaders see *this* America. A fine walk
by the seaside at Dar-es-Salaam or a view of the Indian Ocean
from Mr Yusuf Ali's bungalow on the seaside at Tanga will
give them an idea of the infinite possibilities of India—an idea
which cannot be given by hundreds of books or articles.'

This was not just the Dream of a fanatic. In Kenya itself,
Mr A. M. Jeevanjee, one of the Indian leaders said in 1910:
'I would go so far as to advocate the annexation of this African
territory (Kenya) to the Indian Empire, with Provincial Government under the Indian Viceroy. Let it be opened to us, and in
a very few years it will be a second India.' In 1921, the *East
African Chronicle*, which was at that time the official organ of
the Indian Congress in Kenya, published an article visualising
the future when Kenya would be Indian administered, and
drawing a parallel between such a position and that of South
Africa administered by Dutchmen. The Aga Khan himself, in
an addendum to Gokhale's political statement, suggested that
East Africa be set aside for Indian colonisation.

At the root of the so-called 'Indian Question' in Kenya was
a clash between two Dreams, the solution to which had wider
Imperial implications. Was Kenya to be European or Indian?
And was development to be based on European or Indian
foundations? In Canada and Australia, the white settlers had
already reserved the right to decide what class of non-Europeans,
if any, would be permitted to settle in their countries. In South
Africa, too, restrictive measures against the Indians were
already operating, making the Indian a mere sojourner. The
strength and virility of the British Empire was seen to reside
in its homogeneous European stock. Was Kenya prepared to
undermine the Empire by allowing racial admixture?

The European settlers were determined to resist such a
policy. They demanded an increasing measure of self-government for themselves, in order to deal with 'the Indian menace.'
They got the Colonial Office to reserve the Highlands, on the
pretext of administrative convenience, for European settlement.
Racial segregation was introduced in towns. They wanted an
end put to Indian immigration. The Indians, in their turn,
demanded complete political and electoral equality.

It is in this wider context of a clash between two rival civilisations that the decision to transfer the headquarters of the East
Africa Protectorate from Mombasa to Nairobi in 1907 must be
considered. Established in 1896 as a transport depot, Nairobi

replaced Mombasa as the headquarters of the Uganda Railway in July 1899. Mombasa, on the other hand, had had a long and distinguished history and was the centre of a long-established Swahili culture. It would have been contradictory for the Protectorate Government, which was bent on creating a new society based on British values, to have used Mombasa, with its Oriental background, as a base. Whereas in Tanganyika the coastal Swahili culture was gradually extended from Dar-es-Salaam and other coastal towns to embrace the whole country, in Kenya, the founding of Nairobi, in effect, meant the rejection of Swahili culture and its replacement by a European culture. This fact, together with the geographical position of Nairobi, especially its close proximity to European settlement areas, soon turned this old safari camp into a dominant centre of African and European politics.

But it was not only the large number of Indians which had made it difficult for Kenya to become another Australia or Canada. Even more important for the future was the fact that there were already in Kenya, unlike Australia which was in-habited only by hunters before the advent of the white colonists, societies that were highly developed socially. Most of them had lived in the country for over 300 years. It was, therefore, in-correct to suggest, as many British administrators and European settlers did, that there was a clean slate on which they could write anything they liked. Indeed the very concept 'Protectorate' implied a recognition of the existence of viable African societies, whose interests had to be protected.

Some of Eliot's officials such as Ainsworth, Jackson and Bagge had, in fact, recognised this. Contrary to the views of their superior, they maintained that the first duty of the administration was to safeguard African interests, and that settlement must take second place to this.

But these were voices crying in the wilderness. The 'White-man's Country' concept gradually gained general currency in the administration and among the settlers, many of whom were Transvaalers. It was becoming increasingly clear that Kenya could not be another Australia: but there was much hope that it could be another South Africa. The Protectorate government began, therefore, to look to South Africa for legislative prece-dents. Much of the Kenya Highlands was to be reserved for white settlement; 'native' reserves were to be established; and a Commissioner for Native Affairs was appointed in 1907. In

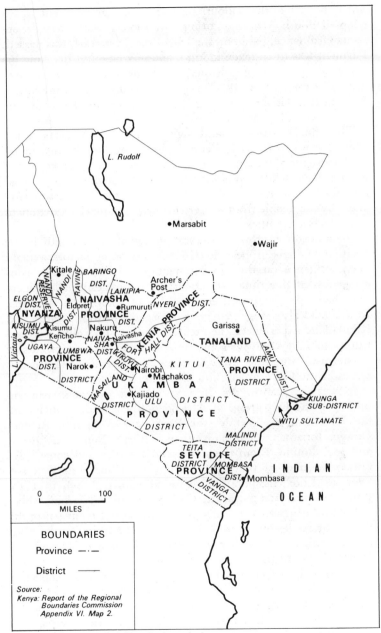

Figure 23 Kenya: Administrative boundaries as at 1909

order to solve the labour problem, the government again
adopted South African solutions. In 1906, a Masters and Servants Ordinance, based on the law of the Transvaal, was passed.
Payment was to be made in kind, and any labourer breaking his
contract was to be imprisoned. Through taxation the 'native'
was to be forced to work. This was the beginning of ordinances
for contract labour that were to culminate in the notorious
Northey Circulars of 1919.

The impact of this racialist legislation on the Africans varied
from district to district. Central Kenya was most affected by
land legislation and the labour laws were felt most keenly in
western Kenya. This would explain why, throughout the colonial
period, the major political grievance in central Kenya was land
and why the people from western Kenya have played a dominant
role in labour politics.

In addition to this legislation designed to strengthen the
position of the European in Kenya, two other factors made a
deep influence on the development of African political consciousness at this time. Missionary activities, especially education, had by 1920 produced a new élite among the Africans.
In this field also, western Kenya, especially central Nyanza and
Kikuyuland experienced the greatest impact. This élite accepted
European values and for some time acted as the chief agents of
Westernism. But from 1921 onwards, they became the greatest
critics of the Government and of Western values.

In western Kenya, the C.M.S. Mission station at Maseno
produced the first group of African political leaders, including
the Rev. Simeon Nyende, the Rev. Ezekiel Apindi, Reuben
Omulo, Jonathan Okwirri, Mathayo Otieno, Benjamin Owuor
and Joel Omino. From the same school earlier had come John
Owalo, founder of the first Independent Church in Kenya—
'Nomiya Luo Mission'. Before founding his church in 1910,
John Owalo had taught at the C.M.S. school in Nairobi, where
he had Kenyatta as one of his pupils. In central Kenya also, the
first political leaders were 'mission boys'. Harry Thuku, and
his associates such as James Beauttah, Jesse Kariuki and Job
Muchuchu were Christians. So was Jomo Kenyatta.

An equally important factor was the Africans' collective
experience during the 1914 to 1918 war. Small numbers were
enrolled in the regular military units, while the majority, about
165,000, were employed as porters in the Carrier Corps. The
groups most affected were the Kikuyu, Luo and Kamba. The

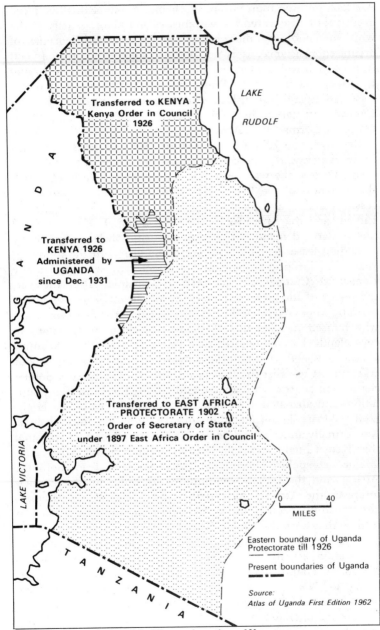

Figure 24 The evolution of the Western boundary of Kenya

Africans became more aware of themselves as a distinct racial group; they discovered the weaknesses and heterogeneity of the white men and, even more crucial, they learnt the importance of organised resistance. It is not without significance that several African political leaders in the 1920's and 1930's, including Jonathan Okwirri, first President of the Young Kavirondo Association, and Joseph Kangethe, later President of the Kikuyu Central Association, had either fought or served in the Carrier Corps in German East Africa.

By 1918, the African was restless. He had fears about his future which were soon confirmed by the actions of the Government. During the war years, the settlers had cleverly exploited the weakness of the British government to obtain several concessions aimed at consolidating their power against both the Indians and the Africans. In 1915 the Colonial Office accepted the settlers' demand for greater security of land tenure by extending leases of land from 99 to 999 years. In the following year, the Europeans' demand for direct representation in the Legislative Council was accepted in principle. After the war, the policy of the paramountcy of European interests was intensified by Major-General Sir Edward Northey, the new Governor, who himself had led the allied forces against the Germans in Nyasaland. He nominated two Europeans to the Executive Council, issued the notorious Northey Circulars on labour recruitment to assist the European settlers, introduced a Soldier Settlement scheme with a view to doubling the European population, and alienated a further 4,560 square miles in the Highlands. Most significant, the country, now renamed Kenya, was formally annexed and declared a Crown Colony. It appeared that Kenya might, after all, become another South Africa.

The new policy engendered sharp reactions from both the African and the Indian communities. In order to protect their interests, the Africans formed their first political organisations almost simultaneously in Nyanza and Nairobi. It is important to note that both the Young Kavirondo Association, founded in 1921 by the former students of Maseno, and the East African Association, established in Nairobi by Kikuyu Muslims, such as Mwalimu Hamisi and Abdulla Tairara, and other Africans living in Nairobi, especially the Baganda, were transtribal organisations. The former was dominated by the Luo and Luyia and operated in a rural environment, while the latter, though urban, was dominated by the Kikuyu, especially after

Harry Thuku had taken over the leadership in mid-1921. These two contrasting areas remained the dominant centres of African politics until 1960.

The Young Kavirondo Association was soon diverted from its radical policies by Archdeacon Owen, Archdeacon of Nyanza from 1918 to 1944. It was renamed the 'Kavirondo Taxpayers' and Welfare Association' in 1923, and henceforth, it devoted much of its energies to welfare politics. In central Kenya on the other hand, although Thuku was arrested and deported to Kismayu in 1922 and his organisation proscribed, much of what he stood for was soon revived by a new organisation called the Kikuyu Central Association, founded in Fort Hall in 1924. Neither of these organisations as yet questioned the colonial system: they were chiefly concerned with obtaining redress for specific grievances.

The Indian opposition to European rule took the form of demanding equality of treatment for the two immigrant communities. They opposed the policies of residential and land segregation, and of restricting Indian immigration. They demanded direct and adequate representation on the Legislative Council, based on a common roll. They argued, with much justice, that separate representation would perpetuate and intensify racial antagonism. In these demands, they were supported by the Indian Government.

The Europeans defended their segregationist policies on the ground that neither the Indian nor any other section of the community—since they were not members of the ruling race—'have the same status or can claim the same rights as appertain to British colonists in a British Colony such as Kenya'. 'To grant the Indian more representation than is sufficient adequately to meet his own interests,' one of the settlers wrote, 'would automatically put the direction of the affairs of the Colony into the hands of two antagonistic cultures'. They also added that the promotion of Oriental influences would be detrimental to African interests. In this last contention, they were supported by the Church in Kenya and in Britain. If their requests were not granted, they warned, they would take the law into their own hands.

It was this European-Indian struggle for the possession of Kenya that constituted the so-called 'Indian Question'. To solve it, a special conference was called in London by the then Colonial Secretary, the Duke of Devonshire, in 1923. Both

Europeans and Indians were represented, and each tried to win sympathy by invoking the principle of safeguarding the interests of the only group that was not represented, the Africans.

The resulting White Paper satisfied neither of the protagonists. The European demand for self-government was rejected; the policies of residential segregation in townships and immigration restriction were to be abandoned; but the policy of land reservation in the Highlands was to continue. The Indians, on the other hand, were granted five representatives only in the Legislative Council, these to be elected on a communal roll. Thus the Colonial Government made it clear that Kenya would be surrendered neither to the Indians nor to the European settlers. It was to remain a responsibility of the Imperial Government, which would hold it in trust for its inhabitants. In the famous words of the White Paper: 'Primarily, Kenya is an African territory; and His Majesty's Government think it necessary to record their considered opinion that the interests of the African natives must be paramount, and that if, and when, those interests of the immigrant races should conflict the former should prevail. Obviously, the interests of other communities, European, Indian or Arab, must be severally safeguarded . . . But in the administration of Kenya His Majesty's Government regard themselves as exercising a trust on behalf of the African population, and they are unable to delegate or share this trust, the object of which may be defined as the protection and advancement of the native races.'

In trying to solve one form of racial conflict, the White Paper in effect created a more serious form in proclaiming the policy of 'the paramountcy of native interests'.

The Age of Separate Development, 1923 to 1952

The major challenge facing Kenya during this period was the future of its tri-racial population, European, Indian and African. Had one community to advance at the expense of the others? Were the Indians to be squeezed out by the other two groups? Or could Kenya develop an harmonious amalgam where each community would be complementary to its fellows and all three could render their appropriate contribution to the well-being of the social whole? These are some of the basic questions that policy-makers had to bear in mind constantly.

The theory of separate development was a logical sequel to

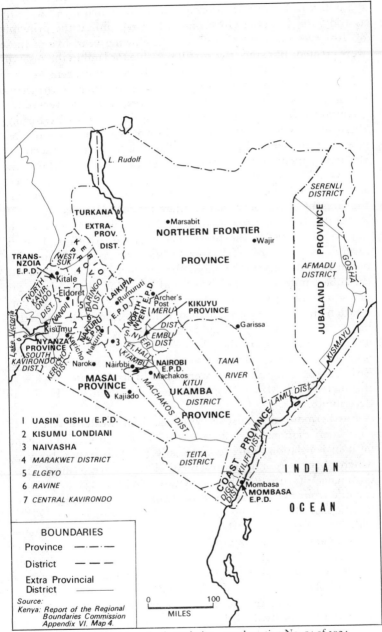

Figure 25 Kenya: Administrative boundaries—proclamation No. 54 of 1924

the policy of land reservation on racial and tribal lines. As early as 1905, the Imperial Government had recognised the principle of 'Reserves for natives', and in the following year, five of these were created. But since it was still possible for land in the reserves to be alienated, the Africans naturally felt apprehensive over their land. Although the Crown Lands Ordinance of 1915 gave statutory recognition to 'native' Reserves, it also increased the feeling of insecurity and unrest among the Africans by turning them into tenants-at-will of the Crown, who could be dispossessed at any time. In order to allay this feeling of insecurity, the government finally agreed in October 1926 to delimit the reserves. The boundaries of twenty-three of them were gazetted, and they could be alienated only by the local government with the consent of the Secretary of State for the Colonies.

But it was evident that in many areas, the land set aside would not be adequate for the future needs of the Africans. Indeed, several of these reserves were already over-populated. The population density in Kiambu, for instance, was about 400 to the square mile in 1919; in Nyeri and Fort Hall, it was about 212 per square mile; in central Nyanza about 165; and in Bunyore location in north Nyanza, it had reached 1,000. On the other hand, the average European farmer occupied about 500 acres of land in 1925 and in the whole of the 'White Highlands' only 9 per cent of occupied land was under cultivation. Thus even as early as 1926, the reserves were already inadequate; and with the increase in African population, the position was bound to deteriorate.

Furthermore, the discovery of gold in western Kenya in 1931 soon demonstrated to the African the futility of placing faith in legislation which could easily be altered by a body on which they were not represented. The Native Lands Trust Ordinance of 1930 was hurriedly amended in 1932 in order to exclude from the Reserves the land containing minerals. To the question of the inadequacy of the 'Native' Reserves was thus added the problem of their security. Land was still a major political and racial issue in Kenya.

In April 1932, the Secretary of State for the Colonies appointed a Commission to investigate certain matters concerning land problems in Kenya. In particular, the Commission was:
 (a) 'To consider the needs of the native population, present and prospective, with respect to land, whether to be held on tribal or individual tenure . . .

(b) To define the area, generally known as the Highland, within which persons of European descent are to have a privileged position in accordance with the White Paper of 1923.'

The Chairman of the Commission was Sir W. Morris Carter, and their report was published in May 1934.

Undoubtedly, the Report gave great satisfaction to the European settlers; 16,700 square miles of good land was to be reserved exclusively and permanently for the European settlers. In 1939 the boundaries of the White Highlands were gazetted. Also, the Reserves which were left substantially as they were before 1934, were to cease to be designated as Crown Land and were to be known as Native Lands. In other words, the Commission's recommendations, which were accepted by the British government, implied that Kenya was to be partitioned into two racial blocs, African and European. And in the African sector, all economic, social and political developments were to be conducted on tribal lines. Racialism and tribalism thus became institutionalised.

What did the British and Colonial governments have in mind in advocating the policy of separate territorial development? Were they thinking of transferring political power to Africans in their areas? Or was it rather to be what has been called 'the policy of racial separation and guardianship of whites over the natives'? A brief review of the facts would show that it was the latter.

The 1923 White Paper had declared that Kenya was primarily an African country. This declaration posed the question: Was Kenya to be developed largely by the Africans? The European settlers were already demanding that white settlement must be the economic backbone of the Colony. On the other hand, West African countries and Uganda were being developed by the Africans themselves, under the guidance of a small number of Government officials and a small number of traders and companies. At the other extreme, there was the case of South Africa, where the African had been deprived of the bulk of the land and had by force of circumstances been driven to become largely a wage earner engaged in mining or on European land. Which of these policies was to apply in Kenya?

It was argued that neither alternative suited Kenya. Instead, the 'dual policy', that is, complementary development of non-native and native production was recommended. Mr L. S.

Amery, when Colonial Secretary, defined the dual policy as 'a policy which recognises our trusteeship both to the native population—whom we had found on the spot and whom it was our duty to bring forward and develop in every possible way—but also our trusteeship to humanity at large for the fullest development of those territories and towards those in particular of our own race who had undertaken the task of helping forward that development'. This was tantamount to a rejection of the 1923 paramountcy policy.

Lord Delamere, the Kenya European leader, contended that the corollary to the dual policy must be separate development. And the latter, according to him, was 'based on a perfectly rational desire to protect a civilised standard of living from an economic competitor on a lower grade of life'.

Although in theory both African and non-African production were to be encouraged, in actual fact, only European production was promoted in Kenya. A prospective European farmer had adequate provision made for training, and he could obtain low interest loans from the Land Bank and direct grants for the purchase of capital farming equipment. Additional aid to European farmers was provided by government-sponsored agricultural research, maize and wheat subsidies, government-sponsored marketing schemes and transport facilities.

It is worth noting that Uganda's exports in 1934, for instance, amounted to £3¾ millions, while the Kenya exports amounted to less than £2 millions. It is also worth remarking that, of Uganda's exports, more than £3 millions came from African agriculture, mainly cotton, while in Kenya not more than £300,000 worth of exports came from African production, and more than half of these from the export of hides. Would it not have paid Kenya from a purely business point of view to concentrate on stimulating African production for export? And even if the Government was committed to the dual policy, it would still have paid the country to accept the consequences of such a policy with the promotion of balanced development both African and European. But this was not the case.

The racial approach which we have noticed in the economic field also applied to the provision of social services. Medical services, education and even sports were organised on strict racial lines, with the Europeans always getting the best services, the Indians the second best and the Africans having to do with whatever was left over. In 1938, for example, an Education Department Memorandum said the aim of European education was 'to provide a good general education for all children who do not attend private schools between the ages of 6 and 16 years'. The aim of Indian education was 'to provide an eight years' course of primary education—for all children of six years of age and over'. In the case of the Africans, the Memorandum reiterated the policy first enunciated by the Colonial Secretary in a Command Paper in 1925, which said that 'The first task of education [African education] is to raise the standard alike of character and efficiency of the bulk of the people, but provision must also be made for the training of those who are required to fill posts in the administrative and technical services, as well as those who as chiefs will occupy positions of exceptional trust and responsibility'. The emphasis in African education on producing clerks and other junior officials for the Colonial administration is evident.

The same Memorandum estimated that only about $12\frac{1}{3}$ per cent of African children of school age were receiving any education at all. Of this number, 96,983 were in sub-elementary and elementary schools, 3,059 in primary, and 176 in junior secondary schools. There was no African attending a college or a university. Thus by 1938 only the fringe of the problem of African education had been touched. By contrast there were already several well-established and well-equipped secondary schools for Europeans; and every year a number of students from these schools went to British universities on government bursaries.

Such discrimination would have been defensible if the Europeans were willing to tax themselves in order to pay for these expensive social services. The fact is that, although most of these services were provided from the Central government funds, the Europeans were, throughout this period, very re-reluctant to tax themselves. If we take education again, we find that in the case of Africans the Local Native Councils paid for much of this education levying special education rates to run elementary schools and to subsidise primary schools. This was necessary because they received very little in direct grants from Central funds. Successive Annual Reports show that the amount spent on education from Central funds per head of the African population fell between 1932 (the first year in which Arab figures were separated from African) and 1936:

1932	64 cents.	1935	50 cents.
1933	50 cents.	1936	44 cents.
1934	50 cents.		

For the Europeans, the figures for 1929 and 1930 were 852 and 800 shillings respectively.

Looking at the budgets of the local authorities, through which most of the social services were provided, it is evident that whereas the Local Native Councils rapidly and willingly assumed major financial responsibilities, the European District Councils rapidly became, in the words of a Commissioner for Local Government, 'little more than agents for the expenditure of Government funds'. In 1945, for instance, 97 per cent of all European District Council Revenue came from Government and military grants, while of the Local Native Council revenue only one-seventh came from the Government and one-third came from rates on the people.

Nor was it true, as many Europeans contended, that most of the Central funds came from non-African sources. The principal source of Central Government revenue was taxation. Between 1925 and 1936, for example, taxation accounted for between 71 and 77 per cent of the net revenue. The two principal items of taxation were Customs Import Duties and African Hut and Poll Tax, which between them accounted for over 70 per cent of the total yield of taxation. The yield from the two items from 1925 to 1936 was as follows:

	Customs Import Duties	African Hut & Poll Tax
1925	£679,727	£537,478
1926	741,374	558,044
1927	830,550	570,783
1928	915,282	564,405
1929	949,725	539,641
1930	815,286	591,424
1931	698,584	530,877
1932	597,262	515,277
1933	581,770	557,791
1934	611,606	514,480
1935	690,380	502,302
1936	775,010	537,219

On top of direct taxation, it should be remembered that the African paid indirect taxation, which must have increased as he became more familiar with and dependent upon imported goods. It is therefore evident that the African community was not only paying more taxation in proportion to their resources than the other communities in Kenya, but also that much of the revenue derived from them was being diverted to non-African services.

This was, in fact, the conclusion of Lord Moyne who made an exhaustive examination of the financial situation of Kenya in 1932. He found, for instance, that since 1926 the Local Native Councils had voted £33,381 for the provision of school buildings to make up for the insufficiency of Government grants, 'although accommodation on a very generous scale has quite properly been found entirely from Central funds for the school buildings of the European and Indian communities'. He also noticed similar anomalies in the case of road, medical and agricultural grants. 'On examining the general structure of these Colonial services,' he concluded, 'and the proportion of cost due to the provision of such conveniences as motor roads, municipal water supply and general scale of Government and municipal services, comparing also the services in settled areas with those provided in neighbouring areas where European interests are less dominant, I have formed the opinion that in the development of the undivided or colonial services in Kenya the prevailing bias has been towards the convenience of a civilisation in which the native so far shares little of direct advantages.'

The theory of separate development faced its greatest challenge in the political field. It was generally assumed that for many generations the European element must have a major influence in the direction of the Government and that the proper line for African political advance was in Local Government. The African, in other words, was to be restricted to local and tribal politics. But the system of Local Government itself had to conform to the theory of separate development. Consequently, three different types emerged, one for the European settled areas, one for the African Reserves and one for the urban areas.

Apart from the District Road Boards, there were no proper local government bodies in the 'White Highlands' until 1929. Before that date, in 1926, Sir Edward Grigg had appointed a Commission of Inquiry under Mr Justice Feetham, a former Town Clerk of Johannesburg and a member of the 1915 South

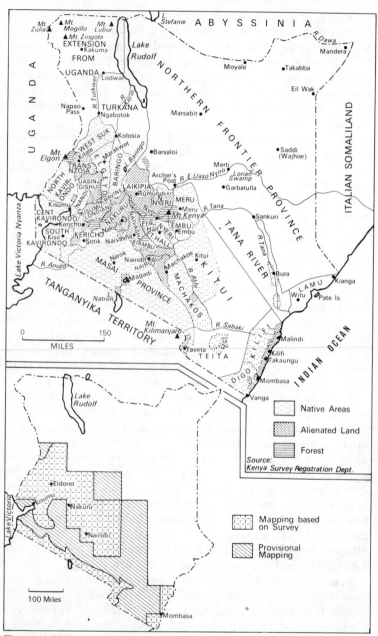

Figure 26 Native and alienated areas 1938

African Local Government Commission 'to make recommendations as to the establishment or extension of Local Government' in the Settled Areas and the Municipalities.

The Commission's Report endorsed the view that local government in Kenya should be developed along racial lines. It recommended that seven European District Councils should be established. Only six Councils (Nakuru, Uasin Gishu, Nairobi, Kisumu-Londiani, Naivasha and Trans-Nzoia) were established in 1929 to 1930, after the passing of the Local Government (District Councils) Ordinance in 1928. The seventh Council, the Aberdare District Council, was set up much later in January 1939.

As local authorities, they were a dismal failure. Although empowered under the law to impose rates, they did not do so except for a specific purpose, such as a hospital. Up to 1945 they failed to provide social services for the over half a million Africans who lived in the Settled Areas. As the Europeans gradually lost political power at the centre after 1952, they fell back on these Councils, which became a kind of political citadel.

The development of local government in the towns was also bedevilled by the theory of separate development. Besides the Swahili towns at the coast, urbanism was a new phenomenon in Kenya, and was a direct consequence of European settlement and Indian commercial activities. Africans might work in the new towns but they were not expected to live in them. The planning and development of all Kenya's towns during this period was based on the assumption that the African workers in the towns were sojourners who could be housed in periurban shanty settlements. Urban Local Government was therefore controlled by the Europeans.

Nairobi, for example, which had been declared a Township in 1903 and became a Municipality on 15 July 1919, was largely controlled by a European-dominated Council which had been instituted in 1928. In a Council of twenty, the Indians had seven representatives and the rest were Europeans. And although Africans were in the majority in the town, they had no direct voice in the affairs of the Nairobi Council until 1946. The result was a proliferation of tribal welfare associations, especially in the 1930's. Since there was little hope of obtaining reasonable social services from the Council, the Africans turned to self-help schemes organised on a tribal basis. In 1936, for example, the Commissioner for Local Government said in his

Annual Report that 'Native Associations based on districts are increasing and are, on the whole, well-organised and useful.' These Associations were also the channels for the expression of African opinion, and they were to prove useful during the post-1945 period in the mobilisation of nationalist forces.

Because of the long history of Mombasa and the high degree of racial admixture that had taken place, the bitterness which characterised the politics of Nairobi was lacking. Otherwise, the pattern here as in other Kenya towns such as Nakuru, Kisumu, Eldoret, Kitale, Nyeri, Nanyuki and Thika, was similar to that of Nairobi. In all these towns there were definite segregationist policies in planning residential areas.

In the African Reserves, the Ordinance setting up Kenya's local councils (the first in any African colony) was introduced by Governor Sir Robert Coryndon, and it became law in September 1924. The Local Native Councils had the District Commissioners as ex-officio Presidents and chief executive officers. Starting with a system of nomination, the elective principle was soon introduced, and by 1948 the elected members had attained a majority in all the councils.

During the period under consideration, these Councils constituted the theatre in which the drama of African politics was played. As we have noted earlier, it was government policy, supported by the Missions, to confine African politics within tribal channels. The Administration therefore saw the new Councils as an instrument for controlling the politicians. In the words of the 1924 Native Affairs Department Report, 'the Councils . . . should go far towards counteracting any mischievous tendencies which might develop in native political societies, for representations made to Government by the latter would in the ordinary course be referred to the former in the first instance.'

African politicians, on the other hand, saw in the new Councils a useful forum for ventilating their grievances. Political organisations such as the Kavirondo Taxpayers' and Welfare Association and the Kikuyu Central Association enthusiastically sponsored candidates for these Councils.

By the 1930's, the politicians had become disillusioned with the Councils which, in their view, had become mere tools of the District Commissioners. The latter used them to pass unpopular agricultural and other by-laws. It was also becoming obvious that the major political problems facing the Africans were not local but national, and the Councils were impotent over such issues.

Towards a Crisis, 1940 to 1952

Just as the First World War had precipitated a political crisis in Kenya, so did the Second World War. With the imminent threat of Italian invasion from Somaliland, a total ban was placed on African political activity. Political organisations which had emerged in the 1930's in different parts of the Country— the Ukamba Members Association, the Taita Hills Association, the North Kavirondo Central Association—as well as the old Kikuyu Central Association, were proscribed, and their leaders detained at Kapenguria.

The Europeans were again quick to exploit a war situation to consolidate their position. Their influence on the Executive Council and on the various committees and Statutory Boards increased enormously. Forced labour for Africans was introduced on European farms. In March 1943 some 16,000 conscripted Africans were in employment. Of these, about three-quarters were employed on private undertakings. When questions were asked how coffee and tea plantations came to be considered 'essential undertakings' for which labour might be conscripted, the Secretary of State replied that:

'The main object in declaring these two important industries in Kenya to be essential undertakings was in order that they might be maintained in operation on a scale which would enable the Colony to play its part in meeting the food supply requirements of the United Nations, including those of the large numbers of refugees and prisoners in East Africa.'

For this conscript labour a minimum wage of 8 to 10 shillings was laid down, or 9 to 12 shillings for long periods of service.

In June 1943 the Agricultural Production and Settlement Board was divided into two Sections, an Agricultural Production Section to carry on the work of organising agricultural production in the war effort and a Settlement Section 'to encourage and plan for increased white settlement in the Colony.' The membership of this Settlement Section consisted of Major Cavendish-Bentinck as Chairman, two officials and fourteen European 'unofficial residents'.

At the end of the war, Sir Philip Mitchell introduced a

'Membership' system which meant that the European unofficial members of the Executive Council could now be given portfolios. And the first to be given to European settlers (Agriculture and Local Government, to Cavendish-Bentinck and C. E. Mortimer respectively) were those which affected the Africans most intimately.

All these political gains by the Europeans were being acquired in a radically changed environment. The rapid widening of political horizons, the growth of the educated class and the prospect of rapid social and economic development among Africans, all imposed the need for a critical re-examination of administrative policy. The new African leaders were no longer satisfied with *ad hoc* measures aimed at redressing specific grievances within the colonial framework which had hitherto characterised African politics. They were now questioning the legitimacy of colonialism itself. Such figures as Eliud Mathu, James Gichuru, B. A. Ohanga, W. W. Awori, J. D. Otiende and F. W. Odede, were educated people who could hold their own with any European. The ex-soldiers who joined them after demobilisation also produced leaders whose horizons had been greatly enlarged by their wartime experiences overseas. This group, which included Fred Kubai, Bildad Kaggia, Dedan Mugo, and later Dedan Kimathi and Stanley Mathenge, was more active in the trade unions. Could these people be confined to tribal politics?

This question had been answered in the negative by the Africans themselves towards the end of the war. On 1 October 1944, thirty-three people drawn from most Kenya tribes attended a meeting in Nairobi at which the Kenya African Union was founded. This was to announce to the world that national politics had arrived. In 1947, Kenyatta, after a long absence in England, took over the leadership of K.A.U. Despite the advice of Sir Philip Mitchell to him to 'begin by seeking election to the Local Native Council of the area where he proposed to live, and make a start in local government,' it was clear that Kenyatta, who for several years had been preoccupied with Pan-African problems, could not be localised.

The question which soon faced the African leaders was whether independence in Kenya could be won by constitutional means. Mr E. W. Mathu had been nominated to the Legislative Council in October 1944. He was soon followed there by F. W. Odede. But it soon became clear that the ex-soldiers as well as the former leaders of the Kikuyu Central, the Ukamba Members, and the Taita Hills Associations were dissatisfied with the politics of the Legislative Council. They demanded a more radical approach. The arrogant attitude of the Europeans and the Government tended to justify the belief of the radicals that non-violent methods could not succeed in Kenya. Even as late as 1950, Governor Sir Philip Mitchell could still say that 'the people whom it is customary to describe in this country as the educated Africans are people with the sort of education that our children have by the time they are twelve years of age.' He was still determined to keep the 'native' in his place.

In desperation, the African turned to violence as a last resort. The 'Mau Mau' movement was thus a desperate attempt by a desperate people to change a system of economic and social injustice which had been a marked feature of Kenya history.

Since about 1940 responsible opinion in both Kenya and Britain had been entertaining grave anxieties about the future. The *East African Standard* had warned in 1943:

'We are beginning to see cracks in the imposing structure that has been erected so quickly in a quarter of a century . . . Right at the foundations is the African and his land . . . policy in the European areas is secondary to policy in the native reserves . . . If policy in the native areas is faulty, if over-crowding continues and grows, with recurring and increasing fragmentation of the land as generation succeeds generation, if on the one hand we have the pressure of the inescapable demand for better living standards and on the other increasing difficulty facing an African who has to make the wherewithal out of soil which is steadily deteriorating, it takes little imagination to see that there is trouble ahead.'

By the beginning of 1952, this touble was just round the corner. With thousands of acres of land lying idle in the 'White High-lands', the so-called squatters were being evicted from the settlement areas and sent to the already overpopulated and greatly eroded Reserves. In towns, although the cost of living rose by 40 per cent between 1949 and January 1952, the minimum wages rose only from 7 shillings 62 cents per week in 1949 to 14 shillings 13 cents per week in 1952, plus a house and medical attention. The house referred to consisted of a small unfurnished room where between four and five people were herded together. Agricultural workers who formed about 40 per cent of the total of African workers and who were employed almost entirely by

Europeans, had an average wage of 4 shillings 24 cents per week. In addition to their wages they got rations which normally consisted of $1\frac{1}{2}$ pounds of maize flour.

The Government Native Affairs Report of 1951, published in 1952, analysing the grim situation facing the Kenya African said,

'The process of solving this problem' (referring to land hunger among Africans) 'and of producing a settled and contented wage earning population, the majority of whom must live in urban conditions, has not been helped during 1951 by inflation which has gone on with even faster increase . . .'

In the Report, the District Commissioner, Fort Hall, explained that 'it is this steady lag of wages behind cost of his needs that deters young men from entering steady employment and causes them to prefer to live in whole or in part on their wits.' An increase in offences against property in Nakuru District was attributed by the District Commissioner to low wages and the high cost of living. The Provincial Commissioner for the Coast Province stated that 'crime in the Province has been on the increase. . . . The increase is probably due to unemployment and the increase in the cost of living rather than to an increase in any real criminal tendency in the individual.'

Those who regard 'Mau Mau' as an atavistic escape from modernity or as a barbarous tribal cult would do well to ponder the words of Robert Gardiner in his book, *A World of Peoples*. Writing about the Africans' political rights he says, 'Here we come, I think, to the crux of the misunderstanding that has led to so much rancour and so much bloodshed. For it has been the conviction—conscious and unconscious—of many colonising powers that on the other side of the confrontation there is nothing. Too often have they failed to recognise that even the poorest people, even those whose way of existence is evidence of a complete inability to meet the challenge that nature poses to man, even people such as these can have their own dignity and can be jealous of it.'

The Mitchells of Kenya had assumed that there was nothing on the other side of the confrontation. They soon discovered that the African had his own dignity, and he was jealous of it.

The Period of Reconciliation, 1952 to 1963

The declaration of the state of emergency in 1952 meant, in effect, that the policy of separate development had failed. It also meant that the British policy of devolving responsibility upon the people in the Colony, i.e. upon the Colonial officials and the settlers, had failed. An alternative policy had to be found.

The years between 1952 and 1960 are therefore crucial for a proper understanding of the post-independence Kenya. A new Kenya society had to be built. But one cannot build a new society on injustice. There was a long heritage of discrimination to contend with and there was the bitterness engendered by the 'Mau Mau' rebellion. Was reconciliation between the races possible?

In working out the new policy, it was necessary for the Colonial Office to play a more dominant role than would have been the case otherwise. In the eyes of the Africans, the Colonial Government had been discredited, and there was little hope that any agreement could be worked out. Initiative therefore reverted to the Colonial Secretary. In 1954, 1957 and 1960, successive Secretaries of State for the Colonies promulgated new constitutions for Kenya (the Lyttleton, the Lennox-Boyd and the Macleod, constitutions). All three were multi-racial in form. Britain, in deference to the wishes of the white settlers, maintained that parliamentary democracy could not work in the plural societies of Kenya, Tanganyika, and Central Africa, if civilised standards were to be kept. 'Multiracialism' or 'partnership' was therefore evolved as the system of government suitable for these areas.

To the Africans, accepting the policy of 'multi-racialism' meant accepting the injustices of the past. They wanted the government to open up the chances of a decent life for their people. This meant land redistribution, expansion of African education, making available job opportunities for Africans, etc. In short, the African leaders demanded that their people be given a chance to attain equality. To achieve this, non-racial rather than 'multi-racial' policies were necessary.

What is important to remember is that the shock of 'Mau Mau' had created the right atmosphere in that the Imperial Power was now willing to talk with the African leaders. In the course of these dialogues, power shifted from the Europeans to the Africans. The first African Minister, Mr B. A. Ohanga, was appointed in 1954. And in the 1960 Constitution the majority of Ministers were African.

But it would be misleading to give the impression that after 1952 everything else simply followed. With the political leaders of the Africans detained, with the failure of the policy of 'association' and with the emergency continuing, the Africans had to find a way of continuing the struggle under these difficult situations. Bitter constitutional battles were fought in Kenya and London. And the fact that the Africans were, by 1960, victorious speaks much for the dedication and tactics of their leaders during these eight difficult years.

African political parties which had been prohibited since 1953 were again allowed, except in the Central Province, in mid-1955. But they could be formed only on a district basis; and the government declared that such district organisations would later be allowed to join together in some form of loose organisation. In December, this policy was challenged by Mr C. M. G. Argwings-Kodhek, the first African lawyer in Kenya. He formed in Nairobi a body called the Kenya African National Congress, which declared that the Government's policy of limiting associations to the district level would encourage tribal feeling and prevent the development of any national sense. The Government refused to register it, and Kodhek had to content himself with a Nairobi Congress.

The only body which could speak for the Africans across the Colony was the Kenya Federation of Labour. Under the youthful though vigorous leadership of its General Secretary, Mr T. J. Mboya, the Federation operated to a large extent as a political movement. Its impact was soon felt throughout the country. In February 1956 the Government threatened to proscribe the K.F.L. if it did not stop its political activities. Indeed, the Federation was saved only by the intervention on its behalf with the Kenya Government of the British Trade Union Congress.

Political activities in Kenya were given a new fillip by the first African election, on a limited franchise, which took place in March 1957. Seven Africans were elected to the Legislative Council. In October of the same year, the Lennox-Boyd constitution added to the Africans six more seats, thus bringing them to parity with the elected Europeans. The new constitution also gave them a second ministry. In order to introduce a multiracial sense of representation, provision was made in the new constitution for Specially Elected seats to be chosen by members of the Legislative Council. The African elected members accepted the increased seats but rejected the idea of Specially Elected members. They also refused the ministerial posts.

'Multi-racialism' as a policy was completely unacceptable to the Africans.

In 1959, another serious attempt was made to sell the concept of 'multi-racialism' to the Africans. The initiative this time came from one of the European leaders, Mr (later Sir) Michael Blundell. He published a policy statement in July in which he argued for the ending of all racial barriers, including land barriers. With the encouragement of the Kenya Government, Blundell resigned from his post as Minister of Agriculture to lead a new multi-racial pressure group—the New Kenya Group. At first he was only supported by Specially Elected Africans and Asians. But he soon gained adherents from amongst the moderates of the African elected members. Thus strengthened, Blundell formed a multi-racial party, the Kenya National Party. It appeared that the policy of 'multi-racialism' was at last succeeding, especially since the majority of the African elected members had joined Blundell's party.

The opponents of 'multi-racialism' were not disheartened. In the Legislative Council they formed the Kenya Independence Movement, with Oginga Odinga as President, and Tom Mboya as Secretary. They declared that the membership of their movement would consist thenceforth only of Africans. The battle between African nationalism and settlerdom was about to begin.

Several important changes precipitated the clash. In October 1959, the Kenya Government, in a desperate attempt to assist Blundell's party, declared the objective of the removal of all racial barriers, including that to entry on to land in the Highlands. Immediately the settlers were up in arms. They condemned Blundell and other Europeans with similar views, as traitors. In Britain, a new Colonial Secretary, Ian Macleod, announced that the emergency would end, and that a Constitutional Conference would take place in the New Year.

In the following year at the Lancaster House Conference in London, the battle between the forces of African nationalism and those of European settlerdom was fought. The Africans emerged victorious. The Kenya Europeans regarded this settlement as a major betrayal of their work in the country over sixty years. Under their old leader of the 30's and 40's, Cavendish-Bentinck, they gathered together in the Kenya Coalition in what proved to be a last-ditch rearguard action.

With independence in sight, the Africans had now to agree

among themselves on the kind of society they wished to see established. Here differences soon emerged, resulting in the formation of two political parties, the Kenya African National Union (KANU), destined to be led by Kenyatta, and the Kenya African Democratic Party (KADU), led by Mr Ronald Ngala. The latter claimed to represent the so-called minority tribes; and even the efforts of Kenyatta after his release in August, 1961, failed to give them the assurance they sought.

K.A.D.U.'s fears for the future soon led them to call for the establishment of regional governments *(majimbo)*, and the protection of their interests through a federal constitution. They declared that a unitary state on the Westminster model which KANU favoured would place too much power in the hands of the majority party.

This was the question which was debated at the last Lancaster House Constitutional Conference from February to April 1962. In the end Mr Maudling, the Colonial Secretary, had to impose a compromise. There was to be a strong central government, but with federal provisions for regional governments. Provision was also made for an Upper Chamber (the Senate). On 12 December 1963 Kenya achieved her independence with one of the most complicated constitutions in the world. But the question which KADU raised in 1962 remains unanswered—although KADU is no more: 'What is the best way of protecting minorities in an independent Kenya?'

Conclusion

In this chapter we have been concerned with showing the multi-racial origins of Kenya. We have indicated how most of the economic and social institutions were originally designed to cater for the needs of the different races. Although there was a general awareness from 1952 that different institutions were needed to build the new Kenya, much of the energy was devoted to political reforms. There was insufficient time in which to evolve economic and social structures appropriate to political independence. The result was that when Kenya attained her independence many of the old racialist institutions still existed. The problem of creating a society based on authentic African values is therefore likely to be a difficult one.

Further reading

MUNGEAM, G. H. *British Rule in Kenya, 1895-1912,*
Clarendon Press, Oxford, 1966.

BENNETT, G. *Kenya, A Political History,* Oxford University
Press, London, 1963.

OGOT, B. A. British Administration in the Central Nyanza
District of Kenya, 1900-1960, *Journal of African History,*
IV: 2, 1963, (pp. 249-74).

DILLEY, M. R. *British Policy in Kenya Colony,* Thomas Nelson
& Sons, New York, 1937.

GHAI, D. P. (Ed.) *Portrait of a Minority : Asians in East Africa,*
Oxford University Press, Nairobi, 1965.

ROSBERG, C. G. and NOTTINGHAM, J. *The Myth of "Mau Mau"
Nationalism in Kenya,* East African Publishing House, Nairobi,
1967.

HARLOW, V. and CHILVER, E. M. (Eds.) *History of East Africa,*
Volume II, Clarendon Press, 1965.

BENNETT, G. and ROSBERG, C. G. *The Kenyatta Election :
Kenya 1960-1961,* Oxford University Press, London, 1961.

WELBOURN, F. B. *East African Rebels,* S.C.M. Press, London,
1961.

WELBOURN, F. B. and OGOT, B. A. *A Place to Feel at Home,
A study of two Independent Churches in Western Kenya,*
Oxford University Press, London, 1966.

HOWARTH, A. *Kenyatta—A Photographic Biography,* East
African Publishing House, Nairobi, 1967.

MBOYA, T. J. *Freedom and After,* Andre Deutsch, London,
1963.

KENYATTA, J. *Suffering Without Bitterness,* East African
Publishing House, Nairobi, 1968.

SORRENSON, M. P. K. *Origins of European Settlement in
Kenya,* Oxford University Press, Nairobi, 1968.

14

Tanzania Under German and British Rule

John Iliffe

German Invasion and African Resistance, 1884 to 1898

Great changes took place in East Africa during the nineteenth century, especially in the south, which was to become Tanzania. Some areas were devastated by slave raiding and Ngoni warfare, but elsewhere African societies began to adapt themselves to long-distance trade and European penetration. At the same time, greater changes were happening in Europe as a result of the industrial revolution. Throughout the world, Europe's new economic and military power forced other peoples either to reorganise themselves or suffer defeat and colonial rule. In Asia, Japan escaped colonial rule and carried out its own industrial revolution. East Africa, by contrast, was partitioned into European colonies. This happened for three main reasons: the ambitions of individual Europeans, the responses of African societies to European pressure, and the hopes and fears of European governments.

The southern part of East Africa came under German rule between 1884 and 1898. Before 1884, German interest in this area was limited. The idea of conquest came from an individual, Carl Peters. He visited East Africa late in 1884 to obtain 'treaties' over land on which Germans could settle. When he returned to Germany in 1885, his government declared a Protectorate over the area inland of Sadani in which he had travelled. The German government did this for two reasons. First, it was quarrelling with Britain, and wanted to use its East African claims as part of the quarrel. Second, it was ignorant of East Africa and feared that unless it took part in the scramble for Africa other European countries might gain some unknown advantages.

Peters organised the German East African Company to rule his Protectorate. In 1888 he forced the Sultan of Zanzibar to grant him the right to govern the coast. The German government helped Peters, but did not want the responsibility itself. Nevertheless, when the coastal peoples resisted in 1888, the Government had to intervene.

The Germans called this resistance 'the Arab revolt', a rebellion of slave traders frightened of losing their economic position. This was partly true, but the movement was really a popular resistance by the coastal peoples to foreign rule, just as they had resisted Portuguese and Arabs before. The resistance began in Pangani in August 1888 and quickly spread along the whole coast. Although it had no central organisation, two main leaders emerged. One was an Arab settler near Pangani, Abushiri bin Salim, an enemy of the Sultan. 'He was brave as a lion', wrote a Swahili poet, 'and intolerant of oppression; where there was trouble, he would be in it.' The other leader was Bwana Heri of the Zigua tribe, who had never accepted Arab rule.

The Company was driven out of all the coastal towns except Bagamoyo and Dar-es-Salaam. The German government was forced to send troops, led by Major Wissmann, who arrived in May 1889. Within two months, he had captured the northern towns. The resistance began to collapse. The Arab aristocrats made peace with the Germans. Abushiri was betrayed in December 1889. 'At the beginning of the rising', he told his captors, 'we all swore on the Koran not to rest until we had driven the Germans out. All the others have broken their word. I am the only one who has remained true to that oath until today.' He was hanged in Pangani. Bwana Heri submitted in April 1890, and the southern coast was occupied soon afterwards. The Arabs who had made peace became German agents in the coastal towns. On 1 January 1891, the German government replaced the Company as ruler of German East Africa.

African resistance forced the German government to replace the Company. It is wrong to think that the European occupation of East Africa was easy, that the Europeans had complete military superiority, that Africans could not influence what happened. The Germans had little money and few troops—never more than 3,000 to control an African population of six or seven million (including Rwanda and Burundi). This had two consequences. First, the German occupation was very gradual. Second, the Germans needed African allies. Because the peoples of German East Africa were not united, such allies existed. Some African peoples co-operated with the Germans, while others resisted. To understand this, one must realise that the objects of both were the same: to retain as much power and independence as possible. Whether an African people resisted depended largely on what it believed to be essential to its existence, and whether the Germans threatened those essential things.

The warlords were among those who resisted. Machemba, the Yao ruler of the Makonde Plateau, defeated several German expeditions until he was overcome in 1899. 'I have listened to your words,' he had written to Wissmann, 'but can find no reason why I should obey you—I would rather die first. . . . I am Sultan here in my land. You are sultan there in your's. . . . I will not come to you, and if you are strong enough, then come and fetch me.' In Tabora, the chief of Unyanyembe, Isike, fought the Germans when they tried to gain control of the town and trade route. In January 1893 the Germans stormed his fortress. Isike blew himself up in his powder magazine.

The most famous resistance was that of the Hehe under their great warrior chief Mkwawa. The Hehe first tried to come to terms with the Germans, but Mkwawa refused to visit the coast. Hehe warriors cut the trade route from Bagamoyo to Tabora, and in 1891 the Germans sent a military expedition to Uhehe, with orders to make peace. Mkwawa wanted to remain free, but hoped to succeed without war. He sent men to offer presents and make an agreement, but the Germans thought these men were coming to fight, and killed them. Mkwawa then ordered an ambush, in which 290 German troops were killed. For three years Mkwawa remained independent, but on 30 October 1894, a very large German force captured his capital at Kalenga. The chief escaped, and for four years he fought a guerilla war. Finally, sick and alone save for two young pages, Mkwawa was found by a German patrol. He shot himself as it approached his camp. With his death in June 1898, the period of occupation and resistance ended. The Germans built powerful forts at strategic points throughout the country. In 1898 they began to demand tax. A new period of administration was beginning.

Yet occupation had taken fourteen years. For those who had resisted, there remained a proud memory which they were to preserve throughout the next sixty years of European rule. Those who had allied with the Germans gained more immediate advantages. Often their power and territory were increased. Mkwawa's rival, Merere of the Sangu, regained his homeland. On Kilimanjaro, Marealle of Marangu, a skilful and ruthless politician, made use of the Germans to become the most powerful chief on the mountain. In Buhaya, power passed to Kahigi of Kianja, who was clever in using the Germans against his rivals. By 1898, through the alliances which the Germans had been forced to make, the balance of power in many parts of German East Africa had been altered to the advantage of those who understood the new possibilities opened by European rule.

German Administration and the Maji Maji Rebellion, 1898 to 1914

By 1898, the main pattern of German administration was established. At its head was the Governor, at first usually a soldier. The colony was divided into districts. Their numbers changed, but by 1914 there were 22. Communications were so bad that almost everything was left to the District Officer (*Bezirksamtmann*). He commanded a small police force or a company of 100 to 200 African troops. He collected taxation, appointed and dismissed African chiefs and agents, judged cases, and administered punishments. Often he ruled with a strong and ruthless hand. Yet the government's power was limited, for it lacked staff and money. On the coast and in areas of European settlement, the administration was quite strong. Elsewhere, two German officers and a hundred troops might face a million Africans. This weakness had several consequences. The Germans feared African risings, and suppressed the slightest discontent with great brutality. In normal times, the District Officer relied greatly on his African allies. Clever men like Marealle and Kahigi could use the Germans to strengthen their own power. Writing of the Chagga, Mrs K. M. Stahl describes the many intrigues by which Marealle persuaded the Germans to defeat his enemies, until he too became the victim of a similar intrigue. The Germans preferred to employ existing chiefs as their agents. Where there were none, they appointed *akidas* to collect tax and try cases.

Because administration was expensive, the German rulers emphasised economic development. They tried three methods: they started plantations of tropical crops, employing many African labourers; they assisted Europeans to farm in the highlands; and they encouraged or forced Africans to grow cash crops in order to pay taxes. German experiments were concentrated along the River Pangani and in the highland areas of Usambara, Kilimanjaro, and Meru. A railway inland from Tanga, begun in 1891, reached Mombo in 1905 and Moshi in 1911. Between 1904 and 1914, a second railway was built from Dar es Salaam to Kigoma. The first plantations grew coffee in Usambara, but the soil was poor and they failed. By 1905 the main crop was sisal. Later, from 1908 to 1912, German planters made large profits from rubber, until the market collapsed. Yet most German administrators preferred to encourage individual European farmers, because plantation labour was scarce, and because they wanted their colony to be a 'white man's country' like Rhodesia or Kenya. Large-scale settlement began in Usambara in 1898, on Meru in 1905, and on Kilimanjaro in 1907. Most of the land was taken from the Masai, some from other peoples. The settlers grew coffee and rubber, but very few were successful. Their main problem was shortage of labour, for they paid low wages. Labourers were recruited from long distances, especially from Unyamwezi. Much deceit and brutality was used. Often the chiefs in the settlement areas were forced to supply labourers. Kinyasi of Usambara abdicated in 1903 rather than do this. By 1913, there were 5,336 Europeans in German East Africa, of whom 882 were adult male settlers. They dominated the Governor's Council, formed in 1904 as the equivalent of a Legislative Council. Few Tanzanians now realise how nearly their country came under settler control. Only the expulsion of the Germans after the First World War prevented it.

African cash crop agriculture began in several ways. Coffee, for example, was introduced to Kilimanjaro by missionaries and spread by African catechists. In Buhaya, coffee was a traditional crop, and was first exported in 1898. Cotton was introduced into Usukuma by a European settler, and became popular about 1911. In 1902 the Governor decided that cotton should be grown in the south of the colony. He ordered that every headman must establish a cotton plot, where all his people would come to work. When the cotton was sold, the workers, headman, and marketing organisation would each receive one-third of the profits. By 1905 this system operated in all the coastal districts south of Dar es Salaam, and also in Morogoro and Kilosa.

The cotton scheme brought great hardship. The land chosen was unsuitable and the crops poor. The work was badly organised and brutally controlled. Virtually no profits were made. Zaramo workers refused the 35 cents they were each offered for the first year's work. In July 1905, the workers resolved to fight. On the night of 31 July, the Matumbi drove their hated *akida* and all other foreigners from their hills. The Maji Maji rebellion had begun. It spread first throughout the cotton area around the middle and lower Rufiji River, then to Uluguru, the Mahenge Plateau, and the Lukuledi and Kilombero Valleys. On 30 August, 8,000 men of the Mbunga and Pogoro tribes, armed only with spears, tried to assault Mahenge fort, to drag away the machine-guns with their bare hands. They failed, with terrible casualties, and this was perhaps the turning-point. Early in September the Ngoni joined the rising, but already its first momentum was lost. By November the Germans had regained control of the Southern Highlands. The rebel area was now divided. In the west, the Germans encircled and destroyed the hard core of Ngoni and Bena leaders. In the east, the Ngindo, among others, fought a long guerilla war until their leader, the elephant hunter Abdalla Mapanda, was shot in January 1907. Then came famine. 'I have never seen such scarcity', a young woman wrote from Masasi. 'I have seen famine, but not one causing people to die. But in this famine many are dying, some are unable to do any work at all, they have no strength, their food consists of insects from the woods.' In war and famine, 75,000 Africans are thought to have died.

Maji Maji was important in three ways. First, it was an attempt to find a new method of regaining independence. Tribal resistance had been defeated because it was disunited. Maji Maji tried to unite people without regard for their tribes. For this it used religion. Every Maji Maji fighter 'drank' the water—normally it was sprinkled on him. This protected him from bullets and committed him to war and brotherhood: *hiyo ni alama ya unamaji*, an applicant was told, 'this is a sign of comradeship.' The water was first distributed by the priests of

Kolelo, a spirit who lived in the Uluguru Mountains. Later it was linked to a belief that a new world was to come, a world without evil, ruled by a new god. 'He will change this world and it will be new', it was said, 'His rule will be one of marvels.' Maji Maji was different from tribal resistance. The Germans called it 'a revolt of the people.'

Yet Maji Maji failed either to regain independence or to preserve the unity in which it had begun. A mass movement needs strong organisation, and the religious organisation of Maji Maji was not strong enough. As German military pressure increased, the movement broke up into its tribal sections. When the Ngoni joined, for example, they fought alone, and were defeated alone.

Perhaps the third point is the most important. After Maji Maji, Africans sought different methods to regain independence. Yet the spirit of protest had been demonstrated, and it remained until independence. Fifty years later, President Nyerere declared: 'They rose in a great rebellion . . . in response to a natural call, a call of the spirit, ringing in the hearts of all men, and of all times, educated or uneducated, to rebel against foreign domination. It is important to bear this in mind . . . in order to understand the nature of a nationalist movement like mine. Its function is not to create the spirit of rebellion but to articulate it and show it a new technique.'

The British in Zanzibar and the 'Arab Revolution', 1890 to 1934

Zanzibar became a British Protectorate in November 1890. Unlike German East Africa, this was no sudden European invasion led by a private adventurer. During the nineteenth century, the Sultan had become dependent on British support, while by submitting to British demands concerning the slave trade he lost the support of his subjects. When threatened by the Germans in the late 1880's, he was forced to seek British protection.

Britain hoped to preserve the sultanate while suppressing slavery. The Sultan was told that Britain would control Zanzibar's foreign relations, while merely 'exercising a friendly influence' in her internal affairs, which would remain under Arab control. But late nineteenth-century Europeans were not content with 'influence' when they detected inefficiency and

injustice. In August 1891 the British consul declared the
Sultan's government 'an embodiment of all the worst and most
barbarous characteristics of a primitive Arab despotism.'
He seized its finances and appointed European officials to control
the government departments. In 1896 the British navy bom-
barded the Sultan's palace to place a British candidate on the
throne. The independence of Sayyid Said's dynasty was broken.

In Buganda, at this date, historians write of a 'Christian
Revolution'. They mean that the Kabaka's power passed to
Christian chiefs. Through their privileged position in education,
land-holding, and administration, these great families became
an aristocracy which dominated Buganda until independence.
A similar process took place in Zanzibar—an 'Arab Revolution'.
Although the British broke the Sultan's personal power, they
wanted Arabs to rule Zanzibar and their new administration
needed trained civil servants. Arabs received special educational
opportunities and the more important civil service positions.
The personal rule of the Sultan was replaced by that of an
educated Arab aristocracy.

While the Arab aristocrats controlled the administration,
their economic position was weakened through the abolition
of slavery. Anxious to preserve the Arab position, British
officials made the 1897 Emancipation Decree as favourable
to the slave-owners as possible. The slave had to claim his
freedom in court. The slave-owner (but not the slave) was com-
pensated—an Arab Association was formed soon after 1900
to ensure this. Since there was little free land, the slave usually
became a squatter on an Arab estate, paying rent in labour.
Nevertheless, the blow to Arab economic power was serious.
Many landowners were already in debt, and throughout this
period the price of cloves was low. Land increasingly passed
from the great estates to African smallholders. As in Buganda, the
aristocracy gained administrative power while losing the economic
strength to support it.

For the Africans, emancipation scarcely fulfilled its hopes.
'Let us rejoice and give thanks', a missionary newspaper had
proclaimed, 'for men are not objects, and all children of Adam
are of the same origin, even the foolish and the weak have their
dignity. . . . Everyone has his rights, his property, his wife, his
dignity, and must not be maltreated without cause. Africa too
will have its day.' For Zanzibar Africans, that day did not come
immediately. Yet new opportunities were opening. The career

of Sheikh Abeid Karume demonstrates this. Born in 1905, he received three years education, and became a sailor at the age of fifteen. By 1930 he had travelled very widely and was already experienced in organising his comrades. In 1934 he was associated with the foundation of the African Association in Zanzibar. This association linked ambitious workers with the small group of mission teachers on the island. It was the first expression of an African political consciousness. For Zanzibar Africans, the age of improvement had opened.

The Age of Improvement, 1907 to 1937

The violence of Maji Maji had failed as a method of regaining independence. New techniques were needed. Between the period of armed resistance and that of mass nationalism, there was throughout colonial Africa an age of improvement, when Africans concentrated on improving their positions, to face their European rulers on more equal terms. They emphasised education, economic development, and political advance in local government. The characteristic man of this period was the educated clerk, teacher, or pastor. The characteristic organisation was the welfare association in which these new men combined together to improve themselves. Improvement often meant westernisation. 'To the African mind,' said one, 'to imitate Europeans is civilisation.' It is difficult to understand such men, but in their quiet, earnest way they made an important contribution to Tanzanian history.

The first recognisable group were the *akidas* appointed after Maji Maji. They were educated in government schools on the coast. Following the German government inland, young coast men staffed the administration and the schools throughout the country. When the British defeated the Germans in 1916 and renamed the colony Tanganyika, a second group emerged. Many had been educated by the UMCA at Kiungani school in Zanzibar, where they received a literary education in English which, after 1918, secured them the best jobs in the new civil service. The outstanding member of this group was Martin Kayamba.

In his career and beliefs, Kayamba was characteristic of the age of improvement. His father was a schoolteacher in Zanzibar, where Kayamba was born in 1891. He was educated at Kiungani from 1902 to 1905. After travelling as a clerk and trader in Kenya and Uganda, and being imprisoned by the Germans, Kayamba was appointed chief clerk of Tanga Provincial Office. Later he travelled twice to Europe and obtained the highest post open to an African in the civil service. While in Tanga, Kayamba founded the Tanganyika Territory African Civil Service Association, in March 1922. The Association later moved to Dar es Salaam, where in 1928 or 1929 some of its members took part in the foundation of the Tanganyika African Association, from which 25 years later, TANU was to be formed. Thus there is a link between TTACSA and later nationalism, but the Association itself, of course, was no mass nationalist movement. It was a club for clerks and teachers, with newspapers and a football team, encouraged by the government. Historically, however, TTACSA was important. It linked these educated men with members of Tanga's coastal society. Kayamba later remembered a visitor to the club who 'was very pleased to see something at last had been done which he never thought he would see, and that was Christians and Mohammedans, Africans and Arabs joining together as members of the association, and all being very friendly.' Further, Kayamba and his group were perhaps the first Tanganyikans to think of their country as a unit, as a future independent state. For Kayamba, political development required self-improvement, and improvement required unity. 'I firmly believe', he wrote, 'that Africans will never progress well unless they realise the necessity for unity.' Yet this progress would give special advantages to a privileged minority. 'Martin Kayamba,' wrote an African newspaper when he died in 1939, 'will be . . . remembered as the selfish African who rose to the highest rank . . . without being of any use to his race. . . . He never bothered about his African brothers.' Kayamba and his circle were not political leaders. They neither represented their people nor demanded independence. But they created an organisation, a central tradition, wider than the tribe, which later provided one foundation for Tanganyikan nationalism.

Similar changes were happening in the rural areas of Tanganyika. New men were emerging from the mission schools, anxious that their tribes should progress, willing to challenge the chiefs whom European administrators supported. These men founded tribal unions in many parts of Tanganyika. The earliest was the Bukoba Bahaya Union.

The first Haya with modern education were men who visited Buganda in the 1890's, who became Christians, learned to read, and returned to Buhaya to found their own church long before Protestant missionaries arrived. Education spread quickly in Buhaya, especially in the northern chiefdom, Kiziba. Two members of the Ziba aristocracy, Fransisko Lwamgira and Klemens Kiiza, proved the ablest men of their generation. The story of how they came to oppose each other shows what was happening in Tanganyika during the age of improvement. Before 1914, Lwamgira was secretary to the German officer in Bukoba. Kiiza worked for both the government and the missionaries. After the war, Lwamgira retained his post, while Kiiza became a trader. In 1925, the British introduced the system of government called indirect rule into Tanganyika. They intended that African tribes should be administered by their own chiefs and elders, under British supervision. They hoped this would encourage political and economic development, without leading to 'detribalisation' or nationalist politics. Indirect rule caused conflict within the tribes between the privileged chiefs and their unprivileged subjects. This happened in Buhaya. Lwamgira was privileged: he became Secretary General to the Council of Chiefs. Kiiza, however, was not. In 1924 he founded the Bukoba Bahaya Union, 'for the establishment of an institution for the development of our country and for the seeking of a system for the simple way to civilisation to our mutual advantage.' The Union became the centre of opposition to the chiefs' privileges. It demanded an educated paramount chief to replace them. At first it had no mass support, but when Kiiza began his own coffee-hulling plant he tried to organise the Haya farmers into a Native Growers' Association. Then in 1936 the chiefs issued orders controlling methods of growing coffee, to prevent disease. The farmers resisted these rules. 'We do not need,' they wrote, 'to be taught how to grow coffee or banana trees or to stop from growing anything in our shambas or our soil.' In one village Lwamgira, the chiefs' agent, was stoned. Kiiza, by contrast, was blamed by the government for the unrest. His Growers' Association collapsed.

This is a complicated but important story. Apart from Kayamba and his circle, this was a period of local politics. Kiiza was not demanding national independence. He wanted power in Buhaya, power to bring progress to Buhaya, power to destroy the chiefs' privileges. For long he lacked popular support.

Then his commercial interests led him to organise the farmers. When the government interfered with their agriculture and the farmers resisted, Kiiza briefly led a popular political movement.

Maji Maji had been a mass movement, but had lacked skilled leadership. During the next thirty years, potential leaders were educated, but they lacked mass support. By 1937, this situation was changing. Under government pressure, the people were coming back into politics. The problem now was to unite leaders and followers into an organised movement.

The Origins of Tanganyikan Nationalism, 1937 to 1954

Nationalism has meant different things in different parts of the world. In East Africa, mass nationalism had three characteristics. First, it aimed to control the political centre of the country, the Legislative Council. Second, the nationalist leaders tried to do this by mobilising mass support and by expressing popular demands. Third, they intended to use their central power and mass support to unite all the people of the country into a single nation, in which there would be economic justice and the only test of full membership would be citizenship—not race, not religion, not political belief. In most parts of colonial Africa, and certainly in Tanganyika, such movements gained independence. But such movements were not bound to come into existence, nor need they have won independence. Colonies can gain independence in other ways. In South American countries in the early nineteenth century, independence was won, not by mass nationalist movements, but by unrepresentative minorities. Early in the twentieth century, Ireland won independence from Britain, not by a mass nationalist movement (a method which had failed) but through a terrorist campaign by a few thousand trained fighters. In South Africa, mass nationalism has so far proved a most ineffective technique to win African freedom. Nationalism was not inevitable in Tanganyika, nor was it inevitably successful. So the historian must explain why a mass nationalist movement came into existence, and why it won independence.

By the late 1930's, Tanganyikans had experience of three types of political action, none of which was nationalist. The political tradition of TTACSA and TAA aimed at the Legislative Council, but had no mass support. Tribal politicians like Kiiza rarely had mass support, and were concerned with tribal rather than national issues. Popular resistance, expressed in Maji Maji or in opposition to agricultural regulations, certainly had mass support, but did not seek control of the Legislative Council. None of these was a nationalist movement, but they were the elements from which a nationalist movement was eventually created. When the three types of politics came together, on 7 July 1954, Tanganyikan nationalism was born. Between 1937 and 1954, the three types of politics gradually became inter-connected.

This was not just the work of educated leaders. The biggest changes took place in the rural areas, for here the people became involved in politics. As in Buhaya in 1937, the people acted because the government interfered with their agricultural methods. In the great world economic depression of 1929 the prices of tropical crops fell sharply. The government urged the people to grow more crops in order to maintain their incomes, but growing more crops threatened to exhaust the land. The government began to make regulations concerning soil conserva-tion, forcing the people to build terraces, to limit the numbers of their cattle, and do many other things which needed much time and work. Sometimes the regulations were foolish. Increasingly, the people resisted. The Shambala of Mlalo, for example, resisted as early as 1946. The most famous incident came later, in 1955, when the government tried to make the Luguru terrace their hillsides, although crops were better where the land was not terraced. In Uluguru there was serious violence. By the 1950's, Tanganyika's farmers were more ready to resist than they had been since 1905.

The farmers were also better organised, for tribal politics had changed greatly. The output of crops, and the wealth of the country, was rapidly increasing. For example, in 1945 Tanganyika produced 7,512 long tons of raw cotton; in 1952, 14,109; in 1960, 34,241. In 1945, coffee exports earned £896,000; in 1950, £3,471,000; in 1955, £6,905,000. This prosperity led to the growth of the co-operative movement. In 1945 there were 79 registered co-operative societies. By 1952 the number had risen to 474. The greatest advance was still to come—the creation between 1950 and 1955 of the Victoria Federation of Co-operative Unions in Usukuma. The co-operatives were of great political importance. Tanganyika's farmers were at last brought together by modern organisations which were not dominated by the chiefs. The co-operative organisers often became local leaders of a new type, progressive and with real mass support. For example, between 1950 and 1953 a new group of political leaders emerged in Lake Province, including Paul Bomani, S. A. Kandoro, S. A. Maswanya and I. M. Bhoke Munanka. At this time, Mwanza was the centre of radical politics for the whole of Tanganyika. These new leaders were different from Kiiza's generation. They were not interested in tribal independence. They were concerned with bigger things, with government's agricultural and marketing policies, with decisions which were made in Dar-es-Salaam. Whether they liked it or not, their local interests forced them to enter national politics, to become the most important men in the nationalist movement. They had practical organisational experience and mass local support from farmers who were increasingly discontented. If they could unite with each other, they could be immensely powerful.

Throughout East Africa, men like these became nationalist leaders. Yet only in Tanganyika was there a single and united nationalist movement. There were several reasons for this. Tanganyika had no dominant tribe and no deep linguistic division. Most important, Tanganyika alone had a central, non-tribal political tradition. When Kenyan or Ugandan politicians moved from local to national politics, they made tribal alliances among themselves. In Tanganyika they joined an existing central political organisation, TAA. This is shown clearly by the Meru Lands Case of 1951. In that year, the government moved 3,000 Meru from their land and replaced them with Europeans. The Meru naturally resisted. They tried three successive methods. First, they formed the Meru Citizens' Union, Freemen, one of whose leaders was Kirilo Japhet, the secretary of the Arusha branch of TAA. They tried to oppose the government as a tribe. When that failed, they appealed to the United Nations, but the British ignored its resolutions. Finally, the Meru turned to national politics. 'Government,' wrote Kirilo Japhet in 1953, 'wants badly to hear the last of our Lands Case, but I have been asked by Mr Kandoro and Mr Nyerere of the Tanganyika African Association to go on safari and tell the whole country about the Meru eviction and my adventures in the United Nations. The eviction woke our Meru people up to the indignity of being ruled without our consent by foreigners. Now we are going to wake up all Tanganyika!' This shows how a local political leader, with mass support, came into contact with the central TAA organisation, with its national outlook. When local support and central organisation joined, nationalism began.

TAA had also changed. Previously it had been 'tea-party politics,' a club for clerks and teachers. After 1945 it gained new strength and militancy from two directions. First, its branches were infected by the new radicalism of local politics. Through these branches, it had been in touch with tribal politicians throughout the 1930's. Now the branches began to demand greater action from the centre—early in the 1950's, the particularly radical Mwanza leaders demanded that TAA headquarters be moved there. Second, leadership was taken over by Makerere-trained intellectuals in Dar-es-Salaam, first by Vedast Kyaruzi in 1950, then by Julius Nyerere in April 1953. On his return from Britain in 1952, Nyerere insisted that TAA could be the nucleus of a mass nationalist movement. Meeting in October 1953, this new TAA leadership decided to reorganise the association, to call it TANU, and to model it on Nkrumah's Convention People's Party.

Seventeen delegates approved TANU's aims and constitution at the TAA meeting of 7 July 1954 in Dar-es-Salaam. They represented the three political traditions from which TANU originated. The new intellectuals were represented by Nyerere himself and by Joseph Kasella Bantu. Kandoro was the delegate of radical Mwanza's leadership. Kirilo Japhet represented the mass politics of the Meru Citizens' Union. The traditions had come together, leaders and people had met—the nucleus of a mass movement existed.

The Triumph of TANU, 1954 to 1961

The problem was now to expand the movement, to hold it together, and to use it to regain lost independence. Maji Maji had failed because it neither expanded sufficiently nor remained united. 'Freedom and unity' was a slogan of the new movement.

TANU spread quickly, for three main reasons. First, its message was simple. 'National freedom, *uhuru,* was an uncomplicated principle', President Nyerere has written, 'and it needed no justification to the audiences of the first few TANU speakers. All that was required was an explanation of its relevance

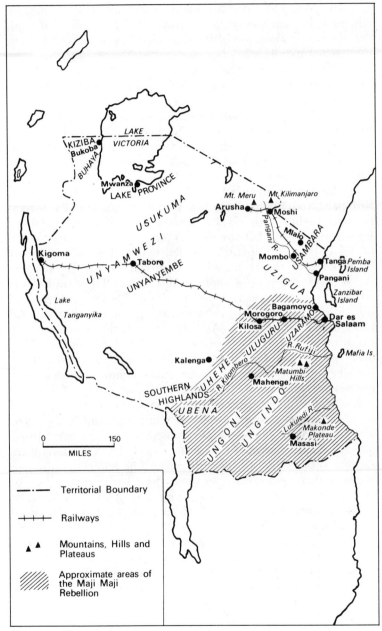

Figure 27 Tanzania

to their lives, and some reasonable assurance that it could be obtained through the methods proposed by TANU.' Second, the movement made use of the existing TAA branches. 'During the last ten months . . .' Nyerere said in March 1955, 'we have tried to organise ourselves. The branches of the former African Association became automatically branches of the Tanganyika National African Union, and they are scattered all over the country.' Third, throughout Tanganyika there was already conflict between the people and their rulers. The people felt the need for action; TANU had only to adapt itself to each local situation, either by taking over an existing popular movement or by organising the people against privilege.

In Buhaya, opposition to the chiefs and to agricultural rules had been continuous since the 1920's. It was led by several political bodies with similar leadership: the Bukoba Bahaya Union, the Kianja Labour Association, and the Bukoba branch of TAA. In 1953 the chiefs ordered that all banana trees must be felled after the crop had been picked, to prevent disease. As in 1937, the people opposed this order. Their leader was Ali Migeyo. The police dispersed one of his meetings and he was imprisoned. In 1954 Mwanza was becoming the local headquarters of TANU. Ali Migeyo's friends consulted the Mwanza leaders. They returned as TANU members, taking over the files, offices, and political programmes of the TAA branch and the Kianja Labour Association. Buhaya's local politics became part of a national movement.

Elsewhere, the transition from local to national politics was more complicated, and needed a new organisation. Kilimanjaro was an example. There the government's land and agricultural policies caused unrest. In 1946 divisional chiefs (*waitori*) were appointed but soon became unpopular. The Kilimanjaro Union opposed them and sought to unite the Chagga in the face of new threats. In 1952 it secured the election of Thomas Marealle as paramount chief. Under his leadership, the Chagga experienced real economic and educational progress, but gradually Marealle became unpopular. He was opposed by TANU and its local ally the Chagga Democratic Party. Marealle was voted out in 1960. Thus on Kilimanjaro, in contrast to Buhaya, TANU established itself through opposition to the political leaders of the early 1950's.

By such means, TANU rapidly dominated local politics throughout the country. By early 1958, some 200,000 members held TANU cards. Now the main problem was not expansion but unity. Nyerere's technique was to concentrate all the movement's attention on freedom, without defining the exact nature of that freedom, for his followers might have disagreed about the definition and the movement might have divided. The most dangerous issues were religion and race. In September 1959 the All Muslim National Union of Tanganyika urged that Tanganyika should not become independent until Muslims had greater educational opportunities, but the organisation was denounced by Muslim leaders. A more dangerous threat, at first, was the African National Congress, which was formed when TANU's annual conference at Tabora in January 1958 decided to take part in elections later that year, under a multi-racial constitution with a limited electorate. ANC was a racialist party which lacked popular following. The majority even of those who disagreed with TANU policy on this issue remained inside the national movement.

At first TANU's strategy was to attack the British through the United Nations. As the movement grew, this became un-necessary. The real battlefield was inside Tanganyika. TANU's power was its mass support. It had to prove to the British that it could make it impossible for them to rule except by armed force, and that TANU could replace the British and rule effectively. By the late 1950's, Britain had ceased to be a major world power. Mau Mau and other colonial rebellions had proved that it was almost impossible—and certainly uneconomic—to suppress nationalism by force. Britain's problem was to hand over political power while retaining her economic interests. The mass nationalist party proved to be the successor Britain was seeking, for it was disciplined, popular, progressive, and led by the ablest men available. In other circumstances, constitu-tional mass nationalism might have been wholly ineffective to regain independence, but in the circumstances, of the late 1950's it was the perfect technique.

TANU first persuaded the United Nations mission which visited Tanganyika in 1954 to accept it as 'a national movement'. With this recognition, Nyerere visited the United Nations in 1955 and 1956 and won international support. By this date TANU was opposed by the government-sponsored, multi-racial United Tanganyika Party. This opposition strengthened and disciplined the movement. TANU was fortunate that until 1958 its victory was not certain, for in African countries like

Uganda, where African rule was certain from an early date, the national movement fragmented. The crucial event in TANU's campaign was its victory in the 1958-59 election. After long argument, both the British and the party agreed that five TANU representatives should become ministers in June 1959. Following a further electoral triumph, responsible government was achieved in September 1960. At midnight on 9 December 1961, the people of Tanganyika regained their independence.

Zanzibar: Background to the African Revolution, 1934 to 1963

Zanzibar's modern history must centre on the revolution of 11 and 12 January 1964, in which the Afro-Shirazi Party leaders gained power and began major changes in Zanzibar's economic and social structure. Its origins go back to the 'Arab Revolution' of the 1890's. After 1945, this group of educated Arabs tried to create a mass political movement to replace the British. They hoped to gain control before the African population became politically conscious. They also believed they were best qualified to create a modern Islamic state. This attempt by a minority to use nationalist techniques to preserve its privileged position can be compared to that of the Ganda leaders at the same date.

In 1948-9 an Arab journalist, Seif Hamoud, revived the Arab Association to demand a ministerial system of government. Between 1949 and 1956 a number of political organisations were formed. Another journalist, Ali Muhsin, united these groups as the Zanzibar Nationalist Party in 1956. A Constitutional Commissioner who visited Zanzibar in 1956 recommended that elections for six seats in the Legislative Council should take place in 1957. This proposal found the African and Shirazi peoples unprepared. The African Association of 1934 had never been an effective political body, and in 1938 a Shirazi Association, based on Pemba, had broken away from it. The African and Shirazi leaders first opposed the idea of elections, but on 5 February 1957, they reunited to form the Afro-Shirazi Union (later the Afro-Shirazi Party). Of the six seats contested in 1957, ASP won three, two were won by independents from Pemba who later joined ASP, and one by the Muslim League. ZNP failed to win a single seat. The five ASP representatives remained a minority in the Legislative Council.

Between 1957 and 1961, three major changes took place.

First, hostility between the parties grew. Afro-Shirazis boycotted Arab commerce. Arab landowners evicted Afro-Shirazi squatters. Second, the Pemba Shirazi leaders broke away in 1959 to form the Zanzibar and Pemba People's Party. Third, Ali Muhsin and the other Arab leaders reorganised ZNP on TANU lines, with a youth wing, social services and all the techniques of mass nationalism. By 1961, ZNP's organisation was balanced against ASP's natural appeal.

The election of January 1961 produced deadlock. Of the 22 seats, ASP won ten, ZNP nine, and ZPPP's three successful candidates split so that each side had eleven representatives. Amid growing unrest, another election was held in June. ZNP and ZPPP formed an alliance. The British added another constituency, in an area dominated by ZNP. The ZNP/ZPPP alliance won thirteen seats against ASP's ten, although ASP polled a majority of the votes. ASP claimed that the election had been corrupt. Tragically, it had been violent. Sixty-eight people were killed.

The final election before independence, held in June 1963, confirmed the 1961 results. Although ASP again received a majority of votes, it won only thirteen seats against its rivals' eighteen. In December 1963 Zanzibar became independent under a ZNP/ZPPP government. The Revolution took place a month later.

Here it is necessary to ask why Zanzibar politics led to violent revolution while Tanganyikan politics did not. Historians have suggested three explanations, based on different ideas of nationalism.

Some historians believe that the main object of a nationalist movement was to unite all the citizens of a country, whatever their race. They feel that nationalism failed to do this in Zanzibar, so that the Revolution was chiefly a racial conflict. 'The essential characteristic of Zanzibar nationalism', it has been said, 'has been its failure to unify Zanzibaris'. Yet nationalists were not concerned solely with unity: they also sought economic justice, which did not exist in Zanzibar under Arab rule.

Other historians believe that a nationalist movement was the political expression of a nation, of a large group of people similar in race, language, religion, and culture. These historians claim that the Revolution was the triumph of the African nation in Zanzibar, that it was a 'nationalist revolution'. The Revolution, writes one, was 'essentially nationalist in character though given the trappings of a socialist or class revolution'. Revolution was necessary because 'imperial domination gave place to a traditional type of reactionary rule, the sole beneficiaries . . . being a small rich class of Arabs.' Yet ZNP was not simply 'a small rich class of Arabs'. Further, the Revolution had not only the appearance but the reality of a socialist revolution.

Perhaps the third explanation is more satisfactory. To be successful, a nationalist movement must bring economic justice to the mass of the people, since it was for this that the people struggled. Privileged political leaders might win independence, but that independence was not complete unless it led on to economic justice. From this viewpoint, the Zanzibar Revolution was the climax of a nationalist movement in which ZNP represented the privileged (especially the landed) and ASP the unprivileged and landless. Whereas in Zanzibar the conditions for economic justice were created by violence, in Tanganyika they were sought by the more difficult method of urgent persuasion.

Further reading

KIMAMBO, I. N. and TEMU, A. J. (Eds.) *A History of Tanzania,* East African Publishing House, Nairobi, 1968. (The most up-to-date history of the country.)

ROBINSON, R. and GALLAGHER, J. *The Partition of Africa,* in F. H. Hinsley (Ed.) *The New Cambridge Modern History, Volume XI,* Cambridge University Press, 1962. (The best brief account of the scramble.)

RANGER, T. O. African Reaction and Resistance to the Imposition of Colonial Rule in East and Central Africa, *History and Politics of Modern Imperialism in Africa,* Stanford University Press, Stanford, 1968. (For the part played by Africans in the process of European occupation, and for the organisation and consequences of resistance.)

GWASSA, G. C. K. and ILIFFE, J. *Records of the Maji-Maji Rising, Part I,* East African Publishing House, Nairobi, 1968. (Contemporary documents illustrating the history of the rising.)

STAHL, K. M. *History of the Chagga People of Kilimanjaro,* Mouton, The Hague, 1964. (Good on the early colonial period, weak after 1918.)

KAYAMBA, M. The Story of Martin Kayamba Mdumi . . . written by himself, *Ten Africans,* Faber and Faber, London, 1936. (Kayamba's autobiography, from which quotations in this chapter are taken.)

LONSDALE, J. M. The Emergence of African Nations, *Emerging Themes of African History,* East African Publishing House, Nairobi, 1968. (The ideas about nationalism used in this chapter.)

LISTOWEL, J. *The Making of Tanganyika,* Chatto and Windus, London, 1965. (Part III for the formation of TANU.)

KANDORO, S. A. *Mwito wa Uhuru,* Thakers, Dar es Salaam, 1961. (Valuable on Mwanza politics and the origins of TANU, by a man who played an important part.)

NYERERE, J. K. *Freedom and Unity,* Oxford University Press, London, 1966. (President Nyerere's most important writings and speeches from 1952 to 1965.)

MWANJISI, R. K. *Abeid Amani Karume,* East African Publishing House, Nairobi, 1967. (An illustrated biography in Swahili.)

LOFCHIE, M. F. *Zanzibar : Background to Revolution,* Princeton University Press, Princeton, 1965. (The most detailed account of Zanzibar politics.)

CLIFFE, L. (Ed.) *One Party Democracy,* East African Publishing House, Nairobi, 1967. (A study of the 1965 general election in Tanzania in its historical context.)

Note : This chapter is based mainly on work which was still unpublished in 1966, but would eventually appear: R. A. Austen and G. R. Mutahaba on Buhaya, M. L. Bates on British administration in Tanganyika, G. C. K. Gwassa and G. P. Mpangara on Maji Maji, J. Iliffe on German administration and Maji Maji, J. A. Kieran and M. Wright on missions, A. Maguire on Sukuma politics, D. Mwakawago on TANU, A. Nelson on the Meru Lands Case, A. H. Redmayne on Mkwawa, S. Rogers and E. M. K. Msella on Chagga politics, and A. R. Thompson on Tanganyikan education.

15

Uganda Under the British

M. S. M. Kiwanuka

By the stroke of the pen which signed the Anglo-German Agreement of 1890, the area north of Lake Victoria, which later came to be known as Uganda, became a British sphere of influence. And by Royal Charter, the Imperial British East Africa Company (IBEA) was authorised to trade as well as to administer this area. The man associated with the rule of the Company in Uganda was Captain Lugard. Though primarily in the pay of the IBEA, he worked hard to further British colonial interests. The Company remained responsible for this area until after the troubles in Buganda when the struggle for power and influence led Catholics, Moslems and Protestants to massacre each other. These troubles and other responsibilities in the East Africa Protectorate (modern Kenya) increased administrative costs enormously and led the IBEA to invite the British Government to assume responsibility. The IBEA like other Chartered Companies elsewhere had done its job, namely of preparing the ground for its home government to take over. Hence in 1893 the Company's flag was replaced by the Union Jack, and soon afterwards an Agreement or Treaty was made between Kabaka Mwanga II of Buganda and Sir Gerald Portal, the first official representative of the British Government.

The Portal Agreement of 1893 invalidated all previous agreements which Kabaka Mwanga had signed. He and his subjects put themselves under British protection, without asking themselves what they were being protected from. The Agreement consisted of many articles and included provision for the assessment and collection of taxes as a responsibility of the new régime. Slave trade was prohibited and the Baganda were thenceforth bound by 'all and every' international act to which Great Britain might be a party! The Portal Agreement which was only provisional was confirmed in 1894 by another Agreement signed by Colonel Colville and Kabaka Mwanga and having almost similar provisions.

The Extension of British Rule and the Reaction of African Rulers

British rule in Uganda spread by force of arms, though, in some areas, military conquest was disguised by a series of agreements. Buganda was to be the centre from which the British octopus spread its tentacles to other parts of Uganda. During Lugard's short stay, he had marched westwards and reinstated Kasagama, the *Omukama* of Toro who had fled to Buganda when Kabarega, the *Omukama* of Bunyoro, attempted to reconquer Bunyoro's rebellious state. Lugard clashed with Kabarega as did his successors. In the process of fighting against Kabarega, the British extended their rule to the west and north-west. Meanwhile, British rule had also been extended to the east and north. As early as 1894 Captain Grant had already established himself in Busoga, and towards the end of the century, Kakungulu, a Muganda veteran general of the religious wars, crossed Lake Kyoga with a large following of his fellow Baganda. These started 'conquering' the regions of Teso and Lango, and eastern Uganda was brought under British rule by the Baganda Agents. By the outbreak of the first British-German war in 1914, British rule had been established over modern Uganda, though there was no regular administration in Karamoja before 1919.

In 1900 another and more detailed agreement was made between the leading Baganda chiefs and the British representative, Sir Harry Johnston*. One of its chief aims was to define the position of Buganda in Uganda, by which it was ranked as a

*This, traditionally known as the *Uganda Agreement,* is referred to below as the *Buganda Agreement.*

Province. We cannot go into all its provisions, but some of the most important ones were in connection with the system of land tenure and the position of the Kabaka and the chiefs. Politically, the Agreement reduced the personal rule of the Kabaka. Henceforth he had to be assisted by his chiefs and the Lukiko. Since the Kabaka at the time was a minor, this provision was actually put into practice. The Kabaka, in fact, became a nominee of the British for he could retain his throne only so long as the colonial régime thought that he co-operated fully with them. From the economic and social points of view, the new system of land tenure created a kind of permanent aristocracy which had not existed before. The introduction of the private system of land ownership is believed to have led to the economic prosperity of Buganda compared with that of other parts of Uganda. Similar but modified agreements were signed in 1900 with the Kingdom of Toro, and with the Kingdom of Ankole in 1904. But no agreement was made with Bunyoro until 1933. Thus with the exception of Bunyoro, the kingdoms came to be known as the agreement states and it was due to these agreements, particularly those made with Buganda, that Uganda owed its status as a Protectorate.

Nearly everywhere in Uganda, colonial rule had been established by force, either directly by the arms of the British or those of their agents, the Baganda. And everywhere this alien rule was resisted with disastrous consequences for the resisters. The most notable were Kabarega, the Omukama of Bunyoro, and Mwanga, the Kabaka of Buganda. As enemies of imperialism, they had to be smashed. Kabarega resisted for nearly ten years, but in 1897 he was deposed and deported, dying in exile in 1923. Although Kabaka Mwanga had originally signed agreements with the British, he finally decided to fight rather than submit to the humiliation of foreign rule. He met with the same fate as Kabarega and died in exile in 1901. In the Ankole area, the King of Igara committed suicide and his neighbour the King of Kajara fled to Tanganyika. The King of Buhweju was killed by British bullets. In Busoga, co-operation was secured by the threat of deposition and deportation. In Teso, Lango and Acholi, alien rule was equally resisted, culminating in the latter district in the Lamogi rebellion of 1912.

But perhaps the greatest threat to colonial rule in Uganda was not from African rulers or resisters, but from the Sudanese troops. Since Lugard first arrived in Uganda at the beginning of the 1890's, Sudanese troops had been gathered by the colonial powers and strategically located. In Uganda as well as in the British East African protectorate, they were Britain's men of action. Lugard used them in Buganda in 1892 to crush the Catholics and they were later used to smash the resistance of Mwanga and Kabarega. They fought in the Nandi country and in various parts of the Rift Valley. All this activity inevitably strained these troops. Under-paid, and with pay in arrears, when called upon to engage in further activities which would have taken them from western Kenya to the eastern borders of the Congo, some companies refused to move any further. A number of regiments mutinied and marched to Busoga. In subsequent fighting, casualties included several British officers. The mutineers held out for about a year, and it was not until Indian soldiers had arrived from the coast and sufficient forces mustered from Buganda that the mutinous soldiers were finally defeated. With the smashing of the African resisters and of the Sudanese mutiny, British rule in Uganda was established with no further challenges.

The Beginning of Administration

When the British took over Uganda, they had no clear plans of how to administer the country. But they found in Buganda the traditional system of a Kabaka heading a hierarchy of chiefs. Though similar administrative structures existed in other kingdoms, the *kiganda* system had acquired a degree of efficiency which was unsurpassed in the whole of the lake region of East Africa. The system impressed the British, and as British rule in Uganda was extended by the Baganda, who generally provided the first chiefs, it was introduced to nearly all other parts of the Protectorate, with varying degrees of success. The Baganda agents, in introducing the kiganda model, were the backbone of the new administration, and everywhere formed the first beginnings of local government. But perhaps to emphasise their role as agents, as soon as the ground had been prepared the British stepped in. Thus in 1901 Kakungulu was replaced and conveniently sent to Busoga where he became the first President and laid the foundation of the office of the *Kyabazinga* (paramount ruler). Practically everywhere, the role of the Baganda as agents of British imperialism provoked reactions which led to violent clashes. Hence between 1902 and 1911 Baganda agents were gradually withdrawn from north-eastern Uganda, though they stayed longer in the administration of the east and west.

The traditional view of colonial rule in Uganda is that in the south the British adopted an indirect system of government. This administrative system endeavoured to vest power in the traditional sources of authority. Thus in areas where there were known traditional chiefs, the British used these to carry out their orders and functions. The degree to which the system was applied differed from area to area and from period to period. Thus in Buganda, where British administrative authority derived from the Buganda Agreement of 1900, the system was believed to be more indirect than elsewhere in the Protectorate. Similarly the power of the chief everywhere was far greater before 1930 than after. In north and in eastern Uganda where there were no large centralised states or traditional rulers whose authority was recognised by many followers, a system of direct rule was adopted. In such areas, the British would appoint a chief even though he had no traditional or hereditary claim to office. It ought to be stressed, however, that the system of indirect rule was as old as mankind itself. It was neither invented by the British nor were they the only colonial power which adopted such a system when it suited them. However, in actual practice, there was little difference between the so-called 'in-directly' administered areas and those which were directly administered. Kings and chiefs, whether traditional or not, were all nominees of the colonial power which would make or unmake them at will.

The Protectorate administration was headed by the Governor, under whom were provincial and district Commissioners. These were assisted by county, *gombolola* (sub-county) and a large number of minor chiefs. It was on such a structure that the local government of Uganda was based. There were local councils which were modelled on the Buganda Lukiko, and their main function was to carry out local administration and to provide a forum for local politics. These councils, however, were unfortunately inefficient, and the men who sat in them were sometimes more interested in preserving their own positions than in efficient administration. After the First World War, the Central Government felt the need to introduce some kind of Legislative Council (referred to below as the Legco). The establishment of such a body was first proposed in 1919 and it was instituted two years later. It was to consist of the Governor, the Chief Secretary, the Attorney General and the Chief Medical Officer. These formed the official side of the council. The unofficial side consisted of two Europeans from the business community of Kampala. The Governor and his three assistants made up the Executive Council. One Indian had been nominated to sit on the unofficial side, but the Indian community had protested against under-representation. Their appeal was cold-shouldered by the Governor and the Colonial Secretary and as a result they boycotted the council when it first assembled in 1921. The Africans, who were the majority and who grew the crops upon which the country's wealth depended, were not represented. Their interests were to be taken care of by the Europeans and Indians, though the latter continued their boycott until the new governor, Sir William Gowers, persuaded them to end it. Hence in 1926, Mr C. J. Amin accepted the Governor's invitation and became an unofficial member of the Council. Meanwhile, the government side had been enlarged by the addition of the Directors of Agriculture and Education.

The Legco obviously was shamelessly racial in composition, representing first the Europeans and second the Indians. Even the unofficial members of the council hardly showed interest in African representation. The attitude of the Uganda Indians in this differed from that of their counterparts in Kenya. It may be argued that the Africans did not show much interest in the new Council. The Baganda, who might have taken the lead, regarded the Legco as an alien institution. They had their own Lukiko (Council) and as long as the new body did not affect the Agreement of 1900, it could carry on without them. Nevertheless, even if Africans had shown interest at this time, the Colonial government would, no doubt, have carried on regardless of their views. The Legco thus continued as a small exclusive body, catering primarily for the Europeans and Indians and only remotely for the African. It was not until 1945 that three African members, one from each province, excluding Buganda, were appointed.

At first sight it seems paradoxical that such a policy should be pursued by a government, which publicly declared that Uganda was to develop primarily as an African country. This 'primarily

African' policy was applied only where it suited British interests. Nevertheless, its implications in other aspects were important. First of all, there was no large scale alienation of land to non-Africans such as that which had taken place in Kenya. Hence there could be only a small European settler community in Uganda, though both Lugard and Johnston had wished Europeans to settle in Uganda as they did in Kenya. Perhaps the most important aspect of this government policy was the decision that the economic development of Uganda would depend on peasant agriculture. Unlike Kenya, the Africans were thus encouraged to grow cash crops such as coffee and cotton which quickly became the mainstay of Uganda's economy. Two European civil servants ought to be remembered for blocking the ambitions of the European planters who were keen to grab the land and introduce plantation agriculture: Mr Simpson, who was the Director of Agriculture from 1915 to 1929, and Mr F. Spire, who was the Provincial Commissioner in the then Eastern Province. Their persistent support of peasant agriculture often provoked bitter opposition from their fellow Europeans. In Buganda, the greatest stumbling block against the would-be settlers was the Buganda Agreement of 1900 which made conditions under which land could be alienated to non-Africans too complicated.

Cotton as a commercial crop was introduced in 1904 by Mr Borup of the Uganda Company, first in Buganda and then in other parts of the Protectorate. By 1910, cotton had already replaced ivory, hides and chillies as the leading export commodity. For a long time, cotton remained the dominant crop, and by 1930 cotton acreage was 304,000. It was not until the 1950's that cotton was replaced by coffee as the leading export crop, but even then it occupied more cultivated land than any other export crop. Uganda is still the leading cotton exporter in East Africa and it must be remembered that it was upon cotton that Uganda's agricultural economy was built. The eastern province has always been the leading cotton area, followed by Buganda. But from the mid-1950's, the Baganda concentrated more on growing coffee. Coffee had been growing in many parts of Uganda before the colonial era, but not as a commercial crop. Other commercial crops such as sugar-cane and tea, which cover extensive acreages in eastern Buganda and Busoga, are grown mainly by Indians, though tea has been introduced in the western region.

Cotton Production 1906 to 1964 (1000s of bales of 400 lbs. of lint)*.

	Uganda	Buganda	E. Region	N. Region	W. Region
1905-6	1				
1910-1	12				
1915-6	22	6	14	2	
1920-1	81	23	46	10	2
1925-6	180	58	93	25	4
1930-1	190	62	94	30	4
1935-6	316	141	135	33	7
1940-1	365		not available		
1945-6	227	127	72	20	8
1950-1	346	139	154	41	11
1955-6	364	120	170	60	14
1960-1	371	71	185	60	14
1963-4	379	53	201	107	18

The development of peasant agriculture has had two important sociological and economic consequences. First, instead of becoming wage earners, the vast majority of Uganda Africans stayed on the land, which even today employs over 80 per cent of the country's population; the farm provided the African with cash income and it remained his source of security. Second, the urban population of Uganda has consequently always been largely non-African. The fact that the majority of the people stayed on the land occasioned a shortage of labour, particularly on the plantations of non-Africans. Thus, until recently, a large proportion of the labour force was non-Ugandan, coming mainly from Burundi, Rwanda and Kenya. Even in industries such as the East African Railways, the labour force was largely Kenyan, from the Nyanza region. From a financial point of view, the Uganda African was generally better off than his counterpart in Kenya and Tanzania, for he shared, though in a very small way, in the economic development of the country. With the money they obtained, the African farmers were able to educate their children.

*Source: A. O'Connor, Economic Geography of East Africa, Bell, London, 1966.

Trade and Commerce

Although Uganda developed as a primarily African country, the bulk of trade and business remained in the hands of non-Africans. The job of the African was to grow the crops which were bought at prices fixed by the government. Price-fixing was usually the result of the influence upon the government of Indian and European traders. Thus the price of cotton paid to the African farmer was sometimes so low that the African lost interest and the acreage decreased considerably. Thus, although by 1918 the total export revenue, mainly from cotton, had reached £1,200,000, less than half went into the pockets of the Africans who produced over 80 per cent of the crop. It was also extremely difficult for the Africans to become middlemen. When in 1920 a Development Commission was appointed to promote commercial and industrial development of the country it was singularly hostile to the advancement of the Africans in every field, not only economic but also educational and political. Non-African Associations of Ginners and Buyers were formed with the avowed aim of keeping prices low. The Buganda Lukiko protested and appealed to the government to protect the growers, but the government quietly connived at the activities of the Indian and European speculators. It was not until African opposition mounted that a Commission of Inquiry was appointed to look into the cotton industry. Although the Commission's report mildly criticised the low prices paid to the growers, it was almost openly on the side of the buyers and ginners. The Lukiko opposed the Report and again appealed to the government to discourage the Buyers and Ginners' Association from paying low prices to African growers. In Busoga, several counties sent petitions to the Provincial Commissioner protesting against controlled marketing which enabled syndicates of Indian buyers to lower the prices. Discontent was widely spread throughout Uganda, even though Africans in other areas were not articulate enough to voice it. Despite these protests, the government, whose declared policy was to develop Uganda primarily as an African country, did little to break the Indian and European monopoly of middle men. Africans were denied an opportunity to enter the ginning industry with the excuse that they were 'entirely ignorant of the ginning system'. When Africans attempted to form buyers' associations, hostility was shown from all non-African quarters including the government. When the associations failed, the government gaily pointed out that the Africans had attempted to run before they had learnt to walk. But as one economic historian has pointed out, there were very few opportunities for the African to learn to walk.*

Adequate transport is the key to economic progress. History and geography had determined the joint development of the railway system of East Africa, and being inland, Uganda had a special interest in the maintenance of an efficient railway link with the coast and so with world markets. Even trade between Kenya and Tanganyika depended not only on lake shipping but also on the railway system. Thus the completion of the 'Uganda Railway' as far as Kisumu in 1902, was a landmark. Not only did it reduce transport costs, but it provided Uganda with a quick link with the outside world. By 1912, the line between Jinja and Namasagali was completed, just when the cotton crop was expanding in the eastern region. Internally, railway development took the form of constructing branch lines to bring traffic from the production centres into the main lines of communication. A line was extended from Tororo to Soroti and in 1948 an extension was made through Western Uganda to the copper-mining area of Kasese. In 1961, the Bukonte-Jinja cut-off was completed; further developments are taking place in the north where the Tororo-Soroti line is to be continued to Lira and Gulu. Railway transport has always been greatly supplemented by water and road. Like the railways, Lake Victoria has always been a major link between Uganda, Kenya and Tanzania. The 'Uganda Railway' was originally completed to Kisumu, and thus the main link between Uganda and the outside world was through Lake Victoria. Internally, Lake Kyoga and the short navigable stretch on the river Nile have always provided excellent waterways. But the increasing efficiency of motor transport must involve a decline in inland water transport. A road system radiating from Kampala, the commercial capital, to other trading centres, was the key to the agricultural development of the country. This was recognised from a very early period of colonial rule, and to facilitate the expansion of cotton growing a programme of road construction was adopted. Today, Uganda possesses one of the best road systems in Africa.

See C. Ehrlich, *Oxford History of East Africa,* Vol. II, pp. 395–475.

Educational Development

It is sometimes assumed that education in Africa began with
the coming of the Europeans. This mistaken belief springs
from the assumption that the Western type of education is the
only system of education. Every community, in fact, has its own
system of education and values. Among Africans, it was usual
for young people to attend meetings of elders and listen to
discussions and even to disputes. The elders would also tell the
history of their ancestors, and in this way the young people learnt
the history, the laws and customs of their own societies, and
appreciated their values. This was one kind of education. The
Western type of education in Uganda was introduced by the
Christian Missionaries as an essential part of the process of
conversion to Christianity. Inevitably therefore the first schools
were Christian schools and were for the sons of chiefs. In the
early period missionary efforts were concentrated primarily in
Buganda and development outside came slowly. The first
boarding Secondary School was opened by the Mill Hill Fathers
at Namilyango in 1902 and it became the prototype for other
schools such as Buddo, Kisubi, Gayaza and others. The last
school was for girls. The curriculum which was designed for
potential leaders was mainly academic, with heavy emphasis on
Grammar and reading of English books, Geography and
Mathematics. Technical schools were also opened.

During the first twenty years of the Protectorate, the Central
Government was mainly concerned with establishing a stable
administration, spending little time and effort or money on
social services. The principal result of this government neglect
in financing education was that non-Christians were generally
neglected in educational development. Hence for many years
the education of the Moslems lagged behind. It was not until
the 1920's that the Government took an interest in the development of education. In 1925, a Department of Education was
started, and the next fifteen years were characterised by a
gradual but steady expansion of schools; the government also
began to subsidise the voluntary agencies which ran the schools.
By the end of the Second World War there had been marked
expansion in the number of schools and in expenditure. For
instance, immediately after the first war, government allocation
for education was £1,250. By 1950, the total estimated expenditure was £75,000 and in 1960 five million pounds were spent
on education.

From the very beginning, education in Uganda had developed along racial as well as religious lines. There were separate schools for Africans, Indians and Europeans. Among the Africans there were separate schools for Catholics, Moslems and Protestants; religious divisions existed also among the Asians. In order to bring an end to this chaotic state of affairs, the Government announced in 1957 its intention to integrate the educational system. And since that date the government has steadily plodded along the road of integration. During the same period, another decision regarding the development of junior and senior secondary education was taken. The rapid expansion of primary education in the early 1950's made it necessary to slow the pace of development in the primary category in order to expand secondary education. Despite this expansion, the ratio of the places available in primary schools has remained one place for nearly every fourteen children.

Why did Uganda achieve so much in educational development compared with many other African countries? It was not because the colonial government did more to develop education in Uganda than elsewhere. Of course, the colonial government has always been proud to quote Uganda, besides Ghana and southern Nigeria as areas where the British developed African education, but much of the credit goes rather to the missionaries. In countries where missionary effort was slow, African education developed very slowly, and particularly where the countries were poor, the colonial governments did little to develop African education. Much more was achieved in Uganda because Uganda was richer and Africans participated in the growing of cash crops such as coffee and cotton. Today education is no longer restricted to the privileged few.

During the same period, medical services expanded considerably. The first hospitals and dispensaries were founded by missionaries, and Mengo Hospital remained for many years the most famous of these hospitals. The missionaries ran also a number of scattered hospitals and other small units. From the earliest period of the Protectorate, the foremost Department was that of Medical Services. Its Director was originally responsible to the Chief Secretary for the administration of the Department and for advice on medical matters generally. At the beginning of the 1950's, the Ministry of Social Services was established to bring about a closer integration of the many different aspects of medical services. Today there are rural dispensaries, district and sub-district hospitals, and mission hospitals. The Central Hospital is Mulago, which cost over £3,000,000 to build and has nearly 900 beds. It has a medical school attached to it, providing medical training for nearly 300 students from all over East Africa and beyond.

The Beginnings of Nationalism

Baganda agents had been removed from north and eastern Uganda as early as 1901, though a few remained until the late 1920's. By the beginning of the 1930's, Baganda agents, wherever they were, were making way for the indigenous chiefs: in Ankole, Kigezi, Toro, Bunyoro, etc. Throughout these areas, a great deal of the reaction to colonial rule was provoked not so much by the British as by their agents, the Baganda. Remotely therefore, these first reactions can be described as the first seeds of nationalism in as much as they were directed against alien rule even though it was represented by the Baganda. For a very long time, Buganda remained the centre of political activity, expressed either against the economic exploitation of the African by the European and Indian businessmen or against the chiefs, even against the Kabaka himself or against certain policies of the central government. The first signs of political discontent appeared before the war of 1914 to 1918.

The Bamalaki, a semi-religious movement sprang up and provided the venue for voicing political discontent. Although this was in all appearances a religious movement, like many such movements it also had political aims. The high-water mark of political discontent came early in the 1920's when the Bataka movement nearly forced a revision of the 1900 Buganda Agreement. The Bataka desired a redistribution of land, and inclusion of a clause which would make ancestral land the property of the clans rather than of the individual heads in whose names the land was registered. The Kabaka, Sir Daudi Cwa II, sympathised with their case and recommended a revision of the Agreement. The Colonial government, however, sided with the existing chiefs whose interests were at stake, and advised the Colonial Secretary to reject the Kabaka's recommendation.

Political activity further manifested itself in the opposition to an East African federation in the 1920's and 1930's because of the fear that Uganda might become another Kenya—a

country dominated by the European settlers. The most vocal
organs at this time were the Buganda Lukiko, the Young
Baganda Association and the Young Basoga Association. During
the 1940's, economic and political discontent increased considerably in Buganda. People wanted more participation in the
direction of their affairs through more representatives in the
Lukiko. At the same time they wanted to get rid of the old type
of chiefs who seemed to be puppets of the colonial government.
Such discontent found an outlet in the Buganda riots of 1945,
and also in the assassination of the Buganda Prime Minister,
Martin Luther Nsibirwa. From that time onwards events moved
fast and the Uganda African Farmers Association conducted a
campaign against exploitation of the African farmers by the
Indian and European businessmen. The agitation culminated in
the 1949 riots which were more serious and better organised
than those of 1945. The Africans demanded that they should
be allowed to market their own crops and also asked the Kabaka
to make the Lukiko more democratic by increasing the representative side to 60 members. At least one thing characterised
the riots of the 1940's: they were confined to Buganda and their
immediate target was the Baganda chiefs. This has created the
impression that they were local movements having nothing to
do with the advancement of Africans in Uganda. What must be
remembered, however, is that Nationalism had to start somewhere. By fighting against economic exploitation of the farmers,
and by denouncing their own chiefs who seemed to be agents of
this exploitation, the leaders of the 1945 and 1949 movements
sowed the seeds of modern nationalism. But for the time being
they were unable to talk in terms of national politics, for they
had less than six representatives in the only national body, the
Legislative Council.

Militant nationalism which brought independence thus took
long to formulate itself because of a number of factors. The
Uganda African, unlike his Kenya counterpart, was never
robbed of his land. Although there was forced labour, it was
never carried to the same extent as in Kenya or other countries
where there were European settlers. But perhaps the greatest
factor militating against a rapid growth of nationalism was the
system of indirect rule and lack of a clear policy on the part of
the British on the future of Uganda. Indirect rule tended to
favour the growth of local autonomy, and the result was that the
British indirectly encouraged federalist tendencies in their

administration. Lack of a central political forum for the Africans, and the British encouragement of local councils meant that the immediate African interests were with local affairs. But by voicing the economic exploitation of the masses, and by demanding increased representation in the Buganda Lukiko, men of the 1940's lighted the tinder which burst into nationalist flames towards the end of the 1950's. After the 1949 riots, the clock could never go back nor even be stopped.

It was Uganda's good fortune at this stage of her political development that at the beginning of the 1950's, there came a governor who was prepared to keep pace with the winds of change. Sir Andrew Cohen had arrived in Uganda in 1952, and early in 1953 proposed constitutional changes in Buganda which if adopted would have led to real representative government. Other parts of the country were also to be affected in varying degrees. In Buganda, more power was to devolve on the government by transferring a number of responsibilities: these were primary and junior secondary schools, rural hospitals, agriculture and veterinary services. In order to cope with these new responsibilities, ministries in the Kabaka's government were increased by three, and in the Lukiko 60 out of 80 members were to be elected, giving it for the first time an elected majority. Sir Andrew's pre-occupation at this stage was to introduce progressive reforms which would give a greater say to the Africans in the running of their own affairs. He at the same time, wished to see a steady development of Uganda as a unitary state. But things suddenly took a sharp turn when, in 1953, the Kabaka, supported by the Lukiko, opposed the idea of an East African Federation, proposed in the Secretary of State for the Colonies' speech of 30 June 1953. It was also at this time that the Kabaka demanded independence and thereby posed a threat to the existence of the colonial government. Hitherto, the colonial government had used the Kabaka as the instrument of suppression of any radicalism in Buganda politics, and even in the reforms proposed by Sir Andrew Cohen the Kabaka was still regarded as a promoter of colonial policy. When by his demand for independence he appeared to be the leader of nationalism, and when he attempted to bring the other rulers in the West to his line of thinking, he clearly became a threat to the colonial government. In November, Mutesa II was deposed and deported to Britain, for 'breaking' the Uganda Agreement which required him to co-operate loyally with the Protectorate government.

Meanwhile, in 1952, the first modern political party was formed. This was the Uganda National Congress, popularly known as the UNC. Its declared aim was to unite all the peoples of Uganda and to bring independence. The kabaka crisis had given a new and sharper edge to the development of nationalist forces. By unceremoniously deporting the Kabaka, Sir Andrew Cohen had made the worst blunder of his political career in Uganda. Overnight, Mutesa became a hero and acquired a measure of popularity which he had never before achieved since his accession in 1940. All politically-minded people saw the governor's action as an affront to the African. The UNC had now a clear target: the immediate ending of colonial rule. It denounced the economic exploitation of the African masses by Indians and Europeans, and opposed East African federation. People all over Uganda were becoming more politically conscious. In 1954 the Democratic Party was founded. At about the same time the Progressive Party, popularly known as the PP was also formed. But the latter two parties lacked the dynamic drive of the UNC, which had such leaders as Musaazi, Joseph Kiwanuka and Abu Mayanja. The UNC was Uganda's burning spear and remained so until about 1958.

At the central level, important constitutional changes were taking place. Early in 1953, Sir Andrew had announced changes in the composition of the Legislative Council. A Cross Bench of ten unofficial members was to be formed and the representative side was to be increased to twenty-eight, of whom fourteen were to be Africans. These changes were not welcomed by all peoples in Uganda. They were in fact not as radical as some contemporary non-Africans believed; the representative side was only half of the total Council. The entire approach to the affairs of Uganda was still racial: for instance the composition of the Council was still in the ratio of 2:1:1, and only two Africans were unofficial members of the Executive Council.

Negotiations for the reinstatement of Mutesa II had led to a new agreement, which attempted to define in a more up-to-date manner the political position of Buganda in Uganda. In these negotiations the Baganda asked for the introduction of direct elections. The request was accepted and incorporated in the 1955 Buganda Agreement. Moving with his extraordinary swiftness, Sir Andrew Cohen announced in 1956 that direct elections would be held in Buganda as an experiment, but that indirect elections would continue to be held in other areas.

But the people from outside Buganda felt that they too should be given the opportunity of holding direct elections and their demand was accepted by the Governor.

Although it was the Baganda who had first asked for the introduction of direct elections while negotiating the 1955 Agreement, they suddenly changed their minds when the time drew near in 1957. The Mengo regime, and the kabaka's government in particular, suddenly realised the political dangers of the ballot box, and therefore opposed the introduction of direct elections 'until certain conditions in the Buganda Agreements' had been fulfilled. Legal fictions were found, such as that the introduction of a Speaker in the Legislative Council was contrary to the Agreement of 1955, and expert lawyers readily made themselves available from Britain to argue Buganda's case. This was in fact a way of perpetuating the positions of the old regime in Buganda politics. The new Governor, Sir Frederick Crawford, was extremely cautious when dealing with Buganda affairs. So he let the Baganda have their own way in this matter, and when direct elections were held in 1958 Buganda did not participate. A system of indirect elections, however, was used whereby the Lukiko nominated the representatives. It was an effective method of control by the Kabaka and the Lukiko on these representatives. It was not long in fact before the Lukiko recalled its representatives from the Legislative Council. With this act, the kabaka's government, then led by Michael Kintu, withdrew Buganda from the centre of Uganda politics. Other districts where the existing regimes felt threatened by the ballot box followed Buganda and opted for indirect elections. Thus no direct elections were held in Ankole. But Mengo's intransigence did not halt the march of progress, for ten districts participated in the district elections, not counting Bugisu, which demanded fulfilment of certain conditions, and Karamoja, which was a special case.

The introduction of the ministerial system in 1955 and of direct elections of African representatives in 1958 marked the real beginning of political progress in Uganda. After these elections, the Legislative Council consisted of twenty-five representatives, fifteen of whom were Africans. The important feature of the post-1958 Council was that, although there were more official members, the Africans had a majority over non-Africans, and there was also a majority of non-civil servants. The political winds of change had began to blow hard.

In 1959, the government appointed a committee to consider

constitutional changes which would pave the way for self-government and independence. The committee was chaired by Mr J. V. Wild, a civil servant, and in December, 1959 it produced its report. The *Wild Report* recommended the introduction of a common roll and the abolition of the indirect rule system of elections. Throughout the country representation was to be on a population basis. The government accepted nearly all the major recommendations and these led to the first country-wide elections. Meanwhile the political scene had been enlivened by the Uganda National Movement which had been launched early in 1959. It was essentially a political movement but it had as many other aims as there were leaders. It declared a trade boycott against non-Africans and very soon it had to back its actions by intimidation and violence. Augustine Kamya took over leadership of the movement, which gave it the mantle of being truly a 'common man's movement'. But it was soon proscribed, its leaders were deported to Karamoja and other parts of northern Uganda, and it finally went underground. The UNM was in many ways a failure for it had neither a programme nor defined aims. However, as the first popular movement in Buganda, it was supported with an enthusiasm which was only exceeded by the *Kabaka Yekka* Movement launched in 1961.

Meanwhile political parties had multiplied with the intense political activity. The once strong UNC had been bedevilled by party squabbles which led to splits, expulsions and counter-expulsions. By 1960, the strongest splinter group was that which became the Uganda Peoples' Congress, led by Mr A. M. Obote. It carried with it some of the radicalism of the old UNC, but this gradually rubbed off. The only major political parties in Uganda in 1960 were the Democratic Party (DP), and the UPC. The former was greatly aided by a change of leadership in 1958 when Mr Benedicto Kiwanuka succeeded Mugwanya as the leader of the Party. But, although these were country-wide political parties, they faced great handicaps in getting themselves established. First of all, Uganda was in many ways an artificial unit consisting of many different tribes. Throughout the seventy years of British rule, little effort had been made to unify the country and develop it as a single unit. The second difficulty was the relative lack of educated manpower. The majority of the educated people were civil servants who were debarred from all kinds of political activity. The DP had another handicap, for it was suspected of masking a Roman Catholic plot, while the UPC was almost non-existent in Buganda. It was with these difficulties that Uganda's two major political parties confronted each other when in 1961 the first country-wide elections were held.

After the collapse of the Uganda National Movement and other Mengo backed political parties such as the United National Party led by Mr Apolo Kironde, the Mengo régime was left without a political party. It was this rather than the 'securing of Buganda's position' which led the kabaka's government in 1960 to boycott the registration of voters and the subsequent election. As a result of the boycott and intimidation, registration in Buganda was very small, which meant that the DP was virtually unopposed and so won the general election with a fairly comfortable majority. The 1961 election opened the way for the first African government headed by the party leader, Mr Benedicto Kiwanuka. Mr Obote led the Opposition. Independence could not be delayed for long and with its approach political activity was intensified throughout the country. Meanwhile, the Mengo régime, realising that they were missing the boat, took steps to correct the unfortunate decision of the previous year. First a party was formed, the *Kabaka Yekka* (King Alone). Its formation provided an outlet for the pent-up emotions of the people of Buganda. A popular movement with a potent weapon in the slogan 'Kabaka Yekka' and the knowledge that it was supported by the Kabaka himself, *Kabaka Yekka* (KY) spread like a wild fire and threatened almost total disaster to the only strong party in Buganda, the Democratic Party. *Kabaka Yekka,* however, was essentially confined to Buganda, having as sole objective the protection of the monarchy.

It, however, won national status when it made an alliance with the UPC and agreed to participate in the constitutional conference which was to produce the Independence Constitution of 1961. One of the major features of the 1961 Constitution was the option given to Buganda to nominate its representatives to the National Assembly instead of electing them directly like other parts of Uganda. As events were to show later, it was dangerous to support the option, because its ultimate aim was to strangle nationalist movements in Buganda. But the immediate aim of ousting the DP served its purpose. In February 1962, elections to the Lukiko took place and the DP, the only major party to contest seats with the KY, was soundly thrashed, winning only two of the 68 seats in the new Lukiko. *Kabaka*

Yekka took the expected decision and opted for indirect elections to the National Assembly.

Things were now moving fast. Self-government was granted in March, and Mr Kiwanuka became Uganda's first Prime Minister. One month afterwards, a general election was held to decide which party was to lead Uganda to Independence. After its defeat in Buganda, the DP's chances of winning the elections were almost nil. They were defeated outside Buganda by the UPC which joined hands with the KY which, with twenty-one members nominated by the Buganda Lukiko, gave the UPC-KY government a comfortable majority. Mr Obote became the Prime Minister, and in September, 1962 led a delegation to London to put the final touches to the Independence Constitution.

Independence and After

On 9 October 1962, Uganda joined the other new nations of Africa as an independent and sovereign state, but there was to be a Governor-General and the Queen was to be the Head of State. In the 1962 Constitution there were a few questions which could only be changed after independence. One of the thorny questions which had been bequeathed to the new government by the colonial power was that of the 'lost counties'. The establishment of British rule had led to the alienation of the counties of Bugangazzi and Buyaga, both of which had been Bunyoro territory then. Although the Banyoro claimed more than the two counties, the government made arrangements to hold a referendum only in those two. This took place in 1964, when the inhabitants of Buyaga and Bugangazzi voted to rejoin Bunyoro. In 1963, Sir Edward Mutesa, the Kabaka of Buganda, was elected the first President of Uganda and Sir Wilberforce Nadiope, the *Kyabazinga* of Busoga was elected Vice-President. By the end of 1964, the government had settled the 'lost counties' issue, and Uganda had an African President, though the Queen was in a vague way still regarded also as the Head of State, for Uganda was not yet a Republic. Meanwhile the UPC had strengthened its position by crossings from KY and DP. These crossings from KY deprived the movement of its intellectual wing, and left the masses with no sound leadership. Daudi Ochieng attempted to turn it into a modern political party, but without success. On the surface therefore, the UPC's position seemed formidable, for the party had won practically every district council election, and the only area where they were almost non-existent was still Buganda. Nevertheless, with the frequent crossings from DP and KY, it looked as if Uganda would become a one party state without even legislation.

But all was not well inside the ruling Party. Dissensions tore it from top to bottom. The annual delegates' conference which elects the party leaders had to be postponed. By late-1965, there were rumours of a *coup d'état,* which set the country on edge. Matters came to a head when in January 1966, Daudi Ochieng brought a motion in the National Assembly demanding an investigation of the financial activities of some leading ministers, including the Prime Minister and Deputy Commander of the Uganda Army. These serious allegations led to the appoint-ment of a Committee of Inquiry which included a number of leading lawyers in East Africa.

By the end of January 1966, it had become clear that there must be an explosion of some kind. Hence in February, during a cabinet meeting, the Prime Minister, Mr A. M. Obote ordered the arrest and immediate detention of five of his ministers. He suspended the constitution and assumed full powers. All this took place before the Committee of Inquiry into Ochieng's allegations had met. The suspension of the 1962 Constitution virtually meant the end of the non-executive President and Vice-President and it was not long before Sir Edward and Sir Wilberforce had to vacate their offices. The 1962 Constitution was finally replaced on 15 April 1966 by a New Constitution. The major change was that Mr Obote became the new President. Other important changes affected Buganda and the Kabaka's ability to direct political movements in Buganda.

Soon afterwards, tension increased between the Central Government and the Buganda Government. Things came to a head when the Lukiko passed a resolution which virtually expelled the Central government from Buganda soil. The situation seemed to have reached a point of no return and it exploded on the morning of 24 May 1966, when Central govern-ment troops invaded and overran the Kabaka's palace. The Kabaka and some of the inmates escaped, but very many others were slain.

Meanwhile all political rallies except those of the ruling party were banned. *Kabaka Yekka* had already been declared illegal and many people were thrown into jail either for alleged rioting during the month of May 1966 or for alleged plotting to over-throw the government. The *Kabaka Yekka* movement will remain one of the most dramatic and interesting episodes in the history of Uganda. It had been formed for the specific aim of protecting the monarchy. It left Buganda without a kabaka and with the country in a state of emergency.

Further reading

LOW, A. D. Uganda: The Establishment of the Protectorate, 1884-1919, pp. 57-122, *History of East Africa,* Volume II, Oxford University Press, Oxford, 1963.

EHRLICH, C. The Uganda Economy 1903-1945, pp. 395-475, *History of East Africa,* Volume II, Oxford University Press, Oxford, 1965.

INGHAM, K. *The Making of Modern Uganda,* Allen and Unwin, London, 1957.

INGHAM, K. *The Economic Development of Uganda,* Report of the International Bank, Baltimore, 1962.

O'CONNOR, A. *The Economic Geography of East Africa,* Bell & Sons, London, 1966.

LOW, A. D. and PRATT, R. C. *Buganda and British Overrule,* Oxford University Press, London, 1960. (See especially pp. 163-178 for valuable comment on Indirect Rule.)

WILD, J. V. *The Story of the Uganda Agreement,* East African Literature Bureau, Nairobi, 1950.

WILD, J. V. *Report of the Constitutional Committee, 1959.* Uganda Government Printer, Kampala, 1959.

APTER, D. *The Political Kingdom in Uganda,* Oxford University Press, London, 1961.

MITCHELL, P. E. Indirect Rule, *Uganda Journal,* Volume IV, 1937, (pp. 101-107).

16

Economic and Social Developments before Independence

Cyril Ehrlich

Three interconnected themes can be traced in the economic and social history of East Africa—the growth of its economies, the policies of its governments, and the welfare of its peoples. Under these main headings we can ask a series of questions. What was the nature and extent of economic development during the colonial period? Which goods were produced with what arrangement of productive factors, land, labour, capital, and enterprise? As the economy grew what happened to its structure, what were the main determinants of this evolving pattern, and what ultimately was the legacy inherited by the new independent governments? How did the colonial governments frame and execute social and economic policies, and with how much success? Finally, to what extent and in what sense were people better off during and as a result of all these changes—what happened to their standard of living? A short introductory chapter cannot hope to provide adequate answers to all these questions, but it might perhaps stimulate interest in and indicate the scope of a neglected subject. It may also provide the reader with some useful background knowledge for a better appreciation of the enormous problems of social and economic development facing East Africans today.

Creating a Cash Economy

At the beginning of our period, in the late nineteenth century, East African economies were simple and poor, based at best on

a traditional agriculture which in good seasons provided sufficient food for the home and perhaps for a limited local market.
In some privileged areas, such as Buganda, fertile soil and
adequate rainfall supported a denser population at a higher and
more assured level of subsistance. Elsewhere, nature was frequently less generous, population sparse, and in bad seasons
men, unaided by physical capital, starved. An essential first
step towards growth, therefore, was the creation of a cash exchange economy, for men do not willingly work to produce more
than their immediate requirements, so building up capital and
raising their standard of living, unless they can find profitable
outlets for these surpluses. Within East Africa, however, such
market outlets were severely limited by various aspects of an
omni-present poverty—low incomes and a general lack of cash,
poor communications, small populations, and an absence of
towns. For these isolated subsistence economies to pull themselves up by their own bootstraps would have been a slow and
arduous process, but the opening of the Suez Canal in 1869 and
the growth of ocean shipping offered an alternative way of breaking this vicious circle of poverty. A comparison with West Africa's
trade links is illuminating. The distance from Lagos to Liverpool
is about 4,300 miles; from Zanzibar to Britain via the Cape is
over twice that distance; the Suez Canal lopped 2,000 miles off
the journey. Now East African products could more easily be
exported to established markets overseas, which promised a
ready source of income to anyone who could supply suitable
goods at competitive prices. The advantages of thus linking
East Africa with the international economy were obvious and
far reaching, but there was an attendant disadvantage. Thenceforth growth and welfare would depend to a very large extent
upon factors lying outside the control of East Africans; while the
quantity of exports would reflect local circumstances and effort,
their *value* would be greatly affected by those world market conditions which still determine the demand for and the price of
most East African products. For example, in 1930 the price of
coffee dropped from about £120 to £70 a ton; the price of sisal
slumped from £40 a ton in 1929 to £20 in the following year,
and then to £12. Such dependence upon markets which are
notoriously fickle has been frequently deplored, but the ad-
mitted defects of this situation when prices fall have been counterbalanced by the enormous benefits of good years like the 1920's
and the great boom of the 1940's and early 1950's. Irregular

income is better than no income. Moreover, this form of dependence should not be confused with the political dependence
imposed by colonial authority. It is, in fact, the prevailing condition of many small independent countries, such as New Zealand
and Ireland, whose foreign trade is a high proportion of their
national income, and whose prosperity therefore depends upon
their ability to exploit the international economy, which can act
as a powerful 'engine of growth' if there is a sufficiently creative
response to its manifold opportunities. There are abundant
examples of this truth in modern economic history, from the
spectacular successes of Denmark and Japan to the more modest
but still impressive achievements of Uganda during the decade
before 1914 and particularly during the 1920's. The production
of viable exports has been the essential basis of whatever material
progress East Africans have enjoyed during the twentieth century.

A Transport Revolution

Before they could benefit from such opportunities, a thorough-
going revolution in transport facilities was an indispensable
first step. Apart from Zanzibar and a narrow strip of coast,
East Africa was landlocked, a fact that goes far to explain its
economic backwardness in the nineteenth century. Water
transport was insignificant, draught animals could not survive,
and the motor-lorry had not so far appeared. The only form of
carriage was the human 'caravan' which was degrading, slow,
wasteful of scarce labour, and absurdly expensive. Therefore,
only goods which were extremely valuable in relation to their
bulk could be afforded transport for any distance: here was a
formidable barrier to trade and therefore to development.
The obvious answer was to build railways, but the necessary
investment would be large, and there was little evidence of a
potential traffic that might attract sufficient funds to such an
enterprise. The German company which began work on the
Tanga-Korogwe railway in 1893 was first in this unenviable
field, and its experience was typical of much of the early history
of railway building elsewhere in East Africa. Difficult terrain,
shortage of skilled labour, inexperience and inefficiency, inadequate materials and machinery, all ensured that progress
was costly and slow. By 1896, the line had progressed a mere

43 kilometres to Muhesa, boasted one train a week, and was earning less than a thirtieth of its running costs. The Government eventually took over and at vast expense pushed the line on to Korogwe by 1902. Meanwhile, the British had made faster, but arduous and expensive progress with the so-called Uganda Railway.

The detailed history of this and later railway lines is familiar or easily available elsewhere. What concerns us here is their economic significance. Since there were no clear prospects of profit and, particularly, no known mineral deposits to exploit, railway projects were unattractive to all but the most optimistic investors, and therefore had to be financed out of public funds. Their principal economic effect was to link East Africa with the international economy by enormously reducing inland transport costs. Thus before the coming of the railway the cost of carrying a typical load from Mombasa to Kampala would account for more than half its final price. The railway and improved transport on Lake Victoria reduced freight costs from England to Kampala by approximately 90 per cent. Deliveries were not merely cheaper, but they were faster, more reliable and more regular. All this was of enormous benefit to import and export trade, for regularity and reliability are essential to modern commerce and they reduce the costly necessity of tying up capital in barren stocks. Railways also made an important contribution to urbanisation. Nairobi was born as a railway base in 1899, providing employment, a market for local produce, and general economic stimulus. There were similar if smaller scale developments at Mombasa, Dar es Salaam, and Tabora. Large labour forces were required for construction; in the building of the Tanganyika central line 20,000 men were employed at peak periods of activity. For the building of the Uganda railway 32,000 workers had to be brought from India (a warning of labour shortages to come). Of these, incidentally, only one-fifth elected to remain after their period of indenture was complete. After their construction, the railways continued to require a large labour force for their operation, administration and maintenance. By the end of our period East African Railways and Harbours, with a staff of some 50,000, was by far the largest industrial employer in the region.

The economic significance of the railways was therefore considerable, but it should not be exaggerated. Their extent was limited in relation to the vast area that needed to be opened up. Southern Tanganyika is perhaps the clearest example of this, but it should also be remembered that the so-called Uganda railway did not actually enter Uganda until the 1920's and had not reached western Uganda until the 1950's. To have done more would have required massive investment which nothing but obsessive philanthropy or megalomania could have called forth. But their limited mileage and inherent inflexibility meant that they failed to provide anything approaching an adequate transport system. It can indeed be argued that the real agents of a transport revolution in East Africa were not the railways but, from the beginning of our period, the bicycle, and during the 1920's, the motor-lorry. The bicycle's contribution to productivity and well-being is self-evident, making it one of the most useful items to be found on the import lists. The lorry, financed by innumerable small businessmen, created a flexible transport system and introduced men to machinery—an innovation of far-reaching educational significance. Its impact was particularly beneficial in eastern Uganda where roads were comparatively good and the cotton crop made great demands on the transport system. Elsewhere, roads remained very poor for most of our period, though a great and expensive effort was made to improve them in Tanganyika during the closing years of colonial rule.

Despite their limitations, however, the railways did remove the immediate barrier to East Africa's joining the international economy. The question then was what could be produced that foreigners would buy in sufficient quantities to provide East Africans with a continuous flow of cash income and with foreign exchange to finance desired imports. The existing trickle of exports, consisting of such natural products as ivory and skins, was no base for economic development, and new commercially viable products had to be pioneered. While this was ultimately desirable for everyone's welfare, for the colonial governments it was an immediate *sine qua non,* for without cash incomes men could not pay taxes in a usable form and without cash revenue government could not function. Early attempts to impose taxes led, at best, to the accumulation of a useless collection of animals and produce. The creation of an exchange economy was thus an essential prerequisite for both economic and political development. During the early years of this century even the modest expenditures of the Kenya and Uganda Governments were made possible only by grants in aid from Britain, and the administration of Tanganyika was subsidised in similar fashion by Germany. Under pressure to reduce these grants local administrators made considerable efforts to find commercial products and men who would produce them. There was virtually no indigenous industry and no mineral deposits had so far been discovered. Therefore the task was one of agricultural policy and development.

Agricultural Policy

Agricultural policy was of vital importance for two simple reasons. First, because agriculture was by far the biggest sector of the economy, and therefore what governments did about it had far-reaching effects upon growth and welfare. Second, because these policies affected or even determined the involvement of Africans in commercial agriculture, and therefore the extent of Africanisation ultimately required when the countries became independent. It should be remembered, of course, that policies were not neat blueprints, imposed after careful planning by a fully informed government. Rather did they emerge as compromises, subject to the delays and pressures of politics, scarcity, and ignorance. Above all, in this as in most aspects of government policy, evolution tended to be slow because it was based upon what has been well described as 'the tranquil assumption of the long-term character of colonial rule'.

The two alternative systems through which commercial crops were produced can be briefly described as 'peasant' and 'plantation' agriculture. Under the first system people already on the land were persuaded or sometimes bullied into adapting their traditional forms of cultivation so as to include the new crops. Uganda's cotton industry is a familiar example of this grafting process by which traditional and exchange economic activities were merged. Under the 'plantation' system large units of land were allotted to immigrants who farmed commercially, employing Africans merely as unskilled labour. In German East Africa much capital, enterprise and skill were thrown into the production of sisal, coffee, and cotton on alienated estates. The Amani research institute, founded in 1902, was typical of the German thoroughness which justified their claim to be 'ahead of British East Africa by a decade in the development of the tropical belt'. In general the choice of system was affected to some extent by the intrinsic qualities and cultivation requirements of different crops, but it was mainly determined by governmental decisions which were in turn influenced by the desire for quick results and by the varying pressures of settler demands. Many crops could be grown under either system, but this fact was usually obscured by special pleading, notably in the case of coffee, which was satisfactorily produced by Africans in Uganda and Tanganyika, while the Kenya government, accepting spurious warnings of crop disease, restricted its cultivation to Europeans.

There were three ways in which governments influenced the pattern of agriculture. First and foremost was the question of white settlement and land alienation, probably the most familiar and certainly the most contentious aspect of colonial policy. Closely linked with this and equally controversial was the 'labour problem'. Existing levels of wages and working conditions were inadequate to attract a sufficient supply of labour for public works, like road building, or for plantations. Governments, therefore, frequently resorted to compulsion, the moral case for which was at least arguable. But planters expected them to exert similar pressures to recruit labour for private employment, where clearly there was no moral case, although 'the dignity of labour' was commonly invoked. Officials reacted to this demand with varying degrees of humanity and circumspection, and missionaries played a notable part in educating British public opinion. The climax of these public airings centred around Keny'a notorious 1921 'Northey circulars', after which officials were unequivocally ordered 'to take no part in recruiting labour for private employment'. But compulsory labour was still occasionally used for public works. In the long run, men's willingness to work on plantations, usually far from their homes, depended less upon government edict than upon the availability of alternative sources of income, a principal factor determining those long distance migrations which are so prominent a feature of African economic life. Here we meet the third form of government influence—the role of agricultural departments. They could serve primarily as information centres for European farmers and planters, as tended to be the case in Kenya and in German East Africa. Alternatively they could actively promote peasant agriculture; but in so far as they succeeded in this they would further increase the planter's labour difficulties and thus incur their animosity. A remarkable example of this was the career of Simpson, who, as Uganda's Director of Agriculture between 1911 and 1929 devoted his considerable energies to building up the cotton industry, despite limited resources and bitter opposition from planters and sometimes even from his superior officers.

These differences between the relative emphasis given to plantation and peasant agriculture form one of the most significant themes in the economic history of East Africa. In Uganda the economy grew on a solid base of African cotton and coffee. From the outset Indians and Europeans were prominent in the processing and marketing of these crops, and Africanisation was delayed until the emergence of co-operatives in the 1950's. But the grass roots of development were indigenous, and when independence came, comparatively little unscrambling was necessary. Kenya was utterly different. African commercial agriculture did not grow significantly until the 1930's, and even then it was given little encouragement by the government. Not until the 1950's, under the Swynnerton plan, was real progress made; African coffee production, for example, a mere 1,000 tons in 1954, expanded six-fold during the next five years. In Tanganyika after the defeat of Germany the pace of development slowed down. There were small cases of African cash income in the desert of subsistence and inactivity. Chagga coffee growers, with the ardent support of Dundas, formed a co-operative in 1924, despite strong opposition along familiar lines from European planters, some of whom advocated a transfer of Kilimanjaro to Kenya! Bukoba was another centre of coffee production; but there was little dynamism in the promotion of African commercial agriculture. By far the biggest industry was sisal, grown on alien owned plantations in which the African's role was solely that of an unskilled labourer, with little education to be derived from his experience, and few prospects of promotion.

The social disadvantages of plantations were therefore considerable. Their principal economic advantage was the possibility that skilled management might get quick results. Against this, however, management costs tended to be high and inflexible, though Indian firms, where they were allowed to farm, tended to be more efficient in this respect. Such inflexibility was a frequent source of failure in times of depression when peasants proved their greater resilience by retreating a little from cash. The long-term social and political advantages of the peasant

system were enormous but entailed certain short-term economic
disadvantages. It was usually a slow and difficult task to persuade
peasants to change their methods of cultivation. This stubborn-
ness was not always a matter of tradition-bound ignorance in
the face of superior scientific knowledge, for traditional methods
frequently embodied the inherited wisdom of the past, and the
new agricultural 'expert' was not always equipped with knowledge that was relevant to local conditions. Since this problem
continues to bedevil traditional agriculture all over the world,
despite the huge international resources that have been thrown
into development programmes in recent years, it is not surprising
that the small, undermanned, and poorly-equipped colonial
departments made slow progress with their pioneering efforts.
Three criticisms can be made of their policies. First, there was
always a tendency to enforce unreasonable quality standards
which were unrelated to the costs of attaining these standards
and to actual market demands. Second, there was a dispro-
portionate concern for soil erosion which made little sense in
an economy where time horizons were short and where land
was usually the *least* scarce of all factors of production. Finally,
official policies frequently laid great emphasis upon the need
to provide an insurance against famine by cultivating such
unattractive crops as cassava. Although it was well-intentioned,
this policy was fundamentally wrong-headed from a developmental point of view. Instead of encouraging market consciousness and the enlargement of the exchange economy, it 'fastened
upon the producer the straightjacket of subsistence production'.
The 1955 Royal Commission's brilliant attack upon this and
similar policies is essential reading for those who wish to understand the intricacies of colonial paternalism.

The Pattern of Development and Trade

Our emphasis upon agricultural *policy* is not intended to suggest
that governments alone were responsible for economic change.
Even in highly centralised economies development rarely takes
place simply as a result of a government's aspirations and plans.
In colonial East Africa foreign trade was the chief motor driving
the economy forward, but the power of this motor had to be
harnessed and transmitted throughout society. At times a
government could provide such transmission directly, as when

the Uganda administration distributed cotton seed and advice to cultivators. But normally the government's task was to provide lubrication for the motor—a monetary system, an apparatus of commercial law, and generally an environment in which men could initiate economic change. In the economic history of many countries such men emerge as leading characters, particularly in times of rapid growth—Arkwright, Carnegie, Ford—and entrepreneurial history is an important branch of the subject. In East Africa most entrepreneurs worked on a small scale, left no records, and are therefore forgotten; only a rare figure like Alidina Visram left his mark. But this anonymity, and later political judgements, should not lead us to underrate the significance of their contribution to economic growth. The value of enterprise and investment in agriculture or mining was self-evident; Williamson's diamonds, for example, were a great contribution to the Tanganyikan economy. By contrast, the trader's role is more obscure. Traders and middlemen were an important group, but their activities, as is common in peasant society, were frequently regarded as parasitic and essentially unproductive. Such criticism stemmed from a basic misunderstanding of the merchant's dynamic role. As a buyer of crops he created markets even in remote areas and injected cash into the economy. By assembling and transporting these small purchases for resale he then provided one of several essential steps on the road to world markets. As a retail trader he made goods available, again in remote areas and in the small quantities desired, which in turn created incentives for further production. If these activities sometimes gave him a power which could be abused, they also demanded skills and the taking of risks which deserved recompense. The fact that Indians tended to be dominant in trade was an additional reason for misunderstanding and mistrust. Towards the end of our period considerable official encouragement and assistance was given to African traders, most notably in Uganda. The expense and many setbacks of such schemes provided fresh evidence that trading was a difficult, skilful, and costly enterprise.

The emerging pattern of development is shown in our Table which illustrates the parallel growth of foreign trade and government revenue in each of the mainland territories. In Zanzibar the story was even simpler since cloves were far the most important source of income. It will be appreciated that a brief table of this kind can give only the barest outline of the quantitative picture. The following paragraphs will attempt to add some details, but students should supplement the figures by their own research. An investigation into the 1950's, when prices and incomes increased rapidly, would be particularly rewarding and comparatively simple as statistics are readily available.

Foreign Trade and Government Revenue 1911 to 1961

UGANDA

	Exports (£m)	Imports (£m)	Government Revenue (£m)	Main Export Commodities as % total exports	
				Cotton	Coffee
1911	0·3	0·5	0·2	55	1
1921	1·5	not available	0·8	85	6
1931	1·9	1·3	1·4	84	8
1951	47·4	22·1	15·8	62	29
1961	46·0	24·5	22·3	43	36

TANGANYIKA

	Exports (£m)	Imports (£m)	Government Revenue (£m)	Cotton	Coffee	Sisal
1911	1·1	2·3	0·7	6	6	20
1921	1·1	1·4	0·9	11	13	22
1931	1·6	2·5	1·5	7	15	43
1951	40·5	31·7	11·9	7	11	58
1961	48·6	39·7	21·9	14	14	29

KENYA

	Exports (£m)	Imports (£m)	Government Revenue (£m)	Maize	Coffee	Sisal	Tea
1911	0·3	1·1	0·7	8	1	0	0
1921	1·8	not available	1·3	7	21	10	0
1931	2·3	4·3	3·0	18	42	10	1
1951	24·1	50·6	23·4	3	17	29	6
1961	35·3	62·5	46·2	0	30	12	11

Imports consisted of capital equipment and consumer goods, such as textiles and shoes, which improved African standards of life. In this connection the advantages of free trade were significant, for poor consumers benefited greatly from the import, for example, of cheap Japanese manufactured goods. Apart from temporary wartime stoppages, the chief impediment to free trade was the protection afforded to Kenya producers of meat and dairy products, which probably had little effect on African living standards. Only in the final decade of colonial rule was there a determined effort to protect such infant industries as Uganda textiles, which harmed consumers, of course, whatever its ultimate benefits in terms of economic growth and diversification.

Exports were narrowly based upon a few agricultural products which were mostly established before World War I and remained dominant thereafter. Their quantity and value rose steadily through the boom of the 1920's, more slowly during depression in the 1930's, and leaped forward after World War II. Tanganyika, however, was particularly unfortunate in failing to share the prosperity of the 1920's, years when the upsets of defeat and the uncertainties of her status as a League of Nations mandate deterred investment and entrepreneurial activity. Thereafter her rate of growth was slower and the living standards of her people tended to be even lower than elsewhere in East Africa. Another notable difference between the countries lay in their balance of trade—the value of Kenya's imports was always considerably greater than that of her exports. This adverse balance of visible trade was financed in two ways. At various times throughout our period there were relatively large imports of public and private capital from overseas which both reflected and advanced the activities of European and Indian enterprise in Kenya. The second source of income not shown in our table were the invisible exports which arose largely from the position of Nairobi as East Africa's main industrial and commercial centre. The expansion of manufacturing and distribution was particularly rapid in Kenya during the 1950's so that by 1960 they accounted for over 20 per cent of the national income. In Uganda and Tanganyika the proportion was very much lower, and dependence upon world markets was therefore greater.

Education and the Colonial Legacy

For the first twenty years colonial governments did little to promote education, though a few schools were opened by the

Germans. Missionaries were, of course, far more active, but evangelism was their main purpose and the literacy which accompanied it was limited and fortuitous. As governments began slowly to accept responsibility the financial problem became acute, for Africans' thirst for education was far greater than could be quenched by local resources. A typical statement was the memorandum of the Kikuyu Central Association to the Hilton Young Commission which stated their willingness to pay 'cesses for . . . the education of the many and the higher education of the few'. But African incomes were not commensurate with such inspirations. In 1924 the Phelps-Stokes Commission argued that expenditure on education 'had been negligible in comparison with the great needs'. There was progress thereafter, particularly in Uganda, where the education bill increased from £8,000 in 1923 to £88,000 by 1933. Tanganyika was less fortunate. Expenditure rose rapidly after 1925 but the depression enforced severe retrenchment after 1932. By 1934 only 10 per cent of children of school age received a regular education, and most of these were offered an insubstantial vernacular course. Even by 1945 the modest proposals of a pre-war committee were rejected as 'far beyond the capacity of the territory'.

After World War II the Colonial Development and Welfare Acts ushered in a far more generous period of aid. Again it was Uganda that set the pace, government expenditure rising from £715,000 in 1950 to over £5,000,000 in 1960. But throughout East Africa the creation of an appropriate system of education proved difficult and elusive. In recent years there has been increasing awareness of the role that education can play in economic development. If costs and curriculum are well adjusted to society's resources and needs it can be regarded as investment in man, more profitable and therefore more worthy of sacrifice than many tangible forms of physical capital. Rarely was this truth grasped until the closing years of our period. Education was more often regarded as a matter of social rather than economic policy, even a luxury which might follow, rather than an essential which must precede and accompany development. When its economic effects were considered it was usually within narrow limits of training for those few jobs which Africans were thought capable of handling. The limitations of colonial education arose therefore from a lack of both finance and relevant ideas. As independence approached concepts of education became more generous but not necessarily more appropriate, except in terms of the immediate objective— training an élite for the Africanisation of the civil service. It is arguable that the British were poorly qualified to provide education suitable for a developing society. Their own system was élitist-fine in quality, deficient in quantity—and export models tended to be caricatures of the domestic product. This was most evident at the university level where costs, standards, and to some extent even curricula, were ill-adapted to East Africa's long term needs. It would be unreasonable and anachronistic to castigate them for this. Africans demanded 'the best' and to a remarkable degree this was given, as defined by the British. But the legacy for the independent nations of East Africa was not wholly beneficial.

What, in conclusion, can be said about growth and welfare during the colonial era? What was the colonial legacy? Except for a few isolated pockets of subsistence the region had joined the international economy and was enjoying some of its benefits. If progress appeared slight after sixty years, it could be remarked that the period was short by the standards of economic growth, and that it had been interrupted by two wars and a great depression. Clearly Uganda was best prepared for independence. Real income per head of the African population was higher, though there were serious regional inequalities. The economy was firmly based on African activity so little economic unscrambling was necessary. In Kenya, African incomes were lower but the economy was more diversified. Africanisation of commercial agriculture and the civil service had at last begun, but the former was impoverished by a half century of neglect, and recruitment to the latter was difficult and costly because of its size and sophistication. Tanganyika's economic inheritance was least enviable. After 1947 the groundnut scheme had done nothing, and an ambitious road programme little, to overcome a harsh geographical environment. By any standards of measurement she remained one of the poorest countries in tropical Africa.

But if the colonial experience had wrought only modest changes in terms of economic growth, it had stimulated wholly new conceptions of human welfare. This gulf between performance and aspiration was the principal and unenviable inheritance of East Africa's new leaders.

Further Reading

EHRLICH, C. *The Uganda Economy 1903-1945*, in V. Harlow and and E. M. Chilver (Eds.) *History of East Africa, Volume II* Oxford, Clarendon Press, 1965.

EHRLICH, C. *Some Social and Economic Implications of Paternalism in Uganda*, in The Journal of African History, 1963.

EHRLICH, C. *Some Aspects of Economic Policy in Tanganyika 1945-1960*, in The Journal of Modern African Studies, July 1964.

EHRLICH, C. *Some Antecedents of Development Planning in Tanganyika*, in The Journal of Development Studies, 1966.

ELKAN, W. *The Economic Development of Uganda*. Oxford University Press, 1961.

HENDERSON, W. O. *German East Africa, 1884-1918*, in Harlow and Chilver (Eds.) *op. cit.*

POWESLAND, P. C. *History of the Migration in Uganda*, in A. I. Richards (Ed.) *Economic Development and Tribal Change*. Cambridge, Heffer, 1954.

WRIGLEY, C. C. *Crops and Wealth in Uganda*, E.A.I.S.R., Kampala. 1959.

WRIGLEY, C. C. *Kenya: The Patterns of Economic Life, 1902-1945*, in Harlow and Chilver (Eds.) *op. cit.*

WRIGLEY, C. C. *The Gross Domestic Product of the Protectorate of Zanzibar 1957-1961*, E.A.C.S.O., 1963.

WRIGLEY, C. C. *The Gross Domestic Product of Uganda 1954-1959* E.A.C.S.O., 1961.

WRIGLEY, C. C. *Domestic Income and Product in Kenya*, Nairobi, 1959.

17

Independent East Africa

Ali A. Mazrui

As independence approached, the term 'East Africa' in the political sense shrank in meaning. It now normally referred to the area consisting of Uganda, Kenya, Tanganyika and Zanzibar. A different colonial background had, by the 1950's, effectively separated Rwanda and Burundi from the stream of the history of the rest of the region.

In this chapter, then, we shall use the term 'East Africa' in its narrow sense. Tanganyika attained independence on 9 December 1961, to be followed by Uganda on 9 October 1962. On 10 December 1963, Zanzibar too emerged into nationhood, to be followed by Kenya two days later.

A month after attaining independence, Zanzibar had a major revolution. The dynasty of Sultans on the island was overthrown, and a socialist era was inaugurated. In April of the same year Zanzibar united with Tanganyika to form the United Republic of Tanzania.

In broader terms, the story of East Africa as a whole since independence has been a complicated struggle for national unity within each country, for economic growth, for social justice, and for regional co-operation between the different countries.

In accounts of modern East Africa there is sometimes a tendency to leave the question of regional unity until the end, and in discussions of regional unity to underestimate the contribution of Uganda to East African integration. This chapter proposes to resist both tendencies.

We shall discuss the question of regional unity first and concentrate on the role of Uganda in that. Our concern here is not with the issue of who is disrupting East African unity but on how that unity came to be there in the first place, and the latter question involves a major historical dimension. The role of Uganda in giving East Africa a recognisable personality is crucial in this, and since we have to be selective in so short a chapter, it is pre-eminently to this issue that we shall first devote our attention.

Uganda's Role in Pan-Africanism

There are few countries whose geographical position has had as big an effect on their political history as has the position of Uganda on the history of eastern Africa as a whole. It has sometimes been argued that Uganda is among the least Pan-African of the countries of East and Central Africa. If Pan-Africanism is defined in terms of strict ideological commitment, this accusation is not entirely unfounded. In the movement since independence to form an East African federation, Uganda's enthusiasm for unification has not been striking. Julius Nyerere once offered to delay Tanganyika's independence if that would help achieve East African federation, and Mzee Kenyatta and his colleagues started negotiating in earnest about how best to achieve that goal. Uganda leaders were, however, suggesting that unless their country was assured her sovereignty, there was no question of her joining an East African federation. This was no different from saying that Uganda did not want to join an East African federation. We must therefore face up to the fact that Uganda has not been in the forefront of Pan-African militancy.

And yet perhaps it is true that some are born Pan-African, some become Pan-African, and others have Pan-Africanism thrust upon them. It is not entirely clear into which category Uganda would fall. What is clear is that by a series of geographical and historical accidents, and by some acts of deliberate policy, Uganda has indeed made a decisive contribution to greater unity along the eastern seaboard of the African continent. Discussing this would be meaningless without reference to East Africa before independence. In an analysis of this kind, there is an iron law of historical continuity which cannot be avoided.

Uganda's contribution to East African integration took a variety of forms. First, it was Uganda's strategic position more than anything else which ensured that East Africa as a whole was ruled by Great Britain and not by another colonial power or combination of powers. As I hope to demonstrate, the fact that Uganda, Kenya and Tanzania were jointly ruled by Britain was itself an important contribution to East African unity. A related element in Uganda's enforced Pan-Africanism is that she is situated at the head of the Nile waters. A third factor is that Uganda, being land-locked, might be increasingly forced to explore new forms of access to her neighbours. A fourth factor in Uganda's Pan-African role is her situation in a sensitive area of Afro-Arab relations, a matter of concern for the continent as a whole. The fifth factor in Uganda's contribution to greater integration in this region hinges on the role of Makerere. This institution of higher learning was closely associated with the emergence of a regional intellectual élite in East Africa which shared a language of political discourse and which is helping to shape the destiny of the three countries of East Africa.

Let us now take a closer look at these factors. In what way did Uganda's strategic attractiveness for Britain later help the cause of East African unity? It would be impossible to grasp the full implications of this first point unless we stopped being naïve about the effects of European imperialism in Africa at large. We often think of imperialism as being an exercise in a policy of 'Divide and Rule'. This view is not entirely false, but it is only one side of the imperial coin. The truth is that if the imperialists divided (as a policy) in order to rule, they also united (in effect) in the very act of ruling. Their intention might very often have been to divide people against people, but administrative convenience frequently resulted in uniting territory with territory. The very momentum and logic of imperial expansion meant adding this piece to that piece of land. But the pieces of land were not empty—they had people on them. And so by putting two pieces of land together they sometimes brought two tribes together in the process.

The natural tendency of imperialism is to prevent the unification of its subjects; and yet an equally natural tendency of imperialism is to prevent an excessive fragmentation of its territory. During the colonial period, the Belgian Government, for example, did not want to see the Congolese united. Yet they did not split up the Congo into a number of small colonies because they wanted the landmass of the Congo to remain one territorial unit. And so it was not until immediately after independence that the Belgians were prepared to encourage Katanga, under Tshombe, to secede from the rest of the Congo. In fact Belgian attempts at Balkanisation came at the time of Belgian withdrawal rather than before. In other words, Balkanisation is an imperialist device, characteristic more of imperial retreat than of imperial expansion.

This view finds further evidence in French Africa. For as long as France was in effective colonial control, her preference was for large administrative areas. But as soon as nationalistic trouble was on the horizon, the French decided on greater administrative decentralisation. Two huge federations of French West Africa and French Equatorial Africa ultimately were split up into nearly a dozen little sovereign states. Again a policy of Balkanisation, or territorial 'Divide and Rule', was more evident in the era of decolonisation than in the days of militant annexation.

And yet, of all the colonial powers, Britain has been the most reluctant to Balkanise her former colonies in the process of withdrawal. British territorial units of administration in Africa were hardly ever as big in size as the old Belgian Congo or the two federations of French West Africa and French Equatorial Africa. Britain did not similarly indulge in blatant Balkanising tricks when she was retreating from Africa either, on the contrary, British policy at the time of imperial withdrawal endeavoured to prevent territorial fragmentation. Both in Nigeria and in East Africa, British diplomacy in the course of imperial disengagement aimed at keeping things together. In East Africa, Britain was so keen on federation that her enthusiasm had to be restrained—lest she should embarrass Pan-African federalists like Nyerere. The East African leaders were so conscious of British keenness to see an East African federation that they even took advantage of it in order to get early independence for Kenya. The East African leaders asked Britain to give Kenya independence before the end of 1963—so that Kenya could join a Federation. And Britain responded positively. This old hand at the game of 'Divide and Rule' was now converted to a policy of 'Withdraw and Unite'.

The moral of all this is that imperialism is not a purely divisive force. On the contrary, where East Africa is concerned, the most unifying single factor has been that the three countries were all ruled by the same imperial power. If Uganda had been ruled by France, Kenya by Britain, and Tanganyika by yet another imperial power, the cause of East African unity would have been twice as difficult. Ugandans would have felt as distant from Kenyans as they do today from Congolese. It was of great relevance for East African integration, not only that all three countries came to fall under the same colonial power, but also that the colonial power happened to be Britain rather than either France or Belgium, which had both also had designs on this region of Africa in the course of the great imperial scramble. Britain even brought forward the independence of British Somaliland to enable it to unite with Italian Somaliland to form the sovereign state of Somalia. All this does not necessarily mean that British rule in East Africa was a good thing. But it does mean that East Africa might easily have had a more divisive colonial power than she actually had.

But in what way was Uganda decisive in ensuring that East Africa was ruled by Britain? Precisely by virtue of her strategic attractiveness. It is not often remembered that the British Government was for a while reluctant to take over Uganda, in spite of pressures from missionaries in Uganda asking for the establishment of a protectorate. Nor was Britain convinced by the arguments of the Imperial British East Africa Company regarding the commercial and economic potential of the region. What sealed the fate of Uganda was the Nile Valley doctrine of the British Foreign Office that whoever controlled the source of the Nile could easily control Egypt as well. A special British Commissioner, who was sent to Uganda to assess the advantages of British intrusion, argued in his Report to the British Government that Uganda was 'the natural key to the whole of the Nile Valley' and had to be 'protected' by Britain or fall into the hands of other powers. The doctrine of the Unity of the Nile became a crucial consideration in the European scramble for Africa. As two distinguished British historians have recently put it, 'almost everything in Africa north of the Zambesi River was to hinge on it'.

When Britain finally decided to establish a protectorate in Uganda, the fate of the rest of East Africa was also ultimately sealed. The road to Uganda from the East African coast was through what later came to be known as Kenya; and so the idea of building a railway to the Lakes became an important factor in Britain's Uganda policy. The very legislation authorising the building of the railway was called the Uganda Railway Bill. The British Government, without an adequate survey, incurred the great expense of building this railway link to the source of the Nile. Why? The answer which came from the British Foreign Minister at the time was this: 'We did so with a perfect consciousness of what we were doing, and for the sake of speed . . . There were considerations of a very cogent character which induced us to desire to finish, at the earliest period possible, what was practically our only access to those regions.'

Having built a railway line, Britain wanted to make it pay; that was the beginning of the policy of encouraging white settlers to come and settle in Kenya. In other words, British interest in Kenya came only as a result of British interest in Uganda. And the fate of both Kenya and Uganda then became intertwined.

Tanganyika had to wait until the end of the First World War before it could be taken out of German hands. But why was it then handed over as a mandate to the British by the League of Nations? In the final analysis, the reason was because Britain was already occupying the contiguous areas of Kenya and Uganda. And so the fate of Uganda, in the long run, affected the fate of Tanganyika too. That all three countries were ruled by the same imperial power helped their sense of community. Otherwise Nyerere today might have been a German-speaking African, or a French-speaking African with a Belgian background. Moreover, there would have been no East African Common Market or Common Services Organisation but for the accident of the British hegemony in East Africa.

Since then, Uganda's place at the head of the Nile waters has had other Pan-African implications. Two of the most important dams in Africa are affected—the Owen Falls Dam at Jinja and the Aswan Dam in Egypt. These waters could easily give rise to serious disputes between the countries which share the River Nile. But it is also possible for the old doctrine of the Unity of the Nile now to serve the new ideal of the Unity of Africa. Certainly the great potential of hydro-electric power in Uganda is already making a contribution to the electrification of neighbouring countries. An even greater contribution of this kind might be possible in the future.

Uganda's land-locked position makes her excessively dependent on Kenya. This is not by itself a bad thing, but every country must try to have more than one good access to the outside world. And just as Zambia is now seeking a new rail link, as well as a possible road connection with Tanzania, so might Uganda have to explore new forms of communication with her neighbours. Her very situation as a landlocked country has a Pan-African dimension. It emphasises for her the need for better and better communications and greater commercial intercourse with her neighbours.

Then there is Uganda's position on the border with the Sudan. It has often been pointed out that one of the worst clashes which could happen in Africa is a deep cleavage between Arab Africa and black Africa. Such a cleavage would not only destroy the Organisation of African Unity but could shake the continent in more profound ways. It happens that the most fragile point of Afro-Arab relations is precisely on the border between Uganda and the Sudan. There are ethnic ties between southern Sudanese and the Ugandans on the border; and with significant numbers of refugees from southern Sudan in Uganda, sympathies could easily lead some Ugandans into supporting the cause of the rebellion in southern Sudan. If this were to lead to an open military clash between Uganda and the Sudan, or even strong tension centering on the racial issue, the whole fabric of trans-Saharan cordiality in the African continent might be in serious danger. But the Ugandan Government has so far resisted all temptations which might endanger Pan-African cordiality at this vital level, taking the position that to condemn secessionism in Katanga and to support it in southern Sudan would be racialistic. In the words of Minister Sam Odaka, 'We cannot denounce racialism in southern Africa and support it when it comes to southern Sudan.' In the very discipline that Uganda has exercised on this issue, she has critically safeguarded the viability of the Organisation of African Unity.

Finally, there is Makerere's contribution to East Africa's integration. Until the eve of independence Makerere was, in effect if not in name, the 'University of East Africa'. It was the top institution of higher learning in the region, and helped to produce a regional intellectual élite. As independence approached, many potential leaders in each of the three East African countries passed through Makerere. These included two who were to be heads of government—Milton Obote and Julius Nyerere—and a significant proportion of the cabinets of the three governments on attainment of independence. Leadership in the struggle for independence was a crucial factor. So, too, among the new African civil servants who were taking up key administrative positions throughout East Africa, the Makerere contribution was often critical and decisive. Among the forces which have helped to give East Africa a sense of political and intellectual integration must surely be included the role of Makerere in producing a regional intellectual élite at a vital moment in the history of the three countries.

All these factors add up to give Uganda a Pan-African status in the history of this part of the continent. Very often Uganda has been Pan-African in spite of herself—a definite case of greatness being thrust upon her. What remains to be seen is whether Uganda can now assume her unifying destiny with greater intent and deliberation.

Internal Unity and Equality

But regional unification, though a major part of the politics of East Africa for many years, is far from being the only theme of significance. The story of independent East Africa has also included the struggle for internal unity, economic development and social justice.

On internal unity, the basic issue has been to find a suitable compromise between love for one's tribe and loyalty to one's nation. These two emotions are sometimes opposed to each other, but need not be; just as one need not stop loving his family in order to love his country, one need not renounce his tribe in order to be patriotic. But the problem in East Africa—as in much of the rest of the continent—has been one of trying to find a suitable balance.

The question of what kind of party-system a country should have is linked to this issue of potentially conflicting loyalties. A two-party system has been suspect in Tanzania, because it was regarded as symbolic of class antagonism, and in Kenya, because it could become a symptom of tribal antagonism. In Tanganyika, Nyerere argued that the Anglo-American systems of government were based on a division between the Haves and the Have-nots, and the party structure reflected that division; Tanganyika should therefore have only one national movement—the Tanganyika African National Union (TANU). But what kind of choice would the people have at election time if there were only one party? On the recommendation of a special Presidential Commission which took evidence from the people on what system of government was best suited to the country, Tanzania in 1965 launched the great experiment of competitive elections within the single party. Members of TANU contested the same seats against each other—and several Ministers lost their seats. It was a great innovation in combining the principle of government by consent with a one-party structure.

Kenya's experiment was different. It rested first on a refusal to outlaw opposition parties. Kenya preferred a one-party structure, but not by legal decree. The first opposition party which Kenya had after independence was the Kenya African Democratic Union (KADU). But the division between this party and the preponderant Kenya African National Union (KANU) was complicated by tribal suspicions. Mr Ronald Ngala, the leader of the smaller party, later decided to dissolve his own party and join forces with KANU. The country then had a *de facto* one-party state until Mr Oginga Odinga and his colleagues withdrew from KANU in 1965 to form a new radical party, the Kenya People's Union (KPU). The party situation in Kenya continued to be flexible. For the time being the nation had decided to leave itself room for different experiments in party-systems without passing special laws which would interfere too much with the inter-play of natural political forces.

The party situation in Uganda has also been flexible. On attainment of independence Uganda was ruled by a pragmatic alliance between Buganda's *Kabaka Yekka* and Dr Obote's Uganda People's Congress. In opposition was the Democratic Party. But the ruling alliance lasted only until Dr Obote felt strong enough to do without his *Kabaka Yekka* partners. During the rest of 1964 Uganda seemed to be on the way towards becoming a one-party state. Crossing the floor in parliament to join the UPC became so common that it appeared to be only a matter of time before the opposition parties liquidated themselves. The climax was the crossing of the Leader of the Opposition, Mr Basil Bataringaya, in December 1964 with several other members of the Democratic Party.

Yet in the course of 1965 new divisions were beginning to appear in Uganda, some of these within the UPC itself. A new confrontation also developed between Buganda and the Central Government. But by the end of May 1966 the Central Government under Dr Obote had prevailed. Sir Edward Mutesa, former Kabaka of Buganda and former President of the country, had left for England. Yet the main task had yet to be completed— that of devising a new political arrangement in Uganda which would assure national unity, including Buganda participation. For this great task the basis was to be the new constitution which Dr Obote introduced in April 1966. In the meantime the country continued to have more than one party, the UPC and the DP, and pragmatic flexibility continued to be the essential policy of Dr Obote's government.

But in addition to these problems of regional and national unity, each East African country was engaged in a struggle to devise the best means of economic development and the best methods of assuring social justice. These too were, of course, connected with national goals within each country and we cannot understand these without looking at national values. If one were to choose the three most important values which are influencing policy and political behaviour in independent East Africa, one would probably list those of equality, development and unity as basic. And of these three, perhaps the oldest in the history of African political movements is the value of *equality*. Today the problem of equality in East Africa is connected with policies of trying to Africanise the economies, as well as with attempts to control the development of great inequalities of income between citizens. But before independence, the idea of equality was at the root of the growth of nationalism itself.

In previous chapters, attention has already been drawn to the history of African resistance to colonial rule. In this chapter, we hope to show how the idea of equality during the colonial period gradually determined the kind of national values which East Africa was to have after independence. National values in East Africa are still fluid and changeable, but the theme of equality is definitely there. We might begin by looking at its origins, and then trace the development of racial integration in East Africa. Of the countries of East Africa, the one which experienced racial segregation at its most elaborate was Kenya. Many of the illustrations of the early history of the idea of equality in East Africa may therefore best be drawn from Kenya's experience. But much of this experience was shared to some degree by other parts of East Africa, and indeed in much of the rest of the continent.

Equality and Segregation

Ideas of equality in Africa had indigenous origins as well as external sources. The latter included the impact of Christianity and the principle of human neighbourliness as also that of Islam which sometimes demonstrated greater racial toleration than was achieved by most Christian Churches in Africa. Internally, there was the historical background of the African who, partly because of relative isolation from other races in the past, and partly because of certain values of fellowship and hospitality within the tribal ways, had not accumulated as many racial prejudices as the paradoxically more 'cosmopolitan' white man. Latest among the channels through which the ideas of equality have entered Africa is that of European Socialism—of the Marxist, the Labour Party and other shades of colour.

Africa has not, of course, been the only area of the world which has witnessed a denial of the principles of equality on grounds of racial differences. The United States in particular has had a continuing racial and constitutional crisis on the issue of civil rights for Negroes. Yet segregation in Africa has sometimes had more complex and varied consequences than even in the United States. In education, for example, the segregation of colonial East Africa was not simply between white schools and non-white schools. Among government schools or government-aided schools in the region as a whole, there were those which were exclusively for Europeans, those for Indians, those solely for Arabs and those for Africans. In addition there were private schools for groups within groups. Among these were Goan schools (for that section of the Asian population which came from former Portuguese Goa), and Aga Khan schools (for those of the Indian Muslim community who were followers of the Aga Khan). Christian Mission schools were also segregated. Mr Tom Mboya, himself a product of a Catholic African school in Kenya, has been known to complain that missionaries had condoned the colonial order in Africa 'to the point of complying with such things as segregated schools and segregated churches'.

As pressures in East Africa mounted for school integration,

the usual argument advanced against it was that integration was bound to 'level down educational standards'. The European schools were the best in the country. If they were to be 'immediately flooded' with children from poorly educated or completely illiterate non-white families, 'the result would not be to bring up the Africans to the level of Europeans, but to bring down European standards of education to the level of the poorest and crudest schools of the nation'. This, it was contended, was a wasteful way of achieving equality. It was like the philosophy sometimes attributed to socialism by its critics— that 'if everybody cannot become rich then everybody must become poor'. Such a philosophy of bringing down the educational standards of East Africa's white population was, so the argument went, short-sighted and misguided for a region which needed highly skilled local people even if they should happen to have a white skin.

Comparing this with American experience, one detects a different kind of reasoning from that which was used in the United States to support segregated schools before the great Supreme Court decision in 1954. Until that year, the American Constitution had been interpreted to mean that people could be segregated and still be equal. Negroes could have separate schools from whites, provided the Negro schools were comparable in quality and facilities with schools for white children. This whole principle came to be known as the 'Separate but Equal' condition of segregation under the American Constitution.

Segregationist argument in old Kenya, for example, rested on a fundamentally different premise—that the standards of the segregated schools were *not* equal, with the admission that the European schools were superior, and that this superiority was on no account to be sacrificed at the altar of the Goddess of Abstract Equality if Kenya was to make the most of her resources of personnel, regardless of race.

In 1954, while Kenya was in the agony of the *Mau Mau* insurrection, the United States was changing its mind about the principle of 'Separate but Equal'. The American Supreme Court decided that the very insistence on segregation implied inequality between races. In any case the segregation in schools had resulted in standards which were *not* equal. With that Supreme Court decision, the American Civil Rights revolution of the mid-twentieth century was launched.

Five years later it was East Africa's turn to start a reappraisal of its own segregationist tradition. Against the thesis that the standards of the region's best schools should not be sacrificed 'for the sake of an abstraction', it was now contended that a temporary lowering of standards of European schools in East Africa was not too high a price to pay for getting the next generation of East Africans to grow up together into less racially-conscious citizens. It was not too high a price to pay for a new East Africa in which no child eager for the best education that the country had to offer would be driven to wish that it had a racially different set of parents.

The segregationists in East Africa have failed. Even the region's best European schools have now embarked on some degree of integration. That in some cases the integration was for a while little more than a 'token', in spite of African independence, is a measure of African patience when a principle has already been accepted. That the Africans have wanted integration at all shows how grossly exaggerated was the assertion sometimes made that African independence would just 'reverse the colour bar'. This assertion might apply to the question of who is permitted to wield political power. Africans might insist on ruling the country to the exclusion of other races. The claim might also be proved correct in certain areas of economic activity—that instead of Europeans and Asians being the economically privileged or dominant section of Kenya's population, discrimination might now be applied to give the Africans a chance to shift the balance of economic power.

Yet the phrase 'Africa's reversal of the colour bar' is still a distortion. It implies a continuation of *social* segregation, as well as a shift in political and economic advantage. One just cannot see the African insisting, as the colonial white man did before him, on segregated schools for Africans, segregated hotels and dancing halls, or segregated restaurants and residential areas. To put it crudely, one cannot imagine the African insisting on a mere exchange of public lavatories. For the African to concede racial segregation at the social level would be to defeat the whole object of African self-assertion. The African government in Kenya—unlike its colonial predecessor—therefore makes a virtue of racial mixture rather than of racial separation. And who knows what greater racial toleration might in time emerge out of this greater social intermingling?

By 1960 the shape of the new East Africa, even in the heart of settler-Kenya, was beginning to be discernible. Racially exclusive hotels were disappearing. Scholarships for study abroad were no longer in racial quotas. The doctors were planning to merge European, Asian and African medical associations which had so far been separate. Into the higher ranks of the civil service there was soon to be a determined policy to introduce as many Africans as possible. Scales of salaries according to race—regardless of similarity of work or identity of qualifications—had already been abandoned. The White Highlands in Kenya, for decades reserved exclusively for white settlers and prospective white immigrants, were soon to be legally no longer 'white'. The Kenya Regiment Training Centre was about to accept its first non-European recruits. The new electroral roll in Kenya, following the first Lancaster House conference of 1960 had not only been substantially integrated, but had also allowed for an elected African majority in the legislature. Even the lavatories were beginning to lose the familiar signs of 'European' and 'Non-European'. And where the signs were still hanging, they could now be ignored with impunity. It was symbolic that even such small details of personal intimacy were beginning to conform with the integrationist principles of the new East Africa.

Self-help and Ideological Toil

But, after independence, new problems of inequalities have presented themselves. It is one thing to narrow the gulf between Africans on one side and Europeans and Asians on the other. But what about the danger of creating new gulfs between Africans themselves? Is there not a possibility of some Africans getting richer too rapidly after independence while others remain poor? Is there not a danger of creating class distinctions between Africans themselves?

One safeguard against this danger is a national ethos which puts a premium on frugality and hard work. Within East Africa the best exponent of such a policy has so far been Tanzania. It is a policy which seems to have deep roots in the ideologies of Tanzania's leaders and has had a consistent history since the country approached independence.

In *Ujamaa: The Basis of African Socialism,* Nyerere claims that in traditional Africa everyone was a worker—a 'worker' not merely as distinct from employer but also as distinct from 'loiterer' or 'idler'. It is not certain that this is a justified interpretation of life in traditional Africa. What is certain is that Tanzania has tried from the outset to utilise the concept of *Work* as a slogan for national mobilisation.

There was first the neat motto of '*Uhuru na Kazi*' or 'Freedom and Work', and then, on independence, came the programme of self-help. Apparently self-help was first considered during discussions on the Three Year Plan envisaged for 1961 to 1964. Some of the external aid expected had not materialised and it appeared more important than ever that a scheme of self-help should be devised. When the Regional Commissioners took office in March 1962, Mr Rashidi Kawawa, then Prime Minister, explained to them the government's desire to get the people to participate in projects which they could undertake without government finance, such as roads and houses. How useful self-help schemes have been economically is not clear, but the idea had other functions apart from economic ones. As Dr Joseph Nye, Jr., once put it in an article in *Transition*:

'Self-help also allowed the Tanganyika Government to release the energies of those who had participated in the struggle for independence, and later to increase the number involved in the political process . . . While no figures are available it is a generally accepted impression that a greater part of the population has been involved in self-help, and it might be called their first contact with "the Tanganyika Nation".'

A later manifestation of the ideology of hard work in Tanzania was in regard to farms. If again we go back to Nyerere's formulation of his socialism in *Ujamaa* we see the following argument:

'Those of us who talk about the African way of life and, quite rightly, take pride in maintaining the tradition of hospitality which is so great a part of it, might do well to remember the Swahili saying: "*Mgeni siku mbili; siku ya tatu mpe jembe*" or, in English, "Treat your guest as a guest for two days; on the third day give him a hoe".'

For not developing their Arusha farms fully, some Europeans there were later to have their farms taken away from them. They were '*wageni siku ya tatu*'—and they had failed to accept the challenge of the *jembe* or hoe. Indeed, the challenge of 'toil' as an ideological concept confronted the native as well as the foreigner. And the concept of toil has now become part of the ambition of maximum utilisation of the nation's resources. On 15 February 1965, the Government of Tanzania once again reiterated the following policy:

'Because of the significant part which the agricultural economy had played in the past, and because of the increased role which it is to continue to play, the government attached great importance to land and its use. It was the greatest single asset at the disposal of the country, and the Government was therefore determined to see that those who had been given land, both indigenous and non-indigenous people, should develop it fully and properly, in the interest of the nation.'

In some ways, this preoccupation with hard and rational work is one of the more attractive aspects of the national ethic of Tanzania. In the struggle for independence the compelling slogan was 'Uhuru'—but Nyerere soon turned it into 'Uhuru na Kazi'. Now the call is for 'socialism'—and the new motto has perhaps become 'Socialism and Sweat'.

Then, in October 1966, came the new National Service in Tanzania, requiring university graduates and products of other major educational institutions to join the National Service for two years and participate in nation-building activities. Here again was an instance of 'ideological toil'—the use of the idea of 'work' as a basis of national commitment and self-reliance.

The culmination of this ethic was the Arusha Declaration of February 1967 which required frugality and self-denial from everyone connected with Government. Every person in authority had to be a worker or peasant in essential status. If he owned an extra house and rented it to a tenant, he had become a landlord and was in danger of losing his status as essentially a worker. But this policy of self-denial by all those in authority, at both national and local levels of government, was phased out a little. Total renunciation of such wordly goods by those in authority could be done gradually over a relatively short span of time. But, at any rate, the idea of self-denial had now become a necessary qualification for holding public office.

Also arising out of the Arusha Declaration was the decision of the Government of Tanzania to nationalise the Banks and then other industries in the country. It was both an assertion of central control of the economy and an attempt once again to narrow the possibility of class privilege in the country.

Nationalisation and Socialism

Take-overs of banks and other industries in Tanzania, when juxtaposed with renewed declarations of economic policy in both Kenya and Uganda, present interesting differences in conceptions.

Two senses of *nationalisation* are becoming effectively operative in East Africa. In one sense—that of Tanzania—'nationalisation' has the usual Western meaning. It means putting economic resources under the control of the state.

But there is another sense of 'nationalisation'—and that is putting economic resources under the control of *nationals*. In the latter sense, the resources might indeed be transferred from foreign hands to the hands of nationals—but not necessarily to the hands of the State. President Kenyatta's major speech at the state opening of Kenya's Parliament on 15 February, 1967 was a reaffirmation of the latter sense of nationalisation—an increasing participation in the economy by nationals of the country.

Linked to the above distinction are also two senses of *public ownership*. One sense of 'public ownership'—that of Tanzania—is the usual Western one. An industry comes under state ownership.

But there is another sense of 'public ownership'—that of trying to make sure that the shares of an industry are owned widely by ordinary members of the public themselves and not by the state. The House of Manji in Kenya, hitherto a family business, converted itself on 16 February, 1967 into a public company and was going to issue 45 per cent of its shares to the public. But how could it be ensured that this 45 per cent was not simply bought by another rich man? Mr Mwai Kibaki, Kenya's Minister for Commerce and Industry, announced at the time that the issue of shares to the public would be handled by his Ministry to ensure that they were available to as wide a section as possible all over Kenya. Prospective buyers would be able to obtain application forms from district officers anywhere in the country.

Mr Kibaki emphasised that the purpose of the Ministry's help in the distribution was to ensure that the shares were available to all Kenyans, not just to people in Nairobi and substantial investors outside. The shares were expected to sell at a par value of twenty shillings and the issue was expected to begin on 1 June. There was also to be some free issue of shares, 60 per cent of which would go to African women who had been employees of the House of Manji.

The Kenya sense of public ownership was, in some ways,

the more novel of the two we have discussed. In order to grasp this point fully, we have to relate it once again to the kind of equality which African nationalism has cherished so far. In their struggle against European rule, Africans did indeed aspire to bring about a world in which no African individual counted for less than an individual from another race. And while they were struggling for that world, African nationalists before independence tried to make sure that neither did an individual African count for more than another African. But independence has now posed these new dilemmas. The ideal of maintaining equality between Africans themselves in a particular country has sometimes come into conflict with the ideal of creating equality between Africans and other races. The former ideal of equality between Africans themselves should presumably dictate a policy aimed against the emergence of an African commercial class. But, in East African conditions, such a policy could mean leaving the profits of the private sector of the economy exclusively to non-indigenous entrepreneurs. Africans in Kenya might then remain equal in poverty between themselves —while the inequalities of income between them on one side and the Asians and Europeans on the other were allowed to persist.

The Governments of Kenya and Uganda seem to have rejected, for the time being, this solution. In April 1965, for example, Kenya's Minister for Commerce and Industry at the time urged the non-African businessmen to identify themselves with African aspirations by inviting Africans to buy shares in their enterprises. Minister Kiano said: 'While we do not discriminate against non-Africans in Kenya, the spirit of give and take should prevail.' Mr Tom Mboya has also repeated the same theme as a reminder to those concerned. Similar attempts to increase African participation in commerce have been made in Uganda.

The Kenya Government Sessional Paper on African Socialism also included a bias towards such a policy. It appeared that what was being urged by the Kenya Government was not so much African socialism as the Africanisation of capitalism. And yet for many Kenyans—as indeed for many Africans elsewhere— African socialism should include the Africanisation of the rudimentary capitalism which has already emerged. There is certainly a great keenness in Kenya and Uganda that there should be greater African participation in commerce. But is this 'equality'? Kenya's Minister for Commerce and Industry has described it as a process of narrowing 'the wide gap between Africans and non-Africans in commerce and trade'. Uganda's President, Dr Milton Obote, has made similar appeals to non-African businessmen—that they should try and get more and more African shareholders. But, while the gap between black East Africans and non-indigenous East Africans is being narrowed, new gaps between black East Africans themselves again might be created.

The Marxist purists might argue that this is not socialism. But the significant thing about socialistic thought in a place like Kenya is not its relationship to Marxism, not even what it expounds in a document; it is what it seems to take for granted. In an ethnically pluralistic society, the first task of socialism, according to this school, is not to abolish class distinctions altogether but to prevent class distinctions from coinciding with racial differences. The problems of class distinctions can be reduced by 'social mobility'. This is the ability of a person to move from one class to another. The very creation of an African business class would be proof that social mobility can be engineered or manipulated by government policy. But while it is possible for an individual to change his class, it is not very easy for any one generation to change its race. 'Racial mobility', or the ability to transfer oneself to another race, is not entirely impossible but it usually involves generations of mixed marriages. The Zanzibar society, for example, has allowed for some degree of racial transfers.

But racial differences, nevertheless, are more rigid than class differences. And if that is so, the first pre-condition of social harmony in a plural society is to make sure that the middle and upper classes are racially mixed. The most important internal revolutions which have taken place in Africa south of the Sahara in the last few years have been the overthrow of the Tutsi in Rwanda and indeed the overthrow of the Sultan's régime in Zanzibar. In neither case was the revolution initially directed against the idea of class distinctions as such. Both Rwanda and Zanzibar had revolutions primarily because their middle and upper classes had not been racially mixed to a sufficient degree, in spite of mixed marriages. It was still possible to think of the Tutsi as the rulers of Rwanda and the Arabs as the élite of Zanzibar.

But would it have been more socialistic to have thwarted those revolutions? Perhaps not. But both in Rwanda and in Zanzibar ethnic minorities held political power out of proportion to their numbers. In Kenya and Uganda, however, political control has already passed to Africans, and with that control the responsibility to prevent, among other things, the victimisation of non-African minorities. Why not take over the Asian shops? Partly because opportunities for Asians in other sectors of national life had already been narrowing; the Africanisation of the Civil Service especially had inevitably been at the cost of the immigrant races. To prevent the Asians also from engaging in commerce might reduce them to a painful redundancy in the life of the country of their adoption.

Why not put Asian businesses under state ownership and still use Asians as Government employees in those enterprises? Partly because once a business becomes a Government enterprise, recruitment for it might become subject to all the usual pressures of political patronage. An Asian competing for a job in a Government enterprise might well be at a greater handicap than if he had been allowed to compete with Africans in private enterprise. There is therefore a sense of 'social justice' in plural African societies which could be best served by attempting to Africanise capitalism through the competitive methods of capitalism itself. Since the Government is engineering the whole competition, this is not pure capitalism. Yet it is not state capitalism either. It is the paradox of state-induced free competition between races. The fact that the new African entrepreneur gets special government encouragement does not negate the fairness of the competition; the immigrant communities have had a head start in business enterprise; only special Government assistance to Africans could counterbalance that start and help to equalise business opportunities between the races. So far the discrimination which Kenya has practised has therefore been, on the whole, discrimination *in favour* of citizens rather than against Asians as such. The so-called "Asian exodus" of early 1968 was basically an exodus of non-Kenyans.

But will the Governments of East and Central Africa limit themselves to this? Kenya's Tom Mboya has asserted that any move to buy up all Asian shops and install Africans 'would hardly be a progressive action.' The ambition for the time being in Uganda and Kenya remains that of creating a racially mixed business class—rather than keeping out the Asians from the class altogether in the days ahead. Given that the ultimate equality which matters to African nationalists is equality between races rather than between classes, the mixing of the middle class can, to many Africans, be defended in intelligible socialistic terms. But there are temptations in the situation which might make African governments more overtly racialistic against immigrant races in the future. When that happens, Africans in these parts would be betraying even their own brand of socialistic equality.

For the time being there is no doubt that both Kenya and Uganda in one way and Tanzania in another way are seeking the elusive ideal of social justice. We cannot as yet be sure which is the more effective way. Tanzania seeks to eliminate economic classes, but there is a risk that she might eliminate economic creativity at the same time. Tanzania has so far tried to create a system which enables every individual to be politically involved. But what about the economic involvement of each individual in the life of the nation? If the state runs everything, can an individual achieve his economic best?

Uganda and Kenya, on the other hand, would like to increase African participation in commerce and thus give to the African individual a chance to become an effective economic agent in his own right. But this too has its risks, opportunities for individual achievement in the economy entail the danger of some inequalities growing in the days ahead.

But East Africa will not innovate unless it is prepared to take some calculated risks. Perhaps it is good for the region as a whole that there are several bold experiments taking place at the same time. The different party systems within each country, the different solutions to tribal problems, the varying relationships between the civil service and the government, and the divergent routes towards equality and social justice, all go to give East Africa a certain richness and inventiveness. In some ways the three countries are drifting apart; in other ways they stand to gain by the lessons of those experiments which are going on independently in each country. Perhaps the cause of East African regional integration is not dying after all; it is merely undergoing the pangs and agonies of profound transformation.

Further reading

TORDOFF, W. *Government and Politics in Tanzania,* Nairobi: East African Publishing House, Nairobi, 1967.

NYE, J. S. JR. *Pan-Africanism and East African Integration,* London and Nairobi: Oxford University Press, London and Nairobi, 1966.

ROTHCHILD, D. and ROGIN, M. Uganda in *National Unity and Regionalism in Eight African States,* (Ed.) G. M. Carter, Cornell University Press, Ithaca, N.Y., 1966, (pp. 337-440).

ROSBERG, C. G. JR. and NOTTINGHAM, J. *The Myth of Mau Mau : Nationalism in Kenya,* East African Publishing House, Nairobi, 1967.

ENGHOLM, G. F. and MAZRUI, A. A. Violent Constitutionalism in Uganda, *Government and Opposition,* Vol. 2, No. 4, London, 1967.

APTER, D. E. *The Political Kingdom in Uganda,* Princeton University Press, Princeton, 1961.

CLIFFE, L. (Ed.) *One Party Democracy,* East African Publishing House, Nairobi, 1967.

ENGHOLM, G. F. and MAZRUI, A. A. Crossing the Floor and the Tensions of Representation in East Africa, Parts I & II, *Parliamentary Affairs,* 1968.

MAZRUI, A. A. *On Heroes and Uhuru-Worship,* (Chapters 2, 5 and 6), Longmans, London, 1967.

ROTHCHILD, D. (Ed.) *Politics of Integration : An East African Documentary,* East African Publishing House, Nairobi, 1968.

18

Contemporary Economic and Social Developments

D. P. Ghai

The attainment of independence has brought about a major shift in the objectives and priorities of the East African countries. Whereas prior to independence, the main focus of nationalist activity was the liberation of the country from colonial rule, the post-independence era has been marked by intense efforts to consolidate national unity and to initiate rapid and balanced social and economic development. The present chapter will identify some of the important social and economic problems facing the East African countries and describe the efforts currently being made to surmount them.

Before addressing ourselves to these problems, it is important to emphasise that in the relatively short period since independence, remarkable progress has been made in all three countries in almost every area of social and economic activity. Apart from the removal of many forms of discrimination prevalent in the colonial era, the imminence or attainment of independence has unleashed vital national energies for rapid social and economic advance. This is evident from a comparison of the conditions in the early sixties with those in later years. The years 1960 to 1962 were throughout East Africa a period of uncertainty, of slackening economic activity, of falling employment and investment, and of stagnant national income, exports and public revenue. In contrast, the years 1963 to 1966 have seen a strong economic recovery, high and rising levels of national income, investment, exports, public revenue and expenditure. All this prosperity is not of course due to independence alone but there can be little doubt that the policies of the East African Governments have made a powerful contribution to the remarkable progress made in the last four to five years.

The social and economic problems confronting the East African countries are manifold and complex. In this chapter it is not possible to deal with them all. In what follows, we shall direct our attention to only a few of the most important.

Rapid Economic Growth

East African countries are among the poorest in the world. The Governments have attached a high priority to rapid economic growth because the fulfilment of cherished social goals such as improved living standards for the masses, universal primary and secondary education, and social security is, in the last analysis, dependent on the wealth of the country.

The Governments' recognition of the primacy of the goal of rapid economic growth is reflected in their policies and in their gearing the machinery of government to cope with rapid economic expansion. Soon after independence, ministries of planning were created in all three countries to give greater cohesion and importance to developmental effort. This was followed by the publication of comprehensive and ambitious development plans in the three countries—Tanzania and Kenya in 1964, and Uganda in 1966. These plans aim to raise the growth rates of the economies considerably in excess of those achieved in the preceding years; for instance, the growth rates of the monetary sector of the economies projected in the development plans of Kenya, Uganda and Tanzania are 7·1, 7·2 and 8·5 per cent respectively, whereas the real growth rates in the monetary sector achieved in the period 1958 to 1962 were of the order 3·5, 3·0 and 5·2 per cent.

The East African development plans also aim to bring about a structural transformation of the economy by increasing the share of industrial activities in the economy. The progress made so far is highly encouraging; the annual growth rates achieved by the monetary economies of Kenya, Uganda and Tanzania in the period 1963 to 1966 are approximately 7·5, 10·3 and 9·6 per cent respectively. If the present pace of economic progress is maintained, there is a high probability that the ambitious goals embodied in the East African development plans will be realised or even surpassed.

Equitable Distribution of Income and Wealth

The goal of rapid economic growth by itself is not enough. From the welfare point of view, it is important that the fruits of growth should be distributed as widely as possible. This is especially the case with East Africa where, for a variety of reasons, there exist enormous disparities in income and wealth distribution. Therefore, the governments in East Africa, while promoting the maximum growth of the economy, cannot afford to neglect questions of income distribution. The problem is complicated by the fact that there is often a conflict between policies designed to accelerate growth and those designed to promote equality. In particular, since the volume of domestic savings is an important determinant of the growth of an economy, and since a large proportion of savings comes from business enterprises and rich people, policies designed to bring about greater equality of income distribution may have an adverse effect on voluntary savings. This effect could of course be countered by policies aimed at increasing compulsory savings, either through taxation or through such devices as marketing boards and workers' investment trusts. In any case, the extent to which the existing disparities in income and wealth distribution can be reduced will depend, on the one hand, on the conflict between growth and equity, and on the other hand, on the priority accorded to a more equitable distribution of income and wealth.

What measures have been adopted by the East African governments to promote greater economic equality, and to what extent have these been successful? It is not possible, owing to lack of information, to provide a quantitative answer to the second part of the question. However, as our answer to the first part will show, there is little doubt that impressive progress has been made throughout East Africa in promoting greater economic equality in recent years.

In order to appreciate the significance of the measures taken to promote greater equality, it is essential to clarify the causes of economic inequality. In the East African type of mixed economy, the two fundamental sources of economic inequality are differences in skills and differences in ownership of assets or wealth such as land, buildings, machinery, stocks and shares, and bank balances. Differences in skills lead to economic inequality because skilled jobs are generally paid much better than semi-skilled or unskilled jobs. The differential between skilled and unskilled wages is particularly high in East Africa where skilled persons are scarce and where the majority of skilled jobs were held in the past by expatriates who had to be paid salaries which would compare favourably with those in U.K. Differences in assets give rise to economic inequalities because assets are generally income earning. A man who has a property or a factory will receive additional income as rent or profits.

Peasants constitute the poorest sections of the population in East Africa. Therefore any policy aimed at promoting greater economic equality must lay primary emphasis on increasing peasant incomes. One of the most important ways in which this can be done is by the progressive conversion of subsistence farmers into farmers growing an increasing range of cash crops for both domestic and overseas markets. An excellent example of this is the record growth in the sale of cash crops and livestock from African smallholders in Kenya, where gross revenue has practically doubled in four years, rising from around £10 million in 1962 to just over £19 million in 1966. In the long run, however, a substantial increase in peasant incomes can come about only through a rise in productivity brought about by improved methods of agricultural production. The development plans and policies of the three East African countries rightly lay heavy stress on increasing peasant production.

In East Africa, greater progress has been made in reducing inequalities where these were occasioned by differences in skills, than where they were occasioned by differences in asset ownership. Wage inequalities may be narrowed by raising the wages of lower paid workers and/or by reducing the wages of higher paid staff. We find examples of both methods in East Africa. The last six years or so have seen a very rapid increase in the wages of lower-paid unskilled workers, especially those in the urban areas, in all the East African countries. This has been the combined result of minimum wage legislation, increased strength of trade unions, and the government encouragement of a high wage economy. This upward movement of wages at the lower end has made an important contribution to reduction in wage differentials.

At the upper end of the wages ladder, progressive Africanisation of better paid jobs, particularly in the public sector, has further contributed to a reduction in income inequalities, since local persons are not entitled to expatriate allowances and fringe benefits. In its determination to reduce economic inequalities, Tanzania has gone further and reduced the salaries of senior civil servants on two occasions: the first one was in 1962 when the Adu Commission on Civil Service Salaries proposed cuts in salaries of senior civil servants; the second occasion was in 1966, when all senior civil servants, along with political leaders, voluntarily accepted salary cuts ranging from 3 to 20 per cent.

In Kenya and Uganda, there has not been any substantial change in the salaries of senior civil servants since 1960. The virtual freezing of the higher salary scales combined with an upward movement of lower salaries and wages, and increases in the tax burden and cost of living, have resulted in a narrowing of income differentials and reductions in the real incomes of persons in upper income brackets. Uganda has a well articulated incomes policy which is laid down in her Second Five Year Plan entitled *Work for Progress*. Under it the government expects to limit annual wage increases for persons earning less than £90 per annum to 3·5 per cent; the relative increase tapers down for higher income groups, with persons earning more than £600 p.a. allowed no wage increases over the Plan period. It remains to be seen how successful the government will be in the implementation of this incomes policy. Tanzania has recently embarked on a comprehensive incomes policy, and a similar policy is under active consideration in Kenya. In the long run, perhaps the most effective method of reducing gross income inequalities arising from differences in skills is by greatly increasing the supply of skilled persons. This is precisely what the East African countries are doing by their emphasis on the rapid expansion of high-level manpower. In years to come, therefore, there will be a natural reduction in income differentials between skilled and unskilled persons, as indeed has happened in all developed countries, and in some developing countries like India where higher skills are not so scarce.

The second approach to a reduction in economic inequalities consists of a more equitable distribution of income-earning assets. Schemes for Africanising agriculture, commerce and industry attempt to bring about a redistribution of assets through a variety of methods. Perhaps the most spectacular example of this is the Africanisation of agriculture in Kenya. This was brought about, as we shall see in the next section, by the purchase of European farms in the Highlands and the settlement thereon of African farmers. Apart from such methods of redistributing assets from the richer to the poorer sections of the population, usually financed in the first place by the state, the only other way of promoting greater equality in ownership of assets, and hence of income and wealth, is through the accumulation of savings by the poorer sections of the population. But the basic poverty of such groups puts a serious limitation on their ability to save. This policy can be successful, therefore, only in the very long run.

It may, of course, be decided as a matter of policy to achieve greater equality by a progressive increase in the proportion of state-owned assets and a progressive decline in private-owned assets. This policy can be implemented by a discouragement of individual accumulation of savings and assets, through heavy income taxes and estates duties, and by nationalisation of private assets. Tanzania is the prime example in East Africa of a country vigorously following this policy, as reflected for instance in the Arusha Declaration and subsequent nationalisation of banks and several large industrial, commercial and agricultural enterprises.

Finally, an important instrument for redistributing income is the pattern of government taxation and expenditure. A system of progressive taxation, which impinges heavily on rich people and lightly on poor, promotes equality in post-tax or disposable incomes. Similarly, a pattern of government expenditure which is biased in the direction of providing social and economic services, such as agricultural extension, education, health and housing, to the lower-income groups could play an important role in increasing the welfare of such groups. The Sessional Paper on African Socialism, which is an important policy document of the Kenya government, attributes a vital role to the budgetary policy in reducing inequalities in living standards among different sections of the population. It is not possible, without a great deal of research, to determine the extent to which the taxation and expenditure policies of the East African governments do in fact redistribute income and welfare from the richer to the poorer groups. Our own judgement is that some such redistribution does take place, but that there is considerable scope for further restructuring of both taxes and public expenditure to make greater impact on the welfare of poorer people.

Africanisation

Closely related to the problems we have been discussing is the question of Africanisation. East African economies, like those of most central and southern African countries, have in the past been dominated by non-Africans, in the sense that a majority of the skills and an overwhelming proportion of industrial and commercial capital have been provided by a small minority of non-Africans. Although there has been a rapid expansion of the African share in the East African economies in recent years, non-Africans continue to play a vital role in these economies.

The African governments on attaining office were, therefore, faced with the urgent need to promote rapid Africanisation in all sectors of the economy. The concentration of economic power and wealth in the hands of a tiny alien minority was ethically wrong and politically explosive. The situation in the three countries varied somewhat. Uganda was, and still is, the most favourably endowed from the point of view of African participation in the economy, while Kenya faced the greatest problem in integrating Africans fully into the modern economy.

The problem in all three countries has been tackled on four fronts, though the relative emphasis placed on each has naturally tended to vary in accordance with the particular circumstances of the country concerned.

The first stage everywhere was the Africanisation of the political system, which marked the emergence and dominance of African political parties, African representatives in national legislatures, and African ministers and heads of governments. This was followed by rapid Africanisation of the civil services of the three countries. Prior to independence, the great majority of higher civil service posts in East Africa were held by Europeans, while Asians tended to dominate the middle ranks. The process of Africanisation of civil services, both at the higher and at the middle ranks, involved crash training programmes and extremely rapid promotion for African officers. It also involved replacement of expatriate officers which was facilitated by generous compensation retirement terms for expatriates. The fact that Britain was prepared to finance the costs of Africanisation directly and indirectly through loans to East African governments materially assisted the orderly progress of a structural change in a major national institution. The achievement is all the more striking when it is remembered that it was carried out at a time when the governments in all three countries were assuming new and complex responsibilities.

The progress made in Africanisation of civil services in the last few years is remarkable by any standards. In Kenya for example, at the time of independence, only one post in seven of the higher ranks of the civil service was held by an African. Even in the lower executive and technical grades less than half of the staff were Africans. By the end of 1966, well over half of the higher ranks, and an average of three-quarters of the executive and technical grades had been Africanised. In the junior ranks the process is almost complete except where particular shortages of skills exist, as for example in stenography. The higher administrative posts are almost completely Africanised. It is only in the technical and professional posts that progress in Africanisation has been relatively slow, due mainly to a lack of Africans with the necessary qualifications. Uganda and Tanzania have also experienced a similarly rapid process of Africanisation of their civil services. With the increase in the supply of trained Africans the next few years should see a virtual completion of the process of replacement of non-citizens by the citizens of the East African countries.

The process of Africanisation of jobs in the private sector has tended to lag behind. Part of the reason for this is that the public sectors in the three countries employ a great majority of the total skilled African manpower. If there is to be balanced Africanisation of better-paid jobs in the entire economy, the governments will have to accept a flow of qualified Africans from the public to the private sectors. Another reason for the relatively slow pace of Africanisation, especially in the middle ranks, has been the failure of most firms to provide the necessary training and promotion to their African staff. However, it must be remembered that in many ways the Africanisation of jobs in the private sector presents much more complex problems than those encountered in the civil service. For one thing, private enterprises are in the business to make profits and are, therefore, naturally reluctant to see any lowering of efficiency and hence of profits such as might be entailed by a rapid pace of Africanisation. Most private firms lack the necessary resources to mount training programmes and to compensate their non-African employees. The situation is even more difficult for concerns such as the smaller, family-based Asian firms. It is, therefore, hardly surprising that it is only the large, international firms which have made any progress in the Africanisation of the better-paid jobs.

The governments of East African countries have introduced a variety of measures to force the pace of Africanisation of jobs in the private sector. In the first place, informal pressure is brought to bear on large firms to Africanise as rapidly as possible. Tanzania, in particular, has worked out an elaborate and comprehensive scheme for phased Africanisation of private sector jobs. Firms are expected to prepare plans, in the light of the policy laid down by the government, regarding training programmes and specific targets for Africanisation. In 1967 the Minister of Labour in the Kenya government announced similar far-ranging proposals for accelerating Africanisation of jobs in the private sector. Secondly, in all three countries, employment permits for non-Africans from abroad are given only after the authorities have satisfied themselves thoroughly that no suitably qualified local candidates are available. Thirdly, the existing immigration and residence laws for non-citizens have been revised to facilitate Africanisation. In 1967 the Kenya authorities announced the replacement of the existing law on immigration and resident permits by one involving new categories of permits. This will enable the government to accelerate the process of Africanisation by controlling the issue and renewal of employment permits for existing employees and businessmen.

Simultaneously with the Africanisation of better-paid jobs in both private and public sectors of the economy, the East African governments have been pressing ahead with increasing the share of Africans in agriculture. Kenya was faced with the most acute problem in this respect. In the past, the cash agricultural sector in Kenya was completely dominated by European settlers. As the land issue had been at the root of most of Kenya's troubles in the past, it was necessary to find a satisfactory solution to this problem in the interests of stability and growth. As is well known, the problem was tackled by a massive resettlement of African farmers on the erstwhile European farms in what was known as the 'White Highlands'. In the last six years or so, approximately $1\frac{1}{2}$ million acres of former European farms have been taken over for 'high density' and 'low density' settlement schemes and for large government and co-operative farms. In addition, many large farms have been bought privately by Africans either as individuals, partnerships or companies, and these total another half-million acres. Under the Million Acre Settlement Scheme, 25,000 African families had been settled on individual plots or co-operative farms by June 1965. The cost of the entire exercise, of land purchase, settlement, and development loans to African farmers has run into millions of pounds. This has been financed by grants and loans from the U.K., and loans from West Germany and the World Bank. It is important to remember that the success of this operation has depended crucially on the availability of the necessary finance.

An important aspect of Africanisation relates to the processing, marketing and distribution of agricultural produce, in which the main instrument for Africanisation in all three countries has been the co-operative movement. Over the years, co-operatives have tended to control an ever-increasing share of the processing and marketing of agricultural products. The governments have speeded this process by providing cheap credit, training facilities and generally preferential treatment to co-operatives. In Uganda, co-operatives have made rapid progress in the ownership of cotton ginning and coffee curing industries in the last few years. Similarly, the co-operative movement in Tanzania has greatly increased its share of cotton ginning, and has a virtual monopoly of the marketing of African produce. At the national level, marketing boards have been established or strengthened to give the governments greater control over the marketing of agricultural products.

With the achievement of a satisfactory level of Africanisation in agriculture and public services, the governments are increasingly turning their attention to commerce and industry. We discussed earlier the problems of Africanising employment in the private sector. Here it is necessary to say a few words about the Africanisation of the ownership of commercial and industrial enterprises. If somehow the necessary finance were available, it would be relatively easy to redistribute the existing enterprises from non-Africans to African businessmen. However, quite apart from the difficulties in the way of raising adequate finance, the East African governments are opposed on economic grounds to a massive buying out of non-African businesses.

In the last few years, the East African governments have been experimenting with a variety of techniques to bring about greater state and African ownership of commerce and industry. Typically these measures have consisted of ways and means of aiding aspiring African businessmen. In Uganda, for instance, African Business Promotion Ltd, a subsidiary of the Uganda Development Corporation, aids African businessmen by making available commercial know-how, subsidised rentals on shops, and cheap and easy credit. Likewise, the Industrial and Commercial Development Corporation of the Kenya government provides advisory services and arranges for loans for African businessmen. Training for African businessmen in Kenya is provided at the Small Industry Research and Training Centre, Nakuru, and at the newly-created Management Training and Advisory Centre in Nairobi. The National Industry Vocational Training Centre has also been set up with the assistance of the United Nations.

Finally, all three countries have set up government-owned trading organisations to trade directly and also to supply African wholesalers and retailers. Tanzania was the first in the field; both Intrata (International Trading and Credit Company of Tanganyika Ltd.) and Cosata (Co-operative Supply Association of Tanganyika) were set up to promote the share of African businessmen and co-operatives in wholesale and retail trade. The National Trading Corporation is the Kenya Government's instrument for accelerating Africanisation by supplying direct to African businessmen a number of commodities in which it has a monopoly.

Despite all these measures, the rate of Africanisation in this sector has been very slow. Part of the reason for this is that for success in commercial ventures experience and hard work are vital prerequisites. We may, therefore, expect that the governments will take further radical measures to speed up Africanisation in this politically sensitive sector. In 1967 the Minister of Commerce and Industry in the Kenya government announced further measures for speeding up Africanisation; these include the construction of new business premises for lease to Africans at low rentals, the channelling of import-export trade to Africans through the Kenya National Trading Corporation, the distribution of locally manufactured goods through African traders, and the conversion of private commercial and industrial firms into public companies. Already in Kenya, a few Asian firms have converted into public companies and made their shares available to Africans. This imaginative move, if followed by others, could be a most important breakthrough in the programme for Africanisation of commerce.

It is likely that as the schemes described above gather momentum and there is an increase in the number and range of African skills and experience, the problem of Africanisation of the economy will have been solved. Thus the racial imbalances in the economy, inherited from the colonial era and disruptive of stability, will have been largely eliminated.

In concluding this section, it is worthwhile making two remarks. Firstly, the successful implementation of the programme of Africanisation will necessarily result in the creation of an African capitalist class and continuation of at least some of the disparities of income and wealth distribution. Of the East African countries, Tanzania is the only country which is making a conscious effort to prevent the creation of an African capitalist class by extending the scope of the public sector. It remains to be seen which of the two types of policies will prove more acceptable and growth-promoting. Meanwhile the chief beneficiaries of Africanisation policies are the fortunate few who have inherited the jobs and assets vacated by the departing non-Africans.

Secondly, it is just as well to remember that Africanisation will result in considerable hardships for some non-Africans, particularly those Asians with little skills and no capital. Most Asians in this group can expect no compensation; and few of them have money stored away in British banks. The irony of the situation is that Africanisation will probably inflict greatest hardships on those non-Africans who are least able to bear them and are most deserving of socialist sympathies.

Rural Development

Recently there has been an awakening of interest in the problems of rural development. The most powerful expression of this in East Africa is to be found in the recently issued Arusha Declaration. The two fundamental ideas behind the Arusha Declaration are self-reliance and rural development. To some extent the development plans of East African countries already reflect the vital importance of the rural sector. But there is something new in the urgency and priority being attached to rural development in current thinking about the appropriate strategy of development for East Africa.

The resurgence of interest in rural development derives from a variety of factors. In the first place, it is felt that in the past far too great a proportion of the nation's resources have been devoted to urban development. This is contrary to principles of equity, not only because urban dwellers are much better off than the rural inhabitants, but, more important, because an overwhelming proportion of East African population lives in the countryside. Secondly, the gap between rural and urban incomes has been widening rapidly in East Africa in recent years. It was some such consideration which prompted the Arusha Declaration to warn, 'If we are not careful we might get to the position where the real exploitation in Tanzania is that of the town dweller exploiting the peasants.'

The concern for rural development has in part been prompted by the failure of rural areas to retain educated persons. The widening rural-urban income differential combined with a variety of other well-known factors has resulted in a large influx of primary-school leavers and others to the urban areas, where they have swollen the pool of the unemployed. The expansion of the economies has not been adequate to provide job opportunities for all those seeking employment in the urban areas. The concern with these trends has led to the advocacy of 'back to the land' policies which are especially noteworthy in Kenya and Tanzania. In Kenya, the official policy is to rely on appeals to persuade people to return to the countryside, whereas in Tanzania more stern measures have been taken to round up all the urban unemployed and to repatriate them to their villages. In Kenya where there is scarcity of land, it is much more difficult to implement a back-to-the-land policy than in a relatively land-abundant Tanzania. But, even there, if this move is to be economically productive, careful plans will have to be made for the settlement of the repatriated urban unemployed.

It is a concern with the above developments which has been the mainspring of the drive towards a more vigorous policy of rural development. What are its essential elements? The most important step would appear to be a concerted plan to increase rural incomes at a pace even faster than that envisaged in the development plans. This in turn would call for harder work and a larger proportion of productive investment in rural areas in the form of increased extension services, provision of better seed, more fertilisers and agricultural implements and a greater emphasis on agricultural research.

Larger investment must be supplemented by an increase in the quality and range of public social services to make the rural areas more attractive places to live in. Some of the important social services are the provision of primary, secondary and technical education, of health centres, and of water, electricity and other modern amenities. Going beyond all these, it would be necessary to raise the status of farmers in the national estimation, and to make farming a respected and high income profession.

It is not possible at this stage to say how fully these new ideas on the urgency of rural development will be reflected in national social and economic policies in East African countries. But some decisive initiatives in this direction have already been taken, particularly in Tanzania, and the widespread acceptance of the new strategy for development gives hope of an early implementation of a vigorous policy of rural development.

East African Economic Relations

A review of the dominant East African economic problems would be incomplete without a reference to recent developments in interterritorial economic relations. Prior to independence, the East African countries had achieved a degree of economic integration which was unique in Africa. The essential elements of this integration were the existence of a common market, a common currency, a largely similar tax structure, and an impressive range of common services including railways and harbours, posts and telecommunications, airways, higher education and certain statistical, tax collection, and research services. The centrepiece of economic co-operation was the East African Common Market, which ensured a free movement of goods, capital and labour among the East African countries. It also implied a common tariff wall against imports from outside East Africa, thus providing local products with a large protected market.

It is to the credit of East African countries that they agreed, unlike certain west and central African countries, to extend these co-operative arrangements beyond the colonial era. There can be little doubt that the whole complex of interterritorial co-operative relations has made a vital contribution to the development of East Africa. But, unfortunately, the last few years have seen a serious dilution of many elements of East African economic co-operation. There are two main reasons for the recent reverses. Firstly, the extent of economic integration achieved in East Africa on the eve of independence could only be successfully continued if each country was prepared to surrender sovereign control over certain crucial instruments of economic policy such as fiscal, monetary and commercial policies. With the attainment of independence, it was merely a matter of time before differences in economic policies and plans, and a desire to exercise greater control over the economy created powerful pressures for greater economic autonomy. The only alternative to this was the surrender of political sovereignty in an East African Federation. This, unfortunately, despite honest and dedicated attempts, has failed to materialise. Secondly, the operation of supranational economic institutions inevitably results in unequal distribution of benefits and costs. The fact that Kenya had been the principal beneficiary of many such institutions, particularly through the common market, created demands in Tanzania and Uganda for certain modifications in their working. It is ironical that Tanzania, one of the most ardent champions of African unity, should have contributed so much to the dilution of inter-territorial economic co-operation.

The story of the retreat from economic co-operation in East Africa is recent and fairly well known. There were complaints in the late fifties from the then Tanganyika, and to a smaller extent Uganda, that Kenya had reaped most of the benefit from the expansion of the manufacturing industry stimulated by the common market. This resulted in the appointment of the Raisman Commission in 1960 to study the working of the common market and common services. Its recommendations led to the creation of the 'distributable pool' whose purpose was to finance some of the services of the East African Common Services Organisation and also to redistribute revenue from Kenya to Uganda and Tanganyika as compensation for the unequal distribution of benefits from the operation of the common market. This apparently was not considered adequate compensation for Tanganyika's continuing and increasing trade deficit with Kenya. Renewed pressure from Tanzania led in 1964 to the negotiation of the 'Kampala Agreement' which made important inroads into the working of the common market in East Africa.

Under the agreement, the countries with a deficit in their

trade balance were permitted to impose quota restrictions on imports from the surplus countries in the common market. Tanzania, and to a lesser extent Uganda, made immediate use of this provision to impose restrictions on a wide range of imports from Kenya. This has had the effect of slowing down the expansion of interterritorial trade, as is clearly shown by 1966 trade figures. In 1965, the three governments appointed a commission, known as the Philip Commission, to review the entire range of economic relations among the three countries.

Their report formed the basis of the 'Treaty for East African Co-operation' signed by the three heads of states in June 1967. The Treaty is an historic document in the history of East African co-operation, and its implementation would do much to reverse the disintegration of East African economic unity seen in the last three to four years. Among the important provisions of the Treaty, coming into operation in December 1967, are the replacement of quantitative restrictions on interterritorial trade by transfer taxes under specified conditions, the creation of an East African Development Bank to promote equitable distribution of industry in the three countries, and the establishment of a number of councils to assist the working of the common services and the common market.

Apart from the modifications in the working of the common market the three governments agreed in June 1965, on the initiative of Tanzania, to introduce separate currencies and separate Central Banks for the East African countries. Similarly, there have been important departures from a common tax policy in the last few years.

Education

It is time now to turn from primarily economic developments to contemporary social developments. In the following sections we shall say something about the problems encountered and progress made in the fields of education, health and housing.

At the time of independence, East African countries were faced with serious imbalances in their educational systems. In particular, there was a severe bottleneck at the secondary school level. In the interests of a more balanced system, and in view of the desperate shortage of local skilled personnel, it was decided to concentrate resources on the expansion of secondary and higher education. The last few years have been a period of unparalleled activity in the expansion and transformation of educational systems in East Africa. Education has undoubtedly been one of the most notable success stories of the post-independence era.

A few statistics will bring out the magnitude of the growth of post-primary school education. In Uganda, the numbers attending secondary schools have risen three-fold in five years, from 6,769 in 1961 to 20,100 in 1966. Likewise in Kenya there has been a nearly three-fold increase in secondary school enrolments, from 21,369 to 59,525 over the same period. This expansion has been greatly aided by self-help efforts; in 1965 alone, over a hundred Harambee Schools came into being to satisfy the unmet demand for secondary school education. The expansion in Tanzania has been less spectacular but is still impressive by any standards: between 1961 and 1966, the enrolments have gone up from 11,832 to 23,800. The progress made in the expansion of primary school facilities has been more limited, because the level reached in the colonial period was considered broadly satisfactory, and also because expansion of primary school education has a low priority on economic grounds.

Along with an expansion of secondary school facilities, there has been a greater emphasis on technical and scientific subjects. This is reflected in the larger proportion of students studying science subjects for Higher School Certificate as well as in the increased number of farm schools, technical and vocational colleges.

At the highest level, a new University College at Dar es Salaam was established in 1961. The University of East Africa, comprising Makerere University College, and University Colleges at Nairobi and Dar es Salaam, came into being in June 1963. It has enjoyed an extremely rapid growth in the last few years: the total enrolments in all categories, degree, diploma and post-graduate, have gone up by 65 per cent, from 2,176 to 3,595, between 1964 and 1967.

The rapid expansion of post-primary education has produced a number of problems. In the first place, an expansion of this order of magnitude could never have been carried out without external help, especially with teachers. The entire system of secondary school education throughout East Africa is heavily dependent on expatriate teachers. This is clearly undesirable, not only because it implies a heavy turnover of teachers to the detriment of students, but also because expatriate teachers are inevitably less conversant with local conditions and problems, and may not have a full appreciation of the appropriate values and attitudes that the secondary schools in East Africa ought to cultivate amongst the students. It is, therefore, vitally important that a higher priority should be given to increasing the number of African secondary school teachers.

Another difficulty in the way of expanding educational facilities in East Africa is the high cost of secondary and higher education; for instance, the capital cost of Makerere College to date has totalled £5,000 per student place; the running cost is £1,000 per student per year which is about thirty times per capita national income! Again, boarding senior secondary schools have in recent years been costing £800 per pupil-place to build, and £100 per pupil per year to operate. Educational costs in Tanzania and Kenya are hardly likely to differ substantially from the above figures. Such high costs of education make it extremely difficult in a poor country to justify a further substantial expansion in secondary and college education. If such expansion is not to eat up an unreasonably large proportion of national resources, it is vital that education costs per student should be drastically reduced. This is not the place to suggest how this may be done, but given the desire to face some radical changes in our educational institutions, costs per student could, no doubt, be lowered considerably without an appreciable effect on quality.

Finally, there is the need to adapt the educational systems to integrate them better with the problems and patterns of life in East Africa. This implies the need not only to turn out more technicians, agricultural experts and other professionals, but also to adapt the curricula in schools and colleges to make them more relevant to local conditions. Already, considerable efforts are being made by the Ministries of Education and the University of East Africa in revising curricula and teaching methods by drawing more on local materials and local problems.

But beyond all these there is the need to make the educational system a better instrument of service to the community by preparing students for the lives they will be leading later. The most searching and far-reaching analysis of the limitations of the present educational systems in East Africa and of their reform to integrate them better with indigenous values and patterns of life has recently been made by President Nyerere in a pamphlet entitled *Education for Self-Reliance*. This pamphlet contains a number of revolutionary proposals to make schools more self-reliant and better integrated with local society and the economy. Whether one agrees or not with Nyerere's vision of the role of education in a developing, socialist country like Tanzania, there can be little doubt that he has exposed serious weaknesses in the present educational systems and has made challenging proposals for their reform.

Other Social Services

Along with education, the provision of other social services has also been stepped up. The development plans of the East African countries contain detailed analyses of these problems and put forward proposals for their solution. In the field of health, greater priority is being accorded to curative rather than merely preventive medicine. At the same time, an attempt is being made to improve the quality of health services in rural areas by a substantial increase in the number of rural health centres and dispensaries, and by a policy of wider dispersion of hospitals.

Another major problem is the provision of housing to cope with increases in population. The quality of rural houses throughout East Africa needs improvement. Community development and self-help is being harnessed to this end. The problem of urban housing was exacerbated by the fact that there was very little building of private houses between 1961 and 1965. This has resulted in an acute housing shortage in all the major cities and towns of East Africa. To counter this trend, governments have taken steps to encourage the supply of houses. National Housing Corporations have been set up by the three governments to build houses directly and also to stimulate building by local authorities. In Kenya the government has established the Housing Finance Company which provides mortgage finance for new houses. Research is being conducted into ways of building houses more economically. The government effort in the field of housing has been too recent to make much of an impact. But as these programmes get under way there should be a substantial improvement in the housing situation in urban areas. But in the long run, an effective solution to the housing problem can only be found in a revival and growth of private building.

Other social services designed to improve the living conditions of the common man include the provision of water and electricity, adult literacy campaigns, and community social centres for those who have hitherto been deprived of them. But it will be many years before each inhabitant of East Africa can avail himself of such basic services.

Conclusion

The picture presented thus far is that of steady progress on a wide front. Some of the most explosive pre-independence social and economic problems have been handled in a progressive, orderly and as far as possible, a just manner. Few would dispute the proposition that the societies that are emerging in the wake of independence in East Africa are vastly superior in justice to their colonial predecessors. Special privileges enjoyed by racial minorities have been largely eliminated. It is true that non-African citizens, in general, do not enjoy the same opportunities of appointment and promotion as Africans, but this to some extent is necessitated by the need to redress past imbalances, and one must hope that discriminations of this nature would disappear over time.

With the passage of time, significant differences are beginning to emerge in the way the various East African countries organise their political, social and economic affairs. Our concern here is solely with social and economic matters. In the colonial days, there was a large measure of agreement in the objectives and methods of social and economic policies in East Africa. With independence, important differences have arisen with respect to appropriate organisation of society and economy for the achievement of what are still basically similar social values and goals. These differences are particularly noticeable between Kenya and Tanzania. In general, the Kenya approach is to work as far as possible with existing institutions and methods, and to adapt them to meet the requirements of the present and the future. The Kenya approach is essentially pragmatic. Tanzania, on the other hand, has launched on bold experiments to bring about major changes in her society and economy. The Tanzanian approach is more informed by ideology and charged with social purpose.

As some of the older problems, such as the promotion of a more prominent African role in the society and the economy, and the resumption of rapid economic growth, are satisfactorily solved, new problems will arise to take their place. The struggle against poverty is a continuing one in East Africa and should absorb the best energies of the present and the next generation. But more specific problems, such as unemployment, an equitable distribution of the fruits of growth, and rural development loom on the horizon, and will require imaginative leadership and sustained effort for their effective solution. If the past performance is any guide, the East African countries should respond to the new challenges with equal wisdom and vigour.

It has been the theme of this essay that the East African countries are basically moving in the right direction and at the right pace. It would appear that, provided they maintain their political stability, they face a bright future.

Further reading

Treaty for East African Co-operation, Nairobi, 1967.

The Economic Development of Tanganyika, Dar Es Salaam, 1960.

The Economic Development of Uganda, Kampala, 1961.

The Economic Development of Kenya, 1962.

Tanganyika Government, *Five Year Plan for Economic and Social Development, 1964-69*, Dar es Salaam, 1964.

ROBSON, P. and LEYS, C. (Eds.) *Federation in East Africa*, Oxford University Press, London, 1965.

Kenya Government, *Economic Planning and its Application to African Socialism*, Nairobi, 1965.

Report of *The Kenya Education Commission*, Part I and Part II, Nairobi, 1965.

Kenya Government, *Development Plan, 1966-70*, Nairobi, 1966.

Uganda Government, *Work For Progress*, Uganda's Second Five Year Plan, 1966-71, Kampala, 1966.

Tanzania Government, *The Arusha Declaration*, Dar es Salaam, 1967.

NYERERE, J. K. *Education for Self-Reliance*, Dar es Salaam, 1967.

Biographical Notes

Edward A. Alpers, A. B. (Harvard), Ph.D. (London) is Lecturer in History at the University College, Dar es Salaam. He has contributed articles to the *Uganda Journal, Azania, Aspects of Central African History,* ed. T. O. Ranger, (1967), and to the Nairobi Conference on East Africa and the Orient. He has completed a pamphlet on *The East African Slave Trade* for the Historical Association of Tanzania. He also is revising his thesis on Yao trade in East Central Africa. He left Dar es Salaam in March 1968 to become Assistant Professor of African History at the University of California, Los Angeles.

Norman R. Bennett, A.B. (Tufts), M.A. (Fletcher School— Tufts), Ph.D. (Boston), is Assistant Professor of History and Research Associate in the African Studies Programme of Boston University. He first visited East Africa in 1959; in 1962 he was visiting lecturer at Kivukoni College, Dar es Salaam. He is the author of *Studies in East African History* (1963) and editor of *New England Merchants in Africa: A History through Documents, 1802 to 1865* with George E. Brooks, Jr. (1965), and *Leadership in East Africa. Six Political Biographies* (1968)—all published by the Boston University Press. He has contributed to the *Journal of African History, Tanzania Notes and Records, African Affairs,* and *Makerere Journal.* He is editor of the American *African Studies Bulletin.*

392

F. J. Berg was born in the United States, educated in the public schools of a small town in the state of Michigan, and took his B.A. with high honours in history at the University of Michigan. Upon completing his undergraduate studies he was awarded a Woodrow Wilson Foundation fellowship to the University of Wisconsin, where he began graduate work in African history, and where he received his M.A. Currently he is completing his doctoral dissertation at the University of Wisconsin, a study of the city of Mombasa during the nineteenth and early twentieth centuries. In 1966 Mr. Berg spent ten months in Kenya carrying out research for his dissertation and was, at this time, affiliated to the University College of Nairobi as a Research Associate of the Department of History.

H. N. Chittick, M.A., F.S.A., was educated at Rugby School and Cambridge University, with intervening war service in the Intelligence Corps. He graduated in 1949, was subsequently called to the Bar and took a postgraduate Diploma in Archaeology. He assisted on various excavations in the Middle East during 1951–52. From 1952–56 he was Curator of Museums in the Republic of Sudan, and carried out fieldwork, mostly on the Christian period. In 1956 he was elected Fellow of the Society of Antiquaries of London. He was later appointed to set up the Antiquities Department in Tanganyika, carried out a general survey of antiquities of the country and began excavations on the coast. In 1961 he was appointed Director of the British Institute of History and Archaeology in East Africa. He completed excavations at Kilwa in 1965 and began work in the Lamu region in 1966. He is the Editor of *Azania,* and the author of *Ghazali, A Monastery in the Northern Sudan,* with P. L. Shinnie (1961), *Kisimani Mafia* (1961), and numerous reports and articles in journals.

D. W. Cohen, B.A., graduated in history from the University of Wisconsin in 1965, having also studied social anthropology at the London School of Economics and Political Science from 1963–64. He is currently engaged in writing his thesis on the pre-colonial history of Busoga, at the School of Oriental and African Studies, University of London. He completed fieldwork in Busoga in January 1967.

Christopher Ehret, B.A. (University of Redlands, U.S.A.), M.A. (Northwestern University), was a Research Associate at the University Colleges of Nairobi and Dar es Salaam in 1967. He was previously engaged in research on the early history of the Highland Nilotes, as Foreign Area Fellow in East Africa. His particular interest is developing linguistic evidence as a source for writing history.

Dr. Cyril Ehrlich is a graduate of the London School of Economics. In 1952 he joined the staff of Makerere College where he introduced the subject of economic history and pioneered its application to East Africa, lecturing extensively in Africa, Britain and the United States. He has published several articles in learned journals and has contributed to the Oxford History of East Africa. In 1961 he left Makerere for the Queen's University, Belfast, where he is now Senior Lecturer in Economic History, but has returned to East Africa several times to research and examine at the University.

Dharam Ghai was educated at the Duke of Gloucester School, Nairobi, Christ's College, London, and at the Universities of Oxford and Yale where he obtained his Ph.D. in economics. He has been a Senior Lecturer in Economics at Makerere University College, Research Fellow, Economic Growth Centre, Yale University, and since September 1966, Research Fellow, Institute for Development Studies, University College, Nairobi. He is now the Deputy Director of the Institute for Development Studies, Social Science Division. He has published several articles on the problems of economic development in East Africa, and a book entitled *Taxation For Development: A Case Study of Uganda*. He also edited, *Portrait of a Minority: Asians in East Africa*. He has been consultant to the Governments of Kenya, Uganda and Buganda on various occasions.

John Iliffe is a graduate of the University of Cambridge. He carried out research in East Africa in 1961–63 and received a doctoral degree from Cambridge in 1965. He then returned to the University College, Dar es Salaam in 1965, to lecture in history and to write on German administration in East Africa, the Maji Maji rising, and Tanzanian nationalism.

J. A. Kieran, B.A. (Liverpool), Ph.D. (London), is Senior Lecturer in History in the University College, Nairobi, at present a constituent college of the University of East Africa. His study of missionary activity in nineteenth-century East Africa is shortly to be published. He is the author of a chapter on East African history in *The Natural Resources of East Africa,* edited by W. T. W. Morgan, and of a chapter on the Church in modern times in East Africa in a forthcoming book on the Church in Africa, edited by N. Q. King. He has also written several articles on East African history.

Ali Mazrui was born in Mombasa, Kenya, in 1933. His early education was at the Government Boys' School, Mombasa, and at Huddersfield College of Technology. He obtained a B.A. with distinction from the University of Manchester, an M.A. from Columbia University, New York, and a D.Phil. from the University of Oxford. He has also been a Rockefeller Foundation Fellow and Visiting Professorial Scholar at the Universities of Chicago, California (Los Angeles), Harvard and Singapore, and at the Indian School of International Studies, New Delhi. He has lectured in Britain, Holland and Sweden, and is now Professor and Head of the Department of Political Science at Makerere University College, Uganda. Dr. Mazrui's published works include *Towards a Pax Africana, The Anglo-African Commonwealth,* and *On Heroes and Uhuru Worship.*

B. G. McIntosh was educated at Prince of Wales School, Nairobi, and Edinburgh University where he graduated with an M.A. Honours degree in history in 1964. From 1965–67 he was Research Fellow in the History Department, University College, Nairobi, under a scheme run jointly by University College and the British Overseas Development Ministry. In 1967 he was appointed Lecturer in History at University College, Nairobi. His Ph.D. thesis will be completed for Edinburgh in 1968.

B. A. Ogot, Dip.Ed. (E.A.), M.A. (St Andrews), Ph.D. (London), is Professor of History and Dean of the Faculty of Arts at the University College, Nairobi. He started his career as Tutorial Fellow at Makerere University College in 1959–60 and was then awarded a Rockefeller Research Fellowship to the School of Oriental and African Studies, London University.

In 1961 he became Research Fellow at the British Institute of History and Archaeology in East Africa, and lectured in history at Makerere University College from 1962–64. In 1965 he became Senior Lecturer and Chairman of the History Department of University College, Nairobi, and was at the same time Director of the Cultural Division of the Institute for Development Studies. He is the Founder Member and National President of the Historical Association of Kenya and is a member of many other learned societies. His published works include *East Africa, Past and Present* (Ed.), *A Place to Feel at Home* with F. B. Welbourn (1966), and *A History of the Southern Luo Peoples, 1500–1900* Vol. I (1967). He has several other works in progress and has contributed articles to numerous books and journals.

Francis Ojany was educated at the Government School, Kisii, and Alliance High School. He graduated from Makerere University College in 1960 with a B.A. Honours Degree in geography, with history as a subsidiary subject. In 1960 he was awarded a Commonwealth Scholarship for postgraduate work in geomorphology, and in 1963 gained his M.A. Degree at the University of Birmingham. He subsequently returned to University College, Nairobi, where he has been Lecturer in Geomorphology since August 1963.

Merrick Posnansky, Professor of Archaeology at the University of Ghana, was in East Africa from 1956–67 and was latterly Director of African Studies at Makerere University College. He was previously Curator of the Uganda Museum and Assistant Director of the British Institute of History and Archaeology in East Africa. He has excavated widely in East Africa on both stone and iron age sites; his most notable excavations being at Lanet in Kenya, Bigo and Magosi in Uganda, and Nyabusora in Tanzania. He was editor of *Prelude to East African History*.

J. E. G. Sutton, M.A. (Oxon.), Ph.D. (East Africa), is Lecturer in History and Archaeology at the University College, Dar es Salaam. Formerly, as a research student of the British Institute of History and Archaeology in East Africa and of Makerere College, he undertook a field survey with excavations of the archaeology of the western highlands of Kenya. The results of this work and its bearing on the history of the Kalenjin and other peoples of the region are explained in several articles, notably in volume I of *Azania* (1966). He is also author of the first paper of the Historical Association of Tanzania, *The East African coast: An Historical and Archaeological Review* (1966).

G. S. Were was educated at the Royal Technical College, Nairobi, the University College of North Wales, Bangor, and the School of Oriental and African Studies, London University. He is currently lecturing in history at University College, Nairobi. He is the author of *A History of the Abaluyia of Western Kenya: c. 1500–1930*, *Abaluyia Historical Texts*, and *East Africa through a Thousand Years*, with D. Wilson.

Index

Published by EAPH P.O. Box 30571, Nairobi, and Longmans
of Kenya Limited, P.O. Box 18201, Nairobi, and printed by
Kenya Litho Limited, Cardiff Road, P.O. Box 775, Nairobi.

DATE DUE